D1600273

Pandita Ramabai (1858–1922)

PANDITA RAMABAI THROUGH HER OWN WORDS: SELECTED WORKS

COMPILED AND EDITED, WITH TRANSLATIONS, BY

Meera Kosambi

OXFORD
UNIVERSITY PRESS

OXFORD

UNIVERSITY PRESS

YMCA Library Building, Jai Singh Road, New Delhi 110 001

Oxford University Press is a department of the University of Oxford. It furthers the
University's objective of excellence in research, scholarship, and education
by publishing worldwide in

Oxford   New York

Athens   Auckland   Bangkok   Bogota   Buenos Aires   Calcutta
Cape Town   Chennai   Dar es Salaam   Delhi   Florence   Hong Kong   Istanbul
Karachi   Kuala Lumpur   Madrid   Melbourne   Mexico City   Mumbai
Nairobi   Paris   Sao Paulo   Singapore   Taipei   Tokyo   Toronto   Warsaw

with associated companies in   Berlin   Ibadan

Oxford is a registered trade mark of Oxford University Press
in the UK and in certain other countries

Published in India
By Oxford University Press, New Delhi

ISBN   019 564 7548

Typeset in Garamond
by Eleven Arts, Keshav Puram, Delhi 110 035
Printed by Rashtriya Printers, Delhi 110 032
Published by Manzar Khan, Oxford University Press
YMCA Library Building, Jai Singh Road, New Delhi 110 001

To the memory of my parents,

Professor Damodar Dharmanand Kosambi

and

Mrs Nalini Damodar Kosambi, née Madgavkar

PREFACE AND ACKNOWLEDGEMENTS

Much of Pandita Ramabai's career bears the imprint of a duality—marginalization at home in Maharashtra where her work for women was pointedly ignored, and made possible only by international recognition and support. A similar duality pervades the recent academic interest in her, which focuses on the better known of her English writings to the neglect of the obscure, and obscured ones and of her far more extensive Marathi works. The present volume hopes to reclaim these lost words of one whose voice has, paradoxically, reverberated across the world for a century, and, in the appreciatively exaggerated words of her friend Dr Rachel Bodley (in the Introduction to *The High-Caste Hindu Woman*), broken 'the silence of a thousand years'.

The genesis of this book was my shocked discovery in late 1995 of Ramabai's (*Ramabai's!*) anti-feminist and seemingly even anti-women ideological stance in *Stri Dharma Niti* and my sharing it with my colleagues at the Research Centre for Women's Studies (RCWS)—mainly Dr Divya Pandey, Dr Veena Poonacha and Ms Usha Lalwani. Their demand for a translation of the full text as a marker of Ramabai's early thinking, buttressed by my friend Ms Aban Mukherji's idea of tracing her dual ideological evolution, resulted in a slim, hastily written volume entitled *Pandita Ramabai's Feminist and Christian Conversions: Focus on Stree Dharma Neeti* published in the RCWS Gender Series in December 1995. Dr Neera Desai, Founder-Director of the RCWS, has since made constructive comments on it in lieu of a review (though Ms Geeta Seshu did review it for the *Indian Express*).

Two other translated pieces, intended as an appendix to my proposed comprehensive book on Ramabai, were the chapters on women and religion in her *United Stateschi Lokasthiti ani Pravasavritta,* made in my free time during a six-week visit as a Distinguished Visiting Scholar to the University of Adelaide, Australia, in 1997. My colleagues there kindly extended their interest in Pandita Ramabai, kindled—or rekindled—by my talks, to the translation. Dr Margaret Allen made many perceptive comments and helped to trace useful background material on Pandita Ramabai and on the women's movement in the West in the Barr-Smith Library of Adelaide University, the State Archives of South Australia and elsewhere. Drs Kay and Robert Schaeffer persuaded me that a translation of the entire book (which I subsequently undertook) would appeal to a readership in the USA, their homeland which they had left years ago. Dr Jane Haggis, Dr Susanne Schech, Dr Susan Magarey, Dr Sue Sheridan and Dr Chilla Bulbeck were generous with their usual warm encouragement. Some materials were made available by Ms Betty Grey, formerly Superintendent of the Mukti Mission at Kedgaon, from the archives of the Melbourne branch of the Ramabai Association.

When the translated pieces acquired an alarming length, I presented them as a book proposal to Oxford University Press, New Delhi. Mr Rukun Advani of OUP was enthusiastic enough to suggest the inclusion of all Ramabai's 'essential' English writings as well. This development led to the retrieval of more works by Pandita Ramabai—including one unpublished manuscript—and refashioning the Introduction, though within a stringent word-limit.

At this juncture, Dr Jim Masselos, on one of his regular visits from Sydney, suggested new ideas (while repeating the old one, with the prerogative of an old friend, that I should get my 'real book' on Ramabai 'out of your system, instead of writing about her in bits and pieces'). But the 'bits and pieces' continued to be written, and presented—as a paper at the Annual Meeting of the American Historical Association in Seattle, Washington, in January 1998, and as talks at some American universities during the lecture tour which followed. During this month-long visit, old and new colleagues and friends were warmly supportive of the project—especially Dr Antoinette Burton, Dr Frank Conlon, Dr Nupur Chaudhuri, Dr Vinay Lal, Dr Philippa Levine, Dr Barbara Ramusack, Dr Guy Welbon, Dr Bill Worger and Dr Lynn Zastoupil. In addition to providing generous hospitality, along with Lynn and Vinay, Barbara also helped to track down references in the Archives and Rare Books Department of the University of Cincinnati Library. Ms Abby McGowan, my former student, helped me to negotiate the half-remembered corridors of Van Pelt Library of the University of Pennsylvania, and also retrieved some materials for me. Work at the Philadelphia Free Library was made possible by the warm hospitality of old friends, Ms and Mr Polly and Harry Fischler of Cherry Hill, New Jersey, during this visit and during an earlier one in December 1995–January 1996 when Drs Mahadev and Judit Apte had also provided equally warm hospitality in New York city for my work at the New York Public Library.

The translations were finalized with help from many friends and colleagues, in many forms—at the Marathi end from Dr S.R. Chunekar and at the English end from Professor Zia Karim and Ms Pareen Lalkaka. As a bilingual expert, Dr Pramod Kale made useful suggestions, and Mr Ramesh Sirkar made a valuable contribution by discussing both the general problems of translation and some of my own translated pieces.

During discussions of earlier drafts of the Introduction, I benefitted especially from the comments made by Dr Neera Desai with her usual readiness to engage in feminist dialogues, and from the insights shared by Ms Rita Monteiro from her Christian and feminist perspective.

For the Introduction and references I have drawn largely upon materials collected over the years from several institutions. In Pune, Jaykar Library of the University of Pune, the library of the Gokhale Institute of Politics and Economics, Bai Jerbai Wadia Library of Fergusson College (from which books were borrowed with the help of my friend Ms Neelima Raddi), the Kesari-Mahratta Trust's Tilak Smarak Mandir, and the United Theological Seminary of Maharashtra have been rich sources of research materials. At the Pandita Ramabai Mukti Mission, Kedgaon, Ms Heather Johnstone, former Superintendent of the Mission, Dr Bobby John, and also Ms Rose Borpujari who worked as a volunteer from the USA, were very generous with their time and effort to make materials available from the Mission's Archives. Ms Betty Jenson, formerly of the Spicer Memorial College, also played an instrumental role. In Mumbai I have consulted the library of the University of Bombay (Fort), the Asiatic Society's library (always 'a home away from home'), the library of the United States Information Services, and that of SNDT Women's University, especially its Juhu Campus branch (where Ms Sushama Paudwal, Deputy Librarian, provided useful reference material).

The RCWS and its tremendous support structure helped the book along in many ways. The Documentation Centre of the RCWS and prompt and willing help from the librarian, Ms Usha Rao, were indispensable. Mr M. Manikandan of the Documentation Centre helped with computer-related matters and printing of the typescript and its drafts, and Usha Lalwani with some of the word-processing. Ms Jyotsna Sanjanwala and Ms Shobha Chitale took care of some of the nitty-gritty details, and everybody else was generally supportive. The RCWS has always lived up to its reputation for an intellectually nourishing and friendly work environment.

On the domestic front, generous moral and practical support was provided by Pareen, Anahita and especially Aban (who also gladly supplied gallons of tea in an effort to fuel intellectual activity) in Mumbai, and by my old and close friend Ms Sindhu Pradhan in Pune. All my friends, particularly Aban and Zia, have had to 'live' with Pandita Ramabai for years because of me, and have accomodated her as an invisible presence in countless heated discussions.

This volume has reached its final form after much thinking about what constitutes the 'essential' writings of Ramabai, and after painful decisions to leave out some favourites among her prolific literary output in the struggle to meet the word-limit. The volume now contains almost as many pages of translations from the Marathi as of Ramabai's original English writings, and will hopefully contribute to a more informed charting of her ideological trajectories—feminist, religious and other—during the quarter-century from 1882 to 1908.

I express my deepest appreciation and gratitude to all those who helped my own intellectual journey during this timespan and who walked at least a few steps with me along the way.

Meera Kosambi
August 1999

CONTENTS

PART IV KEDGAON

INTRODUCTION

In the mystic's spirit of seeing the world in a grain of sand, one may find Pandita Ramabai's whole life (1858–1922) encapsulated in a photograph of her during her last years, head bowed over her Marathi translation of the Bible. In this cultural narrative of conflated contradictions lie embedded several simultaneous readings. The photograph shows an Indian woman sitting on the floor in a pose mandatory for upper caste Maharashtrian women of the time, although the rest of her unconventional appearance—a plain white five-yard sari, a Western-style high-necked, long-sleeved blouse, and short hair—suggests a Bengali Brahmo widow, except for her typically Maharashtrian (and also south Indian) way of modestly covering her right shoulder with the sari.[1] The showcasing of her act of writing serves to privilege her over her contemporaries who did not have access to education and could nurture no literary ambitions. Further exoticizing this unusual blend of customs, cultures and creeds is the intrusive presence of the 'Western' photographer, suggested by the potted palm ubiquitous in contemporary posed portraits. To all these spontaneous readings can be added the fact that the translation of the Bible, Ramabai's magnum opus, marked the apogee of her religious divergence from her orthodox Brahmin origins, via a series of intermediate stages landmarked by her earlier writings. The aim of this book is to present this entire spectrum, which allows us to reconstruct and plot Pandita Ramabai's complex religious, feminist and personal evolution.

The recent resurgence of national and also international academic interest in Pandita Ramabai stands foregrounded against her elision during the last few decades from the mainstream record of Maharashtra's social history.[2] So far this resurgence has left untouched the complex and problematic niche Ramabai occupies in Maharashtra's collective psyche in which pride in her extraordinary learning and fame remains stifled by a sense of betrayal at her conversion to Christianity and subsequent proselytization, as if these were recent occurrences and their wounds still fresh. It is now time for a healing, for a sensitive, unblinkered exploration of her writings and activities from today's secular vantage point.

In a sense this book is a more organized replication of my own journey into Ramabai's fascinating world, which began as an exploration of the region's social-cultural regeneration that had occurred a century and a half ago. The excitement of rediscovering the region's history and culture which I had absorbed during my formative years and education at Pune—the cultural heartland of Maharashtra—and of re-reading the impassioned eloquence of revered public leaders soon gave way to puzzlement as I stumbled upon the militant feminist rhetoric of Pandita Ramabai. She seemed to have inhabited the same age but not shared the same social space; her thoughts resonated well with late twentieth century thinkers—at least feminist ones—but have been almost erased from mainstream records of history. This enigma paved the way for my gradual retrieval of her obscure—and obscured—writings, in the hope of serving several simultaneous agendas: to reconstruct Ramabai's ideological evolution and transformation in interaction with her changing social milieu in order to assess her contribution, to help to 'engender' the social history of Maharashtra by reinscribing women into it and thus broaden its epistemological base and correct the imbalance in historical discourse, and to reclaim a significant part of our feminist heritage.[3]

This volume, planned as a comprehensive source-book of Ramabai's writings, includes her internationally known works in English, *The High-Caste Hindu Woman* (selection 5) and *A Testimony of Our Inexhaustible Treasure* (selection 11) on which, together with her published *Letters and Correspondence*, non-Marathi-speaking scholars tend to place sole reliance in their analyses; importantly, it also includes her other, lesser known and painstakingly retrieved English writings. But its *raison d'etre* is Ramabai's Marathi works—both the well-known and the obscure, recently recovered ones—which appear here in (my) English translation for the first time. They help us traverse an entirely new and startlingly different experiential world in her company. In fact, her writings plot a trajectory involving a hundred and eighty degrees' turn through three clearly contoured phases of cultural transition, starting with an orthodox Hindu world-view which gradually imbricates with a Christian world-view, only to be completely edged out in a final rupture.

From these collected writings (in the original and in translation) also emerges the key to an understanding of Ramabai—the fact of her being positioned simultaneously as an 'insider' and an 'outsider', both within Maharashtra's turbulent social regeneration, and within the larger international project of Christianization. Ramabai shared the ethos and psyche of her reformist contemporaries, but transgressed the boundaries of space, culture and religion—and even of time—through her vision of a gender-egalitarian society. She presented a graphic picture of oppressed Indian womanhood to her Western readers with a trained ethnographer's eye, but without sacrificing her nationalist pride and right to interrogate colonial rule; and she brought news of exciting social and political reforms in the far-off United States of America to her Marathi readers with an empathetic understanding of the prevailing local conditions. The ease with which she straddled the East and West was unique in the heyday of Empire and Orientalism. Hence the imperative to approach Ramabai through both her Marathi and English writings which represent nearly separate cultural spheres and whose juxtaposition alone can throw adequate light on her complex world-view, mindset and personality.

A LIFE SKETCH

Ramabai's intellectual roots go back to the twilight of the (Brahmin) Peshwa reign, to just before Bajirao II lost political power to the East India Company's Mumbai-based government in 1818.[4] However, the multiple Brahmin hegemony, based also on religious, economic and social supremacy, was to survive this event. Ramabai's father, Anant Shastri Dongre, a descendant of Chitpavan Brahmin settlers in Karnataka, was then a promising student at the Peshwa capital Pune. On one of his visits to the Peshwa's palace with his reputed teacher, Anant Shastri was held spellbound by the mellifluous Sanskrit recitation of the Peshwa's wife. He vowed to teach his own wife 'the divine language' from which tradition—and allegedly scriptural injunctions as well—had mandated the exclusion of women and Shudras.

Anant Shastri's attempts were foiled by his uninterested wife, presumably under pressure from his conservative family. Years after her death, he acquired a second wife at the age of forty-four while on a pilgrimage, in a rather cavalier manner (which Ramabai herself marvelled at, though without mentioning names, in her chapter on 'Married Life' in *The High-Caste Hindu Woman*).

Predictably, Anant Shastri's success in teaching his second wife Lakshmibai the Sanskrit language and texts incurred the wrath of his orthodox fellow caste men against whom he defended himself in an assembly of learned *shastris*, citing passages from the sacred texts. He later withdrew to a simple, peaceful life in the forest of Gangamul in Karnataka (having earlier enjoyed patronage from the court of Mysore), ran a residential school and tended rice fields and orchards with his wife's capable help. Of the couple's six children, three survived—Srinivas, Krishnabai, and the youngest Ramabai who was born in 1858.

Launched practically from infancy upon a life of unceasing pilgrimage, Ramabai, along with her family, traversed the length and breadth of the subcontinent visiting holy places and earning a precarious living by reciting the Puranas. Once their frugal needs were met, the surplus money and food received as gifts from devout listeners were offered to holy Brahmins as an obligatory meritorious deed. This life style was punctuated by two unorthodox elements. One, Anant Shastri insisted on giving his daughters a Sanskrit education. In Ramabai's case, this happened through Lakshmibai as he was too old for the exertion. Two, he refused to arrange the customary early marriage for Ramabai, in the aftermath of Krishnabai's unhappy child marriage (an episode described by Ramabai in the chapter 'Woman's Place in Religion and Society' in *The High-Caste Hindu Woman*, without identifying her sister).

A significant consequence of this unconventional upbringing was that Ramabai managed to escape a rigid gender-specific role, unlike her peers who were locked into wifehood and motherhood at an early age, confined to the domestic sphere, subjected to the pressures of the extended family, and denied education or even literacy. Treated as her brother's equal, educated and trained in public speaking before mixed audiences, Ramabai later entered the public, male arena of social reform without hesitation. Again, from early on, her life was anchored in a deep religiosity, with conscience as the sole arbiter of conduct; this explains her later spiritual quest which was coupled with an intellectual curiosity and defiance of dogma. Finally, a life of physical hardship, often at the very edge of survival, forged in her a strength of character and an intense individualism which was, and still is, rare in Indian society—which has rested on collectivity and conformity—and which led her later on to tread a solitary and difficult path to spiritual salvation and contestation of patriarchy.

Despite enjoyable moments that the close-knit nuclear family experienced, the Dongres ultimately paid a high price for their endless travel and rigorous ritual observances. After years of privation and even starvation, Ramabai's emaciated parents died in 1874, victims of a severe famine in the Madras Presidency. (The painful experience of the indignities of starvation, suffered both by its victims and its survivors, was later described graphically by Ramabai in 'Famine Experiences', selection 8.) Krishnabai died of cholera in late 1875, having just undergone the trauma of a lawsuit for the restitution of conjugal rights. The truncated family, Ramabai and her brother Srinivas Shastri, continued the long travels on foot and the ritual austerities. On one occasion, they combated the Punjab winter, in the absence of warm clothes, by burying themselves up to the neck in dry sand on the bank of the Jhelum, as Ramabai narrates in 'Famine Experiences'.

It was their chance arrival in Calcutta in 1878 that catapulted Ramabai into prominence. Her rare Sanskrit learning was honoured and she was bestowed the titles 'Pandita' and 'Sarasvati' by notable scholars after a public examination. She was also inducted into social reform by Brahmo Samaj leaders and delivered public and private lectures on the emancipation of women, drawing heavily upon Hindu texts and mythology, lectures that soon established her fame as a champion of women's education and as a public speaker. But personal tragedy struck again and again. Srinivas Shastri died of cholera in 1880, and Ramabai married his friend (and her own persevering suitor) Bipin Behari Das Medhavi, a Bengali non-Brahmin, Brahmo lawyer. After less than two years of a happy married life in Kochar, Assam, Medhavi also died prematurely of cholera in 1882, leaving the twenty-four year old Ramabai an impecunious widow with an infant daughter, Manorama.

The news of Ramabai's sudden widowhood catalysed the social reformers of Maharashtra into laying claim on their 'native daughter'. She went to Pune (via Madras, to explore briefly the possibility of studying medicine) where she joined the social reform circle of the Prarthana Samaj, which was modelled on the Brahmo Samaj and led by M.G. Ranade. The strength of caste bonds helped Ramabai slide effortlessly into the Chitpavan Brahmin community, as 'one of us' (Ranade 1953: 80).

But a majority of this social stratum also held extremely ortho-dox religious beliefs and was conservative in its social mores; and desired to keep women under strict control. Its patriarchal ideology positioned woman firmly within the domestic sphere as a wife/mother/housewife—underlining her sexual, reproductive and home-making functions—as mandated somewhat ambiguously by the ancient Hindu *shastras* and unambiguously by contemporary social custom, two sources of authority whose relative strength continued to be debated. Prepubertal marriages for girls and immediate post-pubertal consummation of marriage was mandatory in order to harness their sexuality, from its inception, to marriage and motherhood. The highest status for a woman was that of a *saubhagyavati* (or 'blessed' woman whose husband was alive), and a mother of sons, rather than daughters who were considered inferior and undesirable. This status was proclaimed by her appearance—wearing a colourful nine-yard sari and a profusion of ornaments. A woman only with daughters, or one without children had a lower status and was in danger of being deserted by her husband. A widow had the lowest status, especially a child widow or one without children, being neither wife nor mother and thus having forfeited her right to a normal existence. Widowhood was also proclaimed through appearance—having to wear a coarse, plain, borderless maroon sari, denied orna-ments, and disfigured through a completely shaven head which had to be carefully covered. Construed as a result of sins in previous lives, widowhood bore the stigma of inauspiciousness; and the widow became a household drudge expected to live on meagre food, sleep on the floor without a bedding, and spend her time in ritual acts, all calculated to underline her superfluity in patriarchal society (Kosambi 1988; forthcoming).

This tragic figure was to become the focus of Ramabai's future career, although the agency which Ramabai claimed as a social reformer was undercut by her own status as a widow, however unconventional. The entry of a woman, moreover an 'inauspicious' widow with a 'sinful' past and a 'polluting' presence, into public life aroused the outrage of the local orthodox Brahmins (Ranade 1953: 81), which festered over the years and ultimately defeated her.

Ramabai moved rapidly into the male- and upper caste-dominated social reform discourse in Maharashtra and attempted to reinscribe women into it as subjects rather than objects. The movements around caste and gender, the twin axes of reform, had taken largely divergent directions; gender issues had become the preoccupation of the upper castes, whose women were the most oppressed. The recent colonial cultural encounter had introduced reformist ideas of women's 'upliftment' through an amelioration of the coercive customs of child marriage and enforced widowhood, and through education, which had been reserved for Brahmin men until the advent of caste- and gender-neutral English education. But these reforms were to be circumscribed strictly within a patriarchal framework and geared towards making women better wives for the English-educated Indian men expecting companionate marriages, and more enlightened mothers of the future generations who would restore India to its former glory and ultimately to political autonomy. 'Emancipation' of women was thus essentially an investment in societal—that is, male—progress, rather than aimed at bringing about gender equality.

The disparate reform initiatives in Maharashtra coalesced around the mid-nineteenth century under the leadership of 'Lokahitavadi' Deshmukh who operated largely within the Brahmin orbit and 'Mahatma' Jotirao Phule who championed the cause of lower castes against oppressive Brahmin hegemony and also struggled for gender-related reforms (although both shared a generally pro-British ideological stance). In the late 1870s, a more liberal generation of reformers, led by M.G. (later Justice) Ranade and Professor (later

Sir) R.G. Bhandarkar, claimed centrestage and sought to introduce social reform through legislation while also mobilizing public opinion. A significant shift occurred in the mid-1880s with the attempt, especially by K.T. (later Justice) Telang, to prioritize political reform at the cost of social concerns (Telang 1886). This was also the thrust of Professor (later 'Lokamanya') B.G. Tilak's politics. Social reform came to be gradually sidelined with Tilak's ascendancy in the national political scene, especially from the 1890s, reinforced by the newspapers under his leadership, the Marathi-language paper *Kesari* and the English-language *Mahratta*. The liberal faction was led by Professor G.G. Agarkar who resigned from this group and started his own weekly in 1888, newspapers being an essential weapon in the battle for social and political reform. Ramabai would initially enjoy the cautious support of even the conservative papers until her own radical activities led to an open split, and it was the acknowledged social reformers who would support her the longest. Significantly, Ranade, Bhandarkar and Agarkar were to later take a tolerant view of Ramabai's conversion to Christianity, while Phule applauded it as a rejection of Hindu bigotry towards women and Shudras and hailed her as their champion (Kosambi 1992a).

Ramabai's reform career in Maharashtra was launched with the Arya Mahila Samaj, established by her on 1 June 1882 in Pune on the rudimentary foundations of an existing women's association. Several branches were opened in the region later. The pioneering venture, intended to mobilize women themselves through 'consciousness-raising' and discussion to demand reform in the oppressive social customs, was supported by the social reformers as a welcome initiative, and opposed by anti-reformers as a threat to male hegemony—the *Kesari* flatly denied women the agency to 'interfere' in the 'men's task of eradicating the evil customs' affecting women (8 August 1882: 5*).[5] This faction was placated by her Marathi work *Stri Dharma Niti* (or *Morals for Women*, its English title given for the mandatory registration of vernacular books) which was published at the end of June 1882, but it opposed her plea before the Hunter Commission on Education in September 1882 for better facilities for women's general and medical education.

With a renewed ambition to study medicine herself, Ramabai planned to travel to England. She took some English lessons and arranged for her stay with the Sisters of the Community of St. Mary the Virgin at Wantage where she was to earn her living by teaching Marathi to the Sisters who would be sent to western India, on the clear understanding from her that she would not convert to Christianity. This progression of events and her voyage during April–May 1883, accompanied by her daughter Manorama and a companion of the Maratha caste, Anandibai Bhagat, was described by Ramabai in a long letter which was later published as a booklet entitled *Pandita Ramabai Yancha Englandcha Pravas* (Pandita Ramabai's Voyage to England') (Ramabai 1988).

On reaching England, Ramabai soon met Sir Bartle Frere, former Governor of the Bombay Presidency, in June 1883 and wrote him a long letter entitled 'The Cry of Indian Women' (selection 2). The letter was an appeal on behalf of the Arya Mahila Samaj, intended for circulation and fund-raising for a proposed 'destitute home' for the women victims of multiple oppression in India. It was probably the first such Indian initiative in England.

Unfortunately, a series of disasters followed. Anandibai Bhagat committed suicide by swallowing poison, but was baptised on her deathbed ostensibly to respect her own earlier wish to convert to Christianity. Still in a deep depression (and probably under pressure, as discussed below), Ramabai herself converted to Christianity at the end of September 1883 and was baptised into the Anglican Church as Mary Rama, along with Manorama (Manorama Mary). Her Anglican patrons and guardians, especially her spiritual preceptress Sister Geraldine, had already decided upon a missionary career for Ramabai, although they were to face unexpected challenges from her on many counts (Kosambi 1992a; 1998c). Then in the midst of a protracted theological debate with the Anglican nuns and even with bishops, Ramabai discovered that her incurable deafness would preclude her from pursuing medical studies. Ramabai was then enrolled in December 1883 by the Wantage Community in the Cheltenham Ladies' College as a teacher-student who would study the natural sciences, mathematics and English, and give Sanskrit lessons in return. Miss Dorothea Beale, the founder-principal of Cheltenham Ladies' College and a champion of women's education (Spender 1983: 447–8), provided empathetic and intellectual support, in contrast to Sister Geraldine's dogmatic stance (and self-confessed inability to relate to Ramabai on her own intellectual plane; *The Letters and Correspondence of Pandita Ramabai* [hereafter, *Letters*], edited by A.B. Shah, p. 5).

After almost three years in England, Ramabai went to the USA at the invitation of Dr Rachel Bodley, Dean of the Woman's Medical College of Pennsylvania, to attend the graduation of a distant relative[6] Anandibai Joshee, who was to become India's first woman doctor (in vicarious fulfilment of Ramabai's own thwarted ambition). Ramabai was instantly lionized in the USA as an internationally reputed advocate of the Indian women's cause. A glowing account of her life and her speech at a special gathering the day after Anandibai's graduation appeared in the American press. While reproducing it *The Mahratta* of Pune (2 May 1886: 6–7) tried simultaneously to undermine Ramabai through a new and enduring installation of Anandibai (whose conformity to convention had been well-publicized) as the icon of educated Maharashtrian womanhood.

Ramabai was to spend two-and-a-half years (from March 1886 to October 1888) in the USA, studying the educational system in Philadelphia and later (after sending Manorama to England and then to India to await her arrival), travelling from coast to coast in order to publicize her plan to open a home for high-caste Hindu widows in India. In 1887 she published *The High-Caste Hindu Woman* as part of her fund-raising efforts. The campaign resulted in the creation of The Ramabai Association of Boston in December 1887, that would support an unsectarian educational institution for child-widows in India; a number of 'circles' across the country (numbering seventy-five in early 1890 according to the Association's *Second Annual Report*) made annual pledges to the Association. The Association in turn pledged financial support for ten years to a secular widows' home.

The educationist in Ramabai surfaced in other ways. In 1888, while still in the USA, she started writing her Marathi book *United Stateschi Lokasthiti ani Pravasavritta* which she completed and published in Mumbai in 1889 (registered under the English title *The Peoples of the United States*). Its purpose was to share with her compatriots her experience of a free and progressive democracy, repeatedly contrasted with colonial Britain.

After sailing from San Francisco, via Japan where she delivered a few public lectures, Ramabai reached India in February 1889. She settled down with Manorama in Mumbai and almost immediately, on 11 March 1889, opened a widows' home, the Sharada Sadan (Home of Learning), at Chowpatty. The enormous venture underscored Ramabai's enterprising spirit, organizational capability and nationalistic credentials and generated excitement in which her conversion was at least temporarily forgotten. All leading social reformers of the Bombay Presidency supported the Sadan; many, such as Ranade, Bhandarkar and Telang, served on its Advisory Board. The general reaction was captured by the *Kesari* (12 February 1889: 3*). It applauded her 'marvellous deed' of collecting funds for the cause of Indian widows in a foreign land, regretted her conversion and the consequent social and emotional distancing, and prophesized that 'if her conduct is straightforward, people will shortly develop a trust in her'.

In November 1890, the Sadan was shifted to Pune for reasons of economy and direct access to the orthodox Brahmin community, a move that sharpened the conservative attack on its secular credentials and for its perceived 'pampering' of widows. In 1891, a storm broke out over allegations of proselytization—a sensitive issue that snowballed rapidly into a regular verbal warfare with all prominent newspapers of the time engaging in 'investigative journalism' by trying to collect information from current or past inmates of the Sadan. In its bitter aftermath, members of the Advisory Board resigned, and most girls were withdrawn from the Sadan by their guardians. The Ramabai Association of Boston sent Mrs Andrews, chairperson of the Executive Committee, to inquire into the matter. Ramabai was exonerated, but the breach between her and mainstream Hindu society—and later, even the social reformers—never healed.

It was mainly outside the orbit of mainstream upper caste society that Ramabai's project of helping widows and deserted women expanded to wider proportions. After a massive rescue operation following a famine in the Central Provinces and Gujarat in 1896, she housed hundreds of the victims in huts at the village of Kedgaon near Pune, on land she had recently bought. Here she opened a new and Christian institution, the Mukti Sadan (Home of Salvation), later expanded into the Mukti Mission. In 1899 she obtained a renewed pledge of support from the reconstituted American Ramabai Association for an unsectarian Sharada Sadan which was later shifted to the overtly Christian Mukti Mission, alongside Kripa Sadan (Home of Mercy, a rescue home for sexually victimized women), a separate section for blind women who were given a general education in Braille and taught useful crafts, and another that looked after aged women.

Ramabai's shift to Kedgaon and focus on lower caste famine victims rather than upper caste widows made her activities peripheral to mainstream society. Her last years were spent in relative isolation, albeit with a gradual *rapprochement* with the numerous Christian denominations that had earlier criticized her policy of religious neutrality. Through incessant activity—running a school and classes to develop income-generating skills of the inmates (which included teaching, nursing, tailoring, embroidery, laundering, weaving of cloth and carpets, gardening, and even operating a printing press), fund-raising and maintaining international networks—Ramabai had built what an impressed Christian visitor described as 'a female kingdom' in which all the tasks 'from top to bottom' were performed by women (*Dnyanodaya,* 28 November 1907: 380*). It had been Ramabai's cherished dream to develop self-reliance in, and provide an alternative shelter for, women whose homes were their 'social universe' but often an oppressive one (Kosambi 1998b). The dream finally came true at Mukti Mission (renamed 'Ramabai Mukti Mission' after her death, and 'Pandita Ramabai Mukti Mission' in 1969), but was to remain outside the reach of upper caste widows whom she had tried desperately to reach.

These shifts were parallelled by her religious evolution. In 1891, during the darkest hour of the storm Ramabai had a revelation in the classic Christian tradition; faith superseded intellectual questioning and her earlier freshness and openness on religious issues gradually rigidified into a proselytizing zeal, as she describes in her Christian confessions, *A Testimony* (1907) and in occasional pieces in her newsletter, the *Mukti Prayer Bell.* She also launched her most ambitious work, a new translation of the Bible from the original Hebrew and Greek into Marathi, during the course of which she also wrote a Greek grammar in Marathi.

But this newsletter, the *Annual Reports* and other writings show a creeping frustration, resentment, isolation and bitterness. They also reveal the fatal flaw in her reasoning—the conviction that Hindu women would flock to her institutions for shelter and realize that their oppression could be remedied only by conversion to Christianity.

The opening years of the twentieth century found Ramabai beleaguered—Sharada Sadan was marginalized, the Mukti Sadan, that housed hundreds of famine victims, was beset by multiple problems ranging from paucity of funds to imposition of discipline, the uniqueness of her pro-women interventions was partly overshadowed by Karve's 'Hindu' Widows' Home opened at Pune in 1896 (and later shifted to nearby Hingne), explicitly intended as an alternative to the 'Christian' Sharada Sadan (Kosambi 1995: 164) and by Malabari's Seva Sadan launched at Mumbai in 1908; its Pune branch, under Ramabai Ranade's management, opened in 1909. But already an international icon of Indian Christianity, Ramabai was able to function as the strongest single pivot and conduit for 'international aid' to Indian women through funds and volunteer workers. During the last two decades of her life, she relied for support largely on these wide international networks. Her social contribution was recognized by the British Government, which awarded her the Kaiser-i-Hind gold medal in 1919.

Her last personal tragedy befell Ramabai in 1921 with the death of forty year old Manorama, an able assistant in all her mother's enterprises and active in setting up girls' schools in Hyderabad state. The following year Ramabai herself passed away at the age of sixty-four, having just completed her Marathi translation of the Bible which was being printed at the Kedgaon press by her specially trained girls when she died.

THE SELF IN RELIGIOUS TRANSITION

Ramabai never documented her rich and variegated life in any great detail. Her earliest available autobiographical sketch (1883; selection 3) is a terse narrative written in Marathi on the eve of her conversion in England and translated immediately into English. It presents the bare bones of her already eventful life. The account was fleshed out with the occasional incident of her childhood related in passing in some episodes about her parents and sister in *The High-Caste Hindu Woman* (1887), and the harsh realities of poverty and starvation in 'Famine Experiences' (1897). Her final word on her own life was *A Testimony* (1907)—another terse autobiographical account, though leavened with a wry humour.

Most conspicuous in Ramabai's later writings (after 1900) is a marked transition, a deliberate effort to re-plot her entire past on the meridian of Christianity. This occurs at various levels. One is the attempt to trace the red thread of Christianity running right through her life as a conscious or unconscious guiding force. Not only does she locate and reconstruct her life entirely within the framework of Christianity in *A Testimony*, she also rediscovers echoes of Christianity in an almost forgotten childhood experience narrated in 'The Word-Seed' (selection 12), in an attempt to lay claim to the Christian core of her personality which had lain dormant under an orthodox Hindu shell.

Although this reconstructed passage to Christianity was imbued with a sense of inevitability, the suddenness of Ramabai's conversion continues to remain a mystery given her public and convincing promise to her Prarthana Samaj supporters before leaving for England not to convert to Christianity. Recent research indicates that 'pressure' to convert, though not necessarily amounting to 'coercion', was exerted on Ramabai (and Anandibai Bhagat) by the Wantage Sisters in the genuine belief that Ramabai was an 'inquirer', who had come to England to make a concentrated study of Christianity away from other distractions prior to actual conversion. This was the basis for their financial and practical support, although Ramabai's understanding of the situation differed significantly (Glover 1995: 71–109). This version is indirectly corroborated by Professor Max Mueller (1899: 127) whom Ramabai visited at Oxford about this time. He found Ramabai in a state of 'nervous prostration' because Anandibai Bhagat had been so frightened by the possibility of forced conversion that she had tried to save Ramabai by attempting to strangle her one night and finally killed herself.

It was in this mood of disappointment, depression and even despair that Ramabai was baptised. The reasons she herself offered for her conversion—'recollected in (Christian) tranquility' many years later—therefore appear to be more in the nature of justifications, though they are by no means unconvincing. They cover the progression from her early disillusionment with the gender- and caste-based discrimination of orthodox Hindu faith, acceptance of Brahmo belief, the proof given by the Reverend Nehemiah Goreh (a Brahmin convert himself) that the Brahmo Samaj was derived not from the Hindu Vedas but from Christianity, the Christian promise of universal salvation without discrimination, and the compassionate deeds of Christians such as the kindness of the Wantage Sisters and the Christian concept of redemption rather than punishment for sinners (Kosambi 1992). Ramabai records her visit to a Rescue Home in London where 'fallen' women, shunned by Hindu scriptures and custom, were being rehabilitated as useful members of society. This was the model for her own Kripa Sadan years later (see selection 10). A hidden but strong dimension of this conversion was loneliness and isolation which increased the appeal of a supportive social structure that she had missed all her life, the need 'to be able to worship together with those whom she loved and who had long been so kind to her' (Max Mueller 1889: 128).

The aftermath of conversion found Ramabai embroiled in a protracted debate with the Wantage Sisters and the Anglican Church. Her primary contestation of the Church rested on issues of theology: her selective acceptance of Christian doctrine and rejection of the miraculous birth and divinity of Christ. The secondary issue was Sister Geraldine's insistence on the need for implicit acceptance of 'the authority of those over her in the Church' (*Letters*: 43), and Canon Butler's that 'to a neophyte in the Faith . . . self-reliance is intensely dangerous' (*Letters*: 76). The third contentious issue was the patriarchal insistence of the Anglicans that as an Indian woman Ramabai could not jeopardize her future chances in India by teaching Indian languages to men. Ramabai contested the authoritarianism of the Anglican Church by insisting that 'I have a conscience, and mind and a judgment of my own. I must myself think and do everything which GOD has given me the power of doing', and claiming that after having 'with great effort freed myself from the yoke of the Indian priestly tribe . . . I am not at present willing to place myself under [a] similar yoke' by obeying the instructions of the Anglican clergy 'as authorized command of the Most High' (*Letters*: 156).

Underneath this friction ran the barely disguised current of racism: the Anglican bishops' generalization about the 'natives' that 'vanity is one of their very faults', and that academic status 'might lead to a little undue self-exaltation' (*Letters*: 43–5); and Sister Geraldine's bitter complaint of Ramabai's 'pride and vanity' which were 'dangerously inflated' (*Letters*: 4), her 'want of candour and sincerity' and her 'deceitfulness' like 'the generality of the Hindoos' (*Letters*: 114–15). Colonial rule formed the core of this problematic relationship, because Christianity was the religion of the conquerors and the Anglican Church itself bore the title The Church of England which, as Sister Geraldine saw, 'would tend to alarm and repel' Ramabai (*Letters*: 406). This is borne out by the opening passages of Ramabai's chapter on religion 'Religious Denominations' (selection 6) in *United Stateschi.* . . .

The second stage in Ramabai's Christian evolution came after many years, during the dismal days when Sharada Sadan was boycotted and she herself discredited even in the eyes of her former reformist supporters. She now saw the deficiency in her intellectual acceptance of Christ without the emotional support of unquestioning faith. In 1891, during these desperate times, she had a revelation, like a burst of light followed by a sense of great relief. It led to a change in Ramabai's attitude to proselytization, and to intense missionary activity. The shift of the Sharada Sadan to Kedgaon, where Ramabai had bought a farm, was caused fortuitously by a plague epidemic in Pune; it facilitated the establishment of the Mukti Mission where hundreds of famine victims were housed and converted. By 1900, the strength of the Mission was close to two thousand and generated a fresh set of problems. The new inmates were drawn from depressed castes, very different from the disciplined Brahmin widows of the Sharada Sadan, and their needs ranged from creature comforts to character building, secular and spiritual education.

This led to the final phase of uncompromising Christianity that saw closer contacts with the Christian communities within India, while maintaining international Christian networks. Ramabai's touching desire to explain the pure essence of the Vedas to fellow Christians (see 'Indian Religion', selection 4) gave way to a total 'othering' of Hinduism across an ideological divide; her experiential world was now refracted only through the prism of Christianity.

THE EVOLUTION OF
A FEMINIST CONSCIOUSNESS

Ramabai entered the gender reform discourse in Maharashtra through *Stri Dharma Niti* as a surrogate male social reformer by virtue of her unusual Sanskrit education, oratory and leadership qualities, all of which had long been a prerogative of men. A natural extension of her lectures to women in the Bengal and Bombay Presidencies on the need for their education, *Stri Dharma Niti* is a guide on morality and deportment for women, featuring the Hindu mythological models of womanhood. It is also a book of general knowledge peopled by historical figures such as Shivaji and Napoleon, and set entirely within the parameters of the liberal tradition espoused by reformist newspapers and magazines of the time. Hence *Kesari's* satisfaction that 'the task of championing the women's cause and of speaking or writing on their behalf, which hitherto fell to the lot of men, has now been undertaken by one belonging to the female sex herself' (1 August 1882: 2*).

The jarring notes in *Stri Dharma Niti,* in view of our image of Ramabai as a militant feminist, are her endorsement of the Sita-Savitri model of femininity and her castigation of the average woman as lazy, stupid and obstinate, and therefore culpable not only for her own but for the entire country's subjection and stagnation. At the same time, *Stri Dharma Niti* also indicates Ramabai's radical divergence from the positions taken by social reformers on two counts: her advocacy of relatively late marriages by mutual choice, and her exposure of the androcentric and misogynist bias of the *dharma-shastras.* The tension between her castigation of women as culpable for their own subjection and her simultaneous exoneration of them as victims conditioned to internalize their subjection, was to be finally resolved in *The High-Caste Hindu Woman,* the product of a cohesive feminist perspective. But a blueprint for this Indian feminist manifesto had already appeared in 'The Cry of Indian Women' (a newly discovered manuscript, published for the first time in this volume). It also details Indian women's oppression through early marriage, marital harassment, desertion by the husband and widowhood, before outlining her proposed 'destitute home' in India.

The mystifying sea-change between *Stri Dharma Niti* (June 1882) and 'The Cry of Indian Women'(June 1883) has no easy explanation. The former was obviously a product of social liberalism advocated by Ramabai's reformist supporters, but at variance with her own reform efforts through the Arya Mahila Samaj which had challenged the patriarchal ideology and practice. It was a development of this incipient feminism, perhaps further reinforced by the early feminist articulations by Tarabai Shinde[7], Anandibai Joshee and Rakhmabai, which found expression in 'The Cry of Indian Women'. In 1882 Tarabai Shinde (1975) had contested the masculine double standards of morality and unabashed misuse of patriarchal privilege, in February 1883 Anandibai Joshee had protested publicly against the denial of educational opportunities and medical care to women (after having privately protested against the general subordination, neglect and dispensability of women), and in 1885 Rakhmabai was to write about the misery of child brides and widows of all ages (Kosambi 1994; 1995; 1996a; 1996b). Both Anandibai and Rakhmabai, part of Ramabai's wide informal network, figure in *The High-Caste Hindu Woman*. With Anandibai's premature death and Rakhmabai's self-imposed seclusion from public life and dedication to medical duties, Ramabai was to alone mount a sustained attack on Hindu patriarchy, although the internationally known *The High-Caste Hindu Woman* was to have a minimal impact in Maharashtra, or the rest of India.

But the major influence that shaped the evolution of Ramabai's feminist consciousness, as reflected in *The High-Caste Hindu Woman*, was her exposure to the more progressive and less assymetrical gender relations that prevailed in England and America. During her later years she stressed what she saw as the gender-egalitarian impulse of Christianity and its compassion to sinners (especially the rehabilitation of 'fallen women'), contrasting these favourably with the discriminatory and less humane Hindu doctrine (see *A Testimony*). But arguably a far greater influence on Ramabai than religion was the women's movement in the West, especially in America. Dr Rachel Bodley and Frances Willard, President of the Woman's Christian Temperance Union (WCTU), were Ramabai's personal friends and office-bearers of the Ramabai Association, and the international WCTU networks were to support Ramabai's reform efforts for the rest of her life. Her chapter on women in the United States 'The Condition of Women' (selection 7) sketches the brave new world she had glimpsed, with only minor flaws. Her description of women in America is a polemical statement of feminist solidarity.

That American society seemed like a utopia to women readers of *United Stateschi* . . . is suggested in the review by Kashibai Kanitkar, the first major female novelist in Marathi and a rarity as a book reviewer, being a woman. Kashibai's review indicates the appeal of the book for both expanding the female readers' horizons and reinforcing their incipient feminism which only needed an outlet for public expression: 'It would be hardly surprising if every one of our countrywomen who reads this book mutters dejectedly that such a golden day will never dawn for us. However, we will have to swallow these words hastily before they reach anybody's ears for fear of committing "treason against men", just as our men are afraid of committing treason when they discuss the government' (cited in Vaidya 1991: 235–6*). The review itself, which established a vantage point qualitatively different from that of male reviewers, was sufficient proof of the progress in women's education since 1882 when the female readership of *Stri Dharma Niti* was expected to be non-existent—although the progress did not necessarily take the direction anticipated or desired by the (male) reformers.

United Stateschi . . . marks the end of Ramabai's feminist writings (except for a brief spark in *A Testimony*) as her religious preoccupations claimed centrestage. It was also the end of her career as a mainstream writer. *A Testimony* and the Marathi Bible hardly reached the general Marathi readership, and her narratives of women's oppression in several reports were intended for a specific, chiefly Western readership.

TRIADIC ENCOUNTERS

While her upper caste contemporaries remained confined within the home which became their 'social universe' (Kosambi 1998b), Ramabai had not only traversed the Indian subcontinent several times over, but also travelled widely within England and the USA, besides visiting other countries such as Japan. (Only a handful of women—or even men—from Maharashtra travelled abroad before 1900, mainly for higher studies: prominent among them were Anandibai Joshee who lived in the USA from 1883 to 1886, Rakhmabai in England, from 1889 to 1895, and Cornelia Sorabji also in England, from 1889 to 1893.) The formative part of Ramabai's social reform career (the period 1883–8) was shaped by her Anglo-American encounters within the larger context of Christian denominational, ideological, and nationalistic tensions.[8]

The Indo-American connection, relatively slight in the late nineteenth century, was heavily mediated by the British colonial link, and was contingent upon it. The conduit for the American presence in India were the Christian Missions that started operating soon after the East India Company's monopoly of trade with India ended in 1813, which allowed the entry of private commercial and religious interests, a history Ramabai hints at in her chapter on religion in the United States, 'Religious Denominations'. The American Marathi Mission, which opened the region's first public school and started the Anglo-Marathi weekly *Dnyanodaya,* extended overt support for British rule in India in an article revealingly entitled 'The Destiny of the White Race', claiming:

It is fortunate for India that it is England that rules over her. No other of the white races is so fitted to fulfil her high mission over so great an empire . . . the mission of the white race to be the instrument through which is carried to the world a pure religion . . . (*Dnyanodaya* 1885: 500).

While Anglo-American religious interests coincided in India, where most Westerners were complicit in the Orientalist, Christianizing project in some way, the experience of an Indian visiting the two countries was often agreeably different, more so in the USA than in England. For Ramabai, the persistent religious friction with some Anglicans in England, with their vested interest in her proposed missionary career in India, was replaced by American tolerance of her non-denominational Christianity; it allowed her to forge an instant and effective bond with her audiences. Her maiden speech in the USA, for example, ended on a 'startling' and 'unique' note when 'the earnest little lady' asked 'an American company of educated and refined men and women to join with her in a moment's silent prayer "to the Great Father of all the nations of the earth" in [sic] behalf of the millions of her Hindoo sisters to whose cause she has given her life' (*Philadelphia Evening Bulletin,* 13 March 1886).

Ramabai was situated radically differently in the two countries. In England, she was always conscious of being a colonial subject— a 'native'. Having objected, in her article on Indian religion in *The Cheltenham Ladies' College Magazine,* to the indiscriminate and derogatory use of the term 'native' to describe all the people of the British colonies, she herself consistently used the term in its original meaning throughout *United Stateschi.* . . . The book amply reflects Ramabai's affinity with the country that had freed itself from the colonial yoke a century earlier—in her glowing description of the American Revolution, her repeated comparisons of America's superior political, economic, cultural and religious situation with England's, and her conspicuous solidarity with both the women's movement in America and American blacks. Across the racial divide her American friends camouflaged their racial awareness of her by a certain exoticization; Ramabai's pale skin and hazel eyes made her acceptable as almost 'one of us'. The first, and generally representative, reaction of Caroline Dall—a feminist activist and writer, biographer of Anandibai Joshee and a friend who donated the sale proceeds of her biography of Anandibai to Ramabai's cause—was that 'Ramabai is strikingly beautiful' and that, apart from her 'white widow's saree ... [t]here is nothing else about her to suggest the Hindoo [i.e. Indian]' (Dall 1888: 130–1). The Brahmin mystique (despite her conversion to Christianity), her acute intelligence and English education ensured her entry into the elite circles of Philadelphia and Boston.

If the perception of the 'civilized' West being the donors of benefits such as education to colonized nations like India was common to both countries, Ramabai received a great deal of concrete help in the USA, especially from Dr Bodley. In a tribute to the Dean after her death, a colleague recalled the 'noble aid' she extended to Ramabai (and Anandibai Joshee), adding: 'Their two names will thus be long linked together—shall we not say immortalized—the one representing the needs of the far East, and the other the Christian civilization and benevolence of the West' (Hartshorne 1888: 21.) Undeniably, Ramabai's international career was launched in the USA, through the help of friends like Dr Rachel Bodley and Frances Willard.

The international publicity that pervaded Ramabai's successful fund-raising in America and the opening of the Sharada Sadan compelled Sister Geraldine to alternate between denying the 'false reports that England had given Ramabai the cold shoulder, and she had consequently turned from England to America' (Letters: 295), acknowledging that 'America stole Ramabai from England', and insisting that 'England and her colonies have hardly been behind America in the gifts they have sent out to Ramabai; and England would have done still more for her, had she had [the] patience to wait and prove the generosity of the English public' (Letters: 423.)

Of considerable interest is Ramabai's ideological location vis-à-vis India, the original point of the triad, which she referred to variously in her Marathi writings, from the initial, Sanskritized Bharatavarsha in Stri Dharma Niti, to the more prevalent Hindustan in United Stateschi. . . . The contemporary Indian response to the question of her 'nationalism' was dominated by the largely hostile view of her conversion and later, of her missionary activity as anti-Hindu and therefore anti-Indian.

Ramabai's own stance remained largely stable over time: starting with patriotic indignation over a few foreigners having reduced millions of Indians to subjection in *Stri Dharma Niti* (1882); to demanding from Frere (in 1883) and the British government financial aid as a right, almost in compensation for having accumulated their wealth by impoverishing India; to a contestation of colonial power as exploitative, mercenary and patriarchal in discussing the Rakhmabai case in *The High-Caste Hindu Woman* (1887); and finally to an attack on the British policy of returning famine victims to the princely states as equalling the barbarity of those who had earlier pushed the widow onto her husband's funeral pyre, in her account of Mukti Mission (selection 9).

In these triadic encounters, Ramabai occupied a terrain permanently at the intersection of religion, culture and reform: as a high-caste Hindu turned Christian, an Indian straddling Western culture with equal facility and a social reformer aiming to alter the societal core of caste and custom.

OPPRESSED INDIAN WOMANHOOD: TRANSPARENCY, TROPING AND GENDERED SUBALTERNITY

Within this international context, diverse issues are raised by Ramabai's narratives of the oppressed Indian woman—as widow, deserted wife, and sexually exploited woman—which filled her reports of the Sharada Sadan, Mukti Mission and Kripa Sadan, as well as her *Letters*.

For her contemporaries, the most acceptable—or least unacceptable—part of Ramabai's contribution was her attempt to rescue the chaste upper caste widow, the noble symbol of Hindu patriarchal oppression, from her marginalized position within the domestic sphere and to reinstate her in a newly created (but still essentially marginal) space in the public sphere, by educating her and training her in professions such as teaching. But the sufferings of deserted and sexually victimized women, of any caste, revealed the far wider, more unpleasant repercussions of patriarchy and demanded a multi-pronged approach; they also laid bare the basic lack of compassion and will within Hindu society to face and solve these problems. Hence Ramabai's charge, in her account of Mukti Mission, that Hinduism could be proud of such martyrs, only if they were willing martyrs. Ramabai herself spelt out her strategy of transparency in her introduction to M.B. Fuller's *The Wrongs of Indian Womanhood*, first published in 1900: to courageously tell the truth as the first step in making women themselves aware of 'the depths of degradation' they suffer, informing reformers about the real condition of women, and raising public awareness about the scene 'behind the purdah' (Ramabai 1984). But transparency was discredited as a dubious, anti-nationalist strategy in a social climate in which the existence of women's oppression within the family, or 'domestic slavery', was vehemently denied (Telang 1886), where the idea of consulting women themselves on issues that concerned them deeply, like the Age of Consent, was considered innovative (Kosambi 1998a), and where a private reformist belief was prudently suppressed by a public conservative stance for 'nationalistic' reasons even by articulate women such as Anandibai Joshee (Kosambi 1996b). Ramabai's exposure and criticism of this defensive nationalist posture as a (sometimes unwitting) attempt at a tacit 'othering' and an occlusion of oppressed women and a stalling of real social reform, was a double-edged sword.

The questions that arise spontaneously but defy easy answers are: Can Ramabai's narratives, whether in her own words or those of the victims, be construed as gendered subaltern articulations? Did she enjoy legitimacy as a representative or mediator of these victims, on the strength of her positionality as a disprivileged widow and a marginalized, converted Christian? Or was such legitimacy undermined by her being simultaneously a privileged, Sanskrit-educated Brahmin and English-educated Christian with an affinity with the hegemonistic Christian community worldwide?

At one level, Ramabai's troping of oppressed Indian womanhood which started with 'The Cry of Indian Women' and continued through the *The High-Caste Hindu Woman* and beyond has still not lost its power because her revolutionary, objective critique of Hindu doctrines and customs (to the extent that they can be homogenized) with a concrete programme to redress women's oppression resonate well with most Indian feminists today. If, lacking today's language of feminism, she couched her analysis in different terms, she still succeeded in 'naming' the problem. At another level, it is easy to accept her generalized and unambiguous attack on patriarchy—whether described as the caste- and custom-based oppression of Indian women, the authoritarianism of the Anglican Church, or the gender-based subjection of an earlier generation of American women. The questions being raised today would not deny the validity of her attack, they would only expand its parameters in their focus on the persistent gender assymetry in American society and the prevalent oppression of women—through wife-beating, desertion and sexual victimization—in Christian communities, both in India and abroad.

The obverse side of this troping is an increasing repetitiveness and forced quality as well as Ramabai's self-conscious underscoring of her unique position as a simultaneous insider and outsider and of her Christian affinity with her Western readers—all of which exude the staleness of a formalized, stylized narrative.

But the real problem lies deeper. Over the years, Ramabai's essentialization of the oppressed Indian woman was itself edged out of the western Indian discourse of social reform and became permanently lodged within a Western, Orientalist, Christian discourse. The basic question it raises is how her Christian idiom and emancipatory, missionary rhetoric is distinguishable from outright Orientalist works on Indian women by Western authors. The nature and extent of the service she was able and allowed to render to the cause of Indian women through this international publicity (quite apart from the fund-raising which it aided) still remains unclear because of her acute marginalization. Hence the allegation that her ostensible motive of helping women only disguised and legitimized her Christianizing agenda.

CONTEXTS AND CONTEMPORARY CRITIQUES

Ramabai's very first book was her Marathi *Stri Dharma Niti* published in June 1882, about two months after her arrival in Pune, followed by the second, revised edition within six months owing to heavy patronage by the Directorate of Education.[9] In her foreword to the third edition, published in 1967, Lilian Doerksen expressed the hope that *Stri Dharma Niti* would be found 'readable and instructive' by readers in the late 1960s because the problems and conditions of India's largely rural women had not changed much since Ramabai's time.

The archaic Marathi of *Stri Dharma Niti* was explained by Doerksen (1967) as being common among the emigrant Maharashtrian Brahmins settled in Karnataka. But it is the heavily Sanskritized style that obtrudes. The Marathi reviewer of the *Native Opinion* complained that 'the authoress, being well-versed in Sanskrit, has filled the book with Sanskrit words which are difficult for the average woman or even man to understand', but conceded that 'the advice given by her to women is worth accepting not only by Hindu women but by Hindu men also' (23 July 1882: 472*). The reviewer for the *Kesari* said less charitably:

We think that even a man learned in Sanskrit would be reduced to helplessness by some passages, what to speak of poor women who are almost drowning in the sea of ignorance! Sanskrit exerts such a powerful effect on this lady's mind that even if she feels favourably disposed towards the chaste Marathi language and decides to employ a simple word, it gets coated at least once with a Sanskrit brush (1 August 1882: 4*).

In the second half of the review, he went further and suggested that 'if Panditabai intends to write more books, she should first make a proper study of the Marathi language' (*Kesari*, 22 August 1882: 5*).

Ramabai's later Marathi work *United Stateschi . . .* shows considerable stylistic improvement. Although she had gained complete mastery over English in the interim and earned praise in the West for the instantly popular *The High-Caste Hindu Woman,* her Marathi style did not quite acquire the ease and fluency of her English, nor the lucidity of her contemporaries' serious (and even ornate) Marathi prose. But the contents were well-received: her 'elegant and heart-stirring' language and 'gripping' descriptions won the approval of the *Kesari* reviewer (7 January 1890: 2*).[10] His reservations were directed at her feminism: 'That Panditabai has given the male sex a lashing is not surprising; it is a bad habit she has formed. Who knows how she is going to achieve her desired goal without men's help!' But the reviewer admitted that Ramabai's 'occasional comments on our present condition', however unpalatable, 'were worthy of serious consideration', that her stated policy of describing only the good qualities of the Americans was sound and should be applied also while 'considering the customs and manners of other countries' (perhaps a reference to her criticism of Indian society), and concluded that there was 'absolutely no doubt that the book is worth acquiring'.

The Indu-Prakash commended the book for its eyewitness accounts and the author's useful and inspiring comments, adding that 'because this book has been written by a person tender-hearted by nature, its language also shows tenderness. Everyone should certainly read it at least once.' It also noted that this was the second book in this genre in Marathi (after Karsandas Mulji's description of England published in Marathi translation) (6 January 1890: 2*).

Remarkably, *United Stateschi Lokasthiti ani Pravasavitta* has been crafted with the language and perception of a Sanskritized, Hindu worldview, half-a-dozen years after Ramabai's conversion to Christianity. It is most conspicuous in the chapter on women, which opens somewhat startlingly by invoking Sita to validate the achievements of American women and views universities such as Harvard as temples of Sarasvati serving an inexhaustible supply of 'the nectar of knowledge'. In fact, the opening paragraph is a masterly statement of authorial location; it manages to fuse nostalgia for a Sanskritic Brahmin childhood (to capture the attention of her inevitably upper caste readers) with a distancing from the same childhood as both a wiser adult and an enlightened Christian who appreciates revered Sanskrit texts as 'ancient literary works' rather than as sacred books, and also with a remarkable knowledge of both popular and obscure Sanskrit works. The invocation of demon-killing goddesses to stress American women's agency also serves to legitimize a similar effort by Indian women by locating it within the existing tradition of empowered female figures.

Given these cultural moorings, the hiatus marked by her later writings shows signs of a painful wrench to uproot some deeply ingrained traits of her personality, in an effort to force it into an entirely different mould. The scars of this cultural and emotional violence are visible. From the time of her conversion, Ramabai had grappled with the complex intertwining of religion and culture, and repeatedly attempted to indigenize Christianity and transform its alien cultural trappings into a more recognizable Indian garb, because she saw its true message as transcending denominational, cultural and racial divides. In this sense, it was a different and somehow alien Ramabai who in her translation of the Bible strove meticulously for a Marathi language shorn of all its Sanskrit words with their inherent Hindu connotations, and who detailed the difficulties in making a faithful translation of Christian ideas into a language 'saturated with idolatrous thoughts' (Adhav 1979: 206). The 'divine language' which had 'coated' Ramabai's prose in 1882, which she had described as 'the most beautiful and the oldest language of my dear native land' (*Letters*: 28) and which continued to pervade her writings until 1889 had become 'idolatrous' two decades later. Thus her retention of the accepted Marathi word *pavitra shastra,* despite its strong Hindu connotations, for this translation marked the last major contradiction in her writings.

The conflicting demands faced by Ramabai of fidelity to the original and readability of the translation also confront us in translating her: her Sanskritized Marathi is often archaic (sometimes even in her own social context, and invariably in ours). Her texts, each of which traverses cross-cultural and international terrains, from India's ancient Hindu past to the contemporary Anglo-American social scene, contain profuse Sanskrit quotes and allusions to the Christian doctrine and denominations. Even the tone and texture of Ramabai's Marathi show a far wider range than her evenly balanced and lucid English prose. *Stri Dharma Niti*, with its unrelieved didacticism, reads like a sermon and parts of *United Stateschi . . .* like a feminist polemic, but without the the compactness of the hard-hitting *The High-Caste Hindu Woman*; both texts are ponderous. An altogether different problem for the translator is posed by Ramabai's feminism—in both its incipient and full-fledged forms—because concepts which have 'a local habitation and a name' today and which slide spontaneously to the tip of the tongue and pen ('gender construction', 'patriarchy', 'empowerment', 'complicity', 'co-option') were couched in different labels a century ago. The task of translating the three pieces proved to be far more challenging and daunting than I anticipated. After juggling with the various concerns outlined above, I arrived at a somewhat complex agenda: to make a readable translation while avoiding anachronisms, to employ some of the vocabulary current in her time and be as faithful to the original as possible in order to retain the flavour of the original, and accomodate the diverse cultural nuances and pre-empt the possibility of an unwittingly distorted analysis of her writings, which might in future be based on these translations.

Ramabai's cultural transition was also reflected in her English writings. Her piece 'Indian Religion' shows her deep attachment for what she perceived as the core of Hinduism and her touchingly keen desire to convey it to unsympathetic (Christian) English readers. Her perception of Hinduism was to rapidly undergo both a feminist and a Christian transformation visible in *The High-Caste Hindu Woman* published the very next year. Designed as an Indian feminist manifesto, *The High-Caste Hindu Woman* tries to balance an incisive criticism of the Indian woman's inferior status in Hindu patriarchal society, with a nationalist defence of India *vis-à-vis* her Western readers. This effort to make the West understand Indian society shows that Ramabai's own understanding of Indian society was facilitated by the American feminist critique of contemporary Western society and her general exposure to the women's movement in the USA, especially through key figures like Dr Rachel Bodley and Frances Willard.

The book had a remarkable international circulation: its 'tenth thousand' was printed within a year of its first publication in June 1887. Newspapers across the ideological spectrum in America carried rave reviews,[11] variously labelling the book 'a cry for help', 'a revelation' to most Americans, a vindication of 'the activity of our Woman's Foreign Missionary Society'. A blend of Christianity and feminism, similar to that of Ramabai herself, ran through Frances Willard's review and was echoed across the Atlantic by Frances Power Cobbe. Evidently, Ramabai's book, while serving her agenda of creating a sympathetic understanding of the plight of Hindu women, strengthened the existing Orientalist, Christianizing agenda.

On arriving in India in 1889, Ramabai found herself and her Sharada Sadan initially accepted by Hindu social reformers of Mumbai and Pune. The later attack and the final boycott marks an end of Ramabai's writings other than reports and circular letters connected with her work, such as 'Famine Experiences' in 1897 and her letter to the 'Friends of Mukti School and Mission' in 1900. Had these eyewitness accounts of the gruesome realities of famine been heeded by her critics, she would probably have been spared further attacks, especially by Tilak who discredited her efforts by describing the rescued famine victims as 'widows caught in Ramabai's net during unprecedented opportunity of the famine years' (*Kesari*, 12 January 1904: 2*). The 'Famine' piece is noteworthy also for her autobiographical details and the second for her criticism of the hypocrisy of both the Princes of the native states and the British officials in dealing with the famine.

The small pamphlets that followed were written in the then usual missionary spirit that discredited Hinduism; together with *A Testimony* and 'The Word-Seed' (selection 12), both of which are Christian reconstructions of her life, they mark her complete transition to a Christian worldview and culture. A review of *A Testimony* in *Dnyanodaya* (19 September 1907: 299*) found the book truly remarkable, its truthfulness authenticated by the trust she received from 'Christians and non-Christians alike'. It went on, 'Had any-one else written this testimony, it would in all probability have contained exaggeration . . . We pray that a reading of this testimony may bring light to the non-Christians and enhance the faith of the Christians.' 'The second instalment of the review (26 September 1907: 308*) suggested that Panditabai should write this testimony in Marathi as well so as to assist 'the growth of the spiritual life of many people in Maharashtra'.

* * *

The Maharashtrian psyche still grapples with the dilemma of understanding, and slotting, Pandita Ramabai. The most conservative verdict is an outright condemnation of her for a betrayal of the cause of social reform and of the reformers. It was endorsed by *Kesari*'s obituary which blames her overriding personal ambition and impatience which led her to succumb to the 'temptation of the missionaries' before testing 'whether or not her achievements could make an impact on the Hindu society', with the result that 'such an intelligent, determined and enterprising woman's achievements helped not the Hindu society but foreign missionary organizations'. It ends by claiming that gender-related reform in Hindu society could be achieved from within, as Karve's Widows' Home and Seva Sadan under Ramabai Ranade's guidance had shown; and that Pandita Ramabai could also have 'proved her capacity for organizational work while remaining a Hindu. But unfortunately this was not to be!' (11 April 1922: 5*).

More liberal verdicts have also bemoaned her conversion as unnecessary, and suggested that Ramabai could have derived emotional and spiritual comfort from the Prarthana Samaj with its *bhakti* tradition, as well as practical support in her reform endeavours. Others have charitably stressed the symbiotic relationship between religious belief and adherence in the pre-secular age which necessitated her conversion. At the other end of the spectrum is the obituary of *Dnyanodaya* (13 April 1922: 117*) which detects a Christian impulse which propelled her to establish a woman's worth in an inegalitarian society, and predicts (with an unfortunately unjustified faith in the verdict of history): 'If the history of Western India during the last thirty years is to be written, there would be no disagreement that Pandita Ramabai would be given a pride of place'.

But all alike have left untouched the obvious, vexed questions: Did Ramabai, as a Brahmin widow, have the same social acceptance, legitimacy and manoeuvrability (even with male support), the same 'agency' to which a Brahmin man like Karve, or the widow of a nationally revered figure like Ranade, could lay claim? Would the reformers have given her the freedom and support to exercise initiative in opening homes for rescued women, famine victims, the blind and the aged? Most of all, would her basically patriarchal male supporters have validated her vision of self-reliant women? And if the Christianity that provided the only moral and practical support in her struggle also totally alienated her from the society she sought to reform, can one adequately gauge the terrible mutual loss?

This brings us back full circle to the conflated contradictions between Brahmanical, Hindu cultural moorings and Christian belief, an insider's empathy and an outsider's critique, attempts to reform a society but only by recasting its religious base, the urge to contest and the need to be accepted, which inhabited Ramabai's personality with an increasing degree of unease. And to the fact that three-quarters of a century after her death, Maharashtrian society, having yet to produce an individual of her stature engaged in social reform on such a vast and variegated scale, still remains unwilling to remember her and unable to forget.

Meera Kosambi

NOTES

1. The term Maharashtra is used here to indicate the Marathi-speaking region which comprised parts of the Bombay Presidency, Central Provinces and Berar, and Hyderabad state.
2. Prominent among the academic writings on Ramabai are Kosambi (1988; 1992; 1995; 1998c), Burton (1995; 1998) and Glover (1995). Numerous full-length biographies of Ramabai have been written since

her death, mainly by Western and Indian Christian authors, including Macnicol (1926), Dongre and Patterson (1963), Sengupta (1970) and Adhav (1979) in English; and Tilak (1960) in Marathi. Among Ramabai's few non-Christian (and Marathi) biographers are 'Prabodhankar' Thackeray (1950) and Sathe (1975). The biographical introductions to her writings by Bodley (1977) and Shah (1977) are also useful.

The shift among historians in Maharashtra is indicated by Ramabai's earlier exclusion from the list of social reformers (Phadke 1975) to her reinstatement (Phadke 1989; Sunthankar 1993). Professor Y.D. Phadke himself attributes this shift to the year 1975 being designated as the International Year of Women and its effect on the Maharashtra state government, which commissioned both his books (personal communication). The Maharashtra State Board of Literature and Culture has made a significant contribution by helping the republication of *Stri Dharma Niti* (1882) by the Ramabai Mukti Mission in 1967 with a grant (covering 75 per cent of the cost), publishing the *Letters and Correspondence of Pandita Ramabai* in 1977, reprinting the *The High-Caste Hindu Woman* (1887) in 1981, *Englandcha Pravas* (1883; 1922) in 1988 and *United Stateschi Lokasthiti ani Pravasavritta* (1889) in 1996.

3. See Lerner (1992) and Shepherd, *et al.* (1995) for problematizing women's history.

4. This biographical sketch is based on Kosambi (1988; 1992; 1995; 1998c), which utilize the English and Marathi biographies of Ramabai as well as her *Letters and Correspondence*.

   In my own text, current place names are used, such as Mumbai and Pune instead of Bombay and Poona; the Anglicized names are used in the translated texts.

5. The quotations marked with an asterisk are my own translations from the Marathi.

6. Anandibai Joshee's maternal grandmother was Anant Shastri Dongre's maternal cousin, as explained by Ramabai (*Indu-Prakash*, 5 August 1889: 5).

7. Tarabai Shinde, who hailed from an elite Maratha family from the Vidarbha sub-region of Maharashtra, remained an enigmatic and reclusive figure who produced only one booklet. The credit for retrieving it and reconstructing her sketchy biography goes to Dr S.G. Malshe.

8. Ramabai's 'triadic encounters' were the subject of my lectures at the University of Adelaide and Flinders University in Australia in August 1997, and at the Universities of Cincinnati and Pennsylvania in January 1998. The text of the lecture is currently being revised for publication.

9. The translation included in this volume is made from the third edition, published in 1967 (a reprint of the second edition, with a foreword and introduction by Lilian Doerksen).

10. This review has been obtained from the personal files of Dr S.G. Malshe, as the issue of the *Kesari* is missing from the paper's archives. Interestingly, an extract from *United Stateschi* . . . describing winter in America was included in a school textbook for Marathi during the mid-1940s (personal communication from Dr Pramod Kale).

11. From the archives of the Pandita Ramabai Mukti Mission; some details regarding the place and date of publication are missing.

PART I

POONA

Stri Dharma Niti (translation)
(June 1882)

1

STRI DHARMA NITI

Dedication

This small book,
written by the grieving widow of Babu Bipin Behari [Das Medhavi],
MA, BL, in memory of her very dear late husband,
is dedicated to her countrywomen with love

PREFACE TO THE FIRST EDITION

The present condition of women in our unfortunate country is too sad for words and will undoubtedly make every thoughtful person's heart melt with grief. The women of this country, being totally helpless and lacking in education, do not understand how to achieve their own welfare; it is therefore necessary for learned people to explain it to them and make them conduct themselves accordingly. Great improvement has already taken place in this country. Educated people are beginning to realise that the country will not progress as much as it should unless women are given knowledge, and they are therefore making efforts for women's progress, which is praiseworthy indeed.

Knowledge of morality and conduct conforming thereto are the doors to human progress, and both are lacking in womankind at present, the chief reason being their ignorance of the *shastras*. *Dharma, Niti, Darshan* and other *shastras* in this Bharatavarsha were written in the very difficult Sanskrit language which is no longer prevalent, so it is well-nigh impossible . . . for the illiterate women of today to obtain the knowledge they contain. Having realised that it is the sacred duty of every thinking person to write about religion (*dharma*), morality (*niti*), moral fables, history, etc in the simple language prevalent in the country [i.e. region], and provide knowledge to women through them, many learned and thoughtful men are writing excellent books in an effort to uplift womankind, which is very heartening. Womankind will be eternally grateful to them for this obligation.

The great tomes containing morals for women are very large and difficult to understand, and therefore beyond the reach of women, as mentioned above. Currently, highly learned men are writing excellent books in simple language in order to provide women with the knowledge of morality. However, these books are still partially incomprehensible, being in the form of parables and moral fables. Women have not yet developed the capacity to understand their essence, act accordingly and improve their own condition. Therefore, realising the acute need to explain their essence, I made an extensive search for a volume of this kind, but without success. This may be due to my own narrow vision, because I cannot imagine that such a great country would have such a small lacuna. Be that as it may. Having then decided to disregard all this and write a small book of this kind myself, relying on my own limited intellect, I have written the present book. It may contain several inconsistencies, repetitions and grammatical errors due to the currently disturbed state of my mind and my limited understanding. But this is my first effort to write a book in the language of Maharashtra, and I hope that, in view of this, wise people will not be too critical of these faults. It is appropriate to mention at this juncture that reviewers are requested to provide an objective and clear discussion of its merits and demerits, so that all possible attention can be paid to emending faults, should an occasion to write a similar kind of book arise in the future.

For the most part, the present book contains everything worthwhile culled from my own experience, the sayings of learned people and the perusal of several volumes on morality. . . . This attempt of mine is intended primarily for women, therefore they are requested to kindly take note of it. The book does not contain descriptions of heroes and heroines or interesting stories as in novels; therefore it will not appeal at all to people who relish such writings. But after drinking in the excessively sweet sentiments of the novels, they might lose their sense of taste; in order to prevent this, I humbly request them to use the present book as a kind of condiment.

The Authoress

PREFACE TO THE SECOND EDITION

After this book was published, there was a great deal of discussion in the newspapers about its merits and demerits. This indicated that in spite of its many faults, the book also contains useful portions. I think this has made my efforts worthwhile. In view of these useful portions, the Hon'ble Director [of Education] bought 500 copies of the first edition, and the rest were bought by the general public. Therefore this second edition has been published, in which many of the faults of wording and sentence structure have been removed. A great deal of criticism was directed towards the excessive use of Sanskrit and unfamiliar words; such words have also been changed for the most part. In addition, minor changes have been made in the original text.

The Authoress

1. THE FOUNDATION

A house built without laying a firm foundation does not last long. Moreover, the builder of such a house is burdened with double the cost and labour, and, in addition, becomes a general laughing stock. While preparing to undertake any task, a person should lay the foundation after firm and mature consideration. Otherwise the task, even though small, will not reach completion; it will unnecessarily lead to public ridicule and personal trouble.

Everyone knows how sorry is the state of our ignorant womankind. Let us consider how it can be improved and how the foundation should be laid.

In this world, the desire for advancement dwells in the heart of every person at all times, and it is natural that this should be so. It is praiseworthy for a person to be content with his station in life in all other things. But in the two matters of knowledge and self-improvement, one should not rest content with what one has. Among all the sentiments which God has given to man, the desire for self-improvement is very great. That is why, even after attaining greatness, man wants to be even greater. It must be said that God has endowed man with this desire for the welfare of humankind, because if every person has such a desire in his heart, he exerts himself for his advancement. If everybody acts in this manner, the whole country is likely to advance.

This above-mentioned desire leads to every benefit if it is directed along the right path in accordance with a person's understanding; otherwise it leads to very great disasters. Therefore every person who feels this desire strongly should think well and direct it along the right path, to the benefit of all. Now, womankind also desires advancement, but in our country, the path of improvement in the condition of women is as good as closed. That is why it is essential to consider how it can be opened.

Some people claim that women are ignorant and weak to begin with, besides being in a state of subjection, and that they do not know what path to follow in order to achieve advancement and knowledge; what can they do in this condition? But proper consideration shows that there is no room for such doubts.

God has given even mute and ignorant creatures, such as animals and birds the capacity to exercise freedom in achieving their welfare. Therefore it is improbable that He has not granted it to human beings who are the greatest among all creatures. In this world, nobody can live without assistance from others. This state is called interdependence. It is natural to all creatures, and thus also to women. But this state cannot be termed total subjection to others.

Most women say that they desire advancement, but lack the opportunity to make efforts in that direction, because they are always dependent on men. This is true to some extent. But self-improvement depends only on oneself. God has given man the desire to become great and similarly, also the capacity to fulfil this desire. All the means of improvement are attainable by human action; they do not entail dependence on others. But a person needs to concentrate his mind and make the effort without being lazy. If women do so, they too will undoubtedly advance within a short time. . . .

In most places on the face of this earth, one finds illustrations which substantiate the English proverb, 'God helps those who help themselves.' God has granted man intelligence and the capacity to think, which clearly shows that these qualities should, in due course, reach ripeness. The more people rely on themselves, the more they advance. . . .

To do a service for others and to accept a service in return does not ever violate independence. Every human being is free to achieve his welfare by concentrating his mind and intellect on a suitable goal. This proves that all human beings possess the capacity to independently achieve advancement through self-reliance. . . .

This chief form of happiness, that is, self-reliance, is at present almost totally lacking in womankind. Although it is seen occasionally among a few women, one should not assume that it benefits the entire female community, or will do so in the future.

Now, if a remedy is to be employed for achieving the progress of our women, who are in a deplorable state, its foundation is self-reliance. Every woman should nurture and cherish it every moment, as if it were her own heart. Then, if all women were to give careful consideration to the obstacles to their advancement and the effects of removing them, and exert themselves daily in this task, they will shortly achieve the same—or even higher—degree of dominance in society that great men have achieved. There is not an iota of doubt about this.

Diligence is a God-given virtue which is so beautiful and beneficial that it helps a person to attain the unattainable and obtain the unobtainable, and thus derive indescribable happiness and honour. In this world, all those who have acquired enduring fame for their great deeds and unprecedented achievements, have done so mainly on the strength of diligence. When such very recent and trustworthy examples are before us, would it not be madness to even entertain the doubt that the female sex will not progress through industry?

Now, some women will say, 'Our entire sex ignores this matter, what then can I do alone? And what results will my efforts yield?' These words are of no use, because all women harbour the same doubt and say the same thing. That is why none of them does anything at all, and all sit idly wherever they are. But if every sensible and saintly woman were to think otherwise, and, heeding my words, say, 'Other women may or may not do anything, but I will exert myself for my own progress and that of other women in my family', what progress could then be achieved by this fallen sex and this country of ours! If a seed as small as a tamarind seed, or one even smaller, is planted in the earth, it grows into a large tree in the course of time, and provides great benefits to people all over the country. Similarly, if every woman plants a small seed of her industriousness, great benefits will accrue to our sex in the course of time.

If every person makes some effort, the whole community progresses; and similarly, if every person looks to others and says idly, 'What can I do alone?', the whole community regresses. We need not go far to see examples of this, they are visible in this very country. Look at the people from Europe who are ruling our country, who control the wealth, life and honour of the twenty-six crore people of our country. They make all the people in Bharatavarsha—from princes to paupers—dance to their tune like wooden puppets. They are not even one-fourth of the population of our country. What, then, has led to this improbable advancement of theirs? All our people, old and young, are stunned by the extraordinary inventions of this [European] community, their adventurous deeds and bravery; and are making all kinds of conjectures about them. The most ignorant among them say that the Europeans possess an element of divinity, that they have miraculous powers and magic incantations, that they control large hordes of demons, which is why they can perform such difficult feats.

Upon consideration, it will indeed appear that it is on the strength of a very powerful incantation that the Europeans accomplish all difficult tasks with only a little effort and thus achieve the progress of their community. What is that incantation? It is nothing but the incessant effort of every person in their community. It is the general characteristic of that people that once they undertake a task—big or small, good or bad—they never abandon it until it is complete. This quality exists in all of them, from prince to pauper, which is why their power is so strong. These people take a handful of earth and turn it to gold! Idleness cannot affect them, which is why they enjoy the happiness of unity and the rare gains which result from it. This discussion of the advancement of the English people is too brief to amount to anything, because, if the reasons for their advancement and their deeds are described in detail, they would stretch into many a Mahabharata, like the Mahabharata of Vyasa. These words of mine should not lead anyone to believe that I praise them needlessly. Because, I know very well that the English have many and strong faults, like the proverb 'Every village has its untouchable quarter'. But their faults are hidden by their love for their country, their unity, diligence, and other virtues, just as, in the words of Kalidasa, the spots on the moon are hidden by the serene and gentle rays of moonlight.

Now, the present advancement of this community is not the result of one person's efforts, or the great efforts of all the people. Every one of their people made some effort and some made great efforts; the collection of all these efforts has led to their advancement, like the high tide of the ocean.

Now turn your gaze from West to East, and see what you find— the twenty-six crore people of Bharatavarsha and the condition of these people! It would be no exaggeration to say that most people in this country do not know how to be industrious and to achieve good results. The proof of this is the present condition of the native people.[1] They lack adventurousness, brilliance, energy, independence. What other lacunae can I point out? To tell the truth, they possess very little that is good. What do they have? They have musical plays, they have hard-earned money to spend on folk theatre and dances instead of eating a good square meal. They have the inclination to slander anybody in their society who undertakes the task of national welfare, and to instigate others to oppose him and to disrupt his effort. They have unsteady minds. They have a thousand such things. This tide of our misfortune continues to flow, God alone knows when it will ebb!

Be that as it may. Now, if you wish to know the chief reason for this misfortune of ours, it is the sloth and lack of diligence among the native people. How will this vast population of twenty-six crores shake off sloth, if it makes no effort at all? If every person, who lies at ease twenty-four hours a day, gives up his sloth for one hour each day and undertakes some work towards his own advancement during this time, it would mean that everyday twenty-six crore hours are spent on the advancement of the country. The advancement of the people of a country is called the advancement of the country. And if such a thing happens everyday, as described above, who would deny that the good fortune of this country will rise again?

Now, among the people of this country, the persons of the male sex do engage in some work or other everyday, for the simple reason that unless they do so, they will not be able to support their families. That leaves the female sex![††] Such is its present condition that, just as the word 'vessel' at once suggests to our mind the meaning 'a large receptacle for water', the moment we hear the name 'the female sex', we naturally think of fault-ridden individuals who are 'lazy', 'stupid', 'obstinate', and so on. When one talks to men, they say, plainly, 'What can one say about you [women]? You sit idly, you don't want to do any work, all you do is hang upon us incessantly and eat three or four times a day, smacking your lips; what else do you need?' . . . Women have to listen quietly to thousands of such remarks from

---

[††]I do not say that all men work and all women sit still; but in truth, rare are the women who, besides cooking and doing other essential domestic chores, engage in other tasks of advancement.

the lips of men. The very memory of these words would make a woman wish that she would be swallowed by the earth so as to avoid showing her disgraced countenance to anybody in the world ever again.

What is the reason for such disgrace? It is that the female sex is lazy. I do not say that women should do the kind of great deeds that men do. The male constitution is hard, strong, and capable of enduring hard work. The female constitution is delicate and somewhat weak. Men should do work which befits their constitution; if they act contrary to it, they will incur public censure. Similarly women should do work suited to their delicate constitution, else they also incur public ridicule. Some women will say, 'We do all our work—sweeping, mopping, cooking, and so on. What other work do we need to do?' The answer to that is: 'God has not given you life only to do work such as cooking; if you think carefully, you will see that there are innumerable other tasks'. This vast worldly life is like a giant whose body has two sides, the left and the right. Of these, the left side is woman and the right side man. When both sides of the body function in unison, one enjoys happiness and well-being. Similarly, when both man and woman do their work properly, domestic life becomes beautiful and happy. The right side of our body is somewhat stronger and we can do more work with our right hand than with our left; similarly, the man, the right side of domestic life, is somewhat stronger than the woman, and also, does more work. If our body is paralysed and the left side becomes useless, we are not able to do any work properly with the right side alone. In the same way, if the woman sits still without doing anything, the man alone will not be able to do any work well in domestic life. See, writing is a task for the right hand. But if the left hand does not hold the paper properly, the right hand cannot write well. Now, some people will object that one can write even if the left hand does not hold the paper. This can be done if the paper is kept on the table or something similar, and a weight placed on it to prevent the paper from shifting; then the right hand can keep on writing comfortably. True, but the time spent on this roundabout method can be used for writing an extra couple of lines with the right hand, if it is aided by the left hand; and the remaining time can be utilized for doing some other good work. Otherwise twice as much time is expended and no other work is done.

Likewise, men require women's assistance in every task in domestic life. At present, men have to do many tasks which could be managed by women if they were educated and sensible. Thus men's time is wasted. They have many other important tasks which they could perform during the same amount of time, but which they cannot for want of time. They spend the time at their disposal only in earning a living. In this manner, nobody performs great deeds, and, naturally, the country does not advance.

. . . If there is such a divine rule that happiness cannot accrue in the absence of mutual help, how can men derive happiness without the help of women, and women without the help of men?

Now you will ask, 'We are happy, and so are men. What more happiness is there to be had?' My dear sisters, by happiness I do not mean eating and drinking. The chief means of happiness is complete independence. How can you call yourselves happy if you do not possess it, and how can the men do so if they do not possess it, being deprived of time to devote to other work due to your sloth? A poet has said, 'All subjection is unhappiness, and independence is happiness'.[Skt][2] Where does independence exist among our people? Consider the female sex first. There is so much dependence [among us women] that we have to go from door to door asking for help from experts in managing even minor chores, such as putting in a few stitches if a cloth is torn, adding the right amount of salt to [preserve] a hundred raw mangoes, or knowing the price to be paid for any item if a Bohori hawker selling small things comes to the door. Otherwise we ruin everything and sit quietly. Suppose Raosaheb has gone out, and a person has come with a message from some gentleman, which is so urgent that important work will be ruined if an immediate answer is not given. Baisaheb is so clever that not only does she not send the messenger back with a satisfactory answer, she does not even possess a good memory or the intelligence to relate the whole matter to Raosaheb when he returns. She could note it down to aid memory, but she knows nothing of the alphabet other than the letters written by the goddess Satvai on her forehead on the sixth day after her birth [i.e. destiny]. Of course, the whole matter is ruined due to delay. Thousands of things of this nature occur every day. Men, who have to manage all these affairs and also earn a living in whatever time is available, find no time to do all the domestic tasks they are capable of doing, and therefore have to buy all the necessities from foreigners. On account of this reason, our country is losing crores of rupees to foreign countries today and being reduced to poverty. Because poverty has spread throughout the country, there are repeated famines and people are physically debilitated. How much work can weak people do? Day by day, the poor creatures are bound to get [increasingly] exhausted and become totally useless in the end. When we cannot use our arms and legs, cannot even lift up our heads without support, and are utterly dependent on another, we are compelled to listen to what he says and behave according to his whims. But is this the end of the matter? No. On the contrary, those people [foreigners] jeer at us because we are incapable of doing anything and look to them abjectly even for petty things. They do not hesitate even to kick our heads if they get a chance.

I wish to finish this section shortly, therefore I will not write more at this juncture. From my brief writings, you will understand how dependent are the women and men of our country. As this subjection is permanently with us, it is obvious that no happiness is possible. The root cause of this unhappiness is that women are too slothful and do not help men as much as they should. Then why would men not subject women, who cannot serve their self-interest, to harsh and shameful rebukes such as mentioned above? If our sex has such faults, we should not hold men at all guilty for uttering even worse rebukes and insults, because we invite such insults upon ourselves. We do not possess important virtues, such as knowledge, industry, etc. which is why we have no standing among men; therefore, men behave as they please in our very presence and do not at all listen to us. This is all true, but it does not become a person to easily submit to such intolerable insults. We are born as human beings on God's earth, therefore we should also conduct ourselves suitably.

So, my dear sisters, let us now together exorcise the ghost of animal-like ignorance which has entered our bodies, with the help of the powerful incantation of diligence. And let us exert ourselves to attain the divine virtues which can be acquired through education. Then, we will shortly get out of our sorry state and achieve a happy state. Do you not feel shame to remain in this inferior condition? How do your lovely and tender hearts endure this extreme sorrow? Even animals thrash about with their legs in order to save their lives when they fall into a well. And you are, after all, human beings.

How then can you not make an effort to uplift yourselves when you have fallen into this dark well of ignorance?

Come, begin to exert yourselves unitedly while there is still time. Nothing is unattainable to an industrious person. I repeat over and over again, 'Be industrious'. Let the blood in your body be heated by your mental energy, and let it course rapidly through every vein. Let people know your liveliness. Let all see the diligence, knowledge, brightness, belief in Truth and in God, duties of the *sati* and other such virtues which your sex possesses, and become struck with awe. Revive the greatness of the ancient saintly women of our Bharatavarsha. You need not go to a battlefield and fight a war. If you fight sloth, which is your enemy, and conquer it, you will have conquered all the three worlds [i.e. Earth, Heaven and Hell]. May the whole world see this great feat of yours and applaud you! Arise, sisters, wake up now. This is no time to sleep. Your night of sorrow is over and your day of happiness is about to dawn. When you open your eyes, you will see light. Why then do you shut your eyes unnecessarily and become blind?

Come, let us all unite and lay the strong foundation of our 'house of happiness' on the summit of the tall mountain of knowledge—a foundation so strong that it will never cave in and our 'house of happiness' will never collapse and be destroyed. That foundation is called self-reliance, that is, depending on oneself. Now, we must not look to others for our advancement. Every woman must exert herself courageously for her own advancement, relying as much as possible on herself. God Almighty, who can crown this effort with success, is our protector.

2. EDUCATION

A person who has no money cannot be happy. What is more, it is difficult for a person to subsist even for a single day without money. That is why very learned men have termed money 'the outer soul'. A man without money is like the living dead. He is ashamed to approach respectable and great people, and to meet them. His body and garments are soiled with dirt and his mind with worries; and his face is without lustre. People repeatedly deride and scorn him, so that he becomes tired of himself and feels that living in this world is like suffering the torments of hell. In sum, a person without money has no happiness in this world. Therefore, every single person should acquire and possess some wealth according to his capacity, if he wants to live happily and honourably in society.

There are many kinds of wealth. Land, grain, cattle, gold, silver, pearls, diamonds and [other] such moveable and immoveable assets are called wealth. Now, it is true that possession of this wealth gives a person many advantages and much happiness; but they do not last forever. Because, all things on earth are destructible and the happiness they provide is momentary. Therefore, an intelligent and thoughtful person should make the effort to accumulate wealth which is indestructible and which provides unending happiness. What wealth is there in this world which cannot be destroyed? Listen to the answer.

Education is indestructible wealth. He who possesses it is the happiest in this world. Like the sun, education gives light to one who is drowning in the terrible darkness of ignorance and is unhappy. You will say, 'We have eyes. We can see in the light of the sun during the day, and the light of the moon, lamps, etc. at night.' But I say that if you have no education, you are blind even though you may have a thousand eyes. You may perhaps see whatever objects there are on this side of the wall before you. But you know nothing about what lies beyond and very far. Why? Because you have only outer eyes, not inner ones. Education cleanses the inner eyes, and their pure flame allows us to see even an object which is far away. Those who are possessed of an education, even though they may be born blind, can see the whole world with their inner eye, and be very happy. . . .

Students should treat their teacher with great respect. They should not laugh unnecessarily and excessively in front of the teacher, make fun of him in his presence or absence, speak immoderately and loudly in his presence, sit with outstretched legs, spit in front of themselves or him, mock him, return a hasty, thoughtless answer, or address him in the singular. One should talk to the teacher with great humility, with a pleasant face, in a sweet voice. One should not utter harsh, false, indecent or deceptive words in his presence. One should not speak unless spoken to, but should speak first while making polite inquiries about his health, or while paying one's respects. One should speak at an opportune time if one needs to get a doubt resolved or get work done, if it has been held up. One should not speak at an improper time or say inappropriate things. One should not be rowdy in the teacher's presence. If he hits or scorns one for one's offence, one should not rebuke him in return. The persons who do not feel angry towards a teacher who rebukes them for the improvement of their faults, but who strive to remove their own faults, are honoured everywhere. Those who do not do so but behave in the opposite manner, do not receive honour.

One should not slander anyone or tell tales. If the teacher rebukes one even though one is not guilty of an offence, one should inform him of one's innocence calmly and humbly. One should show absolutely no arrogance or anger. One should not demonstrate one's innocence through false pretences. One should not accuse another of one's own fault. One should listen to the teacher with attention, and should not disturb him. If one does not understand something, one should ask again. Because, the speech of learned people is full of excellent advice.

One should not allow the mind to wander while studying; one should do one's lessons with proper concentration so that they can be grasped quickly without too much effort. One should not be lazy about studying. Sometimes, those who lack the habit [of studying] need a great deal of effort for the first few days, to do their lessons with concentration, and without sloth. But once the habit is formed, one even begins to feel restless if the lessons are not done. Thus, one should study with a concentrated mind. One should not be lazy, thinking that one will do today's lesson later or tomorrow; because once time has passed, it never returns. It is just gone. If one is lazy and postpones work, it continues to be postponed; it will never get done.

In childhood a person has no domestic or other troubles, and his mind is calm and concentrated. It becomes totally immersed in any subject in which it is involved. This valuable and rare opportunity, which is not available in adulthood, should not be wasted by children. They should acquire this wealth of knowledge as quickly as possible, so that they will not have to endure any suffering in their later life. If not, once this time is lost, it will not come again. When the mind is beset by all kinds of domestic troubles, what knowledge or learning can one hope for? One only repents in vain. Thousands of people are thus ruined only because of their laziness in childhood, and then they have to suffer extreme unhappiness and calamities for the rest of their lives.

You will say that even those who have knowledge are not exempt from unhappiness; what then is the advantage of wasting a happy time in the useless exertion of studies? It is true that learned people are not exempt from unhappiness; but such people do not get scared like fools when faced by a calamity and do not become dispirited or helpless. They are possessed of great courage. They are able to think of timely ways of getting out of the difficulty. Learned people always have a calm mind due to their knowledge, therefore they are also happy; and no trial they encounter affects them too much. In truth, careful consideration shows that he who has a calm mind is alone happy in this world. If one wears shoes, one is not hurt even while walking on thorns; but if one has a tiny splinter in the foot, it will hurt even when one walks on a velvet mattress. . . .

If you possess the wealth of education, you will not feel the need for other wealth. . . . If you are poor, you should remember that you do not possess wealth which leads to happiness, therefore you should obtain the wealth of education in order to acquire it and be happy in the future. Even if, by the grace of God, you are well-to-do you should realize that this state is not permanent; if at some time in the future the cloud of sorrow bursts upon you, you will not have even a hope of consolation. Therefore, be wise right now and strive to acquire an education.

When you learn a lesson from your teacher, try to understand it well. Do not memorize it like a parrot and sit quietly. Do not let your mind touch upon another subject until you have understood the meaning and essence of what you have memorized. How will you benefit if you do not understand the essence of what you memorize? . . .

Some people say that reading a lot of books gives knowledge. Well, if reading a load of books alone gives knowledge, it is a really easy way. Then the boxes, houses and bags filled with books would have become learned. It is not that the reading of many books alone gives knowledge. One gets a lot of knowledge if one studies a little with a concentrated mind. . . .

. . . Many people are lazy and do not do even the work which needs only a little effort. When they see great deeds done by others, they either begin to hate them out of envy; or they say that the other person has a divine gift, or that he is a divine incarnation, which is why he is capable of such deeds, that one is not fated to do such deeds, and they clutch their brows and repine. But they do not realize that fate is not a deity, and that it can be moulded as one wishes. . . . There are many lazy people nowadays who make false claims that the persons described above know the incantations and means of propitiating gods, goddesses, ghosts, spirits, demons, etc. and that they acquired special powers through austerities. But a thoughtful person soon understands how little truth these claims contain. Only fools believe in such tales, and suffer many kinds of troubles. As an example, I will narrate an episode I have myself witnessed.

In the South, near the Tripati [Tirupati] mountain, there is another mountain known as Ghatikachala. The summit of one has a temple of Nrisinha [Narasinha, the fourth incarnation of Vishnu who is half man and half lion], and the summit of the other a temple of Hanuman. There are thousands of gullible devotees there, those who do not make any effort but put their trust in Fate, believe in tales of ghosts, attain great supernatural powers in their imagination, and enjoy their dreams day and night. Such people harbour different kinds of desires in their hearts; some circumambulate the temples a thousand times every day, some fast day and night and perform ceremonies to obtain spells, some give offerings to the sacrificial fire. They waste their valuable time, money and energy, as mentioned above, and obtain nothing except public censure and trouble, needless to say. There was a young man of about twenty years, who had about three or four thousand rupees in his possession.[3] In such a state, instead of making the effort to study, he became totally engrossed in the foolish desire to learn spells and acquire supernatural powers. Within a few days, all his money was spent because he had to provide frequent meals to Brahmins, perform sacrificial rites and other religious ceremonies, etc. according to the instructions of the priests and other selfish, deceitful persons, in order to acquire spells. When money was spent like water in this fashion, how would any of it be left? The man repeatedly observed fasts for twenty-one days at a stretch, without even drinking water, and thus also ruined his God-given physical wealth. In the end, God was not propitiated, needless to say. But sadly, the man foolishly believed the empty tales of lazy people, and wasted his wealth and time, which would have aided his education and advancement. In the end he acquired nothing.

Then he thought of studying, but had neither money nor strength left. When this happened, he repeatedly expressed his regret, but in vain. One felt very sad to hear him. What can one say about such a man's intellect? You should think about this yourself. In sum, the attainment of knowledge, education, wealth, etc. does not depend on imaginary powers, such as charms and spells, demons and ghosts; it depends on oneself. . . .

It is true that a person looks somewhat more beautiful by wearing ornaments, but only while youth lasts. When the body loses its beauty in old age, it cannot acquire beauty by wearing ornaments of gold and pearl; and youth does not last forever. Similarly, wealth, which makes it possible to buy ornaments, does not remain for all time in the possession of all people. Therefore you should acquire the everlasting and inexhaustible wealth of education, and wear ornaments of virtue. These ornaments and the beauty they lend will not diminish at all even if you are ugly, or become poor and old.

There are many things which obstruct studies; chief among them is sloth. It should be totally eliminated. It has already been mentioned that today's task should not be postponed until tomorrow. One way of removing sloth is to appoint a time for each of the tasks one has to do. One should do the task exactly at the appointed time, not earlier nor later; and one should not unnecessarily miss that time. One should go to bed at nine o'clock every night, and get up exactly at four o'clock. One should not sleep more than seven hours. If one sleeps less, the body does not remain healthy. If one follows the habit of sleeping moderately for seven hours, the body remains healthy and is not disturbed by disease. . . .

One should be devoted to the teacher, so that he loves one and explains even inner secrets in a simple manner which one can understand quickly. If one behaves arrogantly with him, he becomes negligent in his teaching. No matter how educated and clever one becomes, one should never imagine that one knows more than one's teacher, nor should one give others such an impression. If one understands a subject very well and if one's fellow-students or others do not, one should not boast about one's cleverness and humiliate them either in front of others or when alone. Because, there is no one in this world who knows everything. There are many subjects which even great scholars like Brihaspati [the preceptor of the gods] do not know. And if a shepherd understands them, it does not prove that he is cleverer than the scholars. One should not be at all arrogant about one's education. In this world there is always someone who is superior to another. Therefore one should not be conceited, thinking that one is great. . . .

When, having completed your studies, you get involved in your duties, do not neglect the education you have acquired and do not forget everything [you have learnt]. How carefully do you not guard an object which you have acquired with but little effort? Then, is it not sad and shameful that you should lose the education which you have acquired with great effort?

Even if you attain a high status, and your teacher occupies a low position, you should not treat him with disrespect. Because, you should remember that the high position or success which you have achieved today, has been achieved only through the favour of the teacher. If you are ungrateful to those who have done you a service, it is a matter of shame for you. There are many in this world who do others a service, but not one of them is like one's teacher. Had you remained ignorant, you would have met with great disasters. But because you acquired knowledge from your teacher, you escaped them. Does he, who saved you from such disasters, not have a high status? . . .

Now I will tell you briefly what you should learn and from whom.

Any branch of knowledge should be learnt from a very intelligent and far-sighted person; because, those who know nothing, cannot teach others anything.

1. You should learn the Grammar of the language you want to master, in order to be able to read and write correctly. Without Grammar, your language will not become chaste nor your enunciation clear.
2. You should study History, in order to understand things such as the customs and morals of people in ancient times and at present, the conditions of all countries, the reason why a country or a person became good or bad, at what time and through what acts, and the effects thereof, etc. If you do not, you will not be able to develop virtues such as learning, inclination to follow the right path, avoidance of sin, etc.
3. All varieties of *dharma shastras* should be studied, in order to understand sin, religious merit, God, the essence of the world, Truth, etc. Otherwise it will be difficult to obtain the indescribable

happiness which stems from a sense of good and bad, from modesty, compassion, charity, love of God, etc.

4. Physics and Geography should be studied in order to understand the state of the sun, the planets, the earth, etc. in this vast divine universe; the marvellous objects and where they exist, the properties of objects, the causes and processes which lead to their creation; different countries and their location, the religion, practices, knowledge, advancement of their people, etc. Otherwise, one who confines oneself to the house, like a frog in a well, will not understand how vast this divine universe is, what laws it is subject to, and the extent of the greatness of the Creator of the universe.

5. Political Economy and Moral Science should be studied in order to understand how to conduct oneself at a specific time and place, and how to be happy by conducting oneself moderately. Otherwise it would be difficult to live honourably in society.

6. One should study a little Medicine and the method of nursing those who are sick or small children, in order to understand how to protect one's own physical health and that of one's children and other people, how to prevent ill health, etc. Otherwise one is likely to cause very great distress.

7. One should study the Culinary Art from expert women of good character within the family or outside, and learn how to cook. One should also learn, whenever possible, how to sew, embroider, sing, etc., from those skilled in these arts. Otherwise one has to humbly request others for help at the last moment. These accomplishments are indispensable for our sex; not possessing them is a matter of great shame.

8. It is essential to have some knowledge of Arithmetic in order to understand the family income and expenditure, the cost of things at a particular rate, etc. Otherwise one is greatly inconvenienced.

In sum, do not ever let it happen that you are unable to manage any task. Try to comprehend a great deal from a little, and obtain a good understanding of the way great people conduct themselves, and the customs and affairs of your country, of your family and of others. If a lowly person has a virtue, cultivate it eagerly, without treating him with indifference. If you have the desire, you can learn even from tiny creatures like a fly or an ant, virtues which will bestow divinity on you in this very human existence.

3. MODESTY

All of you must have heard that people accord high praise to the sea. If they want an apt simile for a great man, they liken him to the sea. Why is this so? At a superficial glance, the sea does not seem to possess any special qualities. It has a very dreadful appearance. Vile creatures which molest people, such as crocodiles, large destructive fish, tortoises, water-snakes, etc. are born in the sea. Also, if any one feels thirsty, can sea water slake his thirst? Not even that. Although the sea is so vast, it does not have the importance possessed by a small stream of sweet water which slakes people's thirst. In view of all this, you will surely think that those who praise the sea are insane. But this is not the case.

The sea possesses two very great and beautiful qualities: one is called depth and the other, keeping within limits. Because it possesses these two qualities, it is regarded as greater than everything else in this world, and is highly deserving of everybody's praise. The nature of these attributes is such that nobody is able to assess what the sea contains, or how much and where. It has great depth. It contains innumerable valuable gems, but it never boasts aloud, as a man would, that it possesses certain qualities. It remains in its usual simple state. It does not show off its importance like man. Second, it never oversteps its boundary. Its water does not swell and overflow even if it rains heavily enough to drown the whole earth, nor does it recede even if it fails to rain for twelve years. But this is not the case with the stream that slakes your thirst. Everyone can see how many stones, quartzes and how much earth it contains. As soon as it rains a little, it swells to great proportions, and flows noisily wherever it finds a way, no matter how crooked its path, roaring with great ardour; and reveals its arrogance. It does not mind anyone at the time. Similarly, if it fails to rain for a couple of days, the poor thing dries up immediately, and is dismayed. Now think this over and decide whether the sea has qualities worth praising, or the stream?

You must have understood the implication of the above example of the sea and the stream. In sum, a man who possesses thousands of virtues does not receive respect if he lacks depth and modesty. All other virtues of such a man fail to enhance his grace; on the contrary, they incur censure. . . .

Some people imagine that religion [*dharma*] and morality [*niti*] are obstacles to happiness, because they prevent one from behaving in a way which makes one happy. They think the same about those who behave in accordance with the *shastras*—that they are not happy themselves, nor do they let others be happy; that they discourage one in everything. But careful thought will show that this belief is highly mistaken. Morality, religion and the followers thereof try to keep worldly happiness within proper bounds, because they firmly believe that any object of the senses leads to happiness only if it remains within its demarcated boundary, and causes inevitable unhappiness if it crosses that boundary. . . .

In domestic life, happiness is momentary and a calamity is likely to befall one at every step. Moderation, self-restraint and caution make one's life a storehouse of great happiness. Therefore, for those who have recently entered domestic life and who have no knowledge of what is good and bad in domestic matters, it is essential to possess the virtues mentioned above. But it is a matter of great sorrow that persons who newly enter domestic life do not respect these virtues very much. When people begin to take their first walk through the market-place of domestic life, they are in such a state of intoxication that whatever they see appears attractive. Because of this intoxication they consider even very bad objects to be very good. The hope of happiness, like a demon, captivates their intellect and makes them blind. Owing to an excessive desire for enjoyment, their minds are always preoccupied and eager.

People intoxicated with the passion of youth are unable to see anything around them. They jump into the well of allurement with their eyes open, in broad daylight. Their mind becomes so thoughtless and arrogant because of the dreadful passion of youth, that it fears nothing. They trust anybody unhesitatingly without understanding his true worth. They have no patience to do any work after comprehending its real importance first; they become quite impatient. Young people trust others easily, because they are not perceptive. They are arrogant because they have no experience of adversity. Once they are engrossed in one thing, they will not let go, because they have not yet experienced disappointment and such other things in domestic life. If, in this dreadful state of youth, they lack moderation and are taken over by sloth, lack of caution, and pleasures of the senses, will they not head for a downfall? O you young women, you are entering the market-place of domestic life for the very first time. Beware, there are many thieves and cheats here. They will lead you astray and rob you of everything. There are two paths here: a good one and a bad one. If you follow the good path, you will attain your welfare; and if you follow the bad one, the consequences are obvious. The good path is straight, broad and leads to happiness; the bad path is crooked, narrow and leads to unhappiness. Now you have to think carefully before choosing a path. . . .

[When] in the minds of young people, greed is a terrible enemy. There are thousands of instances of their losing their life's happiness and even life itself, because of greed for a negligible object. Therefore, one should not hanker after happiness which seems sweet but has dreadful consequences. Concentrate your mind on keeping your conduct utterly pure. In this world there is no wealth like pure conduct. Every human being must guard it very cautiously. . . .

At present you are intoxicated by the passion of youth. You probably think that this time of [your] life, your lovely appearance, beautiful youth, mental energy, wealth, etc. will last forever. But this is a great delusion. You can see clearly that one's days are not all alike. Stages [of one's life] such as childhood, as well as all objects, are impermanent. Do you know how unstable is your youth, whose passion has intoxicated you so much that you are following any path you see, like an intoxicated elephant, without thinking carefully? After a heavy downpour in the monsoon, a small stream gets in flood and looks very impressive. It becomes so strong that large animals such as elephants are carried away by its currents and it causes even big bridges to collapse. But the swell of water that flows on does not return. Moreover, its former impressive appearance, the strength to carry away elephants and bridges, the arrogant deafening sound, all are gone. What remains is only the dirty mud. Such is also the case with your youth. Take care that the water of intoxicating youth does not flood your body and swiftly carry away the bridge of religion. In order to collect the inexhaustible water in the form of chaste conduct in the lake of your life, build a wall around it in the form of self-restraint, so that beautiful lotus flowers of virtue will bloom in the lake and give it an indescribable beauty. But if you fail to constrain your life with moderation, all the water will dry up and only the mud of vice will remain. Then it will shortly begin emitting a foul smell, and nobody will come near you. Do acquire depth like the sea. The only means of doing so is to preserve the purity of your character through moderate behaviour. Now I will briefly tell you how you should conduct yourself in order to preserve your character.

1. At no time should you sit idle. You should always engage yourself in some good task or the other. Your mind will not have a chance to turn to other subjects if you do this. Usually it is lazy people who turn to evil practices; because it is the natural quality of the mind to be involved in one subject at a time; it cannot help but do so. . . . Therefore a person should be cautious and turn his mind towards good deeds. That is why you should not let your mind remain empty.

2. Learn self-restraint. This will prevent any of your activities from overstepping the boundary. If you wish to do something, and if your elders, teachers or guardians forbid you to do it, knowing that it would be to your detriment, then you should refrain from doing it even though you have a great liking for it. Whenever you are ready to undertake any task, seek the permission of your elders first. Get the advice of learned people. Do not do anything in the light of your own ideas. . . .

3. Be humble. There is no other friend on this earth like humility. All objects in this great and unparalleled creation of God sing the praises of humility. The more humble a person is in this world, the greater is his worth. What beauty is possessed by the trees like *mogri*, rose, jasmine, which bow their heads low and touch the ground in humility! There cannot be anyone who does not praise them, cherish their flowers, and keep them near his heart or head. Everybody loves them. . . . There is no one who is greater than all others. No one's egoism can last. Every one has some stigma or fear. What room is there for egoism? Negligible persons like you and me have no worth; even the egoism of sovereign kings, of persons as wealthy as Kubera and learned as Brihaspati, has been dashed to smithereens. Everywhere in the world you will see the triumph of humility and the defeat of egoism. All moveable and immoveable objects in God's creation advise us to be humble.

If a person has an innate humility, not only do his virtues increase, but he also obtains happiness and success. . . . Humility gives joy both to the person who is humble and the person towards whom he is humble. If one makes a mistake for which one is blamed, and if one accepts the blame instead of feeling angry, it will avoid great calamities in the future, such as dissension that arises out of anger. Moreover, one will escape the penalty appropriate to the offence, and will gain the trust and affection of the person one has treated with humility.

4. Pay due respect to your seniors, teachers and people of a similar status. Parents are next to God in venerability. In fact, the happiness you enjoy today through your human attributes and honour in society is the gift bestowed on you by your parents and the teachers who advised you on morality. Otherwise, there are innumerable small particles like you in this world! Nobody pays any attention to them. You are under such an obligation to your parents and teachers that you may never be able to repay them. Therefore, to follow the moral duty according to your capacity and to obey them is to repay their obligations to some extent. Should you fail to do so, it would mean that you have caused unnecessary distress to your mother by being born to such an unfortunate existence in this world. Never should one speak arrogant, vulgar, angry, false words before one's seniors, or display before them anger, greatness or egoism. Whatever they say should be heeded carefully and remembered, and their advice should be followed; this will lead to your welfare. Do not neglect to serve them to the best of your ability. Stand up immediately to show respect, if seniors, teachers and learned strangers come to the place where you happen to be. Walk up and receive them when they arrive; walk a few steps with them to see them off when they leave. Respectful acts towards them, such as salutations, should be done with great humility.

Give due respect also to those who are your equals. If anyone salutes you, do not stand erect like an arrogant person, but bow your head. The custom in our country, by which respects are paid according to the other person's caste, is not proper. Because, in God's creation, respect belongs not to caste, but to virtue. A person, whom you consider to be of a caste lower than yours, may perhaps possess such valuable virtues as are not found in persons even of a caste higher than yours. Therefore, it is best that you should discard such reservations and respect virtue. If there is a person who is younger than you but higher in learning, it is proper to show him respect as if he were older than you. A person becomes great not because of his grey hair, kinship or wealth. Only he who is greater in learning is great. According to the custom of the country, if a person whom you should bless salutes you, do not think that you or your words alone can achieve their welfare; and do not bless them by wishing that they may enjoy a long life, eight sons, wealth, prosperity, etc. Pray very humbly to God that He may achieve their welfare according to His will. You do not possess the power to help or harm others. If you did, you would not want for anything. Before blessing others and [helping them] achieve their welfare, you would have achieved your own. Similarly, you would have laid a curse upon a person you dislike, and removed him from this world. But it is good that helping or harming others is not within human power. Otherwise, one cannot even imagine whether this world would have survived in its present condition, in the face of man's power to curse and favour.

If there is occasion for you to speak, pay due attention to the person you are addressing and speak briefly and appropriately to the occasion, without being confused, and with a pleasant face. Speak the truth, after due consideration. Never say anything which seems like telling tales or which might harm another. Speak only such words which will honour yourself, the other person, and the truth. If anyone comes to meet you, seat him with due honour. Do not seat him on the floor and sit on a high seat yourself. Then ask after his well-being. If the visitor inquires after you in the same fashion, in reply say, 'all is well by the grace of God.' Then only should you speak of other things. You should not share the same seat with your teachers or male strangers. You should stand up if a person of a superior stature visits you; only after he is seated should you sit, with his permission, at one side on a separate seat or on the floor. You should neither sit right in front of the visitor, nor stand. You should not stare straight ahead, but look about you in a proper and modest manner that would not create the wrong impression in anyone. You should adopt a grave manner while talking, walking or sitting, and should avoid shifting your hands, feet or eyes. You should not speak unless you are asked a question; then you should return an answer which is brief, interesting, and appropriate to the occasion. If there is anyone sitting in front of you, do not clear your throat noisily and spit. If necessary, step aside and spit. Do not crack your knuckles in front of others.

You should not sit with outstretched legs, or in an indecent manner. If you have occasion to be close to the face of your seniors or others while speaking, you should hold a piece of cloth in front of your mouth so as to ensure that drops of saliva do not fall on them. While talking to seniors, learned persons and strangers, you should use the respectful plural, and other words indicative of respect. You should not talk to them as if you are issuing orders. If someone does you a service or helps you in any way, you should express your gratitude. You should not speak rudely to anyone. While introducing one person to another, if it is necessary to indicate that person with a gesture, you should not point a finger but point the whole hand with fingers outstretched.

You should not stand in the street and talk to male strangers or others for any length of time. You should not stand at the window or door and look at the scene on the street. If people are talking amongst themselves, you should not pass by unless called, nor should you overhear their conversation. While walking in the street, you should not look from side to side or up, dangle your hands, run, or stamp your feet while walking. You should look down at the street and walk slowly. While walking in the street or passing before strangers, you should drape yourself in a cloth which covers your head and the rest of your body. In olden days, it was customary for women of good families to drape themselves with an additional cloth. But nowadays one sees that in some places, women tuck the loose end [*padar*] of the sari sideways at the waist, and tuck in the pleats of the sari quite high. While washing clothes, etc. they lose all consciousness of their appearance. This is a very bad practice. Women should make an effort to stop this. They should not bathe naked in places where men are likely to be present, like tanks, rivers and lakes. Bathing should be done early in the morning in the dark. It is best that women bathe in a covered place within the house, rather than in the open.

If a woman has to go to an unfamiliar place or through the market-place, she should not go alone, but take with her a relative or a trustworthy person. She should not visit an unfamiliar place or a stranger's house at night unless there is an emergency; and if compelled to go, should be very cautious and take a companion. Women from good families should not go to the theatre or to folk plays. This leads to a violation of their modesty, because not all people present there are decent, and nobody there shows a concern for propriety of speech. Little wonder then, that a visit to such places should tarnish the purity and modesty of women. But the real sorrow and shame is that, these days, some half-educated women visit such places in disregard of their modesty for the momentary pleasure of watching an amusing spectacle, and thus bring a stigma upon all our saintly women. In some places it is customary for women to attend devotional sermons at any time of day or night. Sometimes they even have to sit close to prostitutes there. Because such a place is meant for uplifting the fallen, all kinds of people are likely to go there, including holy men and unholy ones, saintly women and prostitutes, vagabonds and rakes. Therefore there is no choice but to mix with them. There is the probability of being insulted in such places, and this usually does happen. The reason is that many persons of impure conduct go there to fulfill their evil desires, because women are present. Another thing is that the Puranika, Haridasa and others, whom women visit for religious instruction, are often licentious.[4] There are few among them who are educated and learned. . . . Therefore, it is difficult to get good advice from people of such a nature, but on the contrary, they will turn the good thoughts in people's minds to bad ones.

I do not say that all Puranikas and Haridasas have such [evil] propensities. Obviously there is good and bad in everyone, but I have mentioned this only so that women should protect their modesty. They can obtain knowledge of the *puranas,* history and such things at home, instead of visiting such places. They only have to make a little effort and study Sanskrit. And it is very essential that they do so, because all the religious texts of Bharatavarsha have been written in Sanskrit. One cannot get a thorough knowledge of one's religion only by listening to others reading these texts aloud, without reading them personally. It can lead to great calamities if women lack a knowledge of their religion. The language of the *dharma shastras* is simple and sweet, and intelligible to women after a little study. Even if all women cannot learn Sanskrit, it is enough for a few women to do so. It is more convenient for women to hear the *puranas* from other women than from men. Therefore, it is best that women learn this ancient language of ours, and satisfy their eagerness to understand our *puranas,* history, *dharma shastras,* and such other subjects in this fashion. Otherwise, they should hear them from persons who are learned, of a good character, and elderly, either at home or at some such good place. They should never go to the market-place or the temple, where even prostitutes sit near them. Similarly, it is entirely inappropriate for women of good families to cherish a desire to have children or to charm their husbands into submission, and [for that purpose] circumambulate *peepul*, *banyan* or other trees in the market-place or any such public place, or to go to the temples of gods and goddesses like Narsoba, Jogeshwari, Satvai, Mhalsai, Khandoba, etc. The reasons are the same as those given for not going to the theatre, etc.

In some places, thousands of women go for a *darshan* of 'babas' such as Sanyasibaba, Paramahansababa, Brahmacharibaba, etc. The disasters which result from this cannot even be mentioned here. Women of good families should not visit such places which violate their modesty, but go to persons who are learned and of a good character, and obtain from them good advice which will benefit them. Some Hindu women appoint a '*mantra-guru*'. Sometimes there is no saying what these *guruji*s will do, because their character is not generally known. Also, the *guruji*s can do what they like, but their faults cannot be exposed, because gullible women think that doing so will lead them to hell. This leads to great calamities. They do not understand that the *guruji*s who are themselves involved in thousands of affairs cannot release others from this enormous fire of worldy life. If the *guruji*s had the power to save others from sin merely by whispering Panchakshari and Ashtakshari *mantra*s in their ears, why would very learned and religious people have taken the trouble to exert themselves for hundreds of years, suffer bodily pains, give up even royal pleasures, and devote themselves to the service of God? And even if one were to assume that a *guru* is very important, even the Hindu treatises, which blow up the importance of *guru*s, do not say that women must have an unknown *guru*. These treatises say that teachers such as [one's] parents, older brother, father-in-law, etc. are the real *guru*s of women. . . .

Do not waste your time by spending the whole day with neighbourhood women, yawning, sitting with one leg crossed over the other, preparing lamp-wicks of different kinds and discussing dull things such as, 'so-and-so's husband is such-and-such', 'this woman has a crooked gait', 'that woman's nose is crooked', 'my mother-in-law is shrewish'. It is praiseworthy to be friendly with one another and help one another in times of need. It is very bad to gossip instead of finishing one's routine work and devoting one's free time to a good purpose. . . .

In sum, one should conduct oneself properly, and try to preserve one's own and others' modesty and foster mutual love, so as to spend the rest of one's life happily without having to suffer the ill effects of repentance, unhappiness, censure, etc.

4. TRUE RELIGION

'Courage, forgiveness, control over the mind, to abstain from stealing, purity, control over the senses, intellect, knowledge, truth and absence of anger are the ten characteristics of true religion.'[Skt]

True religion is the foremost among all of man's duties in this world. It is the foundation of all things. If a person ignores the earth and makes an attempt to build an edifice in the sky, will his attempt succeed? Never. Also, it is not possible for a tree to stand or live without the firm support of roots. Similarly, a person who abandons true religion in this world, cannot manage. Not one of his tasks will be carried to proper completion; and if, by some chance, it is completed, it will crumble like a clod of earth which is tossed high into the sky and falls to the ground.

. . . True religion possesses the power to protect the world and ensure its welfare; that is why it is called *dharma* or that which maintains. It is absolutely essential for every person to possess a good knowledge of true religion and to conduct himself accordingly. True religion claims such honour in this world that even the people who pretend to be religious are considered especially venerable.

'In this world, true religion is the sole true friend that protects and accompanies man even at the time of death; all else is destroyed along with the body.'[Skt]

In sum, a person's good or bad conduct alone will accompany him, and nothing else, such as wealth or kin; furthermore, even the body, which he thinks of as the 'self' and which he unhesitatingly nourishes even through cruel demonic deeds, does not accompany him. Therefore a person should befriend religion, which gives peace at the time of death. See, an ordinary person finds nothing as dreadful as death. He shudders and feels terrified at the thought of death. At a time like this, a religious person has religion to protect him. It alone gives him peace, nothing else brings peace at such a time. Therefore a truly religious person feels no fear of death; on the contrary, his mind rejoices at the thought. Similarly, sinful people know that they will not obtain the peace of true religion and become very dejected, which is only natural.

Now, by true religion one should not understand the many doctrines such as the Hindu, Muslim, Christian doctrine, etc. These names indicate doctrines and not true religion, because true religion is single in form, namely, conduct that is in accordance with one's conscience, which exists in all human beings, either in the form of a seed or in a full-fledged form. If you consider the Hindu, Muslim, Christian and other doctrines, you will find that there is an identical description of true religion, that is, good conduct and the effects thereof. Only, there are several differences according to the beliefs of their creators. Be that as it may, I do not intend to discuss all those doctrines here. I accept only that [religion] whose foundation of conscience supports many doctrines in the world; and it is my chief intention to propound it. The word 'religion' has been explained above, let us now consider its [ten] characteristics: (1) Courage (2) Forgiveness (3) Control over one's mind (4) To abstain from stealing (5) Purity (6) Control over the senses (7) Intelligence (8) Knowledge, that is, knowledge of God (9) Truth (10) Absence of anger and its other manifestations, such as rivalry, desire to torment others, or hatred. . . .

5. CONDUCT FOR BRIDES

So far, I have briefly described the manner in which the seed should be sown in your early life in order to obtain good fruits in the future. Now let us consider the new life which begins in this very life of yours, and how to conduct yourself in it. God has created the male and female categories among the creatures in this world. If the persons in these two categories do not support each other and live separately instead, God's creation will never be complete. Man and woman are two sides of domestic life. Our body will never look beautiful if it lacks any organ, and we will not be able to perform any task properly, as a complete person can. Similarly, even very learned, brave, wealthy or dispassionate men do not become complete without women. In that [incomplete] state, they are unable to perform any task properly. Because the lack of female assistance where it is required distracts their minds, and having to carry the entire burden of work single-handedly causes over-exertion, it leads to disaster. It is the same with women. It is God's intention that man and woman should support each other, and depend upon each other. That is why He has created a relationship between them, which cannot be fulfilled without mutual assistance. Some do not practise that relationship properly and wilfully behave like animals. Such behaviour, which is contrary to religion, violates God's wish, and this sin incurs suffering, remorse, insults, etc. Therefore, intelligent men and women should enter a very happy and desirable mutual relationship as created by God, in accordance with religion. This kind of relationship is marriage. Now let us consider how and at what time it should be performed.

There are different kinds of marriage customs in different countries. Not all of them can be called good. As an example, observe the marriage custom in our own country. In this country, as soon as a child, especially a girl, reaches the age of nine or ten years, she is married to another ignorant child. At that time, the children are not able to grasp the nature of their mutual relationship, or how to strengthen it, or maintain mutual unity and respect. This ignorance causes discord between them, so that they do not derive the happiness for which the relationship is intended; on the contrary, it leads to great disasters.

Second, the period in a person's life from the age of eight to twenty is suitable for acquiring knowledge. If he gets married during this period, he gets involved in domestic matters. [In this state] he can never undertake a course of study; or if he does so, leaves it half-way. It is very inappropriate to marry at that time, because one's early life, which is a precious period suitable for the pursuit of knowledge, is never available again. [And] human existence without knowledge must be considered inferior to animal existence.

Third, if men and women produce children at an early age, they themselves and their progeny become weak, dull, unintelligent; and they die prematurely in their youth without enjoying a full life. This happens because their dispositions, life-sustaining bodily parts such as blood, flesh, fat, brain, etc., strength, intelligence, and health are not fully developed at an early age. Any unsuitable activity damages such an undeveloped and immature body; moreover, the progeny issuing from it also turns out to be utterly useless.

Fourth, because intelligence is not perfectly mature in childhood, the two who are to be married are not competent to choose a suitable spouse in accordance with their own wishes. They are compelled to spend their life with whomsoever their parents or other similar persons have tied their nuptial knot. The person may be good or bad; nobody even gives it a thought. This is likely to lead to serious ill effects, because love lasts long between persons of equal standing, but not in a relationship of superiority and inferiority. A person will not know whether the [suggested] person is suitable or not, unless he himself makes a decision after proper scrutiny. He will not find the match acceptable if it is fixed by other people according to their wishes, because others do not know his wishes, and are not capable of testing whether the [suggested] person has the qualities which suit him. If such a man and woman whose qualities are opposed to each other's, and who do not like each other, are tied together [in marriage], how will they be happy? Then they would begin to feel that their marriage is not a happy one, but is like the torments of hell, which have fallen to their lot. Unity never exists between a man and a woman of such opposite dispositions. Their minds are ever dissatisfied with each other. The progeny produced by them in this state also turn out to be troublesome, wicked, foolish, ugly and disagreeable. Therefore an abundance of such progeny leads not to domestic welfare but to misfortune. That is why it is not proper that people should practise customs which are contrary to the divine rule, and should invite misfortune upon themselves.

In this world, even animals have the freedom to establish a male-female relationship according to their own wishes; why then should human beings not have this freedom? A marital relationship is not a matter of one or two days, such that if it does not work out, another one can be tried out any time! This relationship is to last as long as both the partners live. Therefore, in such a matter, it is proper that men and women should have equal freedom to do a proper scrutiny according to their wishes, and to establish a relationship which is suitable. One shudders at the thought of the calamities which result because this does not happen. Many a saintly woman suffers agonies because of the bad activities of her husband and commits the terrible sin of suicide, thereby staining her life. And many a saintly man suffers agonies because of his wife's bad behaviour and commits terrible sins like murdering his wife, adultery, etc. Whose fault is this? Not that of the concerned women and men, but of society which assumes an inappropriate leadership, which wrests away their freedom to enter into a suitable relationship according to their own wishes, and which marries them prematurely and thus cuts with an axe the very roots of the tree of their advancement. It is best that this society abandons such faulty practices; otherwise no progress will be achieved even if thousands of remedial devices are employed.

Men and women should marry persons who match their own qualities, [and] when they reach the marriageable age, that is, twenty years, give or take six months to a year. This marital relationship should not be established because of the approval of others, or through expectations of wealth, or because of any other type of inducement. These inducements look attractive from a distance, but have no substance when viewed from close quarters. In such a situation, one should marry a person who seems right in the opinion of people who are more intelligent and far-sighted than oneself, and also in one's own opinion. The chosen spouse should possess a religious disposition, a good appearance, education, virtues, generosity, wealth and love.

Some marry with only an eye to good appearance or wealth; but this is very improper, because wealth and looks do not abide permanently in one place. When they disappear, a person who is enamoured solely of them will follow them wherever they are. How, then, will love for one another remain? And what is the use of arranging a marriage between persons who have no mutual love? That is why marriages should be arranged mainly with a view to a religious disposition, virtues, knowledge, love and generosity, so that such a suitable relationship leads to the utmost love between the spouses. Only spouses who share such indescribable love also share each other's happiness and unhappiness. They alone bring the beauty of heaven to this worldly existence, and can be expected to lead to progress. Blessed are the men and women united in such a well-matched relationship. Their mutual love will never decrease even if they suffer great misfortune. Even during such dreadful times, they are happy with each other's support. Really speaking, love itself is the source of all happiness in this world; a person whose heart lacks it will never be happy. It is on the strength of such, afore-mentioned, love that great men like Ramachandra, Nala and others left behind an unwavering reputation of their noble lives. Similarly, saintly women like Sita, Savitri, Arundhati, Damayanti, Anusuya and others displayed the ultimate devotion to their husbands and left behind a charming reputation of their virtue. Love brings the beauty of heaven to a heart which is desolate like the cremation ground. Therefore, every human being should nurture love in his heart.

Love has numerous manifestations. The love which parents feel for their offspring is called parental affection. The love which the offspring feel for parents, teachers and God is called devotion. The mutual love of siblings and friends is called friendship. The love which generous-hearted, virtuous persons feel for the poor and the wretched is called compassion. The love between spouses who have two bodies but one soul, who share equally in each other's joys and sorrows, is known simply as love. It has no other name, because it has the completeness of love. Other types of love are partial, not complete. The ultimate love is seen between equal and virtuous spouses.

Man should express God-given, heavenly love, and the source of happiness, in a suitable manner. This wealth, which is given by God to man, is not meant to be squandered and wasted, but meant to be spent well and augmented. But it is a matter of great sorrow and shame that thousands of men and women spend this wealth of love improperly! That is to say, they become lecherous and adulterous. Obviously, this does not benefit them. Therefore, every person should think well and avoid spending love improperly, act with caution, and marry a suitable person. He should not betray his spouse's trust and thereby dishonour his love. This is the chief objective of marriage.

The second [objective] is that tenderness, sweetness, and other charming qualities are natural to the fair sex and not to men; similarly, adventurousness, endurance, courage and such qualities are natural to men and not to women. These two types of qualities do not appear to advantage if kept totally apart. See, a man appears very rough if his harsh qualities, like adventurousness, courage, endurance and bravery, are not tempered with tender qualities such as compassion, humility and friendship. Likewise, a woman is very timid and unable to be of use in a time of need if her qualities of humility, compassion, affection, tenderness and shyness are not blended with courage, endurance, truthfulness and brilliance. Therefore men and women should blend their qualities and enhance their beauty. This alone will lead to the development and welfare of domestic life, and is the duty of every person. One person's qualities will not be assumed by another unless the two are in close contact. It is against the rules of society and religion that this should occur outside marriage. Hence it is proper for a person to enter into marriage.

The third [objective of marriage] is that the human heart is very weak, and unable to sustain itself without support. That is why no one is able to live alone anywhere. If a person is endowed with all the means of happiness and left alone in a forest, he will never agree to stay there; but if he has a companion, he will consider himself to be happy even if beset by great calamities. This proves that a companion is essential in domestic life. A companion who is hostile or indifferent, whose opinions do not agree with one's own, who remains unaffected by the other's happiness and unhappiness and does not share them is no companion at all. Therefore a person needs a companion who loves him unwaveringly, who remains unaffected by good fortune or misfortune. In this world, the only such companions are husband and wife; the rest are good for only a short while. A completely sincere mutual friendship, which is possible with a spouse, is not possible with anyone else. That is why great, learned men have said: 'The wife is one half of the husband, the wife is the best friend of all, the wife is the source of the three objects of wordly existence [i.e. religion, wealth and sensual enjoyment], the wife is the source of heaven.' [Skt] This proves that a person cannot get the kind of friend he wants unless he marries. Therefore it is proper to marry.

Thus far I have stated the objectives of marriage. Now let us consider your duties subsequent to marriage. Everybody knows that married couples are happy only if they enjoy mutual love; otherwise there is no end to their miseries. In this society, an evil custom has been traditionally followed; in case a disagreement arises between spouses even in a minor matter, the husband at once slights or even abandons his wife—the very wife who is a lifelong partner in his joys and sorrows, for whom he means everything, who feels she has attained heaven if he speaks well to her—and then he either remarries or starts committing sins forbidden by religion, such as adultery. Even when men behave in this manner, society does not utter a word. They are not subjected to any kind of royal or social punishment. This being the case, men become wanton, because they alone are the protectors and destroyers of women. There is nobody to defend poor, weak women placed in such a difficulty, and to speak out against men. What then can these weak creatures do? There are some courageous, saintly women who endure such transgressions and disrespect, and spend their lives in religious observances. Many commit suicide to end such misery. And many become wanton just like those men and stain their own lives and the reputation of their families by their unholy conduct. Of these three categories, the first is rarely seen, the second is more common, and the third commonest of all.

Such sins arise mostly from the hard-heartedness and wantonness of men. Men are stronger than women, therefore whatever they do is bound to be considered right. But such transgression does not befit their manliness. It is proper for a heroic person to forgive the weak and charm them with affection. If on the contrary, he uses his bravery to kill rather than protect the weak, who will praise him? Such conduct contravenes religion and such a person offends God, because God has given man greater strength than woman not in order for him to oppress her and make her unhappy. It is the duty [dharma] of a man to refrain from insulting women and to charm them with affection and to love them unwaveringly.

Be that as it may; let us now turn to women. There are some foolish women who, in the belief that their husbands do not love them, start searching for remedies to charm them. When engaged in this effort, they find many people who possess remedies to charm a person with spells, incantations, charms, amulets, sacred ash, . . . etc. In order to thus charm their husbands, the foolish women are prepared to do anything that the rogues tell them to do. These women come to great harm at the hands of such people. For example, they waste hard-earned money instead of putting it to good use. These people are wicked and ill-natured; their company leads to a violation of modesty, to many other irreligious deeds, and results in public censure. The wicked people, in order to show that their words are true, give [the woman] some earth, stones, ash, etc., saying, 'Take this medicine and give it to your husband to eat at such a time in such a manner; then he will be entirely under your control.' . . . The foolish women trust the rogues and feed their dear husbands dreadful medicines, which sometimes results in terrible disasters. . . . The character of these women, who try such spells and magical devices, comes to the notice of their husbands; and then the husbands lose whatever love they feel for them. So, it is obvious that the spells are of no use.

There are several magical devices for charming one's husband . . . [which] should be employed by all women, in order to achieve the welfare of all. These valuable magical devices are as follows: first, your conduct should be in conformity with your husband's wishes. Never do anything contrary to his wishes. Do not ever raise your voice in his presence or treat him with contempt. Always do any task that he instructs you to do, as long as it is in conformity with religious precepts, although it may involve hard work. Whatever work he tells you to do at a certain time, should be done without fail at that particular time. You should not arrogantly say that you are unable to do it, or are too tired. If it is totally impossible [for you] to perform the task, you should speak to him sweetly, and humbly show him the reason why you are unable to do it. You should not tell him a lie of any kind, or unnecessarily slander anybody in front of him. Do not slander or trick him, or unnecessarily rebuke him and blurt out whatever comes to mind. Never betray his trust, or prevent him from doing a good deed, or do anything that would hurt his feelings. If you make any kind of mistake, acknowledge it and beg his forgiveness. If he makes a mistake, do not get angry but explain it to him. Serve him lovingly to the best of your ability.

You should never attempt to attract your husband by wearing ornaments and showy clothes. If a person has good qualities, they themselves draw people's minds. Try to attract your husband with your virtues. Do not ever, for any reason, deceive your husband. In this world a woman has no other friend like her husband. He shows you the right path as a teacher would; he sees to your welfare as a father would; he treats you with affection as a mother would. He is worthy of trust, venerable like a god, and as dear as your own life. If you deceive such an incomparable friend, who else do you have in this world, with whom you can behave candidly and be happy? I think that women who deceive their husbands are capable of any evil deed. Therefore, all of you should be candid with your husbands. Do not ever do anything your husband would not like, no matter how profitable. Do not repeat to others the secrets he has confided in you. If your husband speaks unpleasantly to you when you are alone with him, do not carry tales about him to others. If you conduct yourself properly, it will reduce the possibility of mutual discord.

Second, a woman sometimes carries false tales about others (her mother-in-law, father-in-law, sister-in-law, brother-in-law, neighbours, etc.) to her husband in order to turn his love away from them and towards herself. Never do such a thing. Nobody trusts a person who slanders others. . . . If anybody slanders your husband, do not support that person. If the censure is deserved, you should think how to prevent it. It is useless to quarrel with people. Now let us consider your duties to your husband.

You should assist your husband as much as possible in all his activities. After finishing all household chores in time, instead of sitting idly you should always concentrate on doing the tasks that would achieve advancement for yourself, your husband and all the people in the household. When your husband returns home [from work], you should not take him aside and spend time with him on unnecessary talk. It is only proper that you should spend a happy hour or so with him everyday, in amusing conversation. But if this limit is exceeded, it leads not to happiness but to the loss of important work; and the couples who spend their day in such sloth begin to detect many annoying qualities in each other, which ultimately leads to quarrels. Then both mind and body are disturbed, and joy disappears from all activities.

While conversing with your husband, talk about topics like morality, knowledge, religion and God and avoid unnecessary things like slandering others. If you find anything lacking in your domestic life, at an appropriate time suggest that he should make proper arrangements. When his mind is disturbed, for whatever reason, comfort him as much as you can, with sweet words. If he is dejected and disheartened in any enterprise, you should speak words of encouragement to comfort him and give him courage. In times of adversity, you should be satisfied to live with him in the same state that he is in. You should never complain about anything. Many women have the habit of troubling their husbands for ornaments, etc. and of shaming them by boasting about the high status of their relatives (father, aunt's husband, uncle, brother, etc.) This hurts his feelings a great deal and eventually destroys all love; therefore, saintly women should give up such wrong conduct. Just as men achieve fame through their fathers, women achieve fame through their husbands. Whatever the husband's condition—good or bad, poor or rich —is also the condition of the wife. In such a condition, one should not pay attention to the high status of others. A woman, even if her father is a king, does not inherit his rank, but acquires the position of her husband. Therefore the woman who respects her husband and lives in the same condition as he, is honoured and respected by people. A woman who behaves in a manner contrary to this, is not respected, needless to say.

See, in our Bharatavarsha, there lived in ancient times great saintly women like Sita, Savitri, Arundhati, Lopamudra, Damayanti, and others, whose fame still shines in Bharat like the spotless moon. Why? Because they were ever devoted to their husbands and were extremely loving.

Lopamudra was a princess, whereas the opulence of [her future husband] Agastya *rishi* consisted only of a wooden staff, an ascetic's water pot, garments made from the bark of trees, and a hut. But immediately on being married to him, Lopamudra put aside her royal robes, valuable gems and ornaments with which her father had dowered her, and donned garments made from the bark of trees, which were suited to her husband's station; and, detached from all royal pleasures, she followed him into the forest infested with terrible animals such as lions and tigers!

Likewise the devoted wife [*pativrata*] Sita, the brightest ornament of the fair sex, worthy of being remembered at the dawn of each day. Everyone, from children to old people, knows of her fame. There is no simile worthy of her in this world. By giving birth to her, this land of Bharat attained the distinguished title 'The Womb Which Contains Jewels'. When Sita, venerated by all, was married, she had not experienced even in her dreams the unbearable distress caused by the heat of the sun or by severe cold, by the wind or rain. But, in spite of entreaties to dissuade her, she accompanied her husband to fourteen years' exile in the forest in order to honour his father's promise and went to live [with him] in Dandakaranya, which was the abode of terrible demons! Alas! At that time, Sita could not even manage to wear the garments made from the bark of trees, which were suitable for forest life. What did she then do? She held them in her hand and looked at Ramachandra with tears in her eyes. Then Rama himself draped those garments on his dear wife. Immediately, and joyfully even in this sad state, she followed Rama who, after paying homage to his father, took the royal road towards the forest. At the sight of that sorrowful scene, even the stone-hearted could not help weeping. But Sita felt not an iota of sorrow. She believed that the company of her husband would give her the happiness of heaven even while in hell, and being without him even in heaven would give her the torments of hell. Oh, what love was this! What devotion to her husband! Happy indeed was she who possessed such love and devotion to her husband. Later, did Sita escape only with this exile? No. Poor Sita was subjected to every possible humiliation by destiny. But she displayed, even to such a cruel destiny, her utmost love for her husband and her courage! For fear of public censure, her husband abandoned her in the forest. How deeply is one affected by the memory of innocent Sita, in the last stages of pregnancy, deserted in that uninhabited forest! As Bhavabhuti has said, 'Even a stone bursts into tears and the heart of a diamond breaks asunder with sorrow!' [Skt]

But even at a time like this, Sita's love for her husband and her devotion to him did not diminish even one bit. She did not blame Rama for having deserted her in the forest even though she was not guilty. In the belief that her destiny was unpropitious, she sent a message full of moral and religious advice to Ramachandra through Lakshmana: 'Although you have abandoned me, I am your servant. You alone will protect me in this forest, as you protect your other subjects, and I will always be happy to hear your fame.' Oh! What courage, what greatness!

Truly, a country that has produced such a saintly woman [as Sita] is worthy of veneration from the whole world, no matter if that country is small and beset by misfortunes. At present our Bharatavarsha is overcome by misfortune, and possesses nothing to comfort the hearts of its people, which are seared with grief. But we proclaim to the people, shouting proudly in a voice that roars in the sky, that the gem of a woman like the saintly Sita was not born in any other country! Bharatavarsha may be inferior to other countries in all other qualities, but no other country is yet worthy enough to equal it in the matter of the fame of saintly women like Sita. Similar are the lives of other great, saintly women like Damayanti, Savitri, and others. Therefore, women who wish to enhance the greatness of their sex should re-enact the noble and holy life of the saintly women described above, through their own conduct.

As mentioned above, you should not act or speak in a manner which your husband dislikes. But if your husband is prepared to act in contravention of religion, it is your prime duty to give him good advice and dissuade him from such a path. A wife is not really saintly if she agrees with her husband only in order to win his favour, allows him to do as he wishes, and assists him in his proclivities. We call such a woman 'selfish'. Woman is man's greatest friend in this worldly life; he has no other friend like her. A friend should not flatter. If your friend has acquired a bad habit, and even if he would be hurt or angry and displeased if you advise him against it, you should never hesitate to sacrifice your own happiness and to tell [him] the truth in a disinterested manner, for the sake of your friend's welfare. The great poet Bharavi has said, 'It is difficult to find words which are beneficial as well as appealing'[Skt]. If your words or deeds, which conform to religion and lead to welfare, incur your husband's displeasure, so be it. Indeed, you should not fear the displeasure of the whole world, let alone that of your husband. . . .

Many a woman possesses such a nature that when she sees the wealth of others, she begins to hanker after it. This wealth is [merely] good clothes, utensils, ornaments and such things. If her husband has the capacity to provide it, she gives him no end of trouble, having fallen prey to greed. If he does not have such a capacity, she reveals her demonic side and subjects her husband to great disrespect by cursing and abusing him. It is quite improper for saintly women to behave in this fashion, and also contrary to morality. . . . There is greatness, honour and happiness in being content with what one's husband has.

Only a woman who is pure of conduct, in conformity with her husband's wishes and being mindful of religion and God, is fit to be called saintly. Some women avoid conducting themselves in the manner described above, but try to prove their saintliness only by an outward show, such as eating their husbands' leftover food, drinking the water with which their husbands' feet have been washed, and so on. But this does not last long. Outward show disappears quickly, like clouds in autumn [sharada]; soon, their true nature is exposed. Keeping this in mind, you should offer your husband guileless, everlasting love; it will give you everything. There is no one as lowly as a woman who shows outward devotion to her husband, who is her unique friend, and deceives him by guile. While trying to deceive others, she is deceiving herself. I have heard many women say, 'My husband does not love me, he insults me'.

This claim may be just in some rare case; but careful thought shows that in many cases it is not. Women are foolish, they misunderstand what they are told and do the wrong thing. Naturally, this causes a rift between the couple. Therefore, one should speak and act at the proper time and in a proper manner so as to avoid being insulted. If one is always thoughtful and avoids doing something one is not capable of doing, one is never insulted. If your husband is angry, or if his mind is disturbed due to illness, grief, remorse or similar reasons, you should not say anything unwise or inappropriate. When he is angry, you should soothe his mind with calm, sweet words. At a time of grief, remorse or sorrow, you should calm his mind with sweet words appropriate to the occasion. A person becomes dispirited and lethargic if his efforts do not succeed; at such a time, you should comfort him with words of encouragement.

It is a woman's primary duty to assist her husband in every act, every time, by following his inclinations. Only the women who act accordingly may properly be called their husbands' better halves. Women who are selfish and do not help their husbands in any way are not called saintly. Why would unselfish women, who help their husbands every moment, not be loved by their husbands? Why would they not be respected? Where is the vile man who would abandon such a valuable gem and all desirable things he has in his own home, and go elsewhere? Conduct yourselves as described above; then, your husbands will be absolutely charmed. In this world there are two unique spells which conquer people—straightforward, guileless and sweet speech, and behaviour according to another's wishes. Even persons of a demonic disposition are beguiled by these two spells, how would [ordinary] human beings withstand it? It is in our own hands to be worthy of others' respect and love. The way we treat others is the way others will treat us. If one keeps this firmly in mind, one is not likely to be insulted anywhere. If, in spite of all this, one is [insulted], one should not lose courage. Be that as it may. So far I have briefly described how women should behave towards their husbands. Now let us consider how they should conduct themselves at home.

6. DOMESTIC DUTIES

The great learned men of the ancient past have described four different stages of human life, namely celibacy (*brahmacharya*), the life of a householder (*grihastha*), retirement to the forest (*vanaprastha*) and renunciation (*sanyasa*). Among these four, they have treated the householder's stage as the most superior, because a person in this stage maintains those in the other three. In this world, there is no meritorious deed equal to benevolence. A householder is the most benevolent person of all, and therefore the most superior. The householder's stage is the state in which men and women, having married in a suitable manner, live as husband and wife in mutual love. The manner in which a woman should behave towards her husband has been explained earlier. A woman should help her husband in everything. There are many opportunities for doing so, which have been partly described earlier. But the most essential of these tasks, which also carry the greatest responsibility, are domestic duties which are explained here.

Domestic duties are the work of women. They should never neglect them. A home in which women do not perform household work themselves is not a happy home. The wise have said that 'the housewife herself is the home'. A woman does not attain the rank of a housewife merely by virtue of being born into the female sex or by becoming a wife. It is very difficult to earn the title 'housewife'. Women with shallow minds will never attain it. Therefore, women who are intelligent and desire that great title should behave affectionately towards all in the family and conduct themselves wisely.

First, they should abandon sloth. Man has no enemy like sloth. A person dominated by sloth cannot be called a human being, because he is incapable of doing deeds useful to the human state. Similarly, one should allow no place in one's heart for egoism, anger, hatred, greed, violence, abusiveness, deceit, falsehood, impatience, conceit, hypocrisy, selfishness, rivalry, immoderation and other such vices. I will tell you briefly what harm results from all these:

1. Sloth:

If a person is filled with this vice, it wastes a part of his life, which is the most difficult to obtain [again]. . . .

Everday, you should note down what is to be done at what time, and do it exactly at the noted time without fail. Thus, if you do little things on time, you will be able to accomplish many good deeds within a few days. . . . Thoughtful persons should never give a place in their minds to sloth, which is their greatest enemy.

2. Egoism:

The wise have said that certain is the fall of an egoist. Thousands of such examples are before us, but man's mind is so completely veiled by ignorance that he does not see them. Do not be conceited, about anything. One has never heard that conceit, which stems from wealth, honour, strength, opulence, etc. lasts long; nor will this happen in the future. Emperors like Ravana, Haihaya, Duryodhana, Napoleon, Aurangzeb, etc., and great kings known for their bravery, generosity, keeping their promise, strength and pride, have all fallen only due to [their] egoism. . . .

The damage done by the four vices—anger, hatred, rivalry and violence—have been described earlier in section four; but I will again briefly refresh your memory. Women, who are responsible for managing domestic life, should fear the above-mentioned vices like a snake, because a person cannot last where these vices are found. . . . A person who has the vices of abusiveness, hypocrisy, greed, deceit and falsehood is not a human being but is wrongly described as such. Because nobody trusts such a person; and his tongue is stained by always abusing good people. . . . Impatience and immoderation are similar. . . .

Now let us consider how the daily routine and domestic duties should be managed.

You should always get out of bed before the break of dawn, and should not lie down again even if you feel sleepy. Morning sleep fills the body with extreme sloth, and such irregular sleep everyday affects one's health, giving rise to many types of illness. Therefore, you should cultivate the habit of going to bed at the proper time and getting up before dawn; you will then find ample time to do all your work regularly. Otherwise there is a terrible rush and nothing is done properly. Moreover, there is no time during the whole day for even a little rest. A regular routine leaves no scope for ill health. When in good health, you should never sleep more than six hours. . . . If you get up as soon as you wake up, your mind is calm and your body energetic. All tiredness is gone, and the mind has the zest for the daily routine.

As soon as you get up, you should first rinse your eyes and mouth with clean, cool water. All one's body organs are not properly active during sleep, so all kinds of impurities in the body come out through the mouth, eyes, etc., and accumulate there. The saliva in the mouth is very polluted, like poison. If one swallows it immediately after getting up and before rinsing the mouth, it reaches the digestive tract and causes many types of disease. And the polluted dirt and water from the eyes make the eyes droop. If they do not receive the coolness of water, the light of vision will get reduced day by day. Therefore, as soon as you get up, rinse your mouth and eyes properly, dry them with a clean cloth, and then do whatever else you want to do. Do not fail to do this.

At that time, one's mind is cheerful and undisturbed. Because there is no noise of people or rush of work, the mind is concentrated on whatever one does at that time. At such a time, you should recite the name of God, the protector of all, the most compassionate, the father of the world, with a pure mind and with devotion. That Friend of the distressed has protected us before birth in the mother's womb, in that dark chamber where it is not possible even to breathe. Immediately after birth, when we were too weak to eat anything, He created nectar-like milk in the mother's heart, which was filled with indescribable love, in order to sustain our life. As we grow up, He places before us the ready means of our advancement. It is by His grace that we lack nothing. Like [our] parents, He always protects us from calamities unknown to us, and achieves our welfare at every moment. This Ocean of compassion has placed us under immeasurable obligations for which we should express our gratitude by single-mindedly offering ourselves at His feet. This is the sacred duty of every person. A person who fails to do so is ungrateful, and there is no sinner like him in the world. Therefore, recite the name of God everyday at the hour of dawn, sitting in solitude. After single-mindedly offering yourself at His feet, beg His forgiveness for your offences, very humbly and in an abject voice. Pray for the welfare of yourself, your friends, neighbours, enemies, and all creatures in the world, in accordance with His wish. Ask Him to give you good thoughts, and courage to retain a firm desire for religion and truth in all domestic tasks.

You will never be able to repay the benevolence of God; therefore, express whatever gratitude that can be contained in your little heart, and always love Him unwaveringly. Then you will have done at least a part of your duty. After reciting the name of God and saying your prayers, you should think of what needs to be done next. Every task, great or small, should be performed after careful thought. . . . If something new is to be undertaken, one should prepare oneself by consulting experienced people who have done it frequently before. Many women think that it is demeaning to ask for advice, but such egoism is a sign of ignorance.

You should get up early in the morning before everybody else, and clean the house by sweeping away all dirt and rubbish. Just as the human body accumulates dirt, and a number of diseases erupt if the dirt is not washed off for several days, similarly, if all manner of dirt accumulates in the corners of the house and in bathrooms, bedrooms, kitchen, etc., the air in the house becomes polluted. It enters the body when people breathe, and the disease-generating, foul-smelling particles which enter the body with it act like poison. Such a dirty house is the root cause of all diseases. Therefore, all women should be ever mindful of keeping their houses clean. Only women stay at home all the time, therefore they alone are responsible for keeping the house clean, and for the resultant advantages. . . .

For smearing the house with a coat of cow-dung, [the requisite amount of] fresh dung should be mixed with about a quarter of that amount of earth dug up from a clean place, so that it destroys the foul smell and other bad air-polluting qualities of the dung, and also keeps the floor clean. In this manner, the floor of the house, and also the walls—if they are not white-washed with lime—should be smeared everyday or after every four days, so that troublesome insects like bedbugs, mosquitoes and fleas do not breed. If the walls are coated with lime, there is no need to whitewash them again for six months, because lime contains a kind of pungent salt that dispels bad odours. It keeps the air pure and prevents insects that breed in dirt. Acts such as wiping oily hands on the walls, pillars, doors, or door-frames of the house, drawing lines with coal, or spitting and wiping mucus on them, are loathsome to the sight and harmful. You should never do such things, nor allow others to do so.

If there is space in the garden in front of the house or behind, fragrant flowering plants such as the rose, different varieties of jasmine, *bakul, parijatak, tagar,* as well as the *tulsi,* and [fragrant leafy plants, such as] *davana, marva,* should be planted in pots or in the earth, in a decorative manner. One plant should not be placed under another, and no dirty things should be thrown under them. The fragrance of flowers dispels the bad smells in the air, and plants keep the air cool and healthy, so that one feels cheerful and energetic after breathing it.

Among [one's] household duties, tasks such as keeping the house clean should be performed by the housewife herself, or by servants if she can afford them. At this juncture, let us consider how one should behave with [one's] servants.

It has been observed in many places that servants do not obey the mistress of the house, but make fun of her and give her orders as if they were the masters. This is not the fault of the servants, but of the person who treats them [inappropriately]. The people who perform lowly jobs are usually not of good families, and not deferential. Constant bad company makes their minds totally inferior. It is in your own hands to train them and improve their manners, and make them respect you. They will treat you the same way as you treat them.

You should talk to servants in strict moderation, that is, only when necessary. You should never jest and joke with them, laugh without reason, or discuss shameful things with them. Nor should you go to the other extreme and talk to them all the time with an unpleasant face, angrily, harshly, or as if giving orders. You should say whatever has to be said, pleasantly and mildly. If the servant commits an error, you should explain it to him properly in sweet words, and show slight contempt. There is nothing like sweet words and a show of contempt to make servants tractable. There are some who speak very harshly to their servants, and do not hesitate even to beat them occasionally. But this is a cruel thing to do. It makes servants obdurate and stubborn; then they do not fear such a cruel master. Soft behaviour is a weapon for subduing others; there is no other weapon which is as effective. Soft behaviour makes even vile creatures such as lions and tigers tractable like the meek deer; needless to say, it makes man tractable as well. You should never rebuke servants with harsh words, which break the heart and wound the soul. You should treat them with humility and love, so that they will also treat you likewise. You should never be arrogant and show them disrespect. By the grace of God, you are enjoying good days and are able to keep servants who are forced to serve others because they have fallen on bad days. But all [one's] days [will not always remain] alike; it is not possible to foretell who will prosper and who will be in distress. It need not cause surprise if those who are one's servants today become prosperous, while one is visited by misfortune oneself and is compelled to serve them in order to earn a living. . . . Therefore one should never treat a servant in a cruel, improper manner by behaving heartlessly or making him do unsuitable work. You should always show pity and compassion to servants. Console them in their grief. When they are ill, nurse them with affection as a mother nurses her children. Do not scorn them as lowly and dirty. Do not hesitate to go near them when they are ill. Always treat them with compassion, knowing that your relationship with them is like that of parents and children.

Servants try to gauge your inclinations and flatter you; they try to please the master by slandering others, to gain his good will, and to arouse hostility towards others. You should never be deceived by the flattery of such servants and consider anybody to be guilty without seeing his offence for yourself. . . . You should never tell servants confidential things about your husband, mother-in-law, sisters-in-law, relatives and other family members, or slander them in front of servants.

When a servant is to be given something as a sign of satisfaction, it should be given at a suitable time, and with the consent of one's husband, mother-in-law, or similar persons. You should never give anything at an improper time, in an improper manner, or at your own sweet will. If servants have done any work which deserves a reward, you should never fail to give them a reward which is suitable to your capacity and their worth, on a festive or joyous occasion. Not receiving anything in time disheartens them. Servants do not feel affectionate devotion and gratitude for a master who is not pleased by their work and does not reward them, and who treats them cruelly. The servants of such a master do not help him in adversity, but, on the contrary, become his enemies.

You should be very careful in your treatment of servants. You should behave in a manner that will [help you] retain your authority over them. You should not sit on the same seat as them, lie down on the same bed, or allow them to use your clothes. The main thing is that you should be very careful not to let them lose their respect for you. You should not punish them severely for a small offence. It is improper to rebuke or punish them when they are innocent. You should not shift the blame for your or someone else's mistake on your servant and make him share the punishment. Doing so destroys the servant's devotion and affection for his master.

You should not trust servants too much and entrust everything to them. Once a servant of an inferior disposition knows that his master or mistress trusts him implicitly, he tries to swallow everything. . . . In order to know whether a servant is trustworthy, you should always keep him under observation. You should leave some money, eatables and other small things lying around in the house, and let the servants think that you are not watching them or have forgotten them. If the servants think that their mistress is forgetful, and if they are of an inferior disposition, they immediately steal the things which are lying around. One should decide the worthiness of the servants by paying due attention to such acts, and be alert. But one should not do cruel things like dismissing a servant for a small offence. Many times one observes that a servant who is vile in the beginning improves because of the good treatment and moral instruction given by his master. In sum, you should not decide upon the worthiness of a servant as soon as he comes to you. Many servants are trustworthy in the beginning, but become ungrateful when they find an opportunity. Therefore, it is proper that you should always keep them under observation. But you should treat them affectionately in all matters, knowing that your relationship with them is like that of a mother and children.

All the things in the house should be kept tidily and in their proper place so that they can be found quickly and do not get mixed with other things. They should be dusted everyday so that they do not accumulate dirt. All groceries should be cleaned and kept covered or hung in a place where they cannot be destroyed by rats, cats, children, etc. Things which are to be eaten and drunk should not be kept uncovered. If they are uncovered, they get spoiled because dirt and different kinds of insects, like ants, flies, etc. fall into them. When they are eaten, they give rise to a number of illnesses in the body. Grains like lentils and rice, and things like jaggery, sugar, ghee, oil, spices, etc. contain a lot of dirt and dead or living insects. They should be weeded out; ghee and oil should be strained, grain should be husked by pounding, rinsed and cleaned; only then should they be used for eating. Many people eat sugar, etc. without cleaning it, but it is not good to do so. Even if something is not immediately useful, it should not be left lying around; one does not know when one will need what. All things worth keeping should be kept carefully. All things should thus be kept tidily and conveniently, and the house should be kept clean and pleasant to see.

The appearance of the house is the test of a housewife. If a house has everything in its proper place and looks pleasant, everybody immediately knows that the mistress of the house is clever. . . .

All utensils in the house, such as those used for eating, cooking, storing water, drinking milk, etc. and earthen pots for keeping milk, curd, buttermilk, etc. should be rinsed every day by scrubbing them clean both inside and outside. Otherwise they accumulate dirt and [will] spoil their contents. Utensils become slimy. If such dirty utensils are used for drinking water, etc. they can cause illness. Similarly, bed-clothes and garments to be worn should be kept clean. . . . Garments should be washed every day, and bed-clothes after every three or four days.

After cleaning everything in the house completely in this manner, you should always bathe early, at sunrise. The regular habit of an early bath gives the body energy, health and strength. It is better to bathe with cold water, if it agrees with your constitution. Cold water gives special strength and keeps the body healthy. If the weather is cold, if you are running a fever, or if it is raining, you should heat the bath water slightly. But the prevailing custom in this country, of bathing in water so hot as to scald the body, is totally harmful. The practice of pouring water over the head daily while bathing is an excellent one. If it is inconvenient, you should wash the body from the neck down everyday, and wash your hair every two to three days. But before pouring water over the body, you should bend down your head, pour cold water on it, and pat it with the hand so that the head remains cool. If, without doing so first, you pour water only over the rest of the body, all the heat in the body at once rises to the head, and gradually causes terrible illnesses like severe headaches. After wetting the body, you should scrub the whole body with a wet cloth, and wash it. Then you should bathe in a lot of water.

After bathing regularly in this fashion, you should put on clean, dry clothes, not wet ones. You should not stay in water too long; this causes illnesses like body-ache, rheumatism, fever, etc. Clothes should be worn properly so as to cover the entire body. Some women of good families in this country wear ritually pure garments or even ordinary ones in a very bad manner, such as wearing them vertically [or length-wise], tucking in the *padar* [loose end of the sari] sideways, pulling up the sari while working or even at other times, out of sheer habit. This shows great immodesty. See, wearing the garment vertically leaves one thigh uncovered. Also, pulling up the sari exposes one's legs up to the knees. When the *padar* is tucked in sideways, it is small; as there is no practice of doing up the [knotted] *choli* properly in front, the breasts are exposed. Similarly, if the middle portion of the lower border [of the nine yard sari] is not tucked in at the back with proper care, parts of the body, such as the calves, are visible. Therefore, modest women of good families should not wear garments in this fashion. Garments are to be worn primarily for protecting one's modesty. . . . The many shameful words I have written above are very improper in a book. But one is compelled to hang one's head in shame at the sight of the immodest behaviour of women in our country. One's heart is unable to endure such disgraceful conduct in one's own sex; as a result, these words have been regretfully uttered. May all forgive me for this.

It is especially shameful that attention is not paid to [one's] clothing while walking in the street to fetch water, etc. . . . The women here also have the custom of going out into the street without covering themselves with an additional garment [like a shawl]. Similarly, practices such as sitting in the presence of strangers, say in a meeting, without covering one's head, tucking in the *padar* sideways, etc. have become so common that people do not think that they are bad [practices]. But some thought will show that they are really bad. Therefore, women of good families should abandon them. While going out or when compelled to meet a stranger, it is proper to drape an additional garment to cover the whole body from head to foot. There is no such custom in our country [region], but it prevails in North India, and seems really excellent. Therefore it is good that we should borrow this good custom from others. . . .

After bathing, one should perform one's daily routine properly, tidily and quickly. . . . Cooking is the primary and most responsible task of women. If the meal is good, tasty and clean, it provides strength and does not cause illness. Therefore cooking should be done after learning the culinary art well. Similarly, it is necessary to learn which food items are fit to be eaten in which season, so that no illness is caused. In sum, it is for the women to arrange for food and drink so that everybody's health is secure. Therefore they should do so with great care. . . . You should not eat more or better than the others in the house. Whatever eatable is brought home should be divided properly among all, and you should be content with the rest. You should not feel hurt if you do not get a share. In this fashion, you should behave unselfishly in everything. . . .

One's behaviour towards all persons in the house should be modest, affectionate and devoted. One should not be garrulous or quarrelsome. One should not reply in kind if anyone speaks bad words. One should endure everybody's rebukes or wicked behaviour with great courage. One should not speak to anyone with an unpleasant face. If anybody asks a question, one should return an appropriate answer to the occasion, with a pleasant face and with sincerity. One should not say anything without proper thought. One should not tell tales. One should listen to everything others say and keep it to oneself. One should not share a confidential matter with others, or betray anybody's trust. One should not harm anybody; one should not even think of doing such a thing. One should forgive anybody who harms oneself. A wicked deed should be countered not in kind, but by a good deed. One should show devotion to one's mother-in-law, father-in-law, elder brother-in-law, elder sister-in-law and similar venerable persons, as one would to God. One should listen to the advice of all who conform to religion and act accordingly. One should always hold them in affection, and serve them as much as possible. One should never show disrespect to venerable people. One should not laugh shamelessly in front of them, speak immoderate words, sit with arms and legs outstretched, return improper answers, quarrel, act in a self-willed manner contrary to their wishes, show one's mastery while they are in the house, order them about or engage in any other acts that show disrespect. While in good health, one should not allow venerable persons or male strangers to serve one. One should not share a seat with any man other than one's brother, father or husband, or sit close to him in a lonely place. One should not jest or joke with men. . . . One should never abuse anyone or speak cruel, hurtful words. One should not deceive anyone. One should not disrespect the truth. One should not try to achieve one's ends by uttering falsehoods or through bad acts. One should not assist anyone in speaking ill. One should behave mildly and affectionately with everyone, as far as possible. One should treat one's younger brothers-in-law, sisters-in-law, step-children and such other persons with humility and affection. One should not be inimical to anyone, nor let anyone be inimical to oneself.

One should not put work aside and waste time in idleness. One should not stand at the door or window of the house and look upon the spectacle in the marketplace. At no time during the day should one sit idly or lie down. It is very improper for women to sleep during the day. In the afternoon, after everyone has eaten, one should inquire after everyone and then eat oneself. The meal should be moderate and agreeable to one's constitution. . . . Then one should finish the housework, check what is in the house and what is not. Any item that is used up should be ordered immediately and stored properly. A complete account of income and expenditure should be kept. Moderation should be observed in all actions. Expenditure should never exceed income. One should not waste money by squandering it needlessly. . . . Only that which is indispensable should be bought. . . . Money should not be wasted unnecessarily on expensive clothes or other such things. . . . One should not do anything without consulting one's husband; this applies also to spending money. But if he is not at home, one should unhesitatingly do any task which is unavoidable. One should not be afraid to perform any deed thoughtfully and by following the right path. One should never refrain from spending money on good causes, such as religion, benevolence, and national welfare; at such times, miserliness is blameworthy. Saintly persons say that there is no religious duty greater than giving. Therefore all people should give according to their capacity. Gifts should be given not in order to win gratitude but with an unselfish mind. . . .

It is very essential to give food to the hungry, water to the thirsty, clothes to one suffering from the cold, comfort to one in grief, encouragement to one who is dispirited, shelter to the destitute, etc. One should help, to the best of one's capacity, persons who are blind, crippled, mute, without arms, lepers, the aged, the ailing, etc. One should not hurt the feelings of such persons by making fun of them when one sees them, or by troubling them. It should not come as a surprise if one reaches such a state oneself in the course of time. Be unselfish and benevolent to the best of your God-given capacity. This is your essential duty. . . . When you do others a service, you are merely repaying your debt to them. . . .

In sum, no one is as happy as a person who is loving and benevolent, because he is worthy of being loved by all. . . . Show compassion to all creatures. If a person does bad deeds and is censured by all, do not blame him, but try to rid him of his vices and bring him on to the right path. Do not censure others in order to show off your own greatness, because no one is without faults. . . . If a few women get together, they usually find fault with other people. Such a propensity leads to undesirable results. First, it does not leave any time for conversation on good topics. Second, valuable time is unnecessarily wasted in censuring others. Third, nobody loves one. Fourth, one becomes known as a reviler and faces acute disgrace. Fifth, it lays the foundation of conflict which is most terrible, the root cause of all unhappiness and the source of misfortune. Therefore, one should not harbour abuse in one's heart, which is the mother of lakhs of terrible calamities. It is [also] improper to harbour the conceit that one is superior and others inferior. . . .

One should make a list of all the things in the house, and keep them carefully. If anyone borrows anything, one should note down in a memory-book or in a book of accounts, who has borrowed what, when, for how long, and when it was returned. This avoids confusion and aids memory. Similarly, one should keep a detailed account of salaries paid to the washerman, milkman, servants, etc. The habit of borrowing is very bad. . . . In our country, it is the custom everywhere to borrow money and squander it on celebrations. But it leads to great disgrace and other such terrible calamities. Nobody thinks of these, which is a sad thing. Great kingdoms have been lost due to unlimited expenditure; what then can one say about an ordinary person? Therefore, every person in our country should spend his money on the right things instead of squandering it; he should spend carefully and also save in the knowledge that whatever is left over will be useful to him or to others when the time comes. If all people do so, this country will become wealthy again, and the terrible hardships we have to suffer frequently due to famines and such other catastrophes will reduce. The poverty of the people in this country is the cause of all calamities. Therefore, it is everybody's essential duty to eradicate it totally.

After completing all the housework in this manner, one should also rest for a while, because a person gets tired after working the whole day, and one's health suffers if there is no rest. But it should always be kept in mind that moderation is to be observed in all one's actions. . . . Just as money should be spent carefully and well, so should time. It is possible to regain lost wealth, but lost time cannot be regained, as everybody knows.

After everybody has had the evening meal, one should finish all work and inquire after everyone in the house. Then, after everybody has gone to bed, one should close all the doors, etc. and carefully put away anything that is out of place. Before going to sleep, one should think about the tasks one had listed out for oneself in the morning, about the tasks which were done and [those] left undone, about their results, etc.

One should not be immersed in household duties and be lazy about seeking the way to one's welfare. One should read moral philosophy, stories containing spiritual knowledge, the *shastras* that are within one's comprehension, newspapers, etc.; store in mind whatever good advice one finds in them, and keep one's mind tranquil, intent on excellence and devoted to religion. . . .

One should go to sleep at a regular time, that is, one watch [about an hour and a half] after the night starts, and get up at the right time, that is, one watch before the night ends. While performing all the household duties, one should always remember that God, our judge, is always near. One should not trespass against Him. If one does bad deeds unknown to others, they may not come to light. But God is omniscient, He watches us. It is impossible for one to commit a bad deed without His knowledge and escape punishment. Keeping this in mind, one should try to conform to religion in all one's actions.

7. THE NURTURE AND CARE OF CHILDREN

Thus far, I have briefly discussed the thoughts which occurred to me regarding domestic duties. At the present, let us consider how to nurture children and what kind of upbringing to give them.

This above-mentioned duty is the most important among all one's domestic duties. Therefore, women should perform it with very mature and clear thinking. The brave Napoleon Bonaparte was once asked by someone: 'How is it that your country, France, is the greatest among all the countries in this world? What is the reason for such extraordinary deeds of your countrymen and for their flourishing condition?' That thoughtful warrior briefly replied: 'Our mothers elevated our country and all of us to this condition.' This reply of his is very brief, but upon deliberation it becomes clear that every one of its letters contains all the meaning of great tomes such as *Mahabharata*. Truly, life and death, welfare and wretchedness, superiority and inferiority of the offspring, depends upon its mother.

Usually, all people inherit their mother's qualities to a greater extent, because, from the time of conception to the time of birth, the child's body grows out of the flesh and blood of its mother. Later, as long as it is unable to eat other things, the infant is sustained by her milk. Therefore, a person has a large share of his mother's blood. Likewise, he gets her nature [as well] along with it. Later on, children always learn whatever their mothers say and do, and behave in a similar manner. This proves that if the mother's constitution, character and conduct are good, the children also turn out well, and if not, the children will naturally turn out bad. Why have the people of our unfortunate Bharatavarsha become so dispirited, weak and dependent nowadays? Their ancestors were so brilliant, brave, dutiful and independent; why have these people, belonging to the same lineage, reached such a plight? If anyone asks us this, we will clearly reply that the reason for this is the lacklustre constitution of [our] women, who have been reduced to a state of animal-like ignorance and undeserved slavery by the wrong deeds of the selfish, short-sighted men of this country! Most men in this country believe that women should not be allowed to have any kind of knowledge; if they become knowledgeable, they will prevent the licentious behaviour of the men who will then lose their superiority. With this in mind, they have written the *dharma shastras,* which favour the self-interest of men, which state that, 'Women are not entitled to study the *shastras*; they should live with their husbands as servants; only service to the husband gives them salvation.' Furthermore, they force women to behave accordingly and prevent them from undertaking any good deed, by repeatedly writing and uttering words that revile women, as for example, 'Women are evil, reckless, deceitful.' Men do this in order to achieve their self-interest, but, in effect, manage to cut off their own feet with an axe. A person gets no learning without education; in the absence of learning, he will never acquire qualities such as independence of mind, brilliance, truthfulness, religiosity, etc. which lead to prosperity. Can the people who lack these attributes themselves produce progeny whose constitutions are elevated and vigorous? Can barren land, where only grass can grow, produce a sweet mango tree? Then, if the mothers in this country have a lacklustre constitution, how will their progeny be vigorous? Medical science has stated that 'The exact form, constitution, mental disposition, etc. of the woman and man at the time of conception are acquired by the progeny.' This statement is literally true. At any given time, a person's state of mind is reflected in his physical activities. Little wonder, then, that the reproduction of progeny will follow this rule.

The current state of our country proves this. In this country, men's minds are always filled with inferior feelings about women. Therefore, men do not have open minds, but only make an outward show of deceptive friendship; and, with a feeling of superiority, exercise power over women as they like. Women themselves, oppressed by such behaviour, do not possess good minds. Due to their permanently servile condition and ignorance, their minds are unclean, dull, lacklustre and untruthful. A desire for religion, love of God and adventurousness cannot exist in such unclean minds. Let the readers consider how the progeny will turn out if produced by parents of such an inferior disposition and brought up by mothers endowed with the excellent qualities mentioned above. . . .

At present, some educated nationalist men fill the whole wide world with their roars, orating in a voice like the rumbling of clouds, that: 'Our country is in great distress, it should be uplifted in such-and-such a manner by [people] learning the arts and skills. In the past there were great, mighty people in this country, who were independent, but today we are living in subjection and are dependent on others. Now, all of us should exert ourselves unitedly for the welfare of our country', etc. But is this going to yield any results at all? All their oratory comes to naught. Those who hear their words, receive them through one ear and discard them through the other, and, as if afraid that these words from the world of oratory would stick to their bodies, they shake their garments before going home! When ten persons come together, they only waste their time by talking about words like 'Freedom!', 'Glory!', etc. like idle talk in a gathering of Brahmins. But this talk does not result in any action. How would it? Their impatient disposition, which they have inherited from their parents, has no trace of virtues such as courage, keeping promises, sense of duty, etc. The above-mentioned words that they utter are not their own; they have been produced by observing the behaviour of the English people and by reading books, newspapers, etc. written in their language. How long will their influence last? One should just listen to the prating of these people. They say, 'Our ancestors were great.' We say, 'Yes! That is true! Your ancestors, and also ours, were great and tall like seven palm trees; but why are you giving yourselves airs? If you do not possess qualities to match their greatness, your talk only proves that your being born in their lineage has disgraced it. Your ancestors illuminated the world with their virtues, like the flame of a lamp; and you blacken the face of your motherland, like soot from that lamp. Is this not so? What was the reason for your ancestors being so brilliant?' The reason was that in their time nobody thought of women as servants. They imparted knowledge to women, and inculcated in them qualities such as brilliance, [etc]. They did not behave licentiously and in a self-willed manner, contrary to the interests of women. They protected the rights of women completely. Therefore women acquired virtues, lived in contentment, and were happy like queens, even [while] in poverty. Also the progeny produced and brought up by them were brilliant, religious, and honoured their promises. Now, if the people of our country want to restore this old state of affairs, they should give up their misguided selfishness, and improve the fundamentals. They should try to inculcate virtues in women and should not deprive them of their just rights. Women will then acquire an energetic and vigorous disposition. Later, their progeny will acquire their virtues and disposition, and grow up to be trustworthy, courageous and dutiful. Then, their efforts will deliver the country from its wretched state and revive its fortunes. Nothing will be achieved by thousands of declamations, assemblies, etc. until this happens. If one repeatedly cuts off the roots of a tree while showering nectar on its top, how can one hope to obtain fruits from it? And how wise would the people be who cherish such a hope? Be that as it may, we will now turn to our chosen topic.

The women of our country do not know how to take proper care of children, so the future prospects of the children's constitution are spoilt from the beginning. Therefore, mothers should take great precautions to ensure that their children are nurtured in a manner conducive to their good constitution.

First, mothers of infants should observe every kind of self-restraint. They should completely give up eating in a self-willed manner food that is harmful, excessive, stale, dry, or spicy; and also give up other immoderate physical acts. If this is not done, the mother's milk goes bad. Drinking such milk gives the infant indigestion, which, in turn, produces all kinds of diseases. All food eaten is concocted in the digestive tract in order to produce blood. That blood spreads through the whole body, and forms the very life of a person. The eating of a bad food preparation results in gastric heat slowing down, and the food remaining undigested; this disrupts all bodily processes. Naturally, then, diseases are produced. A child has limited digestive power; if its diet is disturbed even slightly, it immediately contracts a serious illness. Again, it is very difficult to treat children's diseases. A proper diet reduces the probability of disease. . . . One should never give a strong medicine for a slight complaint, or give medicine for a complaint that is likely to disappear by itself, or give the wrong medicine at the wrong time. Women should, therefore, acquire a good knowledge of common diagnostic medicine. When they are not able to understand the problem, they should consult a traditional physician [*vaidya*] or a medical doctor. . . . Second, women should firmly bear in mind that vows, amulets, charmed cords, or sacred ash given by holy men as blessings, and such other remedies do not help at all.

Now let us speak of the regular care of children. Children should be bathed everyday in clean and lukewarm water; cold water is even better, if agreeable to their constitution, because a cold water bath gives physical strength and energy. It is customary to massage the child's body with oil before the bath. But excessive oil should not be applied; it makes the body slippery and blocks the removal of dirt from the pores of the skin. If excessive oil is applied, it sticks to the body even after the bath. When dust settles on it, the body becomes even more dirty. While applying oil, it is customary to put a drop or two in the child's eyes. Experienced women claim that oil makes the eyes water, which cleans them and cures eye diseases. But this does not happen. On the contrary, it makes the child cry more, because the sharpness of the oil smarts the eyes and is harmful. Some women pour very hot water on the baby's body, almost scalding it, and hurt that tender body even more by massaging it roughly. Even when the babies start crying in pain, these women do not leave them alone! Such heartless behaviour is not proper in a compassionate person. Therefore they should stop doing this. Experience shows that when the body is rubbed lightly and bathed in pleasantly warm water, children become cheerful. . . . Many women are fond of adorning their children's bodies with ornaments, but do not pay attention to the cleanliness of their bodies and clothes. . . .

Many women are in the habit of breast-feeding their infant as soon as it starts crying, without finding out why it is crying. This disturbs the regularity of the child's feed, and its frequency prevents the milk from being digested. This causes many complaints of the stomach. Therefore, infants should be suckled only at regular times. . . . Similarly, while putting a baby to sleep, mothers in this country feed it opium to keep it quiet; this is a very bad and harmful practice. If the habit of consuming intoxicating substances is acquired in childhood, it is difficult to get rid of it soon. Feeding children opium intoxicates them and they lie down in a lethargy all the time. . . .

There are four chief ways of protecting children's health:

1. Plentiful and clean water, which the skin needs, should be used for bathing the child after massaging its body and washing it clean. . . . Garments soiled by faeces and urine, or by sweat, oil, etc. should never be used. They should be washed everyday before being used. This keeps children clean, comfortable and happy.
2. Free and clean air to breathe: Children should never be kept in a malodorous and confined place which is like a dark prison cell. . . .
3. A timely and moderate diet agreeable to the stomach [should be provided].
4. The proper amount of natural sleep is necessary for the growth and development of the brain.

Mothers should guard their children properly in infancy, as described briefly above. . . . Every infant's mother should understand that proper protection of her children is her essential duty. If she has to sacrifice all other happiness in doing so, it does not matter, because the protection of children is the repayment of a debt. It has to be done at any cost. One's own parents have exerted themselves to nurture one, and have thus imposed a burden of obligations on one, which can never be repaid. One should try to discharge at least a part of it through devotion and service to them, and through the nurturing of one's offspring. . . .

Mothers must be very careful when the children start to grow and begin to speak and commit acts of different types. The seed of future actions is sown in childhood; the fruits, in the form of well-being or wretchedness, accrue when the person grows up. . . .

Childhood and the indistinct physical disposition during childhood are like a ball of clay. They will turn out good or bad according to the way they are moulded. . . .

Therefore, it is a mother's duty to sow the seed of virtue in their [children's] hearts in childhood. There are thousands of examples of the ill effects that result if the mother does not try to cure her child of bad habits. Therefore, a mother should try to give her child a good upbringing, and with great caution, until it is able to speak and understand everything properly. Be that as it may; now let us consider how to start a good upbringing.

First of all, a mother should be very careful to ensure that her speech, actions and general behaviour are faultless in every way, and should try to ensure that the behaviour of the rest of the people in the house is likewise. . . .

When Peter the Great, the famous king of Russia, became really great, he performed countless deeds for his country, because of his natural right-mindedness. He acquired many arts and skills, and left behind immortal fame through his behaviour, which was worthy of imitation by all kings. But, although inherently right-minded, he had spent his childhood in bad company and was not well brought up; so he was unable to control man's [six] 'enemies', such as sexual passion, anger, etc. [along with desire, affection, pride and envy]. While under their influence, he would engage in many acts unworthy of him. . . . Therefore, he frequently uttered the sad words of repentance: 'I did not receive a proper upbringing in childhood, therefore I am unable to bring myself to the right path.' . . . This proves that if children turn out badly, it is not their fault but the fault of the people who watch over them. Children learn what they are taught.

When children are old enough to talk, the mother should teach them to speak in a truthful, sweet and polite manner. She should not use untruthful, crooked, cruel and impolite words in the presence of children, nor allow others to do so. She should not allow her children to go near people who are in the habit of using such words. . . . In the course of conversation, many women casually use bad, abusive and vulgar words directed towards their children and others. After hearing them everyday, children develop the habit of speaking the same way, and are unable to rid themselves of the habit, no matter what they do. . . . There are great school masters who point out the right path to everyone, impart knowledge, and raise to great fame their pupils who are the pillars of the edifice of future progress. These same school masters also curse their errant pupils with abusive language, referring to their mothers and sisters, in order to show off! . . . It is the custom of this country to say to a child, as soon as it is able to talk, things like: 'What type of husband or wife do you want?'; 'How does so-and-so walk?'; 'How do you mock someone?'; 'When will you marry?'; 'Slap your mother'; 'Kick so-and-so'; 'Bring such-and-such a thing without so-and-so's knowledge', etc. All these things appear trifling to the people here, but they do not imagine, even in their dreams, to what disasters they are likely to lead. . . . The last Nawab of Bengal, Suraj-ud-daula, was brought up by his grandfather; he acquired bad habits from childhood because of his pampering and because of bad company. When he grew up, he ruined his country and ultimately himself through his bad qualities, as can be seen clearly from a reading of history. . . .

Children should not be allowed to keep bad company. When small children seek out other children to play with, they should be allowed to play only with good children, never with mischievous ones. . . . In order to control their children, some women beat them severely or employ other such cruel methods; but this warps the children's minds and is a very improper thing to do. Children lose all love for their mother as a result of untimely, severe beatings and unnecessary intimidation. For the same reason, they feel no respect for her when they grow up. Beating makes children obdurate. . . . It is very foolish to try to win over children or others by harsh methods. Mildness is a great weapon. Mild behaviour makes even cruel creatures like lions humble and obedient to man. As far as possible, children should be given good advice in a mild manner, and put on the right path. . . . Children should not be spoilt needlessly, it prompts them to turn to wrong ways. . . . In life, no other stage is as pure and straightforward as childhood. Children are pliable at this stage [of their lives]. It is the mother's duty to give her offspring good training in childhood. The mother's conduct is like a mould which shapes the thinking, disposition and conduct of the children. . . . The mothers of our country should follow the example of women like Sumitra, Vidula, Kunti, etc. in training their offspring well from childhood so that they will acquire high status and fame later in life.

All children are alike. One should treat all children under one's supervision, even other people's children, like one's own, safeguard their interests, and put them on the right path. Children should not be allowed to quarrel among themselves for any reason at all, because baseless enmity caused in childhood follows a person into adulthood. . . . Kunti, the mother of the Pandavas, had five sons, three of her own and two of her rival wife's. From their childhood when they were under her supervision, to the time when they grew to be independent and became monarchs, she gave them all an equally good upbringing, without discriminating between her own and others, with the good intention that there should be no hostility among them, and that their mutual love should continue to grow more firm. . . . This was the sole reason why those brothers held one another more dear than their own life. . . .

Sumitra had a son, Lakshmana. When her rival wife's son, Rama, started out on his exile to the forest, she could not let her only son Lakshmana go; even so, she gave him good advice and told him to accompany Rama. She said: 'Think of Rama as Dasharatha [their father], Sita as myself, and the forest as Ayodhya. And, O my son! Go happily with Rama.' What advice! What a sense of duty! Who can be happier than children who possess a mother so saintly, so mindful of religion, and so able to point out the right path! . . .

. . . Therefore, the people who suffer at the sight of our country's distress should try to train the mothers of our countrymen to become well-behaved and knowledgeable. Then, their children will learn from their mothers how to be virtuous and dutiful, and, on reaching adulthood, uplift this fallen country of ours.

8. THE ULTIMATE GOAL

Nobody continues to remain in the same state forever. We can see nothing in this ever-changing world that stays in the same condition from beginning to end. The most brilliant object we can see, for which there is no equal, is the sun. Its light illuminates the moon, the stars and the earth. Even this indescribably brilliant sun does not remain in a changeless state. Sometimes it shows black spots, sometimes it is covered by the shadow of ordinary clouds, sometimes it is eclipsed by the moon which hides it. The sun revolves day and night, together with the planets and their satellites, which also revolve. The earth revolves, so do the moon and the stars. The mountains, seas, large and small rivers on this earth undergo transformation every moment, in accordance with the laws of Nature. With the change of seasons, trees are decorated with their native riches such as leaves, flowers and fruits; and, after a while, they are turned into wood and burnt. The human body changes its shape in different stages such as childhood, youth and old age; and experiences states such as waking, sleeping, dreaming, living and dying. History testifies to the variable condition of nations and of their people at different times for different reasons. All these things mutely advise man every moment regarding the transformation of things: 'O man! See our state and abandon your ignorance. Understand that nobody retains the same state forever, and do your duty. What is to happen cannot be avoided. Do not harbour conceit about anything.'

A person is quite terrified when he is in distress, and cannot think of what to do. At a time like this, even great, courageous, learned men lose their wits and do the wrong thing. What then can one say about tender-hearted, weak women, when such distress befalls them? Therefore, let us briefly consider how women should behave during a time of adversity. Far-sighted, learned men of ancient times have said, 'One should be afraid of danger only before it strikes; but, once confronted by it, one should overcome it through appropriate measures.' [Skt] . . . While in a happy state, a person should read books of advice written by learned people; and, if he gets an opportunity to spend time in the company of a great man, he should also seek advice about how to act during adversity. He should also think well on this matter when his mind is calm, and make great effort to cultivate abiding and unflinching courage. . . .

The condition of all creatures is like a water-wheel—once full and once empty, once high and once low. Such is also the transformation of our state [of existence]. . . . The great warrior Napoleon Bonaparte originally started from a low state, but perfomed great feats in the course of time through his efforts, and became the emperor of France. Even after reaching this high position, he was compelled to live as a prisoner in a gaol, owing to the turning wheel of time. At the time, he had no one to help him or to comfort him with a few sweet words. Had he been a weak-minded person, he would immediately have died of a broken heart at this dreadful time. But he possessed great courage and endurance. Even in this helpless, adverse condition, he showed no anxiety, but, inspired by great courage and heroism, said: 'Why worry? Even though alone in this gaol, I do not feel fear or abandon hope. Misfortune is but a herald of good fortune. (Misfortune indicates that good fortune is on its way.) I shall certainly escape shortly, and avenge myself on all my enemies single-handedly.' Oh, what courage!

We do not even need to look to other countries for such instances of courage in the face of adversity; they abound in our own country. A leader was born 255 years ago in this country of ours, who revived the fallen Bharatavarsha—Chhatrapati Shivaji Maharaj. His birth literally justified the title held by Bharatabhumi, namely 'the womb containing jewels'. He also, like Napoleon, started from an ordinary background and reached kingly status through his own efforts. Later, the cruel emperor Aurangzeb, that snake who tormented his subjects, arrested him and kept him imprisoned together with his son. They had no chance to escape; even so, that heroic warrior kept up his courage, and effected his escape through great effort. He became a terror for the Mughal dynasty of the Pathans, revived his kingdom and his people, and became immortal through his noble reputation. Many more such instances could be given, but are not mentioned for lack of space.

When visited by a calamity, a person is unable to see what acts are proper or improper, and is likely to take the irreligious path. But a person should not do so, no matter what the calamity. Irreligious acts do not lead to any good. . . . Jesus Christ was killed by wicked people who nailed him to the cross; but he felt absolutely no fear or sorrow at that terrible time. Even while dying on the cross in such a pitiable manner, with a steady mind and calm heart, he prayed to God the Father for the welfare of all creatures, and endured all agonies with great courage; but he did not slide from the religious path. Such a person is called religious!

The reason why such great, religious persons are visited by terrible misfortune is that they are under divine grace. If they are not tested through such occasions, the world would not realise their true worth. . . .

Many people blame God for the great and small calamities which befall the common man by the will of God. Some say that God is merciless, that there is no justice in His kingdom, that He brings needless misfortune upon innocent creatures. But God is never merciless to any creature; all creatures are the children of God. Even a lowly person is not pitiless towards his children, how then can one say that God, who is an ocean of mercy, is pitiless? It is true that calamities which befall people are caused by the will of God, but that does not prove that God is merciless. Nothing happens in His just kingdom without a reason. The calamities that befall people are also not without a reason. They have the following four reasons:

1. To shed light on the true worth of good people, as has been briefly described above.

2. To make human beings understand the value of happiness. A person who is happy since birth does not understand the value of happiness; he is like a stone statue untouched by the experience of happiness. Without the darkness of night, the world would not realise the happiness and benefits of sunlight. Without bitter things, one would not know the taste of sweet things. Similarly, without the occasional experience of unhappiness, nobody would understand the value of happiness. . . .

3. To understand the suffering of others. Persons who are always happy become arrogant, troublesome and cruel. Being happy themselves, they are unable to understand the condition of those who are unhappy; therefore such people usually harass others. If many human beings in this world had been happy and had started to harass others due to their inability to understand their unhappiness, then there would have been no peace on earth. . . .

4. To pay the penalty for the wrongs one has done. If a kingdom has thieves, cheats and suchlike people who harass others, and if

they are not given their just punishment by the king, they do not lose their evil propensity; this results in terrible misfortune. . . . Therefore, he who is guilty should be given the punishment he deserves; then his evil habit gets broken to a large extent, even if not completely, and others get some peace and quiet. There are many rulers in this world, and it is improbable that they would award punishment that is exactly appropriate to the offences, known and unknown, committed by all. People commit great sins in secret, and pretend to be good and innocent in front of others. If the omniscient God does not punish them suitably for their offences, then they would never give up their evil propensity. . . . Some people repeatedly pray to God for happiness which they do not deserve, and then blame Him if He does not grant it. This is greatest ignorance of all, because it is useless to imagine that God, who has arranged for [every]one's sustenance even before one is born, does not know better than they do. It is a transgression to request something else while He is making proper arrangements to give us whatever we need. God is ever desirous of our welfare. He will never give us anything which is not conducive to our welfare. . . .

. . . God is supremely compassionate and the support for all. Blessed is the person who trusts in Him, and who, without letting his mind be distracted, spends his life in devotion to Him and in achieving the welfare of all creatures.

NOTES

1. The word *deshi* has been translated as 'native'; elsewhere, Ramabai employs the commonly used, Sanskritized word *etaddeshiya*.
2. All Sanskrit quotations in the text are marked as [Skt].
3. This young man was Ramabai's older brother Srinivas Shastri, as shown by her other accounts.
4. A Puranika is a public narrator and expounder of the sacred texts known as Puranas, and a Haridasa is a performer of stories of gods with music and chanting.

PART II

ENGLAND

The Cry of Indian Women
(June 1883)

An Autobiographical Account
(September 1883)

Indian Religion
(1886)

2

THE CRY OF INDIAN WOMEN[*]

To The Hon'ble Sir Bartle Frere Saheb Bahadoor

Honoured Sir,
While I was in India, I have at various times heard of your renown. The Indian people would never be able to obliterate from their minds the various good deeds done by you while Governor of the Bombay Presidency. I, as an Indian female, am so greatly obliged to you for the acts of kindness done to my country.

I cannot say how much I feel delighted at your kindly granting me an interview today, even though you had an urgent appointment elsewhere. Honoured Sir, I am not much accustomed to the presence of great men, and so was not able to pay you all the respect you deserve. But I hope you will kindly excuse these faults of mine, with that generous mind with which you so kindly granted me the interview.

While in India you must have come in contact with millions of Indians working under you, and I am a poor insignificant being living in a corner of that country. It is quite plain that I could not have had

[*]Reproduced from a xerox of the handwritten translation in the Archives of the Pandita Ramabai Mukti Mission, Kedgaon, with very minor modifications.

the honour of your acquaintance. It will thus strike you with what audacity I write this letter to you. In answer to this I will try to explain in the best way my narrow intellect can suggest.

It was only today that I heard from yourself that you were in India for fifty years. Is not that dear country of my birth, where you passed half your life, and its people entitled to your friendship? If so, the people, whether rich or poor, bear towards you feelings of friendship. And this right of mine I for my part will not let go. And for this reason only I made myself bold to write this letter. And if in doing it I have been mistaken, you will kindly pardon me.

It is rather ridiculous for a person like myself to give information about Indian matters to you who have lived in India for so many years, and who are older than myself and possess superior knowledge. Yet the object of this letter is not to inform you but to present you the picture of the female comunity of India, as to their condition, which I beg leave to mention briefly.

The females in India consider it to be a result of sin to be born a female; and I myself endorse this view, because I think that the condition of women in India is not better than that of animals in hell. By this I don't mean to say that all women in India are miserable. Though there are many women in India that are happy, yet considering the entire female population of India, the happy ones are very few. I will try to give you an idea of the life of a Hindoo woman.

To commence with, the Indian people seem to think that no one ought to have a female child born to him. The supposed reason is that there is no use of a female in this life. Though this belief is not universal, yet it is general. If a female child happens to be born to anyone, there is a feeling of sadness. And it is sometimes observed that the parents of female children treat them badly. The reason for it is not that they are wanting in parental affection, but that they follow the general tide of opinion. As the girls grow older, their fathers feel them to be more burdensome. There is a saying that 'it is more difficult to rear up a girl than to keep an elephant'. The meaning of it is that the girl becomes of no use to the father, to rear her up without any corresponding gain being very difficult. It is quite right that no one should like to spend his money and energy without reason; but I fail to understand the reasonableness of the notion that it is difficult to bring up a girl because she does not happen to be of any use to the parents. One is obliged to keep silent, only thinking how ignorant such people are of the utility of women in a household. The Indian people do not take the same amount of care for the education of their girls as they do of their boys. Because it is not only considered to be of no use to give education to girls, but it is the general belief that girls rather spoil by education. Those learned men who call themselves 'reformed', and who are well aware of the benefits of female education, even they do not give the same attention to the matter as they ought, through fear of sacrificing their own interests. While delivering public lectures, they deplore the ignorant state of Indian females, and when brought face-to-face to great *Saheb-lokes* (Englishmen) express themselves as to the great want of female education in India; but when the matter comes to be put into practice, they do not act up to their precepts. Learned men, even though they know the great necessity of female education, 'hurl their daughters into the well of ignorance in a cruel way', through fear of being outcasted and laughed at by ignorant people if they were to give a high education to their sisters and daughters.

And thus it is that people rid themselves of their daughters by marrying them [off] at an early age, following the general practice. When a girl has attained the age of ten or eleven, she has to live with her husband's family. For the time they live with their parents they pass a tolerably happy life. But when these girls are married there is a life of misery in store for them in the future. Those that lead happy lives after marriage are very rare, and are considered to be very fortunate. Young children not even able to speak well, are snatched away from the lap of their mothers and thrown into the crush of worldly life.

In our country it is not the custom for a man to live separate[ly] from his family when married. Though it is difficult to decide whether the custom has good or bad effects, yet it will not be improper to say that from the want of it in India, millions of women kill themselves by suicide on account of the ill-treatment by their mothers-in-law. There are very few mothers-in-law that treat their sons' wives as their own daughters. In India a mother-in-law and daughter-in-law hold the same relation towards each other, as there is between a cat and a rat. There is no hope for a girl to receive education when she has gone to her husband's house. A girl, when she has gone to her husband's house, unlearns all she might have learnt while with her father. There is no occasion offered to girls to receive their education, for while young their lives are spent in [enduring] the cruelty of their mothers-in-law and sisters-in-law; and when they have grown up and live under the control of their husbands, they are engrossed in the cares of their households. Whether young or old, women are given a harsh treatment by their mothers- and sisters-in-law who may themselves have had to undergo a similar treatment. It cannot be said that this is a natural failing with all women. They commit these wrongs because they lack a good education. They cannot well remember the injuries they received in their very young days, but when they have grown up they do not pay much heed to the past wrongs if their husbands behave well towards them.

But in India well-behaved husbands are scarce. Women try their best to please their husbands, because on them depends their entire happiness. They feel and very naturally so, as if they were in heaven, if their husbands were to look with a pleased eye towards them. In our country the choice of a husband or wife rests with the parents, because at the time of marriage the couple, being very young, is not naturally able to make its own selection. When they grow old they do not feel satisfied with the choice made by others; owing to which the husband and wife bear ill-feelings towards each other from very slight causes. And when such is the case, the men instantly supersede the first wife, and marry another, even leaving the first one in the house. One cannot describe the miserable plight into which the first [wife] is thrown. If any man does not feel inclined for a second marriage, he takes to a mistress.

The state of the wives of such men is greatly deplorable. These men treat their wives in the same way as from history we know the Spaniards treated the Indians in America. In India when women are married, their husbands stand to them in the place of their parents, sovereign, and owner. If they treat them badly there is no one in the world to protect them. When it becomes known that a wife is not liked by her husband, the inmates of the house and even the neighbours ill-treat her on various pretexts. She is treated like a female slave that may be purchased. Though it requires no common courage to bear such treatment, there are some women of a patient temperament that put up with this unbearable suffering without grumbling. There is not a single day that passes, without recording that their husbands beat them like animals and call them names.

Some wives, when they feel the treatment [to be] unbearable, live apart from their husbands, or die a suicidal death; and in their great distress they do not find suicide a difficult deed. And there are some ignorant women, who not knowing the boon of this human existence, cling to an immoral life. They do not, by any means, like that greatly sinful life, but in their deplorable state, no other remedy suggests itself to them.

During the lives of their husbands the wives bear all the pain that is inflicted on them. And if through misfortune their husbands die in their lifetime, there is no end to their misery. On [the] one hand the sorrow of the death of their husbands is unbearable, and on the other the ill-treatment they receive at the hands of all is really great. The indignities to which widows are subjected in India is indescribable. All people look on them with disgust. [People] seem to think that it is a fault of theirs because [of which] their husbands have died (as if they themselves had killed their husbands), [and] that it rested with them whether their husbands be dead or living. They believe it to be inauspicious to see the face of a widow. On occasions of pleasure [such] as a marriage ceremony a widow dare not show her face, for it is believed that if the bride were to see the widow on the occasion of her marriage she is likely to become one herself. Some people, while going away to some other part of the country or starting out for some business, stop going if they come across a widow because they believe that some mishap will occur to them. Widows are allowed but one meal a day. It is considered sinful for a widow to eat oftener than once in a day. If there be a widow in a household there is considered to be no need for a servant-girl in it. It is considered to be a widow's duty to be working all day and night like a female slave. A woman if she happens to be a widow in her youth is not allowed to marry again. She is shut up day and night in a dark house. These demons in the shape of human beings don't content themselves with this treatment, but deprive the poor helpless widows of their natural ornament, the hair on their heads. It is believed that if [those] women were to wear hair on their heads, the messengers of death tie their deceased husbands with it. Thus the poor helpless widows, to relieve their deceased husbands from the supposed confinement, have to remove the hair from their heads. Women that become widows soon after their marriage are not aware of this belief and so are reluctant to remove their hair, but they are forced to get their heads shaved by the people in the house, or others. After doing this cruel act, and feeding them only once a day, those people shut them up in the house, thus trying to enclose every chance of their satisfying their carnal desires.

In times of such difficulty even, there is no subduing of human nature. Though the widows are not considered as human beings yet they are in fact so. Those of a strong mind bear this misery with fortitude and pass the remainder of their lives in devotion to God. But all are not so strong-minded; not being able to bear the distress arising from widowhood, some widows give themselves up to an immoral life, and a great many secretly lead the same sort of life; thus committing great sins [such] as infanticide and abortion. It is just that such women are abhorred by people; but it does not enter the mind of anyone that a great share of this sin rests on the shoulders of men. The whole blame of the matter is thrown on women, even though the men that do it know the common saying that it needs two hands to clap. Howsoever great a sin a man may commit, it is considered that he is pure, but women are considered to be impure in their very nature. It is a common saying that 'a man is a lump of gold and a woman is an earthen pot'. The meaning of it is that even if gold were to fall into a dirty matter, its value is not lessened, but if an earthen pot were to be at an impure place no one would even touch it. Men don't [merely] say this proverb, but act up to it as well. In illustration of this I narrate briefly a story:

Last year a widow was with child in the town of Kolhapur. When this sin of hers came to light, the name of the man that participated in the sin became known as well. If this man's name had come to be known by one or two [persons] only, he should not have had to suffer for it; but as the matter came to be talked about by the whole community, it became evident that he could not be admitted into the caste without doing some penance; and so he was taken [back] into the community as a pure man by the Brahmins on his paying a fine of only twenty rupees! I believe that the man [having been] purified is now living a happy life in his community. What must be the condition of the ill-fated widow? There is no penance for her sin. No one would ever condescend to touch her, not even look at her. Now she has lost forever the happiness of her life and that inestimable boon of this life, viz. her good name, which is more valuable than life itself. Her whole living is now turned useless.

Oh, my dear brethren, are not you and we children of the same Almighty? Do you ever bring into your minds this wretched condition of the ill-fated female community of ours? It is not simply that the condition of these helpless and ignorant females is bad, but that you are to a degree responsible for the sins that they commit in this life. In your country of England, there are various means of protecting these destitute persons from their sins and offering them shelter. In this country your widows can remarry. Males and females can make their own choice of partners and marry according to their own wills. Poor helpless females, instead of resorting to an immoral life for their subsistence, can retire into a home for destitutes. Your people cannot marry a second wife while the first is living; and they do not treat widows in the same disrespectful way as our people do. But alas! what a miserable existence is it of women in India!

Oh, India, owing to thee how many people have become happy? Millions of foreign people have acquired riches through thee, and have become happy; but oh India, there is no shelter for thy daughters! Alas, to whom should we resort for redress? Who would, alas, take the trouble to wipe off the tears from the eyes of the helpless Indian women! In India there are 21,000,000 females, widows and married, and it is likely that the cry of these helpless women will not be vainly spent. One could bear the shock of a thunderbolt falling on the head, but it requires a very hard heart to bear with ease the drops of tears falling down the eyes of the helpless widows. But blessed be my countrymen, who will not feel a jot for these poor widows! Some kind-hearted people have set the practice of re-marrying widows, but owing to the sternness of our caste, their attempts have been rendered futile. In former days there was the practice of Suttee (burning widows), but Government having put a stop to it, has left us in a worsening state of existence. It would have been far better to be burnt once [and] for all, than being scorched gradually in the fire of misery for the whole of our lives; such exclamations of sorrow are frequently heard coming from the mouths of millions of women. Oh you English brethren of ours, since you have saved us from immediate death by the prevention of Suttee (widow-burning), you can as well now render the rest of our existence happy by some means! Is it proper that one of our sex, the great Queen Victoria should be the Sovereign of England and Hindoostan, and that we, women, should be subjected to this unbearable torture? You have conferred various boons on Hindoostan and in return she has made your country wealthier. You ought not to treat us with contumely. The help that we ask from you ought not to be considered by you as a mere gift. We take you for our brothers and all assistance from you as a matter of right. Some of our countrymen would give us a helping hand, but our country being very poor, we would not be able to procure the required support; and so it is that now we have come with outstretched hands to claim your succour.

Last year I was at Poona and have established there a female association called Arya Mahila Samaj. This Association is working now even and has its branches at Bombay, Ahmedabad and Viramagaum[?]; and it is hoped that in a few years to come branches of this Association will be spread throughout India. The objects of that Association are three—1st, to put a stop to the marriage of children; 2nd, to prevent a man re-marrying while the first wife is living; 3rd, to give help to destitute women; and to encourage female education.

The accomplishment of the first two objects requires the countenance of the Government and the consent of the entire community; and so just now we do not make ourselves anxious about them. The third object is feasible just now, and we try our best to accomplish it as much as possible, and direct our energies to its achievement.

It is our intention to found an extensive home for widowed and helpless women, at Poona. If such a home is established, it will be resorted to by thousands of females. For the maintenance of so many people, and to provide them with clothing and an attached school where they can receive education, and in short to keep going an establishment of the kind would require us to have a capital of 500,000 rupees. We, the members of this Arya Mahila Association are poor, and our countrymen who favour this project of ours are as well without money, and so we are not able to raise the whole required amount. We will try every means to collect some portion of it in India, and it is our earnest desire that our English brethren should contribute four-fifths of the amount and give us a helping hand. If one such 'home for destitutes' is established at any place in India, there is a likelihood of it being followed by many others by way of example. If great men like your own worthy self were to take into your hands the work of collecting the above amount, it can be very easily carried out. We ask you to give us your assistance by bringing this petition of ours to the notice of our and your sovereign Queen Victoria, our future sovereign the Prince of Wales, Mr Gladstone and other great men of note, so that this deserving object of our Association be accomplished. What you will do for the poor and helpless women of India with one hand, God will return it to you thousand-fold with thousand hands.

Honoured Sir, I am a poor, helpless, ignorant and weak being. I by my own self would not be able to do much good to my sisters in India. But I feel thankful to Almighty God for having offered me the opportunity of enabling the cry of distress of the female sex of India to reach your ears. I have not the power of relieving the poor helpless females of my country from their misery with money, but am prepared to give my powers and life for the object. Is it possible that yourself and fellow-countrymen of yours would not redress the grievances of your Indian sisters? I hope and feel that this adventurous mission of mine of bringing to you this cry of my Indian sisters would not prove useless, having left my own dear country and come to your land after travelling over six-and-a-quarter thousand miles. Is it possible that my hopes would be frustrated at your hands? No, never!

The state of Indian females that I have tried to show in this letter of mine, . . . [has been shown] in a very succinct way. If the distress of those helpless creatures were to be told [even] in a superficial kind of way, it would fill a volume. I think no human being would be able to do justice to their state of misery by describing it. I have travelled a great deal in India and that in a very modest way [i.e. without comforts or conveniences]. I have witnessed with mine own eyes the condition of the females in India. I believe you have as well seen something of the condition of the Indian females, but I don't suppose you have travelled like myself on foot two thousand miles to see the deplorable state of these females in India. If you should be kind enough to relieve the distress of these poor Indian sisters of yours, they will for ever be mindful of your kindness.

In conclusion I beg to take leave of you by wishing you every blessing from God, and that the Almighty may give you the power and will to give us your aid.

Your most obedient servant
Ramabai
Member of the Committee of the Arya Mahila Association

P.S. I hope you will be kind enough to get this letter of mine translated into English and distribute copies of it among your English friends; by doing which I shall feel greatly obliged to you.

I am living just now in St. Mary's Home at Wantage.

[London, 11th June 1883]

3

AN AUTOBIOGRAPHICAL ACCOUNT*

I was born in Mangalore District, in a forest named Gangamul, on the Western Ghats in April 1858. My father's name was Anant Shastri Dongre. He belonged to the caste of the Chitpavana Brahmins, and was a good scholar in the Sanskrit Shastras. When he was a lad of about sixteen years of age, he went to the teacher of the Peshwa Baji Rao for instruction, [who] was a great learned man named Ramchandra Shastri. In this capacity he had access into the palace of Baji Rao. There he became acquainted with the wife of Baji Rao, Shrimati Varanasibai Sahiba, who was learning Sanskrit with Ramchandra Shastri. This roused my father's attention to the cause of female education. When he came to manhood, he was honoured for his learning in Mysore, and other States, and received the title of Shastri. According to the present custom of our country, he was married in his childhood, so he could not carry out his desires as to female education with his first wife. Many years after her death, he married my mother, when she was nine years of age. Her name was Lakshmibai. From the time of their marriage, my father began to educate my mother. At that time, that is to say fifty years ago, in

*This piece has been reproduced from *The Letters and Correspondence of Pandita Ramabai*, pp.15–18, with the kind permission of Popular Prakashan, the copyright-holder.

the Mangalore District, there had been nothing done by the English Government for the improvement of the people. All classes were against female education, and the prejudice clings to them still (e.g. I have received a letter last month from my half-brother, disapproving of my coming to England to learn English, etc). When my father began to teach my mother Sanskrit and Dharma Shastras, the people in the neighbourhood disapproved of it, and threatened to put him out of [their] caste but he would not heed them and as he was in no way beholden to them, he pursued his own ways. When they found they could in no way prevail with him to leave off educating my mother, they went to the Dharma-Guru (a spiritual teacher) and brought the matter before him, begging him to enforce the law against my father, because he was a breaker of their sacred laws and customs. So my father was sent for by the Dharma-Guru and was asked his reasons for breaking the law. My father replied by asking the Dharma-Guru: 'What is written in the Dharma Shastras which in any way forbids the education of women?' But the *dharma-guru* could give no satisfactory answer, so my father remained in [his] caste. Several years after, when [he was] at Swade (Soday), a village in Karnataka, where [there] is a monastery of one of the Dharma-Gurus, several Pandits and a Dharma-Guru were assembled to discuss the matter. There my father proved from the Dharma Shastras that women must be educated and learn their own Dharma Shastras. He received from the assembly a statement to this effect with their signatures affixed.

My father gave my mother a good education in Sanskrit and taught her the Dharma Shastras. She had six children but three died in childhood. I was the youngest, my elder sister and brother were both educated by my father and mother. As I was a good deal younger than they, I could not learn with them. According to the present custom of the country, my sister was married in her childhood, but as my father intended to keep her and her husband in his own house, her marriage did not hinder her education. She and my brother were both well educated in Sanskrit.

When I was old enough to receive instruction, my father was too infirm to teach me, so I received from my mother all the education I had in my youth. At the age of eight, she began to teach me Sanskrit. My parents found that marriage in childhood was a hindrance to education, so I was not given in marriage when I was a child.

You will ask me here why I did not follow in my sister's footsteps and was not married in my childhood? My father had taken a lad of needy parents to be the husband of my sister, for the reason that he might keep him and educate him with his daughter. Had he given her in marriage to the son of a wealthy and influential Hindu, she would have had to live with her father-in-law and be brought up in ignorance. The boy turned out [to be] dull and would not take to his studies and finally he ran away from my father's house; this marriage ended in a life of unhappiness to my sister. So my father resolved that he would not do the same in my case, and as he would not part with me, I remained unmarried. This was contrary to the present Hindu custom, but though his friends and neighbours constantly reminded him of this, he paid no attention to them. In 1874, I lost both my parents within two months of each other. We were living then in the Madras Presidency. After their death, because of the persecution which was carried on against us on account of my not being married and because he advocated female education, we were obliged to leave our country [region]. After a few months my sister died of cholera, and my brother and I travelled for six years in various parts of India. In our travels we were obliged to go on foot, not having the means to afford ourselves conveyance. In this way we went a distance of 2,000 miles, and thus we had a good opportunity of seeing the sufferings of Hindu women and were much touched by their sorrows. We saw it not only in one part of India, but it was the same in the Madras Presidency, Bombay Presidency, Punjab, the North-West Province, Bengal, Assam, etc. This made us think much of how it was possible to improve the condition of women and raise them out of their degradation. We were able to do nothing directly to help them but in the towns and villages we often addressed large audiences of people and urged upon them the education of the women and children. In order to be able to converse with the different races we were obliged to learn Hindi (as it is a general language in India) and Bengalee. In the year 1880, when we were in Dacca, my brother died, and then I was alone in the world. Six months after, I married a Bengalee gentleman, Bipin Behari Das [Medhavi]. He was a great friend of my brother, and I knew him two years before I married. He was born in the Sylhet District in Assam, and belonged to the caste of Shudras (the fourth of the Hindu castes). He lost both his parents in childhood and was brought up by his uncle until he was 14 years of age. From that time, he continued his education by his own industry and perseverance. For some time he was Headmaster of the Government Normal School in Assam. After this he entered the Calcutta University [where] he obtained the degree of MA and BL. After this he became a pleader and followed this profession until his death. It was against the Hindu religion for me, being a Brahmin, to marry a Shudra, but neither my husband nor I believed in the Hindu religion, so we were married under the Civil Marriage Act.[1] After our marriage, we lived together in Cachar (Silchar) in Assam, for 16 months. In 1882, my husband died of cholera, leaving me with one little daughter. After his death, I had to pay off his debts; then I went to the Bombay Presidency and lived there for a year. During that time my countrymen helped me and they were willing to maintain me in independence, but my wish was to come to England and thus fit myself for a life of usefulness, in order to benefit my countrywomen. I had not money to pay my passage, so I wrote a book [*Stri Dharma Niti*] and published it. The Government kindly bought 600 copies of it (which was great help to me) and other copies were sold by booksellers. In this way I received sufficient money for my passage, but how to support myself and [my] child in England I knew not. It was my good fortune to become acquainted with the Wantage Sisters working in Poona; so I asked them if they would help me, and they promised to do so. Now I am staying in Wantage with them, and they are kindly supporting and teaching me. I am very grateful for their kindness. If my health allows me to carry out my plans, and it is God's will that I should do so, it is my intention to study medicine in England in order to benefit my countrywomen and with the hope of inducing some of them to follow my example. As I was by birth a Brahmin, my religion was at first Hinduism. Then for a time, I was a Theist, believing that Theism was taught in [the] Vedas. In the last two months, however, I have accepted Christianity and hope shortly to receive Holy Baptism.

NOTES

1. The Civil Marriage Act (III of 1872) legalized marriages performed according to the Brahmo rites, and allowed marriages between persons who did not profess any specific religion or between those of different religions.

4

INDIAN RELIGION[❖]

M any of my Christian friends are full of eager desires to be of use to the natives of India, and to bring to them the light of Christian truth. They have often asked me questions regarding missionary work, and the Christianizing of India, which it has been impossible for me to answer in a way intelligible to them, owing to their almost total ignorance of all matters of Hindu thought and religion. Some English have such comprehensive classifications of the human race—they have been known to bring under the same category the skin-clad, flat-headed inhabitant of the North American continent, and the descendant of the ancient Aryan race of Central Asia. Some have even a more comprehensive mind still, and embrace under one term 'native' inhabitants of India, America, Africa, Australia, and all the islands of the Pacific. One evil result of this confusion is, that the stories related of one race are often supposed to be true of another—all alike are 'benighted heathen' and the same treatment is given to all. Some missionaries

❖Reproduced from *The Cheltenham Ladies' College Magazine*, no. XIII, Spring 1886.

The editor [of *The Cheltenham Ladies' College Magazine*] has in some degree translated the thoughts as well as the language into a more vernacular form. But the article was in the first place written, and after correction finally revised, by the writer.

go out to teach those of whose language and philosophy, and modes of thought, they are utterly ignorant; with whom they have no sympathy, because they cannot feel what are their difficulties. Such was hardly, it seems to me, the method of the apostles. In the first ages of Christianity, St. Paul became to the Jews as a Jew, to the Greeks as a Greek. Christ tells us He came not to destroy, but to fulfil—and God's method of work seems to be ever to build on the old foundations, keeping that which is good, and destroying only that which is evil, decaying, ready to perish.

It grieves me to think how much harm is done, how opponents are encouraged in error, by finding that those who profess to teach are unable to enter into their thoughts, and to answer their questions. They cannot believe that missionaries, who will not take the trouble to understand them, can really care for them, and sincerely desire their good; that contempt which is ever the offspring of ignorance, always alienates and hardens—only sympathy born of understanding, will ever make them open their hearts to light. It seems to me that it has become something of a fashion for kind-hearted young ladies (of gentlemen I will not speak) to think they will easily convert 'the natives'. Imagine for a moment that the relations were reversed—that a Hindu lady, inspired with a desire to convert the English, should at once proceed to London, in utter ignorance of the Christian faith, only firmly convinced of the truth of her own. Would her assertion that the Vedas are inspired books be accepted by any? Would not Christians require her to show them in what respects her faith was superior to theirs? Yet there are lady missionaries who think themselves qualified to teach Hindus, with no more knowledge of their faith than our imaginary Pundit has of Christianity.

Happily some missionaries, though not all, do study that teaching which God has given to us in past ages, through the sacred writings of India, and they are able to help my countrymen to see more of the divine truth. . . .[1]

I can quite understand, now that I have become accustomed to Western thought, how repulsive are some of the sacred symbols of Hindu mythology. I can, however, assure Christians that to the pure-minded these are mere abstractions, or if the[ir] origin is thought of, they are merely the expression of the sacredness of all life, of the consecration of the family. . . .

Since I desire that the races, whom God has in His providence placed in such intimate relations with one another, should understand one another better—believing that it will be for the happiness of both, and that each has something to learn from the other—I, who have adopted the Christian faith, and entered sympathetically into the elevated spiritual teachings of that faith, am anxious that my Christian friends should know, too, what is good and true and beautiful in the teachings of our books, though I would be far from palliating, or attempting to excuse, much of the abominable teachings of Brahmanism, and would acknowledge with gratitude to our Lord, that He is [the]Mediator between God and men, the Way, the Truth, and the Life, the Light. . . .

I cannot, of course, in a short article hope to do more than interest my readers so far as to make them desirous to read large works.[††]

Before beginning my comments, it will be convenient to give a table of the principal books. The Hindu Scriptures are much more voluminous than those of the Christians—they consist of hundreds of books by different authors. . . .

The Vedas	⎡ Rig-veda Yajur-veda Sama-veda Atharva-veda ⎣

The Brahmanas (the Leviticus of the Hindus)

Upanishads (philosophical treatises)

The Vedanta and Yoga Sutras Bhagvad-gita, Anugita, etc ⎤	later philosophical writings

Sutras (early laws)
Smritis (later laws)

The Ramayana The Mahabharata ⎤	Epics

Puranas, i.e. old writings ⎤	Bible of the later mythological Brahmanism

†† Amongst those specially interesting I may mention the Hibbert Lectures and 'India, What Can It Teach Us?' by Professor Max Mueller, *Religious Life and Thought in India* by Professor Monier Williams, or his smaller book published by the SPCK [Society for the Promotion of Christian Knowledge]. Those who desire to really

The oldest part of the Hindu Bible is the Rig-veda. Scholars agree in the opinion that its composition began as early as the sixteenth century BC. The doctrine of the Rig-veda is, if we read it superficially, polytheistic, but the underlying thought is monotheistic. It has been clearly shown that the doctrine which the Indo-Aryans held previous to the Vedic age was monotheistic. The Rig-veda, however, speaks of thirty-three gods, of whom Agni (Fire-god), Indra (Rain-god), and Surya (Sun-god), the Vedic Triad, are chief. The Rig-veda is a collection of hymns composed in honour of, and prayers addressed to, these gods. The prayers are generally for prosperity, for increase of cattle, for offspring, for good crops, etc., e.g.

> Will you then, O Maruta, grant unto us wealth, durable, rich in men defying all onslaughts—wealth a hundred and a thousand-fold, always increasing?[tt]

But there is one remarkable prayer which, like the 'Hail Mary' of the Roman Catholics, is frequently repeated—at least thirty times daily by the Brahmans; it is addressed to the Sun-god, and runs thus:

> Let us meditate on the excellent glory of the Divine vivifying Sun; may he enlighten our understandings. (Rig-veda III, 63–10.). . . .

It is true the Vedic people believed in many gods, but the foregoing hymn will show that they believed only one Deity to be the supreme Lord of all gods, but this one Lord was not designated by one particular name only. It depended upon the choice of the worshipper to elect his own god from among the thirty-three, and adore him as the supreme, and worship all others as his servants. This is the chief feature of the religion of the Hindus to this day, and it seems to me that this implies a fundamental belief, that all the gods worshipped under different names are one, and that there is but one God. So I would argue with Hindu polytheists as St. Paul [did] with the Jews, that monotheism is

---

study the subject can refer to the twenty volumes of *Sacred Books of the East* in the Cheltenham Library. The translation of one of the great epics of the Hindus, the Mahabharata, has been kindly presented to our College by Babu Protab Chunder Roy of Calcutta. A good analysis of the Ramayana is given in Wheeler Talboy's *History of India*. There are translations of Indian poems into English verse by my talented countrywoman, Toru Dutt, also a Christian, and some by Mr Arnold and Mr Griffith. *The Land of the Vedas* is out of print, but there are smaller books published by the SPCK and the Religious Tract Society.

[tt]*Rig-veda*, translated by Professor Max Mueller.

implied in Vedism, as Christianity in the law. I would show that the teaching of Christ is far more one in spirit with that of the ancient Rishis than with that of those who profess to be their disciples, but have overlaid their teaching with a mass of superstition and idolatry. It is quite clear that when hymns in praise are addressed to several divinities, the worshipper thinks of them as different manifestations of the same Omnipresent Spirit. This is a thought surely not incomprehensible to Christians, for whom the glory of the Father shines forth in the person of the Son, and for whom the indwelling Spirit is the indwelling of Christ. This is proved by the following hymn. It is addressed to Agni (Fire-god), but he is identified with two other persons of the Hindu Triad, Indra (the Lightning) and Surya (the Sun-god). . . .

The Hindus were from the first firm believers in immortality. . . . The Vedic worshipper was also conscious of sin, and sought forgiveness. . . . The Rigveda inculcates charity: 'The kind mortal is greater than the great in heaven.'

Of the later teachings of the Brahmans regarding caste, there is almost nothing; nothing of the cruel widow burnings or the exclusion of women from the sunlight. On the contrary, it is taken for granted that they are, as well as men, thinking beings, and even in the later Upanishads we find ladies conversing on equal terms with men on subjects of religion and philosophy. I think this may have something to do with the fact that these works are pronounced by modern Brahmans too sacred for us women to read; it is thought undesirable that the high-caste women of today, who are utterly secluded and forbidden to speak to any men except to very near relations, should read in the Aranyaks [a class of religious and philosophical writings associated with the Brahmanas] of ladies conversing with great sages, such as Yagnavalkya, especially [that they should read] of Gargi, who like the English princess St. Hilda, exercised authority over Brahmans, priests, and monks. I remember, when a child, being forbidden to repeat the sacred texts, which I had picked up by hearing my brother and other pupils of my father repeat them. The Aranyaks are so sacred that not a single text from them is pronounced in the presence of women, even of the Brahman caste, much less in that of a Shudra.

We find traces in the Vedas of the later Vedanta philosophy, which is pantheistic. The pantheistic teaching has undergone many changes of form, but began to manifest itself in the thought of the Hindus in very early times. . . . When the poetical expression was represented by a symbolic form and worshipped, we can easily see that a pantheon would be developed out of pantheism. Indeed, idolatry has developed to gigantic proportions, as one might see it would from such a doctrine; the Upanishads were written as a protest against it. Christians find great difficulty in understanding Hindu thought, and even the Christian Scriptures may, to those who have not the same spiritual conceptions, seem to fall in with their own ideas, and therefore justify their own conclusions, because they are unable to conceive [of] the Christian doctrine of transcendency and creation. If missionaries quote such words as 'God is above all, through all, and in all', a Hindu will say, 'Then we may certainly worship all, the Mountain, the River, the Tree, much more the living creature, e.g. the cow, and any image of God, which we have consecrated by prayer.' It seems a great step from the poetical, nominalistic pantheism of the Vedas to the coarse idolatrous realisms of modern Hinduism, yet the latter is only the degenerate offspring of the former.

Though the authors of the Rig-veda believed in thirty-three principal and many other gods, and sacrificed and addressed hymns to them, there is no trace of idol worship. I may perhaps explain the growth of idolatry thus—The worshippers in the exuberance of the religious imagination, seem to have become dissatisfied with the worship of an abstract conception, and even of One who seemed afar off. They could not even rest in the worship of the Omnipresent Spirit, through the three visible objects of the Great Triad, the Fire, the Light [Lightning], the Sun. So a symbolic image was made. . . . Thus, to express almighty power, a figure was made with many hands; or, to express omniscience, a five-faced figure was made looking every way; or strength was expressed by a lion-headed man. These symbolic forms soon became to the worshipper realised conceptions, so that they thought of the God as having such a body. Since the sun is visible, and his worshippers can address their prayers to him, standing as it were face to face, one can hardly feel the necessity for making a picture or statue of him; but the worshipper's mind was not satisfied by looking, or by prostrating himself before the sun. He felt he was not doing the Lord as much service as he might.

But how could he express his gratitude and make his god, so far above him, partake of his goods? He wanted the god to dwell in some form on the earth, and he wanted to show his devotion by offering him everything he felt to be good, e.g. a comfortable bed, rich garments, precious jewels; the devoted servant must offer the best he has to his god. Hence the necessity for making a statue of the god. He then can wash the statue, dress, adorn, put [it] to sleep, and offer meals to it, and wait upon it, as a servant waits upon his master. This, of course, is all done to the idol, as being the representative of the sun; all the while the worshipper thinks that he is doing service to the sun in the sky, and that this service, imperfect as it is, is yet acceptable to the sun. Again, seeing that the sun bestows on him in various seasons, various gifts, he begins to worship the sun in twelve different manifestations, for there are twelve months in the year, and the devoted servant would give him twelve names, significant of twelve benevolent characters. He would do all in his power to show his love to the god. He would keep feasts in his honour, make processions, give him a ride in the great chariot, etc. All this seems so natural to him that he has never once thought he can be doing wrong. And if we enter into his spirit it would not seem wrong to us either.

Why, then, he asks, should idolatry be considered wrong? We answer, because such devotion, instead of elevating the worshipper's mind, only helps to degrade it. For the symbols do become to him real things, and the worshipper gets to think the god needs the daily meals, washing, clothing, etc. Even the Hebrew prophets had to correct the foolish thought of those who offered sacrifice, imagining that God needed anything from man, instead of graciously accepting worship as a part of His child's education. Of course, as soon as idolatrous rites are introduced, the spiritual conception is degraded, and becomes a false one, God is made 'like unto some corruptible thing', and this plainly is sinning against God.

When worship was extended to every visible thing, a vast mythology grew up, such as we find in the later religious institutions, and this led the Hindus to what may be called universal idolatry, since everything in the universe is the manifestation of God. Thence arose three forms of the religion which Professor Monier Williams calls the Mythological, Ritualistic, and Nomistic Brahmanisms. Time and space alike do not permit me to dwell upon these forms now.

NOTES

1. Long quotations from Reverend Peter Percival of the Society for the Promotion of the Gospel, Professor Monier Williams and Professor Max Mueller have been omitted.

PART III

UNITED STATES OF AMERICA

The High-Caste Hindu Woman
(1887)

Religious Denominations and Charities in the USA
(1889)

The Condition of Women in the USA
(1889)

5

THE HIGH-CASTE HINDU WOMAN*

To the
memory of my beloved mother
Lakshmibai Dongre
whose influence and able instruction
have been
the light and guide of my life
this little volume
is most reverently dedicated

---

*The text of this book has been reproduced *verbatim*, but a very few minor changes have been inevitable. The original chapters are treated here as sections, because the whole book has become a chapter in the present volume; and the list of contents has been omitted.

In Memoriam
Anandibai Joshee, MD
Daughter of Ganpatrao Amriteswar
and Gangabai Joshee

Born in Poona, Bombay Presidency, India, 31 March 1865 (Child-name, Yamuna Joshee).

Married Gopalrao Vinayak Joshee, March 31st, 1874 (Wife-name, Anandibai Joshee).

Sailed from Calcutta, India, for America, April 7th, 1883, being the first high-caste Brahman woman to come to the United States. Landed in New York, June 4th, 1883.

Graduated in medicine, from the Woman's Medical College of Pennsylvania, March 11th, 1886, being the first Hindu woman to receive the Degree of Doctor of Medicine in any country.

Appointed, June 1st, 1886, to the position of Physician-in-Charge of the Female Ward of the Albert Edward Hospital, in the city of Kolhapur, India.

Sailed from New York, to assume her duties in Kolhapur, October 9th, 1886.

Died in Poona, India, February 26th, 1887.

1. PREFATORY REMARKS[††]

In order to understand the life of a Hindu woman, it is necessary for the foreign reader to know something of the religion and the social customs of the Hindu nation. The population of Hindustan numbers two hundred and fifty millions and is made up of Hindus, Mahomedans, Eurasians, Europeans and Jews; more than three-fifths of this vast population are professors of the so-called Hindu religion in one or the other of its forms. Among these, the religious customs and orders are essentially the same; the social customs differ slightly in various parts of the country, but they have an unmistakable similarity underlying them.

The religion of the Hindus is too vast a subject to be fully treated in a few paragraphs; it may be briefly stated, however, somewhat thus: All Hindus recognize the Vedas and other apocryphal books as the canonical scriptures. They believe in one supreme Spirit, Paramatma, which is pure, passionless, omnipresent, holy and formless in its essence, but when it is influenced by Maya, or illusion, it assumes form, becomes male and female, creates everything in the universe out of its own substance. A Hindu, therefore, does not think it a sin to worship rivers, mountains, heavenly bodies, creatures, etc., since they are all consubstantial with God and manifestations of the same spirit. Any one of these manifestations may be selected to be the object of devotion, according to a man's own choice; his favourite divinity he will call the supreme ruler of the universe and the other gods, servants of the supreme ruler.

Hindus believe in the immortality of the soul, inasmuch as it is consubstantial with God; man is rewarded or punished according to his deeds. He undergoes existences of different descriptions in order to reap the fruit of his deeds. When at length he is free from the consequences of his action, which he can be by knowing the Great Spirit as it is and its relation to himself, he is then re-absorbed into

---

[††]The translation of the sacred texts quoted throughout this work are those found in the well-known *Sacred Books of the East,* edited by Professor Max Mueller, Clarendon Press, Oxford.

the spirit and ceases to be an individual; just as a river ceases to be different from the ocean when it flows into the sea.

According to this doctrine, a man is liable to be born eight million four hundred thousand times before he can become a Brahman (first caste), and except one be a Brahman he is not fit to be re-absorbed into the spirit, even though he obtains the true knowledge of the Paramatma. It is, therefore, necessary for every person of other castes to be careful not to transgress the law by any imprudent act, lest he be again subjected to be born eight million four hundred thousand times. A Brahman must incessantly try to attain to the perfection of the supreme knowledge, for it is his last chance to get rid of the misery of the long series of earthly existences; the least trifling transgression of social or religious rules however renders him liable to the degradation of perpetual births and deaths.

These, with the caste beliefs, are the chief articles of the Hindu creed at the present day. There are a few heterodox Hindus who deny all this; they are pure theists in their belief, and disregard all idolatrous customs. These Brahmos, as they are called, are doing much good by purifying the national religion.

As regards social customs, it may be said that the daily life and habits of the people are immensely influenced by religion in India. There is not an act that is not performed religiously by them; a humorous author has said, with some truth, that 'the Hindus even sin religiously'. The rising from the bed in the morning, the cleaning of teeth, washing of hands and bathing of the body, the wearing of garments, lighting the fire or the lamp, eating and drinking, and every act of similar description, is done in a prescribed manner, and with the utterance of prayers or in profound silence. Each custom, when it is old enough to be entitled 'the way of the ancients', takes the form of religion and is scrupulously observed. These customs, founded for the most part on tradition, are altogether independent of the canonical writings, so much so that a person is liable to be punished, or even excommunicated, for doing a deed forbidden by custom, even though it be sanctioned by religion.

For example, eating the food prepared by persons of an inferior caste is not only not forbidden by the sacred laws, but is sanctioned by them.[††]

[††]'Pure men of the first three castes shall prepare the food of a householder' (Brahman or other high caste). 'Or Shudras (servile caste) may prepare the food under the superintendence of men of the first three castes.' (*Apastamba II, 2, 3. I, 4.*)

At the present day, however, time-honoured custom overrules the ancient laws, and says that a person must not eat anything cooked nor drink water polluted by the touch of a person of inferior caste. Hindus transgressing this rule instantly forfeit their caste, and must undergo some heavy penance to regain it.

Without doubt, 'caste' originated in the economical division of labour. The talented and most intelligent portion of the Aryan Hindus became, as was natural, the governing body of the entire race. They, in their wisdom, saw the necessity of dividing society, and subsequently set each portion apart to undertake certain duties which might promote the welfare of the nation. The priesthood (Brahman caste) were appointed to be the spiritual governors over all, and were the recognized heads of society. The vigorous, warlike portion of the people (Kshatriya, or warrior caste) was to defend the country, and suppress crime and injustice by means of physical strength; assisted by the priesthood, they were to be the temporal governors in the administration of justice. The business-loving tradesmen and artisans (Vaisya, or trader caste) also had an important position assigned under the preceding classes or castes. The fourth, or servile class (Shudra caste) was made up of all those not included in the preceding three castes. In ancient times persons were assigned to each of the four castes according to their individual capacity and merit, independent of the accident of birth.

Later on, when caste became an article of the Hindu faith, it assumed the formidable proportions which now prevail everywhere in India. A son of a Brahman is honoured as the head of all castes, not because of his merit, but because he was born into a Brahman family. Intermarriage of castes was once recognized as lawful, even after caste by inheritance had been acknowledged, provided that a woman of superior caste did not marry a man of an inferior caste; but now law is overruled by custom. Intermarriage cannot take place without involving serious consequences, and making the offenders outcasts.

The four principal castes[††] are again divided into clans; men belonging to high clans must not give their daughters in marriage to

---

[††]'There are four castes—Brahmanas, Kshatriyas, Vaisyas, and Shudras.' 'Among these, each preceding caste is superior by birth to the one following.' (*Apastamba I*, 1, 1, 3, 4.)

'The Brahmana, the Kshatriya and the Vaisya castes are the twice-born ones, but the fourth, the Shudra, has one birth only; there is no fifth caste.'(*Manu*, X, 4.)

men of low clans. To transgress this custom is to lose family honour, caste privileges, and even intercourse with friends and relatives.

Besides the four castes and their clans there are numerous castes called collectively, 'mixed castes', formed by the intermarriage of members of the preceding; their number is again increased by castes according to employment, as scribe, tanner, cobbler, shoemaker, tailor, etc., etc. Even the outcastes, such as for example the sweeper, have their own distinctions, as powerful among themselves as are those of the high castes. Transgressors of caste rules are, from the highest to the lowest, subject to excommunication and severe punishment. Offenders by intermarriage, or change of faith, are without redemption. It must also be borne in mind that if a Brahman condescends to marry a person of lower caste, or eats or drinks with any of them, he is despised and shunned as an outcaste, not only by his own caste, but also by the low-caste with whose members he has entered into such relation.[1] The low-caste people will look upon this Brahman as a lawless wretch. So deeply rooted is this custom in the heart of every orthodox Hindu that he is not in any way offended by the disrespect shown him by a high-caste man, since he recognizes in it only what is ordered by religion. For, although 'caste' is confessedly an outgrowth of social order, it has now become the first great article of the Hindu creed all over India. Thoughtful men like Buddha, Nanak, Chaitanya and others rebelled against this tyrannical custom, and proclaimed the gospel of social equality of all men, but 'caste' proved too strong for them. Their disciples in the present day are as much subject to caste as any other orthodox Hindu. Even the Mahomedans have not escaped this tyrant; they, too, are divided into several castes, and are as strict as the Hindus in their observances. Over a million Hindu converts to Christianity, members of the Roman Catholic Church, are more or less ruled by caste. The Protestant missionaries, likewise, found it difficult in early days to overcome caste prejudice among their converts, and not many years ago, in the Madras Presidency, clergymen were compelled to use different cups for each separate caste when they celebrated the Lord's Supper.

The Vedas are believed by the devout Hindu to be the eternal, self-existing word of God, revealed by Him to different sages. Besides the Vedas, there are more than twenty-five books of sacred law, ascribed to different inspired authors who wrote or compiled them at various times, and on which are based the principal customs and religious institutes of the Hindus. Among these, the code of Manu ranks highest, and is believed by all to be very sacred, second to none but the Vedas themselves.

Although Manu and the other law-givers differ greatly on many points, they all agree on things concerning women. According to this sacred law, a woman's life is divided into three parts, viz.: 1st, Children; 2nd, Youth or married life; 3rd Widowhood or old age.

2. CHILDHOOD

Although the code of Manu contains a single passage in which it is written 'A daughter is equal to a son' (*Manu,* ix, 130), the context expressly declares that equality to be founded upon the results attainable through her son; the passage, therefore, cannot be regarded as an exception to the statement that the ancient code establishes the superiority of male children. A son is the most coveted of all blessings that a Hindu craves, for it is by a son's birth in the family that the father is redeemed.

Through a son he conquers the worlds, through a son's son he obtains immortality, but through his son's grandson he gains the world of the sun. (*Manu,* ix, 137.)
    There is no place for a man (in heaven) who is destitute of male offspring. (*Vasishtha*, xvii, 2.)

If a man is sonless, it is desirable that he should have a daughter, for her *son* stands in the place of a son to his grandfather, through whom the grandfather may obtain salvation.
    In western and southern India, when a girl or a woman salutes elders and priests, they bless her with these words: 'May thou have eight sons, and may thy husband survive thee.' In the form of a blessing, the deity is never invoked to grant daughters. Fathers very seldom wish to have daughters, for they are thought to be the property of somebody else; besides, a daughter is not supposed to be of any use to the parents in their old age. Although it is necessary for the continuance of the race that some girls should be born into the world,

it is desirable that their number by no means should exceed that of boys. If unfortunately a wife happens to have all daughters and no son, Manu authorizes the husband of such a woman to supersede her with another in the eleventh year of their marriage.[††]

In no other country is the mother so laden with care and anxiety on the approach of childbirth as in India. In most cases her hope of winning her husband to herself hangs solely on her bearing sons. Women of the poorest as well as of the richest families are almost invariably subjected to this trial. Many are the sad and heart-rending stories heard from the lips of unhappy women who have lost their husband's favour by bringing forth daughters only, or by having no children at all. Never shall I forget a sorrowful scene that I witnessed in my childhood. When about thirteen years of age, I accompanied my mother and sister to a royal harem where they had been invited to pay a visit. The Prince had four wives, three of whom were childless. The eldest having been blessed with two sons, was of course the favourite of her husband, and her face beamed with happiness.

We were shown into the nursery and the royal bed-chamber, where signs of peace and contentment were conspicuous. But oh! what a contrast to this brightness was presented in the apartments of the childless three. Their faces were sad and careworn; there seemed no hope for them in this world, since their lord was displeased with them, on account of their misfortune.

A lady friend of mine in Calcutta told me that her husband had warned her not to give birth to a girl the first time, or he would never see her face again, but happily for this wife and for her husband also, she had two sons before the daughter came. In the same family, there was another woman, the sister-in-law of my friend, whose first-born had been a daughter. She longed unceasingly to have a son, in order to win her husband's favour, and when I went to the house, constantly besought me to foretell whether this time she would have a son! Poor woman! She had been notified by her husband that if she persisted in bearing daughters, she should be superseded by another wife, have coarse clothes to wear and scanty food to eat, should have no ornaments, save those necessary to show the existence of a husband, and she should be made the drudge of the whole household. Not

---

[††]See Chapter IV [Section 4 in this reproduction: Women's Place in Religion and Society].

unfrequently [sic], it is asserted that bad luck attends a girl's advent, and poor superstitious mothers, in order to avert such a catastrophe, attempt to convert the unborn child into a boy, if unhappily it be a girl.

Rosaries used by mothers of sons are procured to pray with; herbs and roots celebrated for their virtue are eagerly and regularly swallowed; trees and son-giving gods are devoutly worshipped. There is a curious ceremony, honoured with the name of 'sacrament', which is administered to the mother between the third and the fourth month of her pregnancy for the purpose of converting the embryo into a boy.

In spite of all these precautions, girls will come into Hindu households as ill-luck, or rather nature, will have it. After the birth of one or more sons girls are not unwelcome, and under such circumstances, mothers very often long to have a daughter. And after her birth both parents lavish love and tenderness upon her, for natural affection, though modified and blunted by cruel custom, is still strong in the parents' heart. Especially may this be the case with the Hindu *mother*. That maternal affection, sweet and strong, before which 'there is neither male nor female' asserts itself not unfrequently [sic] in Hindu homes, and overcomes selfishness and false fear of popular custom. A loving mother will sacrifice her own happiness by braving the displeasure of her lord, and will treat her little daughter as the best of all treasures. Such heroism is truly praiseworthy in a woman; any country might be proud of her. But alas! the dark side is too conspicuous to be passed over in silence.

In a home shadowed by adherence to cruel custom and prejudice, a child is born into the world; the poor mother is greatly distressed to learn that the little stranger is a daughter, and the neighbours turn their noses in all directions to manifest their disgust and indignation at the occurrence of such a phenomenon. The innocent babe is happily unconscious of all that is going on around her, for a time at least. The mother, who has lost the favour of her husband and relatives because of the girl's birth, may selfishly avenge herself by showing disregard to infantile needs and slighting babyish requests. Under such a mother the baby soon begins to *feel* her misery, although she does not understand how or why she is caused to suffer this cruel injustice.

If a girl is born after her brother's death, or if, soon after her birth, a boy in the family dies, she is in either case regarded by her parents and neighbours as the cause of the boy's death. She is then constantly addressed with some unpleasant name, slighted, beaten, cursed, persecuted and despised by all. Strange to say, some parents, instead of thinking of her as a comfort left to them, find it in their hearts, in the constant manifestation of their grief for the dear lost boy, to address the innocent girl with words such as these: 'Wretched girl, why didst thou not die instead of our darling boy? Why didst thou crowd him out of the house by coming to us?; or why didst not thou thyself become a boy? It would have been good for all of us if thou hadst died and thy brother lived!' I have myself several times heard parents say such things to their daughters, who, in their turn, looked sadly and wonderingly into the[ir] parents' faces, not comprehending why such cruel speeches should be heaped upon their heads when they had not done any harm to their brothers. If there is a boy remaining in the family, all the caresses and sweet words, the comforts and gifts, the blessings and praises are lavished upon him by parents and neighbours, and even by servants, who fully sympathise with the parents in their grief. On every occasion the poor girl is made to feel that she has no right to share her brother's good fortune, and that she is an unwelcome, unbidden guest in the family.

Brothers, in most cases, are of course very proud of their superior sex; they can know no better than what they see and hear concerning their own and their sisters' qualities. They, too, begin by and by to despise girls and women. It is not a rare thing to hear a mere slip of a boy gravely lecture his elder sister as to what she should or should not do, and remind her that she is only a girl and that *he* is a *boy*. Subjected to such humiliation, most girls become sullen, morbid and dull. There are some fiery natures, however, who burn with indignation, and burst out in their own childish eloquence; they tell their brothers and cousins that they soon are going to be given in marriage, and that they will not come to see them, even if they are often entreated to do so. Children, however, soon forget the wrong done them; they laugh, they shout, they run about freely, and are generally merry when unpleasant speeches are not showered upon them. Having little or no education, except a few prayers and popular songs to commit to memory, the little girls are mostly left to themselves, and they play in whatever manner they please. When about six or seven years of age they usually begin to help their mothers in household work, or in taking care of the younger children.

I have mentioned earlier the strictness of the modern caste system in regard to marriage. Intelligent readers may, therefore, have already guessed that this reason lies at the bottom of the disfavour shown to girls in Hindu homes. From the first moment of the daughter's birth, the parents are tormented incessantly with anxiety in regard to her future, and the responsibilities of their position. Marriage is the most expensive of all Hindu festivities and ceremonies. The marriage of a girl of a high-caste family involves an expenditure of two hundred dollars [i.e. about six hundred rupees] at the very least. Poverty in India is so great that not many fathers are able to incur this expense; if there are more than two daughters in a family, his ruin is inevitable. For, it should be remembered, the bread-winner of the house in Hindu society not only has to feed his own wife and children, but also his parents, his brothers who are unable to work either through ignorance or idleness their families and the nearest widowed relatives, all of whom very often depend upon one man for their support; besides these, there are the family priests, religious beggars and others, who expect much from him. Thus, fettered hand and foot by barbarously cruel customs which threaten to strip him of everything he has, starvation and death staring him in the face, the wretched father of many girls is truly an object of pity. Religion enjoins that every girl must be given in marriage; the neglect of this duty means for the father unpardonable sin, public ridicule and caste excommunication. But this is not all. The girl must be married within a fixed period, the caste of the future husband must be the same, and the clan either equal or superior, *but never inferior*, to that of her father.

The Brahmans of Eastern India have observed successfully their clan prejudice for hundreds of years despite poverty; they have done this in part by taking advantage of the custom of polygamy. A Brahman of a high clan will marry ten, eleven, twenty, or even one hundred and fifty girls. He makes a business of it. He goes up and down the land marrying girls, receiving presents from their parents, and immediately thereafter bidding goodbye to the brides; going home, he never returns to them. The illustrious Brahman need not bother himself with the care of supporting so many wives, for the parents pledge themselves to maintain the daughter all her life, if she stays with them a married virgin to the end. In case of such a marriage as this, the father is not required to spend money beyond his means, nor is it difficult for him to support the daughter, for she is useful to the family in doing the cooking and other household work; moreover, the father has the satisfaction *first*, of having given his daughter in marriage, and thereby having escaped disgrace and the ridicule of society; *secondly*, of having obtained for himself the bright mansions of the gods, since his daughter's husband is a Brahman of high clan.

But this form of polygamy does not exist among the Kshatriyas, because, as a member of the non-Brahman caste, a man is not allowed, by religion, to beg or receive gifts from others, except from friends; he therefore cannot support either many wives or many daughters. Caste and clan prejudice tyrannized the Rajputs of North, Northwestern and Central India, who belong to the Kshatriya or warrior caste, to such an extent that they were driven to introduce the inhuman and irreligious custom of female infanticide into their society. This cruel act was performed by the fathers themselves, or even by mothers, at the command of the husband, whom they are bound to obey in *all* things.

It is a universal custom among the Rajputs for neighbours and friends to assemble to congratulate the father upon the birth of a child. If a boy is born, his birth is announced with music, glad songs and by distributing sweetmeats. If [it is] a daughter, the father coolly announces that 'nothing' has been born into his family, by which expression it is understood that the child is a girl, and that she is very likely to be *nothing* in this world, and the friends go home grave and quiet.

After considering how many girls could safely be allowed to live, the father took good care to defend himself from caste and clan tyranny by killing the extra girls at birth, which was as easily accomplished as destroying a mosquito or any other annoying insect. Who can save a babe if the parents are determined to slay her, and eagerly watch for a suitable opportunity? Opium is generally used to keep the crying child quiet, and a small pill of this drug is sufficient to accomplish the cruel task; a skilful pressure upon the neck, which is known as 'putting nail to the throat', also answers the purpose. There are several other nameless methods that may be employed in sacrificing the innocents upon the unholy altar of the caste and clan system. Then, there are not a few child-thieves who generally steal girls; even the wild animals are so intelligent and of such refined taste that they mock at British law, and almost always steal girls to satisfy their hunger.

Female infanticide, though not sanctioned by religion, and never looked upon as right by conscientious people, has nevertheless, in those parts of India mentioned, been silently passed over unpunished by society in general.

As early as 1802, the British government enacted laws for the suppression of this horrid crime. More than forty years ago Major Ludlow, a kind-hearted Englishman, induced the semi-independent States to prohibit this custom, which the Hindu princes did, by a mutual agreement not to allow anyone to force the father of a girl to give more dowry than his circumstances should warrant, and to discourage extravagance in the celebration of marriages. But caste and clan prejudice could not be overcome so easily.

Large expenses might be stopped by law, but a belief, deeply rooted in the hearts [of], and religiously observed by the people for centuries, could not be removed by external rules.

The Census of 1870 revealed the curious fact that three hundred children were stolen in one year by wolves from within the city of Umritzar [Amritsar], all the children being girls, and this under the very nose of the English government. In 1868, an English official, Mr Hobart, made a tour of inspection through those parts of India where female infanticide was most [intensly] practised before the government enacted the prohibitory law. As a result of careful observation, he came to the conclusion that this horrible practice was still followed in secret, and to an alarming extent.

The Census returns of 1880–81 show that there are fewer women than men in India by over five million. Chief among the causes which have brought about this surprising numerical difference of the sexes may be named, after female infanticide in certain parts of the country, *the imperfect treatment of the diseases of women in all parts of Hindustan, together with lack of proper hygienic care and medical attendance.*

3. MARRIED LIFE

It is not easy to determine when the childhood of a Hindu girl ends and the married life begins. The early marriage system, although not the oldest custom of my country, is at least five hundred years older than the Christian era. According to Manu, eight years is the minimum, and twelve years of age the maximum marriageable age for a high caste girl.[tt] The earlier the act of giving the daughter in marriage, the greater is the merit, for thereby the parents are entitled to rich rewards in heaven. There have always been exceptions to this rule, however. Among the eight kinds of marriages described in the law, there is one form that is only an agreement between the lovers to be loyal to each other; in this form of marriage there is no religious ceremony, nor even a third party to witness and confirm the agreement and relationship, and yet by the law this is regarded as completely lawful a marriage as any other. It is quite plain from this fact that all girls were not betrothed between the age of eight and twelve years, and also that marriage was not considered a religious institution by the Hindus in olden times. All castes and classes could marry in this form if they chose to do so. One of the most noticeable facts connected with this form is this: women as well as men were quite free to choose their own future spouses. In Europe and America women do choose their husbands, but it is considered a shame for a woman to be the first to request marriage, and both men and women will be shocked equally at such an occurrence; but in India, women had equal freedom with men, in this case at least. A woman might, without being put to shame, and without shocking the other party, come forward and select her own husband. The *svayamvara* (selecting [one's] husband) was quite common until as late as the eleventh century AD, and even now, although very rarely, this custom is practised by a few people.

I know of a woman in the Bombay Presidency who is married to a Brahman according to this form. The first wife of the man is still living; the second wife, being of another caste, he could not openly acknowledge as his religiously wedded wife, but he could do so [i.e. acknowledge her] without going through the religious ceremony had she been of his own caste, as the act is sanctioned by Hindu law. The lawless behaviour of the Mahomedan intruders from the twelfth century AD, had much to do in universalizing infant marriage in India. A great many girls are given in marriage at the present day literally while they are still in their cradles; from five to eleven years

[tt]A man aged thirty years shall marry a maiden of twelve who pleases him, or a man of twenty-four a girl of eight years of age. (*Manu*, ix, 94.)

is the usual age for their marriage among the Brahmans all over India. As it is absurd to assume that girls should be allowed to choose their future husbands in their infancy, this is done for them by their parents and guardians. In the northern part of the country, the family barber is generally employed to select boys and girls to be married, it being considered too humiliating and mean an act on the part of parents and guardians to go out to seek their future daughters- and sons-in-law.

Although Manu has distinctly said that twenty-four years is the minimum marriageable age for a young man, the popular custom defies the law. Boys of ten and twelve are now doomed to be married to girls of seven and eight years of age. A boy of a well-to-do family does not generally remain a bachelor after seventeen or eighteen years of age; respectable but very poor families, even if they are of high caste, cannot afford to marry their boys so soon, but even among them it is a shame for a man to remain unmarried after twenty or twenty-five. Boys as well as girls have no voice in the selection of their spouses at the first marriage but if a man loses his first wife, and marries a second time, *he* has a choice in the matter.

Although the ancient law-givers thought it desirable to marry [off] girls when quite young, and consequently ignored their right to choose their own husbands, yet they were not altogether void of humane feelings. They have positively forbidden parents and guardians to give away girls in marriage unless good suitors were offered them.

To a distinguished, handsome suitor of equal caste should a father give his daughter in accordance with the prescribed rule, though she has not attained the proper age. (*Manu*, ix, 88.)

But the maiden, though marriageable, should rather stop in the father's house until death, than that he should ever give her to a man destitute of good qualities.(*Manu*, ix, 89.)

But, alas, here too the law is defined by cruel custom! It allows some men to remain unmarried, but woe to the maiden and to her family if she is so unfortunate as to remain single after the marriageable age. Although no law has ever said so, the popular belief is that a woman can have no salvation unless she be formally married. It is not, then, a matter of wonder that parents become extremely anxious when their daughters are over eight or nine and are unsought in marriage. Very few suitors offer to marry the daughters of poor parents, though they may be of high-caste families. Wealth has its own pride and merit in India, as everywhere else in the world, but even this powerful wealth is as nothing before caste rule. A high-caste man will never condescend to marry his daughter to a low-caste man though he be a millionaire.

But wealth in one's own caste surpasses the merits of learning, beauty and honour; parents generally seek boys of well-to-do families as their sons-in-law. As the boys are too young to pass as possessing 'good qualities', i.e. learning, common-sense, ability to support and take care of a family, and respectable character, the parents wish to see their daughter safe in a family where she will, at least, have plenty to eat and to wear; they, of course, wish her to be happy with her husband, but in their judgment that is not the one thing needful. So long as *they* have fulfilled the custom, and thereby secured a good name in this world and heavenly reward in the next, their minds are not much troubled concerning the girl's fate. If the boy be of rich or middle-class people, a handsome sum of money must be given to him and his family in order to secure the marriage; beside this, the girl's family must walk very humbly with this little god, for he is believed to be in-dwelt by the god Vishnu. Poor parents cannot have the advantage of marrying their daughters to boys of prosperous families, and as they *must* marry them to someone, it very frequently happens that girls of eight or nine are given to men of sixty and seventy, or to men utterly unworthy of the young maidens.

Parents who have the means to secure good-looking, prosperous men as their sons-in-law, take great care to consult the horoscopes of both parties in order to know the future of their daughters; in such cases, they are anxious to ascertain, over and above all things, that the girl shall not become a widow. If the daughter's horoscope reveals that her future husband is to survive her, the match is considered very satisfactory; but if it reveals the reverse, then a boy having a horoscope equally bad is sought for, because it is sincerely believed that in that case the guardian planets will wrestle with each other, and, as almost always happens, that the stronger, i.e. the husband's planet will be victorious, or else both parties will fall in the conflict, and the husband and wife [will] die together. A friend of mine informed me that three hundred horoscopes were rejected before one was found which agreed satisfactorily with her sister's guardian planet. Undoubtedly many suitors, who might make good husbands for these little girls, are for this reason rejected, and unworthy men fall to their lot; thus, the horoscope becomes a source of misery instead of blessing.

It not unfrequently [sic] happens that fathers give away their daughters in marriage to strangers without exercising care in making inquiry concerning the suitor's character and social position. It is enough to learn from the man's own statement, his caste and clan, and the locality of his home. I know of a most extraordinary marriage that took place in the following manner:[2] the father was on a pilgrimage with his family, which consisted of his wife and two daughters, one nine and the other, seven years of age, and they had stopped in a town to take rest for a day or two. One morning, the father was bathing in the sacred river Godavari, near the town, when he saw a fine-looking man coming to bathe there also. After the ablution and the morning prayers were over, the father inquired of the stranger who he was and whence he came; on learning his caste, and clan, and dwelling-place, also that he was a widower, the father offered him his little daughter of nine, in marriage. All things were settled in an hour or so; next day the marriage was concluded, and the little girl placed in the possession of the stranger, who took her nearly nine hundred miles away from her home. The father left the place the day after the marriage without the daughter, and pursued his pilgrimage with a light heart; fortunately, the little girl had fallen in good hands, and was well and tenderly cared for beyond all expectation, but the conduct of her father, who cared so little to ascertain his daughter's fate, is none the less censurable.

When the time to conclude the marriage ceremony draws near, the Hindu mother's affection for the girl frequently knows no bounds; she indulges her in endless ways, knowing that in a few days her darling will be torn away from her loving embrace. When she goes to pay the customary visit to her child's future mother-in-law, many are the tearful entreaties and soul-stirring solicitations that she will be as kind and forbearing towards the little stranger as though she were her own daughter. The boy's mother is moved at this time, for she has a woman's heart, and she promises to be a mother to the little bride. On the day fixed for the marriage, parents formally give their daughter away to the boy; afterwards the young people are united by priests who utter the sacred texts and pronounce them man and wife in the presence of the sacred fire and of relatives and friends. The marriage being thus concluded, it is henceforth indissoluble.

Neither by sale nor by repudiation is a wife released from her husband; such we know the law to be which the Lord of creatures made of old. (*Manu,* ix, 46.)

Marriage is the only 'sacrament' administered to a high caste woman, accompanied with the utterance of the Vedic texts. It is to be presumed that the texts are introduced in honour of the man whom she marries, for no sacrament must be administered to him without the sacred formulae. Henceforth the girl is his, not only his property, but also that of his nearest relatives.

'For they (the ancient sages) declare that a bride is given to the family of her husband, and not to the husband alone.' (*Apastamba, II,* 10, 27, 3.)

The girl now belongs to the husband's clan; she is known by his family name, and in some parts of India the husband's relatives will not allow her to be called by the first name that was given her by her parents; henceforth she is a kind of impersonal being. She can have no merit or quality of her own.

Whatever be the qualities of the man with whom a woman is united in lawful marriage, such qualities even she assumes, like a river united with the ocean. (*Manu, ix,* 22.)

Many of our girls, when asked in fun whether they would like soon to be married, would innocently answer in the affirmative. They often see their sisters, cousins or playmates married; the occasion is one long to be remembered with pleasure. Even the poorest families take great pains to make it pleasant to everybody; children enjoy it most of all. There are gorgeous dresses, bright coloured clothes, beautiful decorations, music, songs, fireworks, fun, plenty of fruit and sweet things to eat and to give away, lovely flowers, and the whole house is illuminated with many lamps. What can be more tempting to a child's mind than these? In addition to all this, a big elephant is sometimes brought, on which the newly-married children ride in procession amidst all sorts of fun. Is it not grand enough for a child? Oh—, . . . I shall ride on the back of the elephant, thinks the girl; and there is something more besides; all the people in the house will wait on me, will make much of me; everybody will caress and try to please me. 'Oh, what fun!'

'I like to have a cold, and be ill,' said a girl of four. 'Why, darling?' asked her mother, in surprise. 'Oh, because,' replied the little girl, 'I like to eat my breakfast in bed, and then, too, everybody waits on me!' Who has not heard remarks such as these, and laughed heartily over them? Children like even to be ill for the sake of being waited on. What wonder, then, if Hindu girls like being married for the sake of enjoying that much-coveted privilege! But little do these poor innocents know what comes after the fun. Little do they imagine that they must bid farewell to [their] home and mother, to noisy merriment and laughter, and to the free life of pure enjoyment. Sometimes the child desires to be married when, through superstition, she is ill-treated at home by her nearest relatives, otherwise there can be no reason except the enjoyment of fun that excites the desire in the girl's heart, for when the marriage takes place she is just emerging from babyhood.

Childhood is, indeed, the heyday of a Hindu woman's life. Free to go in and out where she pleases, never bothered by caste or other social restrictions, never worried by lesson-learning, sewing, mending or knitting, loved, petted and spoiled by parents, brothers and sisters, uncles and aunts, she is little different from a young colt whose days are spent in complete liberty. Then lo, all at once the ban of marriage is pronounced and the yoke put on her neck forever!

Immediately after the marriage ceremony is concluded the boy takes his girl-bride home and delivers her over to his own mother, who becomes from that time until the girl grows old enough to be given to her husband, her sole mistress, and who wields over the daughter-in-law undisputed authority!

It must be borne in mind that both in Northern and Southern India, the term 'marriage' does not mean anything more than an irrevocable betrothal. The ceremony gone through at that time establishes *religiously* the conjugal relationship of both parties; there is a second ceremony that confirms the relationship both religiously and socially, which does not take place until the children attain the age of puberty. In Bengal, the rule is somewhat different, and proves in many cases greatly injurious to the human system. In some very rare cases the girls are allowed to remain with their own parents for a time at least. In the North of India, the little bride's lot is a happier one to begin with, she not being forced to go to her husband's home until she is about thirteen or fourteen years of age.

The joint family system, which is one of the peculiarities of Eastern countries, is very deeply rooted in the soil of India. There may not unfrequently [sic] be found four generations living under one roof. The house is divided into two parts, namely, the outer and the inner court. The houses, as a rule, have but few windows, and they are usually dark; the men's court is comparatively light and good. Houses in country places are better than those in the crowded cities. Men and women have almost nothing in common.

The women's court is situated at the back of the house, where darkness reigns perpetually. There the child-bride is brought to be forever confined. She does not enter her husband's house to be the head of a new home, but rather enters the house of the father-in-law to become the lowest of its members, and to occupy the humblest position in the family. Breaking the young bride's spirit is an essential part of the discipline of this new abode. She must never talk or laugh loudly, must never speak before or to the father and elder brother-in-law, or any other distant male relative of her husband, unless commanded to do so. In Northern India, where all women wear veils, the young bride or woman covers her face with it, or runs into another room to show respect to them, when these persons enter an apartment where she happens to be. In Southern India, where women, as a rule, do not wear veils, they need not cover their faces; they rise to show respect to elders and to their husbands, and remain standing as long as they are obliged to be in their presence.

The mothers-in-law employ their daughters in all kinds of household work, in order to give them a thorough knowledge of domestic duties. These children of nine or ten years of age find it irksome to work hard all day long without the hope of hearing a word of praise from the mother-in-law. As a rule, the little girl is scolded for every mistake she commits; if the work be well done, it is silently accepted, words of encouragement and praise from the elders being regarded as spoiling children and demoralizing them. The faults of the little ones are often mistaken for intentional offences, and then the artillery of abusive speech is opened upon them; thus, mortified and distressed, they seek to console themselves by shedding bitter tears in silence. In such sorrowful hours they miss the[ir own] dear mother and her loving sympathy.

I must, however, do justice to the mothers-in-law. Many of them treat the young brides of their sons as their own children; many are kind and affectionate, but ignorant; they easily lose their temper and seem to be hard when they do not mean to be so. Others again, having themselves been the victims of merciless treatment in their childhood become hard-hearted; such a one will do all she can to torment the child by using abusive language, by beating her and slandering her before the neighbours. Often she is not satisfied by doing this herself, but induces and encourages the son to join her. I have several times seen young wives shamefully beaten by beastly young husbands who cherished no natural love for them.

As we have seen, the marriage is concluded without the consent of either party, and after it the bride is not allowed to speak or be acquainted with the husband until after the second ceremony, and even then the young couple must never betray any sign of their mutual attachment before a third party. Under such circumstances, they seldom meet and talk; it may therefore be easily understood that being cut off from the chief means of forming attachment, the young couple are almost strangers, and in many cases do not like their relationship; and if in the midst of all this, the mother-in-law begins to encourage the young man to torment his wife in various ways, it is not strange that a feeling akin to hatred takes root between them. A child of thirteen was cruelly beaten by her husband in my presence for telling the simple truth, that she did not like as much to be in his house as at her own home.

In spite all these drawbacks, there is in India many a happy and loving couple that would be an honour to any nation. Where the conjugal relation is brightened by mutual love, the happy wife has nothing to complain of except the absence of freedom of thought and action; but since wives have never known from the beginning what freedom is, they are generally well content to remain in bondage; there is, however, no such thing as the family having pleasant times together.

Men spend their evenings and other leisure hours with friends of their own sex, either in the outer court or away from home. Children enjoy the company of the father and mother alternately, by going in and out when they choose, but the children of young parents are never made happy by the father's caresses or any other demonstration of his love in the presence of the elders; the notion of false modesty prevents the young father from speaking to his children freely. The women of the family usually take their meals after the men have had theirs, and the wife, as a rule, eats what her lord may please to leave on his plate.

4. WOMAN'S PLACE IN RELIGION AND SOCIETY

The Hindu religion commands:

Women must be honoured and adorned by their fathers, brothers, husbands and brothers-in-law, who desire their own welfare.

Where women are honoured, there the gods are pleased; but where they are not honoured, no sacred rite yields rewards.

Where the female relations live in grief, the family soon wholly perishes; but that family where they are not unhappy ever prospers.

The houses on which female relations, not being duly honoured, pronounce a curse, perish completely, as if destroyed by magic.

Hence men who seek their own welfare, should always honour women on holidays and festivals with (gifts of) ornaments, clothes and dainty food.

In that family where the husband is pleased with his wife, and the wife with her husband, happiness will assuredly be lasting.

For if the wife is not radiant with beauty, she will not attract her husband; but if she has no attraction for him, no children will be born.

If the wife is radiant with beauty, the whole house is bright; but if she is destitute of beauty, all will appear dismal.(*Manu*, iii, 55–62.)

These commandments are very significant. Our Aryan Hindus did, and still do honour woman to a certain extent. The honour bestowed upon the *mother* is without parallel in any other country. Although the woman is looked upon as an inferior being, the mother is nevertheless the chief person and worthy to receive all honour from the son. One of the great commandments of the Hindu Scriptures is 'Let thy mother be to thee like unto a god.'[tt]

[tt]My readers would perhaps be interested to see these commandments; they are as follows:

> After having taught the Veda, the teacher instructs the pupil:
> 'Say what is true.
> Do thy duty.
> Do not neglect the study of the Veda.
> After having brought to thy teacher his proper reward, do not cut off the line of children! (i.e. Do not remain unmarried).
> Do not swerve from the truth.

The mother is the queen of the son's household. She wields great power there, and is generally obeyed as the head of the family by her sons and by her daughters-in-law.

But there is a reverse side to the shield that should not be left unobserved. This is best studied in the laws of Manu, as all Hindus, with a few exceptions, believe implicitly what that law-giver says about women:

It is the nature of women to seduce men in this world; for that reason the wise are never unguarded in the company of females.

For women are able to lead astray in this world not only a fool, but even a learned man, and to make him a slave of desire and anger. (*Manu*, ii, 213–14.)

Women do not care for beauty, nor is their attention fixed on age; thinking 'it is enough that he is a man', they give themselves to the handsome and to the ugly.

Through their passion for men, through their mutable temper, through their natural heartlessness, they become disloyal towards their husbands, however carefully they may be guarded in this world.

Knowing their disposition, which the Lord of creatures laid in them at the creation, to be such, every man should most strenuously exert himself to guard them.

When creating them, [Manu the Creator] allotted to women a love of their bed, of their seat and of ornament, impure desires, wrath, dishonesty, malice and bad conduct.

For women no sacramental rite is performed with sacred texts, thus the law is settled; women who are destitute of strength and destitute of knowledge of Vedic texts, are as impure as falsehood itself, that is a fixed rule.(*Manu*, ix, 14–18.)

Such is the opinion of Manu concerning all women; and all men with more or less faith in the law regard women, even though they be their own mothers, 'as impure as falsehood itself'.

Do not swerve from duty.
Do not neglect what is useful.
Do not neglect the learning and teaching of the Veda.
Do not neglect the sacrificial works due to the gods and fathers.
Let thy mother be to thee like unto a god.
Let thy father be to thee like unto a god.
Let thy teacher be to thee like unto a god.
Let thy guests be to thee like unto a god.
Whatever actions are blameless those should be regarded, not others.
Whatever good works have been performed by us, should be observed by thee, not others.'(*Taittiriya Upanishad*, Valli, i, An. xi, I, 2.)

And to this effect many sacred texts are chanted also in the Vedas, in order to make fully known the true disposition of women; hear now those texts which refer to the expiation of their sins.

'If my mother, going astray and unfaithful, conceived illicit desires, may my father keep that seed from me'[1], that is the scriptural text.(*Manu*, ix, 19–20.)

Such distrust and such low estimate of woman's nature and character in general, is at the root of the custom of seclusion of women in India. This mischievous custom has greatly increased and has become intensely tyrannical since the Mahomedan invasion; but that it existed from about the sixth century BC cannot be denied. All male relatives are commanded by the law to deprive the women of the household of all their freedom:

Day and night, woman must be kept in dependence by the males of their families, and if they attach themselves to sensual enjoyments, they must be kept under one's control.

Her father protects her in childhood, her husband protects her in youth, and her sons protect her in old age; a woman is never fit for independence. (*Manu*, ix, 2–3.)

Women must particularly be guarded against evil inclinations, however trifling they may appear; for if they are not guarded, they will bring sorrow on two families.

Considering that the highest duty of all castes, even weak husbands must strive to guard their wives.(*Manu*, ix, 5–6.)

No man can completely guard women by force; but they can be guarded by the employment of the following expedients: Let the husband employ his wife in the collection and expenditure of his wealth, in keeping everything clean, in the fulfilment of religious duties, in the preparation of his food, and in looking after the household utensils.(*Manu*, ix, 10–11.)

Those who diligently and impartially read Sanskrit literature in the original cannot fail to recognize the law-giver Manu as one of those hundreds who have done their best to make woman a hateful being in the world's eye. To employ her in housekeeping and kindred occupations is thought to be the only means of keeping her out of mischief, the blessed enjoyment of literary culture being denied her. She is forbidden to read the sacred scriptures, she has no right to pronounce a single syllable out of them. To appease her uncultivated, low kind of desire by giving her ornaments to adorn her person, and by giving her dainty food together with an occasional bow which costs nothing, are the highest honours to which a Hindu woman is entitled. She, the loving mother of the nation, the devoted wife, the tender sister and affectionate daughter is never fit for independence, and is 'as impure as falsehood itself'. She is never to be trusted; matters of importance are never to be committed to her.

I can say honestly and truthfully, that I have never read any sacred book in Sanskrit literature without meeting this kind of hateful sentiment about women. True, they contain here and there a kind word about them, but such words seem to me a heartless mockery after having charged them, as a class, with crime and evil deeds.

Profane literature is by no means less severe or more respectful towards women. I quote from the ethical teachings, parts of a catechism and also a few proverbs:

Q. What is cruel?
A. The heart of a viper.
Q. What is more cruel than that?
A. The heart of a woman.
Q. What is cruellest of all?
A. The heart of a sonless, penniless widow.

A catechism on moral subjects written by a Hindu gentleman of high literary reputation says:

Q. What is the chief gate to hell?
A. A woman.
Q. What bewitches like wine?
A. A woman.
Q. Who is the wisest of the wise?
A. He who has not been deceived by women who may be compared to malignant fiends.
Q. What are fetters to men?
A. Women.
Q. What is that which cannot be trusted?
A. Women.
Q. What poison is that which appears like nectar?
A. Women.

[Proverbs]:

Never put your trust in women.
Women's counsel leads to destruction.
Woman is a great whirlpool of suspicion, a dwelling-place of vices, full of deceits, a hindrance in the way of heaven, the gate of hell.

Having fairly illustrated the popular belief about women's nature, I now proceed to state woman's religion. Virtues such as truthfulness, forbearance, fortitude, purity of heart and uprightness are common to men and women, but religion, as the word is commonly understood, has two distinct natures in the Hindu law; the masculine and the feminine. The masculine religion has its own peculiar duties, privileges and honours. The feminine religion also has its peculiarities.

The sum and substance of the latter may be given in a few words: to look upon her husband as a god, to hope for salvation only through him, to be obedient to him in all things, never to covet independence, never to do anything but that which is approved by law and custom.

'Hear now the duties of women,' says the law-giver, Manu:

By a girl, by a young woman, or even by an aged one, nothing must be done independently, even in her own house.

In childhood, a female must be subject to her father, in youth, to her husband, when her lord is dead, to her sons; a woman must never be independent.

She must not seek to separate herself from her father, husband, or sons; by leaving them she would make both her own and her husband's families contemptible.

She must always be cheerful, clever in the management of her household affairs, careful in cleaning her utensils, and economical in expenditure.

Him to whom her father may give her, or her brother with the father's permission, she shall obey as long as he lives, and when he is dead, she must not insult his memory.

For the sake of procuring good fortune to brides, the recitation of benedictory texts, and the sacrifice to the Lord of creatures are used at weddings; but the betrothal by the father or guardian is the cause of the husband's dominion over his wife.

The husband who wedded her with sacred texts, always gives happiness to his wife, both in season and out of season, in this world and in the next. Though destitute of virtue, or seeking pleasure elsewhere, or devoid of good qualities, yet a husband must be constantly worshipped as a god by a faithful wife.

No sacrifice, no vow, no fast must be performed by women apart from their husbands; if a wife obeys her husband, she will for that reason alone, be exalted in heaven.

A faithful wife, who desires to dwell after death with her husband, must never do anything that might displease him who took her hand whether he be alive or dead.(*Manu*, v, 147–56.)

By violating her duty towards her husband, a wife is disgraced in this world, after death she enters the womb of a jackal, and is tormented by diseases, the punishment of her sin.

She who, controlling her thoughts, words and deeds, never slights her lord, resides after death with her husband in heaven, and is called a virtuous wife.

In reward of such conduct, a female who controls her thoughts, speech and actions, gains in this life highest renown, and in the next world a place near her husband.(*Manu, v, 164–6.*)

5. MARITAL RIGHTS

He only is a perfect man who consists of three persons united, his wife, himself and his offspring; thus says the Veda, and learned Brahmanas propound this maxim likewise, 'The husband is declared to be one with the wife.' (*Manu, ix, 45.*)

The wife is declared to be the 'marital property'of her husband, and is classed with 'cows, mares, female camels, slave-girls, buffalo-cows, she-goats and ewes'. (see *Manu, ix, 48–51*).

The wife is punishable for treating her husband with aversion:

For one year let a husband bear with a wife who hates him; but after a lapse of a year, let him deprive her of her property and cease to live with her.

She who shows disrespect to a husband who is addicted to some evil passion, is a drunkard, or diseased, shall be deserted for three months, and be deprived of her ornaments and furniture.(*Manu, ix, 77–8.*)

She who drinks spirituous liquor, is of bad conduct, rebellious, diseased, mischievous or wasteful, may at any time be superseded by another wife.

A barren wife may be superseded in the eighth year, she whose children all die in the tenth, she who bears only daughters in the eleventh, but she who is quarrelsome, without delay. (*Manu, ix, 80–1.*)

A wife who, being superseded, in anger departs from her husband's house, must either be instantly confined or cast off in the presence of the family. (*Manu, ix, 83.*)

Though a man may have accepted a damsel in due form, he may abandon her if she be blemished or diseased, and if she have been given with fraud. (*Manu, ix, 72.*)

But no such provision is made for the woman; on the contrary, she must remain with and revere her husband as a god, even though he be 'destitute of virtue, and seek pleasure elsewhere, or be devoid of good qualities, addicted to evil passion, fond of spirituous liquors, or diseased,' and why not!

How much impartial justice is shown in the treatment of womankind by Hindu law, can be fairly understood after reading the above quotations. In olden times, these laws were enforced by the community; a husband had absolute power over his wife; she could do nothing but submit to his will without uttering a word of protest. Now, under the so-called Christian British rule, the woman is in no better condition than of old. True, the husband cannot, as in the golden age, take her wherever she may be found, and drag her to his house, but his absolute power over her person has not suffered in the least.[3] He is now bound to bring suit against her in the courts of justice to claim his 'marital property,' if she be unwilling to submit to him by any other means.

A near relative of mine[4] had been given in her childhood in marriage to a boy whose parents agreed to let him stay and be educated with her in her own home. No sooner however, had the marriage ceremony been concluded than they forgot their agreement; the boy was taken to the home of his parents where he remained to grow up to be a worthless dunce, while his wife through the kindness and advanced views of her father, developed into a bright young woman and well-accomplished.

Thirteen years later, the young man came to claim his wife, but the parents had no heart to send their darling daughter with a beggar who possessed neither the power nor the sense to make an honest living and [who] was unable to support and protect his wife. The wife too had no wish to go with him since he was a stranger to her; under the circumstances, she could neither love nor respect him. A number of orthodox people in the community who saw no reason why a wife should not follow her husband even though he be a worthless man, collected funds to enable him to sue her and her parents in the Courts of Justice. The case was examined with due ceremony and the verdict was given in the man's favour, according to Hindu law.[††]

[††]In all cases except those directly connected with life and death, the British government is bound according to the treaties concluded with the inhabitants of

The wife was doomed to go with him. Fortunately she was soon released from this sorrowful world by cholera. Whatever may be said of the epidemics that yearly assail our country, they are not unwelcome among the unfortunate women who are thus persecuted by social, religious and State laws. Many women put an end to their earthly sufferings by committing suicide. Suits at law between husband and wife are remarkable for their rarity in the British Courts in India, owing to the ever-submissive conduct of women who suffer silently, knowing that the gods and justice always favour the men.

The case of Rakhmabai, that has lately profoundly agitated Hindu society, is only one of thousands of the same class. The remarkable thing about her is that she is a well-educated lady, who was brought up under the loving care of her father, and had learned from him how to defend herself against the assaults of social and religious bigotries. But as soon as her father died the man who claimed to be her husband brought suit against her in the court of Bombay. The young woman bravely defended herself, declining to go to live with the man on the ground that the marriage that was concluded without her consent could not be legally considered as such. Mr Justice Pinhey, who tried the case in the first instance, had a sufficient sense of justice to refuse to force the lady to live with her husband against her will. Upon hearing this decision, the conservative party [i.e. conservative sections] all over India rose as one man and girded their loins to denounce the helpless woman and her handful [of] friends. They encouraged the alleged husband to stand his ground firmly, threatening the British government with public displeasure if it failed to keep its agreement to force the woman to go to live with the husband, according to Hindu law. Large sums were collected for the benefit of this man, Dadajee, to enable him to appeal against the decision to the full bench, whereupon, to the horror of all right-thinking people, the Chief Justice sent back the case to the lower court for re-trial on its merits, as judged by the Hindu laws. The painful termination of this trial, I have in a letter written by my dear friend Rakhmabai herself, bearing the date [line] Bombay, March 18th, 1887. I quote from her letter:

India, not to interfere with their social and religious customs and laws; judicial decisions are given accordingly.

The learned and civilized judges of the full bench are determined to enforce, in this enlightened age, the inhuman laws enacted in barbaric times, four thousand years ago. They have not only commanded me to go to live with the man, but also have obliged me to pay the costs of the dispute. Just think of this extraordinary decision! Are we not living under the impartial British government, which boasts of giving equal justice to all, and are we not ruled by the Queen-Empress Victoria, herself a woman? My dear friend, I shall have been cast into the State prison when this letter reaches you; this is because I do not, and cannot, obey the order of Mr Justice Farran.

There is no hope for women in India, whether they be under Hindu rule or British rule; some are of the opinion that my case so cruelly decided, may bring about a better condition for woman by turning public opinion in her favour, but I fear it will be otherwise. The hard-hearted mothers-in-law will now be greatly strengthened, and will induce their sons, who have for some reason or other, been slow to enforce the conjugal rights to sue their wives in the British Courts, since they are now fully assured that under no circumstances can the British government act adversely to the Hindu law.

Taught by the experience of the past, we are not at all surprised at the decision of the Bombay court. Our only wonder is that a defenceless woman like Rakhmabai dared to raise her voice in the face of the powerful Hindu law, the mighty British government, the one hundred and twenty-nine million men and the three hundred and thirty million gods of the Hindus, all these having conspired together to crush her into nothingness. We cannot blame the English government for not defending a helpless woman; it is only fulfilling its agreement made with the male population of India. How very true are the words of the Saviour, 'Ye cannot serve God and Mammon.' Should England serve God by protecting a helpless woman against the powers and principalities of ancient institutions, Mammon would surely be displeased, and British profit and rule in India might be endangered thereby. Let us wish it success, no matter if that success be achieved at the sacrifice of the rights and the comfort of over one hundred million women.

Meanwhile, we shall patiently await the advent of the kingdom of righteousness, wherein the weak, the lowly and the helpless shall be made happy because the great Judge Himself 'shall wipe away all tears from their eyes'.

6. WIDOWHOOD

We now come to the worst and most dreaded period of a high-caste woman's life. Throughout India, widowhood is regarded as the punishment for a horrible crime or crimes committed by the woman in her former existence upon earth. The period of punishment may be greater or less, according to the nature of the crime. Disobedience and disloyalty to the husband, or murdering him in an earlier existence, are the chief crimes punished in the present birth by widowhood.

If the widow be a mother of sons, she is not usually a pitiable object; although she is certainly looked upon as a sinner, yet social abuse and hatred are greatly diminished [by] virtue of the fact that she is a mother of the superior beings. Next in rank to her stands an ancient widow, because a virtuous, aged widow who has bravely withstood the thousand temptations and persecutions of her lot commands an involuntary respect from all people, to which may be added the honour given to old age quite independent of the individual. The widow-mother of girls is treated indifferently and sometimes with genuine hatred, especially when her daughters have not been given in marriage in her husband's lifetime. But it is the child-widow or a childless young widow upon whom in an especial manner falls the abuse and hatred of the community as the greatest criminal upon whom Heaven's judgment has been pronounced.

In ancient times, when the code of Manu was yet in the dark future and when the priesthood had not yet mutilated the original reading of a Vedic text concerning widows, a custom of remarriage was in existence.

Its history may be briefly stated. The rite of child-marriage left many a girl a widow before she knew what marriage was. Her husband, having died sonless, had no right to enter into heaven and enjoy immortality, for 'the father throws his debts on the son and obtains immortality if he sees the face of a living son. It is declared in the Vedas, endless are the worlds of those who have sons; there is no place for the man who is destitute of male offspring.' The greatest curse that could be pronounced on enemies, was, 'May our enemies be destitute of offspring.'

In order that these young husbands might attain the abodes of the blessed, the ancient sages invented the custom of 'appointment' by which, as among the Jews, the Hindu Aryans raised up seed for the deceased husband. The husband's brother, cousin or [any] other kinsman successively was 'appointed' and duly authorized to raise offspring from the dead. The desired issue having been obtained any intercourse between the appointed persons was thenceforth considered illegal and sinful.

The woman still remained the widow of her deceased husband, and her children by the appointment were considered his heirs. Later on, this custom of 'appointment' was gradually discouraged in spite of the Vedic text already quoted, 'there is no place for the man who is destitute of male offspring.'

The duties of a widow are thus described in the code of Manu:

At her pleasure let her emaciate her body by living on pure flowers, roots and fruit; but she must never even mention the name of another man after her husband has died.

Until death let her be patient of hardships, self-controlled, and chaste, and strive to fulfil that most excellent duty which is prescribed for wives who have one husband only.(*Manu*, v, 157–8.)

. . . nor is a second husband anywhere prescribed for virtuous women. (*Manu*, v, 162.)

A virtuous wife, who after the death of her husband constantly remains chaste, reaches heaven, . . . (*Manu*, v, 160.)

In reward of such conduct, a female who controls her thoughts, speech, and actions, gains in this life highest renown, and in the next world a place near her husband.[††] (*Manu*, v, 166.)

The following are the rules for a widower:

A twice-born man, versed in the sacred law, shall burn a wife of equal caste who conducts herself thus and dies before him, with the sacred fires used for the Agnihotra, and with the sacrificial implements.

Having thus at the funeral, given the sacred fires to his wife who dies before him, he may marry again, and again kindle the (nuptial) fires.

. . . And having taken a wife, he must dwell in his own house during the second period of his life. (*Manu*, v, 167–9.)

[††]It should be borne in mind that according to the popular belief there is no other heaven to a woman than the seat or mansion of her husband, where she shares the heavenly bliss with him in the next world if she be faithful to him in thought, word and deed. The only place where she can be independent of him is in hell.

The self-immolation of widows on their deceased husbands' pyre[s] was evidently a custom invented by the priesthood after the code of Manu was compiled. The laws taught in the schools of Apastamba, Asvalayana and others older than Manu do not mention it, neither does the code of Manu. The code of Vishnu, which is comparatively recent, says that a woman 'after the death of her husband should either lead a virtuous life or ascend the funeral pile of her husband' (*Vishnu*, xxv, 2).

It is very difficult to ascertain the motives of those who invented the terrible custom of the so-called *Suttee*, which was regarded as a sublimely meritorious act. As Manu the greatest authority next to the Vedas, did not sanction this sacrifice, the priests saw the necessity of producing some text which would overcome the natural fears of the widow as well as silence the critic who should refuse to allow such a horrid rite without strong authority. So the priests said there was a text in the Rig-veda which, according to their own rendering reads thus:

Om! Let these women, not to be widowed, good wives, adorned with collyrium, holding clarified butter, consign themselves to the fire! Immortal, not childless, not husbandless, well adorned with gems, let them pass into the fire whose original element is water.

Here was an authority greater than that of Manu or of any other law-giver, which could not be disobeyed. The priests and their allies pictured heaven in the most beautiful colours and described various enjoyments so vividly that the poor widow became madly impatient to get to the blessed place in company with her departed husband. Not only was the woman assured of her getting into heaven by this sublime act, but also that by this great sacrifice she would secure salvation to herself and husband, and to their families [up] to the seventh generation. Be they even sinful, they would surely attain the highest bliss in heaven, and prosperity on earth. Who would not sacrifice herself if she were sure of such a result to herself and her loved ones? Besides this, she was conscious of the miseries and degradation to which she would be subjected now that she had survived her husband. The momentary agony of suffocation in the flames was nothing compared to her lot as a widow. She gladly consented and voluntarily offered herself to please the gods and men. The rite of *Suttee* is thus described:

The widow bathed, put on new and bright garments, and, holding kusha grass in her left hand, sipped water from her right palm, scattered some tila grains, and then, looking eastward, quietly said, 'Om! On this day I, such and such a one, of such a family, die in the fire, that I may meet Arundhati, and reside in *Svarga*; that the years of my sojourn there may be as many as the hairs upon my husband, many scores multiplied; that I may enjoy with him the facilities of heaven, and bless my maternal and paternal ancestors, and those of my lord's line; that, praised by Apsara I may go far through the fourteen regions of Indra; that pardon may be given to my lord's sins whether he have even killed a Brahman, broken the laws of gratitude and truth, or slain his friend. Now I do ascend this funeral pile of my husband, and I call upon you, guardians of the eight regions of the world, of sun, moon, air, of the fire, the ether, the earth and the water, and my own soul. Yama, king of Death, and you, Day, Night and Twilight, witness that I die for my beloved, by his side upon his funeral pile.' Is it wonderful that the passage of the Sati to her couch of flame was like a public festival, that the sick and sorrowful prayed her to touch them with her little, fearless, conquering hand, that criminals were let loose if she looked upon them, that the horse which carried her was never used again for earthly service? (E. Arnold)

The act was supposed to be altogether a voluntary one, and no doubt it was so in many cases. Some died for the love stronger than death which they cherished for their husbands. Some died not because they had been happy in this world, but because they believed with all the[ir] heart that they should be made happy hereafter. Some, to obtain great renown, for tombstones and monuments were erected to those who thus died, and afterwards the[ir] names were inscribed on the long list of family gods; others, again, to escape the thousand temptations, and sins and miseries which they knew would fall to their lot as widows. Those who from pure ambition or from momentary impulse, declared their intentions thus to die, very often shrank from the fearful altar; no sooner did they feel the heat of the flames than they tried to leap down and escape the terrible fate, but it was too late. They had taken the solemn oath which must never be broken, priests and other men were at hand to force them to remount the pyre. In Bengal, where this custom was most in practice, countless, fearful tragedies of this description occurred even after British rule was long established there. Christian missionaries petitioned the government to abolish this inhuman custom, but they were told that the social and religious customs of the people constituted no part of the business of the government, and that their rule in India might be endangered by such interference. The custom went on unmolested until the first quarter of the present century, when a man from among the Hindus, Raja Ram Mohun Roy, set his face against it, and declared that it was not sanctioned by the Veda as the priests claimed. He wrote many books on this subject, showing the wickedness of the act, and with the noble cooperation of a few friends, he succeeded at last in getting the government to abolish it. Lord William Bentick, when Governor-General of India, had the moral courage to enact the famous law of 1829, prohibiting the *Suttee* rite within British domains, and holding as criminals, subject to capital punishment, those who countenanced it. But it was not until 1844 that the law had any effect upon orthodox Hindu minds.

That the text quoted from the Veda was mistranslated, and a part of it forged, could have been easily shown had all Brahmans known the meaning of the Veda. The Vedic language is the oldest form of Sanskrit, and greatly differs from the later form. Many know the Vedas by heart and repeat them without a mistake, but few indeed are those that know the meaning of the texts they repeat. 'The Rigveda,' says Max Muller, 'so far from enforcing the burning of widows, shows clearly that this custom was not sanctioned during the earliest period of Indian history. According to the hymns of the Rigveda, and the Vedic ceremonial contained in the Grihya-sutras, the wife accompanies the corpse of her husband to the funeral pile, but she is there addressed with a verse taken from the Rigveda, and ordered to leave her husband and to return to the world of the living.

' "Rise, woman", it is said, "come to the world of life, thou sleepest nigh unto him whose life is gone. Come to us. Thou hast thus fulfilled the duties of a wife to the husband, who once took thy hand and made thee a mother."

'This verse is preceded by the very verse which the later Brahmins have falsified and quoted in support of their cruel tenet. The reading of the verse is beyond all doubt, for there is no various reading, in our sense of the word, in the whole of Rigveda. Besides, we have the commentaries and the ceremonials, and nowhere is there any difference to the text or its meaning. It is addressed to the other women who are present at the funeral, and who have to pour oil and butter on the pile.

'"May these women who are not widows, but have good husbands, draw near with oil and butter. These who are mothers may go up first to the altar, without tears, without sorrow, but decked with fine jewels."

It was by falsifying a single syllable that the unscrupulous priests managed to change entirely the meaning of the whole verse. Those who know the Sanskrit characters can easily understand that the falsification very likely originated in the carelessness of the transcriber or copyist, but for all that the priests who permitted the error are not excusable in the least. Instead of comparing the verse with its context, they translated it as their fancy dictated and thus under the pretext of religion they have been the cause of destroying countless lives for more than two thousand years.

Now that the *Suttee* rite, partly by the will of the people and partly by the law of the empire, is prohibited, many good people feel easy in their minds, thinking that the Hindu widow has been delivered from the hands of her terrible fate; but little do they realize the true state of affairs!

Throughout India, except in the Northwestern Provinces, women are put to the severest trial imaginable after the husband's death. The manner in which they are brought up and treated from their earliest childhood compels them to be slaves to their own petty little interests, to be passionate lovers of ornaments and of self-adornment, but no sooner does the husband die than they are deprived of every gold and silver ornament, of the bright-coloured garments, and of all the things they love to have about or on their persons. The cruelty of social customs does not stop here. Among the Brahmans of the Deccan, the heads of all widows must be shaved regularly every fortnight. Some of the lower castes, too, have adopted this custom of shaving widows' heads, and have much pride in imitating their high-caste brethren. What woman is there who does not love the wealth of soft and glossy hair with which nature has so generously decorated her head? A Hindu woman thinks it worse than death to lose her beautiful hair. Girls of fourteen and fifteen who hardly know the reason why they are so cruelly deprived of everything they like, are often seen wearing sad countenances, their eyes swollen from shedding bitter tears. They are glad to find a dark corner where they may hide their faces as if they have done something shameful and criminal. The widow must wear a single coarse garment, white, red or brown. She must eat only one meal during the twenty-four hours of a day. She must never take part in family feasts and jubilees, with others. She must not show herself to people on auspicious occasions. A man or woman thinks it unlucky to behold a widow's face before seeing any other object in the morning. A man will postpone his journey if his path happens to be crossed by a widow at the time of his departure.

A widow is called a 'inauspicious'. The name 'rand,' by which she is generally known, is the same thing that is borne by a Nautch girl or a harlot. The relatives and neighbours of the young widow's husband are always ready to call her bad names, and to address her in abusive language at every opportunity. There is scarcely a day of her life on which she is not cursed by these people as the cause of their beloved friend's death. The mother-in-law gives vent to her grief by using such language that, when once heard, burns into a human heart. In short, the young widow's life is rendered intolerable in every possible way. There may be exceptions to this rule, but, unhappily, they are not many. In addition to all this, the young widow is always looked upon with suspicion, and closely guarded as if she were a prisoner, for fear she may at any time bring disgrace upon the family by committing some improper act. The purpose of disfiguring her by shaving her head, by not allowing her to put ornaments or bright garments on her person, is to render her less attractive to a man's eye. Not allowing her to eat more than once a day, and compelling her to abstain from food altogether on sacred days, is a part of the discipline by which to mortify her youthful nature and desire. She is closely confined to the house, forbidden even to associate with her female friends as often as she wishes; no man except her father, brother, uncles and her aunt-cousins (who are regarded as brothers) is allowed to see or speak with her. Her life then, destitute as it is of the least literary knowledge, void of all hope, empty of every pleasure and social advantage, becomes intolerable, a curse to herself and to society at large. She has but few persons to sympathize with her. Her own parents, with whom she lives in case her husband has no relatives, or if his relatives are unable to take care of her, do, of course, sympathize with her, but custom and religious faith have a stronger hold upon them than parental love. They, too, regard their daughter with concern, lest she bring disgrace upon their family.

It is not an uncommon thing for a young widow, without occupation that may satisfy mind and heart, and unable [any] longer to endure the slights and suspicions to which she is perpetually subjected, to escape from her prison-home. But when she gets away from it, where shall she go? No respectable family, even of a lower caste, will have her for a servant. She is completely ignorant of any art by which she may make an honest living. She has nothing but the single garment which she wears on her person. Starvation and death stare her in the face; no ray of hope penetrates her densely-darkened mind. What can she do? The only alternative before her is either to commit suicide or, worse still, accept a life of infamy and shame. Oh, cruel is the custom that drives thousands of young widows to such a fate. Here is a prayer by a woman doomed to lifelong misery, which will describe her own and her sisters' feelings better than any words of mine. It was written by a pupil of a British Zenana missionary,[5] one of the few Hindu women who can read and write, and one who has tasted the bitter sorrows and degradation of Hindu widowhood from her childhood.

Oh Lord, hear my prayer! No one has turned an eye on the oppression that we poor women suffer, though with weeping, and crying and desire, we have turned to all sides, hoping that some one would save us. No one has lifted up his eyelids to look upon us, nor inquire into our case. We have searched above and below, but Thou art the only One who wilt hear our complaint. Thou knowest our impotence, our degradation, our dishonour. O Lord, inquire into our case. For ages, dark ignorance has brooded over our minds and spirits; like a cloud of dust it rises and wraps us round, and we are like prisoners in an old and mouldering house, choked and buried in the dust of custom, and we have no strength to go out. Bruised and beaten, we are like the dry husks of the sugarcane when the sweet juice has been extracted. All-knowing God, hear our prayer! Forgive our sins and give us power of escape, that we may see something of thy world. O Father, when shall we be set free from this jail? For what sin have we been born to live in this prison? From Thy throne of judgment justice flows, but it does not reach us; in this, our lifelong misery, only injustice comes near us.

Thou hearer of prayer, if we have sinned against Thee, forgive, but we are too ignorant to know what sin is. Must the punishment of sin fall on those who are too ignorant to know what it is? O great Lord, our name is written with drunkards, with lunatics, with imbeciles, with the very animals; as they are not responsible, we are not. Criminals, confined in jails for life, are happier than we, for they know something of Thy world. They were not born in prison, but we have not for one day, no, not even in our dreams, seen Thy world; to us it is nothing but a name; and not having seen the world, we cannot know thee, its maker. Those who have seen Thy works may learn to understand Thee, but for us, who are shut in, it is not possible to learn to know Thee. We see only four walls of the house. Shall we call them the world, or India? We have been born in this jail, we have died here, and are dying. O Father of the world, hast Thou not created us? Or has perchance, some other god made us? Dost Thou care only for men? Hast Thou no thought for us women? Why hast Thou created us male and female? O Almighty, hast Thou not power to make us other than we are, that we too might have some share in the comforts of this life? The cry of the oppressed is heard even in the world. Then canst Thou look upon our victim hosts, and shut Thy doors of justice? O God Almighty and Unapproachable, think upon Thy mercy, which is a vast sea, and remember us. O Lord, save us, for we cannot bear our hard lot; many of us have killed ourselves, and we are still killing ourselves. O God of mercy, our prayer to Thee is this, that the curse may be removed from the women of India. Create in the hearts of the men some sympathy, that our lives may no longer be passed in vain longing, that saved by Thy mercy, we may taste something of the joys of life.

A Hindu gentleman contributes an article entitled 'The Hindu Widow,' to *The Nineteenth Century*. I quote from this as testimony from the other sex, of the truthfulness of my statement, lest I should appear to exaggerate the miserable condition to which my sister-widows are doomed for life:

The widow who has no parents has to pass her whole life under the roof of her father-in-law, and then she knows no comfort whatever. She has to meet from her late husband's relations only unkind looks and unjust reproaches. She has to work like a slave, and for the reward of all her drudgery she only receives hatred and abhorrence from her mother-in-law and sisters-in-law. If there is any disorder in the domestic arrangements of the family, the widow is blamed and cursed for it. Among Hindus, women cannot inherit any paternal property, and if a widow is left any property by her husband she cannot call it her own. All her wealth belongs to her son, if she has any, and if she has nobody to inherit it she is made to adopt an heir, and give him all her property directly he comes of age, and herself live on a bare allowance granted by him. Even death cannot save a widow from indignities. For when a wife dies she is burnt in the clothes she had on, but a widow's corpse is covered with a coarse white cloth, and there is little ceremony at her funeral.

. . .

'The English have abolished sati (suttee), but alas! neither the English nor the angels know what goes on in our houses, and the Hindus not only do not care, but think it good!' Such were the words of a widow; and well might she exclaim that 'neither the English nor the angels know, and that the Hindus not only don't care, but think it good'; for Hindu as I am, I can vouch for her statement that very few Hindus have a fair knowledge of the actual sufferings of the widows among them, and fewer still care to know the evils and horrors of the barbarous customs which victimises their own sisters and daughters in so ruthless a manner; nay, on the contrary, the majority of the orthodox Hindus consider the practice to be good and salutary. Only the Hindu widows know their own sufferings; it is perfectly impossible for any other mortal, or even 'the angels,' (as the widow says) to realise them. One can easily imagine how hard the widow's lot must be . . . when to the continuous course of fastings, self-inflictions and humiliations is added the galling ill-treatment which she receives from her own relations and friends. To a Hindu widow, death is a thousand times more welcome than her miserable existence. It is no doubt this feeling that drove in former times many widows to immolate themselves on the funeral pyres of their dead husbands. (Devendra N. Das, *The Nineteenth Century*, September 1886.)

There is a class of reformers who think that they will meet all the wants of widows by establishing the re-marriage system. This system should certainly be introduced for the benefit of the infant widows who wish to marry on coming to age; but at the same time, it should be remembered that this alone is incapable and insufficient to meet their wants.

In the first place, widow-marriage among the high-caste people will not for a long time become an approved custom. The old idea is too deeply rooted in the heart of society to be soon removed. Second, there are not many men who will boldly come forward and marry widows, even if the widows wish it. It is one thing to talk about doing things contrary to the approved custom, but to practise [it] is quite another matter. It is now about fifty years since the movement called widow-marriage among the high-caste Hindus was started, but those who have practised it are but few. I have known men of great learning and high reputation who took oaths to the effect that if they were to become widowers and wished to marry again they would marry widows. But no sooner had their first wives died than they forgot all about the oaths and married pretty little maidens. Society threatens them with excommunication, their friends and relatives entreat them with tears in their eyes, others offer money and maids if they will consent to give up the idea of marrying a widow. Can flesh and blood resist these temptations? If some men wish to be true to their convictions, they must be prepared to suffer perpetual martyrdom. After marrying a widow they are sure to be cut off from all connection with society and friends, and even with their nearest relatives. In such a case, no faithful Hindu would ever give them assistance if they were to fall in distress or become unable to earn their daily bread; they will be ridiculed and hated by all men. How many people are there in the world who would make this tremendous sacrifice on the altar of conscience? The persecution to be endured by people who transgress established customs is so great that life becomes a burden. A few years ago, a high-caste man in Cutch (Northwestern India) ventured to marry a widow, but to endure the persecution which ensued was beyond his power, and the wretched fellow was soon after found dead, having committed suicide.

Re-marriage, therefore, is not available, nor would it be at all times desirable, as a mitigation of the sufferer's lot. So, the poor, helpless high-caste widow with the one chance of ending her miseries in the Suttee rite taken away from her, remains as in ages past with none to help her.

7. HOW THE CONDITION OF WOMEN TELLS UPON SOCIETY

Those who have done their best to keep women in a state of complete dependence and ignorance, vehemently deny that this has anything to do with the present degradation of the Hindu nation. I pass over the hundreds of nonsenses which are brought forward as the strongest reasons for keeping women in ignorance and dependence. They have already been forced out into the broad day-light of a generous civilization, and have been put to the fiery proof of science and found wanting. Above all, the noble example of thousands of women in many countries have burned the so-called reasons to ashes. But their ghosts are still hovering over the land of the Hindus and are frightening the timid and the ignorant to death. Let us hope that in God's good time, all these devils shall be forever cast out of India's body; meanwhile, it is our duty to take the matter into serious consideration, and to put forth our best endeavours to hasten the glad day for India's daughters, aye, and for her sons also; because in spite of the proud assertions of our brethren that they have not suffered from the degradation of women, their own condition betrays but too plainly the contrary.

Since men and women are indissolubly united by providence as members of the same body of human society, each must suffer when their fellow-members suffer, whether they will confess it or not. In the animal as well as in the vegetable kingdom, nature demands that all living beings shall freely comply with its conditions of growth or they cannot become that which they were originally designed to be. Why should any exception to this law be made for the *purdah* women? Closely confined to the four walls of their house, deprived throughout their lives of the opportunity to breathe healthy, fresh air, or to drink in the wholesome sunshine, they become weaker and weaker from generation to generation, their physical statures dwarfed, their spirits crushed under the weight of social prejudices and superstitions, and their minds starved from absolute lack of literary food and of opportunity to observe the world. Thus fettered, in ninety cases out of a hundred, at the least, they grow to be selfish slaves to their petty individual interests, indifferent to the welfare of their own immediate neighbours, and much more [so] to their nation's well-being. How could these imprisoned mothers be expected to bring forth children better than themselves, for as the tree and soil are, so shall the fruit be. Consequently we see all around us in India a generation of men least deserving that exalted appellation.

The doctrine of 'pre-natal influence' can nowhere be more satisfactorily proved than in India. The mother's spirits being depressed, and mind as well as body weakened by the monotony and inactivity of her life, the unborn child cannot escape the evil consequences. The men of Hindustan do not, when babes, suck from the mother's breast true patriotism, and in their boyhood, the mother, poor woman, is unable to develop that divine faculty in them owing to her utter ignorance of the past and present condition of her native land. Fault finding with neighbours, bitter feelings towards tyran [nical] relatives expressed in words and actions, selfish interest in personal and family affairs, these are the chief lessons that children learn at the mother's knee, from babyhood up to the seventh or eighth year of age.

Again, how does it come to pass that each succeeding generation grows weaker than the one preceding it, if not because the progenitors of each generation lack the mental and physical strength which children are desired to inherit? The father may have been free and healthy in mind, as well as in body, but the mother was not; she undoubtedly has bequeathed the fatal legacy of weakness and dullness to her children. The complete submission of women under the Hindu law has in the lapse of thousands millenniums of years converted them into slavery-loving creatures. They are glad to lean upon anyone and be altogether dependent, and thus it has come to pass that their sons as a race desire to depend upon some other nation, and not upon themselves. The seclusion, complete dependence and the absolute ignorance forced upon the mothers of our nation have been gradually and fatally telling upon the mental and physical health of the men, and in these last times they have borne the poisonous fruit that will compel the Hindu nation to die a miserable and prolonged death if a timely remedy is not taken to them.

Moreover, the Hindu woman's ignorance prevents liberal-minded and progressive men from making necessary and important changes in the manners and habits of the household; bigoted women also prevent their husbands and sons from such important enterprises as crossing the ocean in the pursuit of useful knowledge, or for purposes of trade.

To add to all the disabilities of the Hindu mother in the discharge of her sacred maternal duties, she is as a rule, wholly ignorant of the commonest hygienic laws. It must be remembered that she is herself a girl, scarcely out of her babyhood, when she becomes a mother. At about fourteen, fifteen or sixteen years of age she cannot be expected to know all that is necessary in order to take good care of her child. The first and second children of this young mother usually die, and if they survive, they are apt to grow up to be weak and unhealthy adults. Until they are seven or eight years of age, the children of the household are left to themsleves without anyone to take care of them, and no influence is exerted to mould their character at this most interesting and important period of life. Who but an intelligent and loving mother can do this all-important work for her children at that age?

Having thus far endeavoured to bring to the notice of Western women the condition of a class of their oriental sisters, I now desire to direct their attention definitely to our chief needs. After many years of careful observation and thought, I have come to the conclusion that the chief needs of high-caste Hindu women are: first, Self-Reliance; second, Education; and third, Native Women Teachers.

1. Self-reliance:

The state of complete dependence in which men are required by the law-giver to keep women from birth to the end of their lives makes it impossible for them to have self-reliance without which a human, being becomes a pitiful parasite. Women of the working classes are better off than their sisters of high castes in India, for in many cases they are obliged to depend upon themselves, and an opportunity for cultivating self-reliance is thus afforded them by which they largely profit. But high-caste women, unless their families are actually destitute of means to keep them, are shut up within the four walls of their house. In after-time, if they are left without a protector, i.e. a male relative to support and care for them, they literally do not know what to do with themselves. They have been so cruelly cropped in their early days that self-reliance and energy are dead within them; helpless victims of indolence and false timidity they are easily frightened out of their wits and have little or no strength to withstand the trials and difficulties which must be encountered by a person on her way toward progress. But it is idle to hope that the condition of my country-women will ever improve without individual self-reliance; therefore, is it not the duty of our Western sisters to teach them how they may become self-reliant?[5]

2. Education:

The lack of education among the women of India can be fairly realized by scanning the Report of the Educational Commission for 1883, and the census returns of 1880–81. Of the 99,700,000 women and girls directly under British rule, ninetynine and one half millions are returned as unable to read and write, the remaining two hundred thousand who are able either to read or write cannot all be reckoned as educated, for the school-going period of a girl is generally between seven and nine years of age; within that short time she acquires little more than an ability to read the second or the third vernacular reading-book, and a little knowledge of arithmetic which usually comprehends no more than the four simple rules. It should be remembered that the two hundred thousand women able to read or write are the 'alumnae' of the government schools, mission schools, private schools conducted by the inhabitants of India independently, private societies and Zenana mission agencies all reckoned together. It is surprising how even this small number of women can have acquired the limited knowledge indicated, when we consider the powers and principalities that are incessantly fighting against female education in India. Girls of nine and ten, when recently out of school and given in marriage, are wholly cut off from reading or writing, because it is a shame for a young woman or girl to hold a paper or book in her hand, or to read in the presence of others in her husband's house. It is a popular belief among high-caste women that their husbands will die if they should read or should hold a pen in their fingers. The fear of becoming a widow overcomes their hunger and thirst for knowledge. Moreover, the little wives can get but scanty time to devote to self-culture; anyone fortunate enough to possess the desire and able to command the time is in constant fear of being seen by her husband's relatives. Her employment cannot long be kept secret where everyone is on the lookout, and when discovered, she is ridiculed, laughed at and even commanded by the elders to leave this nonsense. Her literary pursuits are now at an end unless the proceedings of the elders be interfered with by her progressive husband; but alas, such husbands are extremely rare. Our schools, too, are not very attractive to children; the teachers of primary schools (and it is to these schools that girls are usually sent) are but nominally educated, and do not know how to make the lessons interesting for children. Consequently a great many of the girls who have been educated up to the second or third standard (grade) in these primary schools make it their business quickly to forget their lessons as soon as they find an opportunity. Shut in from the world and destitute of the ability to engage in newspaper- and useful book-reading, they have little or no knowledge of common things around them, and of the most important events that are daily occurring in their own or foreign lands. Ignorant, unpatriotic, selfish and uncultivated, they drag the men down with them into the dark abyss where they dwell together without hope, without ambition to be something or to do something in the world.

3. Native Women Teachers:

American and English women, as Zenana missionaries, are doing all they can to elevate and enlighten India's daughters. These good people deserve respect and praise from all, and the heartfelt thanks of those for whose elevation they toil, but the disabilities of an unfriendly climate, and of an unknown tongue make it exceedingly difficult for them to enter upon their work for some time after reaching India; and then, 'what are these among so many?' They are literally lost among the nearly one hundred millions of women under British rule to whom must be added several millions more under Hindu and Mahomedan rule. In America and in England we hear encouraging reports from mission fields, which state that a few thousand Hindu and Mahomedan women and girls are being instructed in schools or in their own homes, but these seem as nothing compared to the vast multitude of the female population of Hindustan. In a country where castes and the seclusion of women are regarded as essential tenets of the national creed, we can scarcely hope for a general spread of useful knowledge among women, through either men of their own race or through foreign women. All experience in the history of mankind has shown that efforts for the elevation of a nation must come from within and work outward to be effectual.

The one thing needful, therefore, for the general diffusion of education among women in India is a body of persons from among themselves who shall make it their life-work to teach, by precept and example, their fellow-countrywomen.

8. THE APPEAL

In the preceding chapters [sections] I have tried to tell my readers briefly the sad story of my country-women, and also to bring to their notice what are our chief needs. We, the women of India, are hungering and thirsting for knowledge; only education under God's grace, can give us the needful strength to rise up from our degraded condition.

Our most pressing want, and one which must immediately be met, is women teachers of our own nationality. How can these women teachers be supplied? I have long been thinking over this matter and now I am prepared to give answer.

Among the inhabitants of India, the high-caste people rank as the most intelligent; they have been a refined and cultivated race for more than two thousand years. The women of these castes have been and still are kept in ignorance, yet they have inherited from their fathers, to a certain degree, quickness of perception and intelligence. A little care and judicious education bestowed upon them will make many of them competent teachers and able workers. That this statement is not altogether visionary on my part, has been proven by the gratifying results of careful training in the person of Chandramukhi Bose, MA, now lady principal of Bethune School, Calcutta, Kadambini B. Ganguli, BA, MB, and also others who have successfully passed their examinations in Calcutta University. The professors of the Woman's Medical College of Pennsylvania will bear testimony to the ability of the late Dr Anandibai Joshee. Had her life been spared a little longer, she would have shown–the world that the Hindu woman, in spite of all drawbacks, equals any woman of civilized countries.

Again, according to the census of 1881 there were in India 20,930,626 widows, of all ages and castes. Among these were 669,100 widows under nineteen years of age, viz.:

[Nine and] under nine years of age	78,976
From 10 to 14 years of age	207,388
From 15 to 19 years of age	382,736
	669,100

Girls of nine and ten, or thirteen years of age, whose betrothed husbands are dead, are virgin widows, and these, if of high-caste families, must remain single throughout life. Now, if there were suitable educational institutions where young widows who might wish to be independent of their relatives and make an honest living for themselves, might go to be instructed in useful handiwork, and educated [as] teachers, many horrid occurrences might be prevented, and at the same time, these widows would prove a welcome blessing to their countrywomen. But alas!, institutions have not been founded anywhere in India where high-caste widows can receive shelter and education.

In the year 1866, an eminent English lady Miss Mary Carpenter, made a short tour in India, with a view to find some way by which women's condition in that country might be improved. She at once discovered that the chief means by which the desired end might be accomplished was by furnishing women teachers for the Hindu zenanas. She suggested that the British government should establish normal schools for training women teachers and that scholarships should be awarded to girls in order to prolong their school-going period, and to assist indigent women, who would otherwise be unable to pursue their studies. In response to Miss Carpenter's appeal upon her return to England, the British government founded several schools for women in India, and in honour of this good lady a few 'Mary Carpenter Scholarships' were endowed by benevolent persons. These schools, which I have personally inspected, were opened to women of every caste, and while they have undoubtedly been of use, they have not realized the hopes of their founder, partly because of the impossibility of keeping caste-rules [i.e. observing one's caste practices] in them, and partly on account of the inadequacy of the arrangements for attendance. When a high-caste widow takes it upon herself to go to school, she cannot hope, except in cases which are extremely rare, to receive any kind of help from her own relatives; so she is thrown out a penniless, helpless, forlorn creature, to face the world alone. If then she is so fortunate as to be sheltered in a normal school and is awarded a [scholar]ship, she finds this scarcely enough to keep her from starvation, its money value being from twelve to twenty or twenty-five dollars per year; but she cannot get even this scanty support from the Education Department, unless she pass[es] a certain examination. How can an illiterate widow hope to pass that examination?

Besides these government normal schools for women, of which at the present time, there are probably six throughout India, there are a few foreign mission schools where a woman may find shelter and instruction, but if she be an orthodox Hindu by faith, and of a respectable family, she will on no account take refuge with people of a strange religion and country. There are exceptions of course to this statement, but as a rule, a high-caste Hindu woman prefers death to this alternative. She knows that if she goes to live with missionaries, she must lose caste, and that she must study their Bible, and perhaps in the end be induced to forsake her ancestral faith and embrace a strange one. No woman of any religion, in which she firmly believes, whether it appear to others to be true or false, would violate her conscience simply for food and shelter. That the fear of being tempted to abjure one's religion, for the sake of worldly gain should prevent many an excellent Hindu widow from going to foreign missionary schools is undoubted. She honestly believes that if her life is rendered intolerable by domestic misery she can drown herself in some sacred river by which deed she will not only escape the wretchedness of this life, but her past sins will be forgiven, and a place in heaven secured, but to forsake her ancestral religion under any circumstances would doom her to eternal perdition in the world to come.

Is there then no way of helping and educating these high-caste widows? Can none of these obstacles be removed from her path? Yes! they can be removed, and the course which in my judgment can most advantageously be taken in order to succour the widows and the women of India in general, may be stated as follows:

1. Houses should be opened for the young and high-caste child-widows where they can take shelter without the fear of losing their caste, or of being disturbed in their religious belief and where they may have entire freedom of action as relates to caste-rules, such as cooking of food, etc., provided they do not violate the rules or disturb the peace of the house wherein they have taken up their abode.

2. In order to help them make an honourable and independent living, they should be taught in these houses to be teachers, governesses, nurses and housekeepers, and should become skilled in other forms of hand-work [sic], according to their taste and capacity.

3. These houses should be under the superintendence and management of influential Hindu ladies and gentlemen, who should be pledged to make each house a happy home and an instructive institution for those who seek its opportunities.

4. The services of well-qualified American ladies as assistants and teachers should be secured in order to afford the occupants of the houses the combined advantage of Eastern and Western civilization and education.

5. Libraries containing the best books on history, science, art, religions and other departments of literature should be established in these houses for the benefit of their inmates and of other women in their vicinity who may wish to read. Lectureships should also be established in the libraries, and the lecturers should be engaged with the distinct understanding that they do not speak irreverently of any religion or sacred custom while lecturing in that house or library; the lecturers should embrace in their topics, hygiene,

geography, elementary science, foreign travel, etc. and the lectures should be designed primarily to open the eyes and ears of those who long have dwelt in the prison-house of ignorance, knowing literally nothing of God's beautiful world.

It is my intention after my return home (which I trust I may be within a year from this time) to establish at least one such institution. I am fully aware of the great responsibility the trial—and it may be [a] failure—will involve; but as someone must make a beginning, I am resolved to try, trusting that God, who knows the need of my countrywomen, will raise up able workers to forward this cause, whether I succeed in it or not. The great majority of my countrypeople being most bitterly opposed to the education of women, there is little hope of my getting from them either good words or pecuniary aid.

For the present, it is useless to reason with high-caste Hindu gentlemen concerning this matter; they only ridicule the proposal or silently ignore it. There are some among them who would certainly approve and would help to carry the idea into effect, but they must first realize its advantage and see its good results. One must have the power of performing miracles to induce this class of men to receive the gospel of society's well-being through the elevation of woman. Such a miracle, I have faith to believe, will be performed in India before the end of the next ten years, and if this be true, the enterprise will prove self-supporting after that period with only native aid. There is even now a handful of Hindus entertaining progressive ideas, who are doing all they can to reform the religious and social customs of Hindustan and who will, without doubt, support my work from the beginning; but they have little with which to forward the cause except their personal services.

An institution of the kind indicated, where the pupils must be supported and the foreign teachers liberally paid for their services, cannot be founded and afterwards kept in a flourishing condition without money. Therefore I invite all good women and men of the United States to give me their help liberally in whatever way they may be able for a period of about ten years; it is my solemn belief that it is the most sacred duty of those who dwell in this highly-favoured land to bestow freely talents of whatever kind they may possess to help forward this educational movement. I venture to make this appeal because I believe that those who regard the preaching of the gospel of our Lord Jesus Christ to the heathen so important as to spend in its accomplishment millions of money [sic] and hundreds of valuable lives will deem it of the first importance to prepare the way for the spread of the gospel by throwing open the locked doors of the Indian zenanas, which cannot be done safely without giving suitable education to the women, whereby they will be able to bear the dazzling light of the outer world and the perilous blasts of social persecution.

Mothers and fathers [in the United States], compare the condition of your own sweet darlings at your happy firesides with that of millions of little girls of a corresponding age in India, who have already been sacrificed on the unholy altar of an inhuman social custom, and then ask yourselves whether you can stop short of doing something to rescue the little widows from the hands of their tormentors. Millions of heart-rending cries are daily rising from within the stony walls of Indian zenanas; thousands of child-widows are annually dying without a ray of hope to cheer their hearts, and other thousands are daily being crushed under a fearful weight of sin and shame, with no one to prevent their ruin by providing for them a better way.

Will you not, all of you who read this book, think of these, my countrywomen, and rise, moved by a common impulse, to free them from lifelong slavery and infernal misery? I beg you, friends and benefactors, educators and philanthropists, all who have any interest in or compassion for your fellow-creatures, let the cry of India's daughters, feeble though it be, reach your ears and stir your hearts. In the name of humanity, in the name of your sacred responsibilities as workers in the cause of humanity, and, above all, in the most holy name of God, I summon you, true women and men of America, to bestow your help quickly, regardless of nation, caste or creed.

NOTES

1. Ramabai was evidently speaking from personal experience, having earlier married a non-Brahman, whom she described in A *Testimony* as 'belonging to the Shudra caste'. Ramabai herself had no family left at the time, but the couple were ostracized by her husband's family.
2. This episode describes Ramabai's own parents' marriage at Paithan.
3. In fact, this ancient injunction advising the husband to drag his errant wife home, was cited by *Kesari* during the Rakhmabai case for the Restitution of Conjugal Rights which Ramabai mentions in this chapter (together with her sister's, similar, case). See Kosambi (1996a).

4. The reference is to Ramabai's older sister Krishnabai.

5. Zenana missionaries were the women missionaries who had obtained the family patriarchs' permission to teach the women in their secluded quarters. Special Zenana missions were also established by several Christian denominations for the purpose of reaching women in their homes.

6. Ramabai's next book, a Marathi description of the United States, with a detailed account of the American women's movement, was designed to serve just this purpose.

6

RELIGIOUS DENOMINATIONS
AND CHARITIES IN THE USA
(translated from *United Stateschi
Lokasthiti ani Pravasavritta*)

In England the denomination known as the Church of England
is integrated with the power of the monarchy. The King or Queen
of England must belong to this denomination, and all the subjects of that country must bear the expenses of its bishops, etc. The
Government extracts a heavy tax from them, whether or not they
belong to that denomination, and donates it to the bishops of 'The
Church' and their disciples. This practice of extracting forced obei-
sance, in a progressive country like England, is very strange indeed.
It is even said that the bishops and other clergymen of the Church of
England who go to our country to perform ecclesiastical duties for
the Government are paid fat salaries from the Treasury of India,
although I do not know whether this is true. If it is, then that too is
a marvel.

In the United States, no religious denomination is integrated with
the power of the people,[1] therefore all the people here[2] accept any
denomination which agrees with their own way of thinking; and the
money they give for defraying the expenses of the churches, clergymen,
etc. of that denomination, is given voluntarily. The Government does
not levy a separate tax on them on account of religion. Even so, religion
is not any the less strong here than in England. In England, only the
Church of England gets high respect, because it is the denomination

supported by the monarchy. The adherents of that denomination turn up their noses at the followers of other denominations as 'dissenters' (i.e. holding different beliefs). In the free States of America, no one publicly accords greater respect to one denomination than to another, because no one has heard of any particular denomination as being especially favoured by those in power.

Many people in England claim that people would become irreligious, if the Government did not provide for the support of religion. But this claim of the English is totally false, because in England there are 144 churches per 100,000 people[3], whereas in the United States there are 181 churches for the same number of people. This disproves the claim that religious belief is less strong in the United States, where religion is not supported by the Government.

In the year 1880, there were 92,000 churches in the United States, of which more than 80,000 were built by Protestants and the rest belonged to the Roman Catholics. The total moveable and immoveable property of all these churches amounts to 350,000,000 dollars, or more than about 1,000,000,000 rupees. There are a total of 77,000 clergymen of various denominations. About a hundred and fifty years ago, there was a strong denominational discord in this country. The Puritans of Massachusetts felt a deep hatred for the followers of other denominations. They persecuted many Quakers. They accused women of many other denominations of witchcraft and burnt them alive; they hanged some people and imprisoned others. They whipped some like animals right in the streets, and exiled others after wresting away their property. In the year 1705, the State Government of Virginia passed a resolution that whosoever denies that God is a Trinity and that the Bible is a divinely inspired book, should be punished with three years' imprisonment. And should he deny these things yet again, it should be made very difficult for him to get Government employment, etc.

In the latter part of the eighteenth century, when the American people were trying to sever their political ties with England and become independent, they put aside their internal denominational differences and acted unitedly. In the fear that their country would acquire a permanent stamp of English political power and of 'The Church' if they did not act in accord at the time, they abandoned their denominational differences, put up a united fight against England and became independent. For the same reason, even now these people disregard denominational differences and act unitedly, and will continue to do so. It is not that there is no denominational prejudice in this country. However, because equal freedom is available to all in matters of religion, people prefer not to pay undue attention to and argue about each other's beliefs, and enjoy a great deal of mutual social intercourse. Therefore one would find more examples in this country than in England, of people belonging to different denominations who have friendly dealings with each other. . . . The people here have largely given up the habit of looking for faults among those belonging to other denominations in their own country and religion. Most of the people in the United States are Christians among whom there are two chief denominations, Roman Catholics and Protestants, and numerous subdivisions. Their differences may be denominational, but not religious. These denominational differences do not obstruct any work for the national good.[††] One finds cases of husband and wife or parents and children, in the same family, belonging to different denominations, although their natural love for one another remains undiminished.

Since the establishment of the nation of the United States to the present day, no single religious denomination has received special patronage from the Government; nor will this happen in the future. The Government is concerned with religious denominations to the same extent that it is with medicine, agriculture or general trade and commerce, and not more. . . .

[††]The people of our own country should give this matter serious thought. Although we belong to different denominations and religions, we can and must unite in the work of the national and public good. We may believe that by following a particular religion or denomination we will go to a special, superior place in the next world, and our neighbours who belong to another denomination or religion will go to a quite different place; but such a belief should be limited to the next world. At least in this world we have to live in the same country and on the same earth. At least in this world we do not find that the excellent divine gifts, such as sunlight, rain, wind, earth, etc. are available only to us and not to those of other [religious] beliefs. When we can see that the Divine Grace which is shown to us, is shown in exactly the same degree to our brothers and sisters belonging to other religions and denominations, why should we not treat them with friendship, courtesy and love? Why should we not unite in the work of national and public good? Hindus, Mahommedans, Christians, Shaivites, Vaishnavites, devotees of Ganapati, Shias, Sunnis, Episcopalians, Presbyterians, Methodists, Unitarians, Trinitarians and believers in thirty-three crore gods—all these should put aside religious animosity and unite themselves in order to serve the country.

In England there is . . . an unfortunate practice, that every church owns large landed property, that is to say, that land has been assigned to each church. This land is leased out to other people as a source of income; the leaseholder can utilize the holy land for any unholy purpose, as long as the church earns an income. There are many liquor-distilleries and liquor-stores on such land. How very surprising that the money which is to be utilized for saving people is acquired by destroying people! Here [in America] there is very little land attached to churches. Some years ago this country also had the practice of leasing church lands to all and sundry. There was a Methodist church in which people would sing psalms above while the basement was rented for storing liquor. Another strange thing was that, while this country was engaged in the slave trade, these [church] people did not feel ashamed to accept money from the sale of slaves, and spend it on church expenditure and on good deeds like evangelization. They were firmly convinced that God had created the Black people of Africa, like cattle, for their own wilful use; why then should it matter if the money from their sale was used for religious deeds? In our own country, the three [upper] castes including the Brahmans also believed that the people of the Shudra caste were created by God only to serve them, and that such service was their only means of salvation. People in a state of barbarity always hold such evil beliefs. For a person to make others toil for him mercilessly without payment, and, moreover, to act as if he has conferred a favour on them by allowing them to serve him and thus opening the way for their salvation—is this not barbarity? Equally barbaric is the utterly demonic practice of selling human blood and using the proceeds for the salvation of other people and for evangelization. It is a matter for rejoicing that such practices have now ceased altogether in the United States.

Here, the expenses of churches as well as those of the clergy are defrayed from charitable donations by the people. The preacher of a church that has a congregation of five hundred gets an average monthly salary of two hundred dollars. In addition, persons appointed to look after the church also have to be paid high salaries. The chairs, benches, lamps, mats, carpets, etc. in the church also cost a great deal. (The churches here are very well decorated.) The congregation pays a contribution to cover all this expense. Every Sunday, after the morning and evening service, the persons appointed by the managing body of the church go around the congregation with plates in hand; it is customary for people to put whatever money they can afford in the plate, to be used for religious purposes. There is another way of earning money which should be mentioned here, although I do not approve of it. A rent is charged for the benches or chairs in the front portion of the church; they are reserved for those who pay. It is not proper that such trade should be carried on in the Lord's prayer-house, and that only the rich should be in a better position to hear the sermon. A great deal of money is earned in this manner. At pilgrimage places like Gaya, there is a nonsensical belief that only the ancestors of one who pays the priests well, attain a higher state; this is a similar belief. It is not to be supposed that all the people who rent the front pews are religious; there are many hypocrites among them. It is considered a sign of gentility, that is, refinement, to go to church every Sunday with one's whole family. So there are many people who go to church, even without piety in their hearts. There are also many here who give to charity only for the sake of publicity. For their generous charitable gifts they may not be awarded lengthy honours by their Government, such as Baronet, GCSI, CSI, CIE, etc. awarded by our Government there [in India]; however, they do get a great deal of publicity in the newspapers.

Not even all these means can defray all the expenses of the church, therefore the women here employ various means to collect large amounts of money for religious expenditure. Women constitute two-thirds of the congregation; and about half the money needed for church expenses comes from them. I think it is doubtful whether these religious organizations would have been able to continue to function in the absence of women. Men are not concerned about the livelihood of the clergy as women are. In our country, women are never empty-handed when they attend Purana recitals or go to the temple. They place some money, betel-nut, flower, fruit, or at least a handful of rice before the Puranika. (When menfolk go to the temple, they usually content themselves by sounding the bell with their empty hands.) Thus most of the priests and Puranikas are supported by the charity of women. Even so, the . . . pious Puranikas tell people: 'Women are inherently evil. The Creator has made them by combining everything that is evil in Creation. They are shackles on men's legs, and the cause of the destruction of religion. Those who desire salvation should not see their faces. Women should not have the right to study the Shastras, they should not read the Vedas, they should not preach;

women alone are the cause of men's destruction in this world.' Indeed the conduct and preaching of these Puranikas show the height of gratitude! In olden times, even in this country, men harboured similar derogatory and strange beliefs regarding women. They said that women should never preach. Many people went so far as to believe that women should not even sing psalms. Although this belief has not yet disappeared altogether, it is on the decline. Of the total of 77,000 preachers in the United States, 165 are women. Twenty years ago, there were hardly four or five. At the time it was considered to be highly improper for a woman to preach.

Like Christians in other countries, these people also observe Sunday as a holy day. On Sunday, trading and businesses are closed in almost all places. . . . All Government offices, public and private schools, and factories are closed on Sunday. On that holy day, religious men and women go to church, pray to God and listen to sermons. They consider evangelization to be a part of their religion, and invite everybody to their churches. Although there is no religious education in schools, most people teach their children religion at home every day. . . The schools held in churches every Sunday for preaching to children and adults are called Sunday Schools.

The people here are also greatly concerned about preaching to the new settlers in this country, and about leading them on the right path. The societies which evangelize in this manner are called Home Missions. There are a large number of men and women who work day and night to evangelize, with utmost sincerity. They believe that a person cannot obtain spiritual salvation except through the Christian religion; therefore they spend a great deal of money on propagating their religion in foreign countries. Hundreds of men and women in this country have left their homes, comforts and conveniences, etc. only for the sake of religion, to travel far and wide for the welfare of people in foreign countries. About a hundred years ago, some American missionaries went to our country. At the time the [East India] Company Government did not allow them to evangelize within their territories. They made no headway in Bengal and Madras [Presidencies]. Many of them lost their wives, and they suffered great hardships. Then they came to Bombay [Island]. Even there the Government did not wish them to stay. But in the end the English Government allowed them to stay for fear of public censure if they drove out of their territory the harmless people who had come to evangelize.[4] The climate of Bombay did not agree with them, nor was the Government favourable to them; and the local people hated and harassed them. They had no protector in that foreign land, and their own country was far away. Also, the means of travelling to and from their country were not as widely and easily available as now. In spite of all these obstacles, they continued their work. At present they have thirty to thirty-five societies in India. Their efforts are in accordance with the words of Christ: 'Go ye into all the world, and preach the gospel to every creature.' It would be totally wrong to suppose that all those who contribute money to such evangelical work are rich. It is the poor who help a great deal in this work. Here the rich are not much concerned about religion; . . . In New York, there is a huge play-house, known as the Italian Opera House, built by seventy rich local residents. It cost 9,800,000 dollars, to which 140,000 dollars each were contributed by those seventy! They spend money on luxuries; help for evangelization comes from the poor.

Although these people are convinced that those who are not Christians will go to eternal hell, they spend only 5,500,000 dollars on this effort. Today, there are at least ten million people in the United States who listen to sermons in churches and belong to one of the Christian denominations. Their wealth increases by about 310,000,000 dollars every year, and they own one-fifth of the total wealth of this country, which amounts to 8,728,400,000 dollars (that is, 26,185,200,000 rupees). Such wealthy people spend only 16,500,000 rupees per year to support evangelization. This religious expenditure is only 159th part of their wealth. It is very little compared to the tremendous wealth of the people in this country; and the greater share of it is borne by the poor rather than the rich, and especially by poor women. The women here make great effort to collect this amount. In this country, ten million people drink liquor worth nine hundred million dollars (that is, 2,700,000,000 rupees) every year, and smoke tobacco worth 1,470,000,000 rupees. This shows that tobacco and liquor enjoy greater importance than religion in this country. This is sad and deplorable indeed. The societies for temperance and moral instruction here make great efforts to eradicate both these vices in this country. I pray to God to grant them success and to free this beautiful country from the grip of Demoness Liquor, Fiend Tobacco, and Immorality.

The religious people in our country give alms to everybody who begs. It is good to give to the destitute, but after assessing who is truly deserving; this is not done in our country, with the result that beggary has become rampant. Our virtuous ancestors have said, 'Alms given to an undeserving person are wasted; they incur sin.' But who pays any heed? Suppose there is a fat *bairagi* [religious mendicant who has renounced the world]; if anybody gives him money, he will spend it on smoking *ganja* [dried hemp flowers]. The addiction to *ganja,* which has already ruined him, passes on from him to children and to other people, because there are many who follow the example of such holy men! Therefore, this is how charity to unsuitable persons promotes idleness and vice in the country, and the country sinks to a lowly state. I have visited many places of pilgrimage myself, and also seen the system of charity there. Alms given to the priests there are undeserved; these priests reduce their patrons to poverty. The priest who extracts the most from his patron in the name of religion is considered learned and regarded as very 'clever' and wise.

The people here have a custom of giving to charities, which is very different from ours. Here, nobody wanders through the streets, begging. Popular opinion and the laws of the land are openly opposed to begging. Alms are not given to anybody who comes to the door to beg. Blind and lame, weak and aged persons sit in the street selling matchboxes, strings, mirrors, and other small things. Some good-hearted person buys a thing or two from them and pays a little more than the actual price. These people do not give to those who beg; but that does not mean that they are not compassionate. They are very particular about giving only to the deserving. People in villages and cities collect money through contributions in order to support those who are destitute, crippled, or too weak to work. In addition, the inhabitants also have to pay a small tax for charitable works, which they pay willingly. This money is handed over to the local societies which manage charities, called Boards of Charities. The men and women who manage these societies are elected by the people; they are highly respectable, honest and pious, and do their work with great care and concern. The management of these Boards is similar to that of other societies. Of the money spent on charity in the country, half comes from the people and half from the Government. All this money is spent only on those who are truly crippled and unable to earn a living. . . .

In our country, begging has increased greatly because of the practice of thoughtlessly giving alms to mendicants, who have become lazy owing to their addiction to *ganja*, tobacco, etc. and to such others who are capable of work but remain idle. . . . In the United States, no one who has any capacity to work receives alms. The tenet of their religion is: 'He who wants to eat, must work.' In our country there is no limit to laziness, anybody gets food without doing anything. A person only needs to smear ash all over his body, let his hair grow into long tangles, wear bead necklaces, or don saffron robes. As a holy man, people feed him free of charge. Our people consider it to be an important part of religion to beg, and to give alms to those who beg. . . . This does not happen here. Everybody works according to his capacity; even small children go about selling newspapers, loudly announcing the important news items. Some shovel snow in winter. Even destitute widows earn their livelihood. Their small children do all kinds of work to help their mothers. Here, even begging is turned into a form of work. There are people called gypsies who are beggars like the *kaikadis* [5] in our country; but they entertain people by playing instruments, etc. Many beggars make monkeys or bears dance in order to amuse people. There are asylums here which give shelter to old people and children who are destitute. Even there, suitable work is provided.

There is a large number of consumptives here. Drinking and the use of tobacco are among the chief causes of this disease; even so, these people do not rid themselves of these twin vices! Our people are also rapidly imitating these two vices and becoming terribly debilitated. The reason for our Raosaheb to be in delicate health, or the reason why Raosaheb has a headache and is unable to meet vistors, is liquor! This vice leads to havoc at home, loss of honour outside, and a waste of money; and it carries one to Lord Yama [the deity of Death] quite soon. Even so, our people are getting involved in these vices. Great indeed is our desire for imitation!

Many people here are sick because of these two vices. Some say that their spleen is affected! Some say that they cannot digest food! Some say that they have no strength! Thus, the bodies of many people, who are addicted to liquor and tobacco, have become the very lodging-houses of numerous diseases, especially consumption. Such sick persons are sent to Poor Houses. Going to a Poor House is considered to be very shameful here; there are many who say that they would rather die than go to one, and who act accordingly. There are some here who would shoot themselves but not live in these homes for destitutes. Even these sick people are made to do light work in these places, such as watering flowering plants. Self-esteem reigns supreme everywhere here. These people sincerely feel that they should not eat at the expense of others. Here nobody gives or receives money without a proper reason. In our country, most people do not even know what self-esteem and self-respect mean. They would accept anything given free, without any qualms, and say that it will tide them over the next few months. They will borrow, and if unable to repay the debt, say that they will do so in their next life. But they feel no compunction about the fact that they would be compelled to be reborn in order to repay the debt!

The number of beggars who come to the United States from other countries is very large. Of all the inhabitants here, one-seventh are foreigners; of the criminals in the country, 30 per cent are foreigners. The chief reason is that foreigners do not get work quickly, and are prompted to commit acts which lead them to the 'rent-free house'. There are not many physically defective people here, who have to be supported by the general public; because those who migrate to this country leave their own only if they are strong enough. In the United Kingdom of Great Britain and Ireland, 33 persons per thousand require public support. In the United States only five persons in the same population require public support, that is, one person in every two hundred. . . . This immediately gives [us] an idea of how low the extent of beggary, and how much work, there is in this country. I think that in our own country, the proportion of beggars must be even a hundred and fifty per cent! Now, there are a lot of outsiders in the United States. That means that there is quite a mixture of all kinds of people here. There is also a large population of Negroes, who were formerly sold here as slaves. Among the Negroes, there are very few beggars or persons requiring public support. This is a good example of how a people become industrious once they get the freedom that they lacked earlier. There are many professionals among the Negroes; some are lawyers, some barristers, some businessmen, others engaged in some profession or another—all are hardworking. It is not yet twenty-five years since the slaves were freed; but already they have equalled other people in every field. This is a perfect illustration of all the advantages which flow from granting freedom to people. The people who favoured the traffic in slaves claimed that the emancipation of Negroes from slavery would bring a terrible disaster upon the country, that they would ruin the country, that begging would become rampant, robberies would increase, that peace would be shattered. But happily, not one of the things predicted by them happened. There are those who are not qualified to do any work in spite of being able-bodied; the religious societies here consider it their duty to make such people work, and provide them training. One-third the amount spent on beggars in England, that is, 18,000,000 dollars are spent on beggars in the US. This figure shows that there are very few beggars here. Some of the reasons why there are very few beggars in the US are as follows. Only those who are able to work emigrate to another country. There is plentiful land here which can be brought under cultivation. This is why there is a lot of work, and a hard-working person would not ever starve anywhere. Laziness has no prestige here. . . .

In olden times, convicts from Austria, Germany and England were shipped to the United States, but now the Federal Government has made very strict laws regarding beggars and immigrants. They forbid such criminals, beggars and persons who are lazy or unwilling to work, from entering the country. . . .

There are very few physically defective people here, that is, those who are blind, mute, lame, crippled, etc., as mentioned above. There is one blind person in every 2,720 people, and one mute in every 2,094. Although it is proper to give alms to the blind, if they receive some education and start working according to their ability, it benefits the nation and reduces poverty. There are many schools for the blind here. Every state has at least two or three schools for the blind; all their expenses are paid by the State Government. In these schools, the blind are given an education through the sense of touch. The blind have a very sharp sense of hearing and touch; all their perception is concentrated in these senses. They have a quick grasp. The blind do weaving and many other kinds of work. I have brought with me some articles made by them. They are taught Geography. Globes and maps are specially made in order to give them knowledge through touch. They are taught Mathematics. The kindergarten method of education has worked wonders for the education of the blind! There are many among the blind who sing and also many who play musical instruments. I heard a blind person play the organ in church, which sounded very sweet. The parents here take very good care of their children's eyes, etc. The mothers in our country put drops of oil in the children's eyes and smear then with lamp-black; this is not done here. There are also a number of schools for the deaf and mute. Even in the task of educating them, the imaginative people here have made the utmost progress! There is a school for them in New York, which has 500 students. Their education seemed to me to be a marvel. There was a boy in the school who was deaf and mute, and also blind. The man who showed me around the school, also showed me this severely disabled boy. He touched his hand with his own fingers and told him, 'An Indian lady has come to see you, talk to her if you wish.' In a trice, he wrote a few sentences about me on a machine called the 'typewriter' and brought the paper over. My guide gave me the paper, which I have carefully preserved. On it the boy had written in brief my name, that of my country, and my purpose in coming to this country, and also expressed his pleasure at my visit. I was utterly amazed to see this, and felt that if a miracle could happen in this world, this was it! Besides these, there are numerous orphanages and industrial schools here. There are schools also for feeble-minded children. There are altogether 430 homes and schools of different types for the weak, the destitute, etc. There are fifty-six schools for the blind and the mute, and thirty schools for feeble-minded children. All the school teachers teach their students very carefully and with great understanding.

The people here believe that works such as improving the conditions in prisons, visiting the prisoners, advising them, etc. are pious deeds. In our country, people believe that they have no connection whatsoever with prisoners; moreover, they probably think that such a connection would bring shame upon them. Therefore nobody ever goes to a prison to inquire after them. One cannot say that absolutely all the people who go to prison are criminals. (And so what if they are? Why should we not visit them in prison to inquire after them?) An innocent person might also have occasion to go to prison. Who can know with absolute certainty whether or not he will have to go to prison? I have not yet seen a prison in India. Earlier I knew nothing at all about the prisons there, but got some idea from Mr Agarkar's 'Hundred and One Days in Dongri Prison' after the affair at Kolhapur.[6] Fifty years ago, the prisoners in the US were treated very badly. In most cases they were locked up in dungeons or mines. Even children were tormented in different ways by putting chains around their necks and shackles on their arms and legs. In short, there was a great deal of ill-treatment all around. But since good, pious men and women started visiting them, these prisons have become like our Zenanas. I have seen the prisons here. They are clean and have been made safe from fires. The prisoners are turned into useful people. They are advised to conduct themselves properly after being released. There are libraries for them. There are pots of flowering plants. Every Sunday is a holiday, when they pray. Good people treat them with compassion, in the belief that they have come to this pass owing to a lack of proper upbringing by their parents. There are several societies of such good people. There are many reformatories for children. The first such home was established in 1824. In 1874, there were thirty-four such homes, on which eight million dollars were spent. During these fifty years, a total of 91,402 children have been reformed, and about 70,000 children have turned out to be industrious and respectable. Moral education is provided in these homes. Great care is taken to avoid bad qualities being passed on from one to another. The prisoners here do not receive much corporal punishment, but they do get chained. In many States, electrocution is used for capital punishment, instead of hanging. When a prisoner is released after serving his term, he receives all the rights of a citizen.

There are many hospitals of different types here, for those suffering from different diseases, and also many for ordinary patients. The Government pays their expenses, and many hospitals are run at public expense. Pious people visit the patients and cheer them up in many ways. Some women visit infirmaries and sing sweet songs and psalms, and read religious books to the patients. Some tell stories and the news, some read out newspapers, some play sweet instruments, some give sweets, some give fragrant flowers. The custom of giving flowers has become popular here. The society which gives flowers is called the Flower Mission. I have seen the pious woman who first had the idea of giving flowers. She has been bed-ridden for about ten years, because of paralysis. Even so, she still performs many such pious deeds. There is real compassion here. In our country, nobody knows what real compassion means. There are many patients there, and many hospitals are being built for them. It would be very good if someone were to visit them and speak to them sweetly, inquire after them, give them flowers, etc. We are eager to imitate the Americans and other Western people in matters like drinking, smoking and talking of atheism. If, instead, we imitated their good qualities and customs with eagerness, how greatly it would benefit us and our country!

NOTES

1. In the earlier part of the book Ramabai gives a glowing account of the American republic and the people's power, contrasting it with the English monarchy. This contrast runs like a red thread through the book.
2. Ramabai wrote most of the book in 1888 while she was in the USA; hence the reference to the Americans as the people 'here'.
3. Here, and in some other places, Ramabai quotes figures in lakhs and crores (sometimes in words), which are converted in the translation into numbers and presented in the Western style for the sake of universality. The figures that follow show that one dollar was equal to three rupees at the time.
4. Missionary activity was initially forbidden by the English East India Company in Mumbai Island (the only territory under its control in western India), until the Company's monopoly of India trade was ended in 1813. The American Marathi Mission was the first on the scene and opened the very first public school in Mumbai in 1815 (*Gazetteer of Bombay City and Island*, III: 101–5).
5. *Kaikadis*, a caste whose traditional occupation was making twig-baskets, also earned money through acrobatic performances in the streets.
6. The involvement of Agarkar and Tilak, as editors of the *Kesari* and *The Mahratta*, respectively, in the Kolhapur Libel Case stemmed from their support to the young prince against his Diwan who allegedly maltreated him with the connivance of the British Resident. In the court case that followed, Agarkar and Tilak found the documentary evidence in their possesssion to be forged and their informants unwilling to testify; they were sentenced to prison in July-October 1882. Agarkar's account of prison life, published in 1882 as a booklet, was the first of its kind in Marathi (Agarkar 1986, III: xiii-xix, 1-37).

7

THE CONDITION OF WOMEN
IN THE USA
(translated from *United Stateschi*
Lokasthiti ani Pravasavritta)

A s a child, I took great delight in listening to marvellous tales,
just as other children do. Who does not enjoy the legends,
the Mahabharata, Bhagvata [Purana], Ramayana, Adbhuta
Ramayana, Jaimini, Ashvamedha, and other such ancient literary
works popular in our country? Who would not find them inspiring?
And who would not yearn for the strength to perform similar feats?
But there would be few children and adults who do not realize, to
their disappointment, that such feats are beyond them because of
their lack of strength, general ignorance and lack of resourcefulness;
and, besides, that the tales themselves are but imaginary. If we are so
delighted and eager to read imaginary tales and marvels, why should
we not be eager to read accounts of real events? Seven years ago, I
had not the slightest inkling that I would really be able to witness
goddesses like Sita, endowed with the strength, comparable to that
of Haihayarjuna, to block the force of a great river, and able to slay
invincible demons like Ravana with their hundred or thousand heads.[1]
But, happily, in the course of time I was able to witness such wonderful
things and now have the opportunity to present at least a brief
account of them to my countrymen and women.

Some months ago I chanced to see the book *Society in America*
written by the famous and scholarly Englishwoman Harriet

Martineau. She wrote the book when she returned home after visiting America in 1840 and observing the society here.[2] While describing the condition of native[3] women, she has said: 'They (women in this country) receive no higher education at all; moreover, all avenues of acquiring it are blocked for them. The highest reach of their education consisted of [accomplishments such as] singing, playing musical instruments, a little reading and writing, and needlework. They enjoy no social or political freedom. Should they suffer the misfortune of widowhood or poverty, they have no recourse but to undertake work like sewing, cooking, domestic service or similar lowly work; or to marry or remarry against their will. The laws of this country take no cognizance of women's existence at all. Women are mere prisoners of men, like bought slaves. There is no exception to this in political matters and in the eyes of the law; only in social life might there be an exception, though a very rare one.'[4] . . . The one sentence, that 'women are mere prisoners of men, like bought slaves', clearly reveals the pitiable and dreadful plight of native women about fifty years ago. The courage, powers of endurance and unceasing effort that enabled these women to lift themselves out of this condition can be adequately described only by a Sarasvati [Goddess of Learning] descended upon our earth; a mortal like me, with her limited intellect, cannot do them justice.

Thus far, kind and philanthropic people have accomplished great deeds (like the abolition of slavery, promotion of the temperance movement, etc.) in the face of terrible adversity; but the emancipation of women was a deed far more difficult than them all. Because, it is obvious that to purchase slaves like livestock, make them work without wages and block their worldly and spiritual progress is very reprehensible and cruel. Also, everyone knows that vices such as drinking cause physical and mental ruin. The harm done by these things is immediately visible to all; but the harm done by the slavery of women is generally not noticed. Like a mysterious heart disease, it remains invisible even as it continues to destroy the heart of human society. Most people think that women are living not in slavery, but in a state natural to them. The belief that women are not oppressed and that their condition need not be any different from the present one, is so deeply entrenched in everybody's mind that it is impossible for anybody to even imagine how evil their condition really is. What is worse, even women themselves believe that their condition is as it should be. In the past, when African Negroes were slaves in America, many of them held similar beliefs: 'We may be enslaved, but this alone is our source of happiness; we are low and abject compared to everybody else, and we are utterly dependent on our masters, who have the power of life and death over us.' In this belief, they quietly endured even the worst kind of humiliation. This state of mind is the ultimate in slavery. One cannot even begin to imagine how evil is slavery which destroys self-respect and desire for freedom—the two God-given boons to humanity!

How true is the claim of many Western scholars that a civilization should be judged by the condition of its women! Inherently, women are physically weaker than men, and possess innate powers of endurance; men therefore find it very easy to wrest away their natural rights and reduce them to a state that suits them [i.e. men]. But, from a moral point of view, physical might is not real strength, nor does it signify nobility of character to deprive the weak of their rights. Among the barbaric or semi-barbaric people of the past and present, physical strength is seen to be generally supreme. 'Might is right' is their creed. . . . But, as a country advances in knowledge and compassion, brute strength declines in importance, people begin to regard intellectual strength as superior to physical strength and accord a higher status to venerable customs and common wisdom than to the pompous scriptural precepts of 'pretentious fools'. Such people do not consider it right to grasp the property and rights of others just because they are weaker. For them, justice means protecting the weak, forgiving those who harm them instead of retaliating, and being modest rather than arrogant about their natural strength. Thus, as people progress and expand their knowledge, they naturally develop greater innate compassion and morality. For the same reason, the tradition that believes in exercising arbitrary power over women on the grounds of their weakness is considered barbaric; and as men gain wisdom and progress further, they disregard women's lack of strength, honour their good qualities, and elevate them to a high state. Their low opinion of women and of such other matters changes and gives way to respect. Thus, the progress of a country can be accurately assessed from the condition of its women.

According to the natives, the social conditions in England and among the Americans who have immigrated from that country are the very best, because their women are honoured everywhere and because they regard men and women as equals. And those who profess Christianity claim that women acquired a high status because of the Christian religion, because women receive no respect at all among the people of other religions, and that women of any community begin to progress as soon as it embraces Christianity. Careful consideration shows that both these claims contain a great deal of truth, but also a great deal of falsehood. The condition of women is not identical among all the communities that call themselves Christian. People like the Russians, Italians, Greeks, French, Swiss, Finnish, English, Americans and others are all Christians; but there is a wide difference in the condition of their women. To claim to be the follower of a religion, and to actually practise that religion are two very different things. Almost all the people in this country call themselves Christians, but not all of them practise the teachings of Christ. The doctrine which Christ taught and the practices He propagated did not differentiate at all between men and women; but that egalitarian view is not accepted by everyone here. Through their view of women's worth and their treatment of women, some people prove that they accept the doctrine of Christ, some that of St. Paul, some that of Moses, and some that of Satan; but all of them claim that they accept the Christian doctrine. The doctrine of Christ, and that of St. Paul who adhered to it, states that there is no difference between men and women in Christ, but that all are the children of God; whereas most of the doctrines prevailing in this country consider women to be inferior to men. Women do not have the right to climb onto the pulpit and preach like men, or to conduct religious services and rites; they have to take the vow of obedience to their husbands during the wedding ceremony; (male) preachers maintain that a husband has supremacy over his wife. This falsifies the claim of all self-styled Christians, that their religion is the cause of the freedom, high standing and honour enjoyed by the women of England and of this country. The religion which has led to women's high state should properly be called by these followers of different denominations, not 'our' religion but simply 'the holy doctrine' or 'the doctrine of Christ' (which is not the prevailing form of Christianity). The prevailing form of Christianity continues to change in conformity with popular opinion. From olden times, the religious heads of different denominations have followed the tradition of shaping religion in the manner of kneading a ball of wax and moulding it into the shapes that appeal to them and to popular opinion. What different shapes these clergymen have given to the Christian religion and how they have changed its essence is clearly seen from the history of the native slaves and women.

The sect known as Quakers, which was founded about two hundred years ago, does not discriminate in this fashion, at least in matters of religion. According to them, God loves men and women equally. God inspires people according to their worth, whether they be men or women; therefore they believe that a man or a woman who feels the divine inspiration should preach. But in other matters, even Quakers considered women to be inferior to men. In 1840, the World Anti-Slavery Convention was held in London and was attended by Lucretia Mott and many other eminent women as delegates of the American Anti-Slavery Society. The meeting, attended by many Quakers, was presided over by one Joseph Sturge, a famous Quaker gentleman. Even in a meeting devoted to such an altruistic cause, he refused to grant the status of delegate to the women who had dedicated themselves totally to the service of the Anti-Slavery Society, sometimes at the risk of their own lives.[5] The reason advanced was the 'British tradition'.

The other day (in May 1888), there was a Methodist meeting of the clergy and laity in New York city, to which many local Methodist societies had sent their representatives, including five well-known women. But they did not receive due recognition at the meeting, the only reason being that they were women. One thing worth remembering here is that two-thirds of the Methodists are women, and that the livelihood of most of their clergy and the charitable works of the sect depend on their support. The same thing applies to other sects. When it comes to religious and charitable works, the task of collecting money for them falls to the women's lot. After completing their housework or the paid employment they have taken up for earning a livelihood, they do sewing, embroidery and make beautiful things, go from door to door and plead with people, collect money and things for charity and philanthropy through all such means, and get together crores of rupees. But then it is men who decide how to disburse this money, and it is men who are the presidents, vice-presidents and other [office-bearers] of the committees appointed for managing the charitable works. It is women who do secretarial and other routine, tiresome work. This is the justice of the Methodists—how beautiful it looks in the clear sunlight of the nineteenth century reform! Among the Christian sects, other than the Congregationalists, Quakers, Unitarians, Universalists, and a progressive branch of the Methodists, women lack the freedom to preach in church, the only reason being that they are *women*! In his Epistle to the Corinthians, St. Paul says in one place, 'Let your women keep silent in the churches.' Therefore women—be they ever so pure, educated, effective speakers, possessed of other excellent qualities, and much more capable than male preachers, but whose only fault is that they are women—are ordered by men to shut their mouths and sit quietly even if they have the divine inspiration to preach.

It is not yet sixty years since the condition of native women started to improve, but even within such a short time they have begun to taste many excellent fruits of their industry and persistent efforts. Even at the time when Harriet Martineau wrote that these women were men's prisoners like bought slaves, and that there was no exception to this rule in political matters and in the eyes of the law, there were one or two women who had already noticed the disrepect shown to their sex and attempted to bring this injustice to the notice of American society. A hundred years ago, the sister of the famous Robert Lee in the State of Virginia, and the wife of John Adams in the Commonwealth of Massachusetts told Government officials clearly that they would not pay taxes because they had no right to vote in political matters. But nobody paid much attention to those things at the time. Later, in 1830, an opinion in favour of abolishing slavery began to be created in this country; since then, the matter of improving the condition of women has also taken shape. In 1832, William Lloyd Garrison first established the Anti-Slavery Society. He, Wendell Phillips and many other eminent speakers gave hundreds and thousands of speeches propounding the injustice of enslaving Negro men and women. The arguments they advanced against the slavery of Africans were also applicable to the slavery of women. With this realization, some brave and adventurous women started delivering speeches in public meetings, espousing the cause of their sex along with that of the Negro slaves.

The year 1832 should be called a golden year, when the slaves' chains received a hard blow and began to break. Similarly, ignorance, the root cause of slavery and the inferior status of women, began to decline. In this good year, a very famous college, known as Oberlin

College, was founded in the town of Oberlin in the State of Ohio. The founders of the College made a rule to generously impart education to all who were interested, without judging their suitability by criteria such as skin colour—whether black, white, yellow or any other—or sex.[6] Not many years have passed since the condition of native women began to improve, but the Sun of their good fortune has begun to acquire greater brilliance with every passing day. Favourable signs are visible that within a few years, they will obtain all rights that men enjoy and that this nation of the United States will become a full-fledged republic. Every day, women are making great strides in social and political matters. . . .

EDUCATION

The chief cause of progress is education. It has been sixty years since education was made available to native women in a small way. It is almost a hundred years since the Englishwoman, Mary Wollstonecraft, stated publicly that women of England should receive an education. In the year 1789, this woman openly claimed that the lack of education was the biggest obstacle to women's advancement in England at the time, and that it was not proper to prevent women from studying. In 1799, a woman named Hannah More wrote several books to publicly state her opinion that it was proper for women to be educated. In 1809, a gentleman named Sidney Smith presented his favourable opinion of women's education before the people, through his books. The two decades from 1789 to 1809 may be called the preface to the history of Western women's education. During these twenty years, the desire for a wide dissemination of women's education sprouted in the hearts of many men and women, and became stronger day by day.

In 1819, the American woman Emma Willard made the first attempt to make education available to her countrywomen. That year she presented an Address to the Senate of New York State with a request to establish a seminary for women.[7] The history of American women's higher education can be said to have started from this date. However, women's higher education itself did not start at this time. Until 1831, almost all the supporters of women's education said that women should get only a general education, because higher education would not only not benefit them, but would destroy their natural modesty, beauty and usefulness to society; and make them arrogant, careless and thoughtless. In 1832, Oberlin College in Ohio made higher education available to women along with men. The founders of Oberlin College set the world an excellent example by dismissing the prevalent, barbaric belief about women's inferiority. The city of Boston, capital of the Commonwealth of Massachusetts, is famous as an old centre of learning in the United States; and scholars from Boston are popularly believed to be very superior and pioneers in matters of progress and public welfare. But not a single girls' college had been established in Boston until 1878. It was only a 125 years after the establishment and great development of Harvard University (at Cambridge, Massachusetts), regarded as the jewel in the crown of America's universities, that permission was granted for Boston girls to enter the most inferior colleges. If, keeping this in mind, one analyses the history of native women's education (which started very recently), one is amazed at the feats achieved by women in the academic field in such a short time.

Now, one should not assume that the general progress in female education in the United States, which one sees today, was smooth. As soon as women began to read a new book, or declared their intention to learn a new branch of knowledge, they would immediately be subjected to curses, censure, criticism, wrinkled noses and meaningful glances every where—from newspapers, preachers' pulpits, the mouths of public speakers, declarations of religious meetings, and from the eyes and tongues of neighbours; and this continues even now. Only a cause which was naturally pure and had the support of eternal truth could hope to endure such a shower of stones and thunderbolts, and survive to this day. . . .

There is a State called Colorado in the western part of the United States, in which a solid, stony, immoveable range of mountains known as the Rockies has spread across the land since time immemorial. It seems impossible to break through it in order to cut a trail and go across. How would a river, [which is] almost a tiny stream, possess the strength to penetrate the mountains? But behold the marvel! The

Arkansas river started quietly to make a way through the Rocky mountains. The sea, the lakes and the rivers of the plains must have felt a sad surprise at its unshakeable resolve, and the sky-high range of the Rockies must have pitied it. The smaller mountains must have deplored and condemned it for this risky venture. But the Arkansas river ignored them all. It was only a small weak rivulet, but its resolve was strong enough to lift even the mountains in its path and fling them away. With persistent effort and strong resolve it defeated even the Rocky mountain. The tiny Arkansas clashed against that impenetrable, unbreakable stone range and carved out a way for itself right through the Rocky mountains! Bravo Arkansas! And bravo American women! Even though weak like this rivulet, lacking the support of scriptures, money, popular opinion or religious tradition, and relying only on the strength of persistent effort and resolve, they clashed against thousands of obstacles a hundred times more difficult, impenetrable and unbreakable than the Rockies, bore tunnels right through them and cut a trail for themselves. I say once again, bravo American women!

The arguments against female education that were advanced and accepted by all, not just twenty-five but even ten years ago, are beginning to fade now. That educated women will become arrogant, neglect housework and child care, be unable to cook; that they lack the necessary physical, mental and spiritual strength to study hard, pass college examinations, and complete their education in good health; that men will have to sit at home if women get educated and enter the professions or get jobs; that men will lose their livelihood; that the world will see an apocalypse—all such objections are now dead, and their corpses are being buried in deep graves. The ghosts of one or two of these objections still appear occasionally before the people and terrify the faint-hearted; but, lacking bones and muscles, brains and life, [these apparitions] soon dissolve into nothingness and disappear!

The foremost among the institutions for women's education in the United States now (in 1888) are the colleges; below them rank the four lower-level arrangements, namely, societies for the promotion of education, lecture series, institutions offering education through correspondence, and the examinations offered by some universities. The details of colleges offering higher and professional education to women in 1886 are as follows:

Colleges established only for women	266
Co-educational colleges	207
Men's engineering and agricultural colleges that admit women	17
Technical colleges	3
Medical colleges	36
Total colleges	*529*
Women students studying in women's colleges	27,143
Women students in co-educational colleges	8,833
Total women students of higher and technical subjects	*35,976*

In addition, most schools offering middle-level education admit girls. They include 117 State-run teacher-training colleges and 36 independent (privately established) teacher-training colleges, which have a combined strength of 27,185 female students.

The primary and general public schools as well as most State-run high schools provide a common education for girls and boys combined.†† Seventy years ago, primary schools for girls had not

††In the year 1818, primary schools for girls as well as boys were established in the United States. During the seventy years since then, native women have made great strides in the field of education; and now thousands of splendid, intelligent, educated women of this country shine like brilliant gems. But this should not lead anyone to suppose that all women here have the educational facilities that (all) men enjoy, and that women's colleges receive the same degree of generous public support that men's colleges do. The details of men's colleges in 1886 are as follows:

Universities and colleges	346
Technical colleges	90
Religious seminaries	142
Law schools	49
Medical, dental, pharmaceutical colleges etc.	175
Total	*802*
Total number of male students	78,185

The cost of men's college buildings, their grounds, equipment, etc. is $ 62,356,638 (or Rs187,069,914), the money invested for the upkeep of these colleges is $ 57,782,303 (or Rs173,346,909), and their annual earnings are $ 3,271,991 (or Rs 9,815,973).

A comparison of these figures with the money invested in women's education reveals a wide disparity between the two. The colleges for women's higher education number 529; [the cost of] their buildings, grounds, equipment, etc. amount to $

been set up, whereas men had free access to education. Men could study not just in primary schools but also get an excellent education and vocational training in high schools, colleges, and technical schools. Today, women of the United States are trying to equal men in education, in spite of popular opposition to female education, and many other obstacles. This is cause for not a little surprise. The census of 1880 shows that in that year, eight per cent of all men (i.e. White American men, excluding Negroes) in the United States were illiterate, while eleven per cent of White American women were unable to read and write. This proves that women are not very far behind men in general education.

A truly large-hearted woman named Mrs Emma Willard had appealed to the legislature of the State of New York for a subsidy to a middle school for women, called the Troy [Female] Seminary, established in 1821; but the Government refused to support this good cause. . . . Today, women are provided with advanced education equal to that of men by many colleges (of which the co-educational ones are indicated by an asterisk): Oberlin College*, Vassar College, Michigan University*, Smith College, Wellesley College, Harvard Annex, Ingham University, Bryn Mawr College, Cornell University*, and many others.[8] This progress in women's education in the United States was achieved not through empty chatter, wishful thinking and meaningless arguments, nor through lounging on soft beds with feather cushions. This golden age for the native women was ushered in by the women champions of education and some liberal-minded men, by facing unpleasant allegations, enduring endless hardships and making persistent efforts.

. . . Fifty years ago, the United States had barely four or five institutions of higher education for women. Today, it is doubtful whether one can find four or five such institutions of academic excellence in the whole country, which refuse admission to women to study along with men. There was a time when people laboured under the absurd misapprehension that women's education was

---

9,635,282 (Rs 28,905,846); their investments and properties are valued at $ 2,376,619 (Rs 7,129,857), and their annual earnings are $136,801 (Rs 410,403).

In 1886, the local, State and Federal Governments gave $ 1,690,275 (Rs 5,070,825) as aid to men's higher education, but not even a single penny to promote women's higher education!

dreadful and dangerous, that it would harm society, that it would make women unnatural and arrogant, and that domestic happiness would then disappear from this world. It was then that some far-sighted, non-partisan and perceptive men and women embarked upon the great adventure of . . . rowing against the current [of popular opinion]. . . .

Many avenues of acquiring an excellent education have recently been opened to women. . . . Nobody, except a half-baked and inexperienced person, dares to claim that women's intelligence is not equal to that of men. Of the elite universities in America, Columbia and Johns Hopkins have crossed the old traditional boundaries and allowed women to pass their thresholds and enter their portals. These universities have conferred their very highest degrees on two excellent women graduates—either out of generosity, or lack of choice—and achieved a rare miracle witnessed 'neither in the past, nor in the future'[Skt]. Harvard University at new Cambridge in the Commonwealth of Massachusetts followed the model of old Cambridge†† and denied women the nectar of knowledge which was gathered from the inexhaustible vessel of Goddess Sarasvati, and which was served to men all the time. Therefore some industrious women attempted successfully to establish an independent college and obtained the nectar from the same inexhaustible vessel, if not inside Harvard, then outside its portals [at 'Harvard Annex'].

In the eastern States, women have gained entry into the best universities, such as Michigan and Cornell; and women's colleges which vie with them, such as Wellesley, Smith, Vassar, Bryn Mawr, have been and are still being founded. In the western States, almost all the colleges and universities admit women as well as men, so that there is no need to establish separate colleges.

Nowhere does one see evidence of higher education having

††Some years ago, women could not get admission to Cambridge University in England. Now, two women's colleges, Newnham and Girton, have been established at Cambridge, and provide a very good education. Women are now allowed to study as men's equals at Cambridge University and sit for examinations. However, the University authorities still retain a residue of the barbarism of their ancestors. They allow women to study and sit for examinations, but deny degrees to the women who pass the examinations—although they have rightfully earned the degrees after years of hard work! Truly unparalleled is the generosity and culture of progressive English scholars, especially those at Cambridge!

impaired women's health or beauty. Let alone small or middle-level colleges, but even colleges like Cornell, Vassar, Wellesley, Smith and Bryn Mawr have thousands of young women in higher education. I have visited each of these places and spent a few days there to investigate these and other such matters, which has convinced me that women are well able to cope with higher education. It does not impair their beauty, nor does it change their delicate, modest disposition and make them unnatural. Many women graduates of these colleges have married and are managing their domestic life very well. They do not neglect their children or housework because they are educated; nor have the husbands of these educated women suffered or been reduced to dire straits, or their homes ruined! I visited many women graduates of the said colleges, saw their homes and made inquiries with their husbands. I was satisfied when the husbands repeatedly said that women should have a good education.

Two years ago, Miss Alice Freeman was the President of Wellesley College.[9] Before she took up this position, the whole world believed that a woman would never be able to manage even a small school as its principal, let alone a college. But Alice Freeman accepted the presidency of a large college with 600 young and promising women students and managed her duties extremely well, to the surprise of the whole world. Her learning was suitably honoured by Columbia University which, after duly examining her, awarded her the PhD—the highest of all university degrees. A sceptic was worried that this president of a large college, having spent a lifetime (thirty years) in education, would be lacking in the knowledge of domestic duties and would not find a husband. True, she is able to run a college and organize large meetings, be a good teacher, debate with renowned scholars on scientific subjects—but of what use is all this? If she cannot marry and manage her husband's home, what is the use of her education? But calm down, all ye sceptics! A learned woman like Alice Freeman could and did find a husband who is himself a scholar of no mean repute. Alice Freeman, the great PhD, is now an excellent housewife. She is knowledgeable about big matters related to the college, but also about small domestic matters. There is no doubt whatsoever that she is able to manage her household and a college with 600 women students! . . .

EMPLOYMENT

The history of women's education during the period 1828 to 1888 is quite extraordinary, interesting and instructive. It has been mentioned above that about sixty years ago Mrs Emma Willard had presented an Address to the Senate of New York State for a Government subsidy to women's schools. In it, Mrs Willard had clearly stated, in keeping with the prevalent popular belief, that higher education was not necessary for women, but general education was essential. The learned Senators of New York disapproved of even this moderate request, and refused any encouragement even to the general education of women. . . .

Some people were of the opinion that a study of Mathematics and Law would derange women's brains and make them ill, that a study of the Sciences would make them lose faith in religion, that a knowledge of Greek would destroy their womanliness and make them rowdy, like men. Some said that no matter what else happened, it was certain that when women were educated, men would lose their livelihood; that men would be compelled to sit at home, mind the babies and sing them lullabies, or do the cooking, because educated women would grab their jobs. Other thoughtful men said that there was absolutely no fear that women would grab men's jobs because they simply lacked the brains to acquire scientific knowledge and put it to use. A headache presupposes a head, and fear of an educated woman would arise if she possessed the brains to acquire a good education; but where would they get the brains?[††] There were other intelligent and experienced men who wondered how women would find the time for studies; and if they did, to what use they would put them.

[††]Women's education in today's United States is beyond anybody's imagination fifty years ago. It has already been mentioned that a study of Mathematics, Law, the Sciences, Greek and other subjects does not seem to have made women unhealthy, insane or unruly, or transformed their womanliness and destroyed their love of domesticity and children. It is true that educated women have taken up diverse types of employment, but that has not ruined the livelihood of men; on the contrary, the number of occupations in the United States have increased a hundred-fold and flourished during the last fifty years. . . .

There is hardly any point in discussing how far these doubts were real or imaginary. A hundred years ago, women in the United States were not able to work as teachers in Government schools because men believed that women lacked the strength to control rowdy children and discipline them. But in 1789, the male Senators of Massachusetts made a new law allowing women to give general education in the State-run public schools— whether to test women's ability to teach in schools or to get the job done at low salaries, it is difficult to ascertain. At that time women were unable to teach anything other than 'a,b,c' and 'one, two, three', because the kind, thoughtful and learned men had, for fear of women falling ill from studying too hard, taken the precaution of drawing up the 'woman's curriculum'. It is difficult to say whether those who studied this curriculum were able to even write a short letter in a grammatically correct language, let alone prepare children for higher studies or impart higher education themselves. In due course, women expanded their knowledge by studying at home, instead of giving up in fear when confronted by a mountain of obstacles and the Chinese Wall of popular opposition. When the status and influence of women teachers and their usefulness in imparting general education were widely recognized, some wise people favoured giving them an education somewhat higher than the 'woman's curriculum' to help them to perform their job well. Even after women were able to get higher education, the positions of college teachers were not open to them until Michigan University opened the golden gates of its Temple of Sarasvati and invited them, along with men, to worship at her throne. Ever since, women have had the opportunity to occupy the positions they are qualified for, such as teachers, professors, college presidents, and others (which had earlier been reserved for men), to give a good account of themselves and demonstrate the extent of their capability and intellectual strength. Now nobody doubts that women will be able to manage schools and train children properly. The triumvirate of local, State and Federal Governments in the United States is so impressed by women's performance that it has entrusted women with primary and middle education of almost all children. Now women teachers are beginning to handle higher education as well. There are a total of 273,000 teachers in the country's public educational institutions (i.e. higher, middle and lower grade schools and colleges), of whom 154,375 are women. In addition, there are women teachers in many private and public high schools, who teach Mathematics,

Chemistry, Botany, Astronomy, Anatomy, Physics and other difficult scientific and philosophical subjects, performing their duties well. Some are college presidents or vice-presidents, some are chiefs of all city schools, some are headmistresses, some 'deans' and some teachers of Moral Science. Some are engaged in writing instructive books on Politics, Philosophy, History, and other difficult subjects.

Some scholarly women are studying not only in the United States but also in the old universities of Europe, and earning praise from the learned people there. Professor Maria Mitchell, Professor of Astronomy at Vassar College, has gained high proficiency in Astronomy, just like the scholar Caroline Herschell; she has discovered new planets, won praise and an excellent prize from the Government of Russia, and made her name immortal among Western astronomers. Professor Jane M. Bancroft has written a thesis on the politics of France, entitled *The Parliaments of Paris*, which has been adjudged the best book on politics by great scholars at universities such as Johns Hopkins, Cornell, etc. The famous Professor Louisa Reed Stowell of Michigan University has gained such proficiency in Microscopy that she has been made a member of the great Royal Microscopical Society of London. Women scholars gain membership as equals of their male colleagues in all the well-known and influential scientific societies in America today.

If it had been prophesied to the learned but somewhat short-sighted Senators of New York sixty years ago that the following half-century would witness women entering the academic field and achieving great feats, and that half the task of imparting education and moral instruction to the countless sons of the United States would be entrusted to women, it would have seemed utterly impossible (like the horn of a hare) not only to the politicians of New York but also to the whole world. The extent to which educated women have advanced national education in the United States after entering the educational field cannot be described or praised enough. To women goes the credit of making the great effort to start the Kindergarten or 'children's garden' method of education which today benefits thousands of children, and which has put a stop to corporal punishment for the tender ones. Elizabeth Peabody and her students taught the Kindergarten method to thousands of women; and wealthy ladies like Mrs Shaw and Mrs Thompson provided financial assistance to teachers like Elizabeth Peabody and helped them with the proper means to put this method into practice. When the local Government of Boston refused to grant premises or expenses for Kindergarten education in its Department of Public Education, Mrs Quincy Shaw, a wealthy and philanthropic lady of Boston, resolved to help in propagating Kindergarten education in her city.[10] She established many Kindergarten schools in Boston in a spirit of charity, and has followed the practice of spending $ 36,000 (about Rs 108,000) on their development every year, for the past twelve years. The Government has now realized the value of this educational method and granted permission to start it in all the public schools. The famous philanthropist of New York, Mrs Elizabeth Thompson, spends up to Rs 200,000 every year on child education and vocational education. She spends most of her income on children's education and lives the simple life of a nun. It is because educated women like Elizabeth Peabody, Mrs Shaw and Mrs Thompson have devoted their energies and money to this noble cause that the system of education in the United States has progressed thus far.

Educated women of the United States serve as teachers in two ways: one is to teach in educational institutions, and the second is to improve people's minds by giving them a moral education through newspapers. Women have taken to the journalistic profession for the last twenty-five years or so. The earlier practice, by and large, was for anybody to write whatever he wanted in the newspapers. There was no special restriction on the use of vulgar language in the newspapers. Educated women did not approve of this, because the papers were read by young boys and even girls; therefore they started to bring all sections of the newspapers, one by one, under their purview. This practice still continues today, and is very beneficial. Every newspaper that has a women's section is very careful to avoid reports unfair to women or articles violating morality. Besides, these newspapers acquire a greater interest because of the sweet language and style used by women. Prominent newspapers such as *The New York Herald, The Philadelphia Ledger, The Boston Transcript, The Boston Herald and The Chicago Inter-Ocean* enjoy strong support from women journalists. Every reputed newspaper invariably has a women's section. Nowadays vulgar language is usually not seen in newspapers. Women are able to discuss matters such as their own and their children's needs, what should be done for the benefit of children and society and which customs should be changed, the ideal school curriculum, the kind of laws necessary for ensuring equal justice for men and women, and so on. From the time of Creation, strong men, in the arrogance of their physical might, had lost their sense of duty and shut women's mouths. But they have opened now, not for the detriment of society but for its good, as people have realized.

Now women are no longer content to run only a section of a large newspaper, but have started independent newspapers themselves. There are hundreds of newspapers run entirely by women. *The Boston Woman's Journal, Chicago Justicia, The Union Signal, Beatrice Women's Tribune, Women's Work for Women, Children's Work for Children, St. Nicholas, Women's Magazine,* and many such papers and magazines are doing very useful work in improving social and political matters as well as public education. The weekly paper *The Union Signal* grew in a novel way. It was started about seven years ago by four or five women with a capital of $ 2,500. At that time, temperance was not a popular subject—nor is it so today—but this paper was started by the officials of the Woman's Temperance Society, and it was doubtful whether it would run. Even so, it seems to have become popular now. It now has a capital of $ 50,000, and over 40,000 subscribers. . . . The future of *The Boston Woman's Journal* was also in doubt, because it supports the view that women should obtain the same political rights as men. Just as the people of the United States opposed women's education thirty years ago, they oppose women's political rights today. But just as women, through ceaseless effort, changed public opinion with regard to education, they are resolved to change it in this regard; and there are signs that their resolve will lead to success. In some places, women are found to be even more suitable in the field of journalism than men. . . .

The greatest benefit arising from women's entry into diverse professions comes from [the rise of] women doctors. Ignorant women are unable to protect their own health or that of their children. This ignorance is very harmful to mankind, which makes it essential for women to possess medical knowledge. But people of the United States used to hold very strange beliefs in this regard. About thirty years ago, when a medical college for women was opened in Philadelphia, people persecuted its founders because they believed that women would be ruined by medical studies, lose their innate delicacy, and become useless for domestic work. Lack of knowledge breeds strange beliefs. . . . Now, thirty years after the founding of the Woman's Medical College [of Pennsylvania], the people of the United States have realized that women doctors are very useful to society. Today, there are over 1,000 licensed women doctors in the United States; their annual net income ranges from $ 100 to $ 50,000. Now women doctors are greatly appreciated everywhere, and people are thoroughly convinced that women are more skilful than men in treating patients.

Let me cite an example of the change in public opinion in this regard. . . . Twenty-five years ago, not even one or two well-known medical associations had women members; now there may not be even one or two reputed medical associations which lack women members.

Whether or not women's brains function competently in difficult scientific subjects such as Medicine will become clear from the following anecdote. There is a prestigious medical association in the United States which gives substantial awards to doctors who write excellent essays on a topic specified by it. Once, the association had invited essays on the topic, 'The Question of Rest for Women During Menstruation'.[11] One of the essays, among the four or five written by candidates at the time of the examination, was adjudged to be the best, and it was resolved to give an award of $ 500 to the author. This author had cleverly signed only with initials rather than the full name. This association was deeply prejudiced against women doctors and had not imagined that women could write such difficult papers. But after the prize was announced, it was discovered that the author was a woman, the famous Dr Mary Putnam Jacobi of New York. After realizing this, the partisan medical association found it very difficult to admit that a woman had written such a good essay and had been awarded the prize. But what could it do? Having already declared its decision, it was compelled to reluctantly give the prize to Dr Jacobi.

The city of New York has a medical college known as the New York Infirmary which is considered to be very prestigious and ranks among the best governmental or independent medical colleges in the United States. Needless to say, its founder is a woman doctor who is counted among the best doctors in the United States. When Elizabeth Blackwell, its founder, returned home in 1850 after studying Medicine and obtaining medical experience in Europe, she saw the acute need for women's hospitals.[12] In the large public hospitals under the supervision of reputed men doctors, women—who were thought to possess inferior brains—were not allowed to study how to treat patients, perform surgery, etc. In 1857, this industrious lady, together with her sister, founded her famous hospital, with a medical college attached to it. She was assisted by other equally industrious and altruistic women. Her example was followed by the women of Boston who founded the New England Hospital for Women and Children in 1862. Newly graduated women work here as well as in the New York Infirmary [as interns] to gain valuable experience of medical practice, by treating patients, performing surgical operations, etc. and by watching the other doctors. Our dear countrywoman Dr Anandibai Joshee spent some time as an intern at this New England Hospital, after graduating from Philadelphia. Following Boston, the women of Philadelphia established a hospital for women and children, attached to the women's medical college there; it also offers internships to newly graduated women doctors. Similarly there are the Chicago Hospital for Women and Children in Chicago, the Pacific Hospital for Women and Children in San Francisco, the Ohio Hospital in Cincinnati, and the Northwestern Hospital in Minneapolis. These seven excellent teaching hospitals in the Northern States, established by women and also run by women, shine with extraordinary brilliance like the seven stars in the constellation of Pleiades in the northern skies, and are a source of great happiness to the men and women who look to them with hope and expectancy. It is good news that the women of England are following the example of the women of the United States in establishing teaching hospitals.

To date, there are thirty-six medical colleges in this country, established only for women. Most of the teaching there is also conducted by women. Many women doctors work as teachers even in co-educational colleges. This proves that the prevalent belief in the United States, that medical education will ruin women, has undergone a change. After women started studying Medicine, medical experts have begun to regard the human body and anatomy as sacred. Before women were admitted as students, anatomy lessons led to vulgar practices which have now ceased altogether, because the modesty and very praiseworthy morals of the women students made the male teachers and students ashamed of their vulgar behaviour. Now the presence of women has improved the teaching style and language of anatomy to such an extent that people want to teach it even to young children of eight or ten.

Another useful profession undertaken by women is the practice of law. In the year 1868, Washington University in the city of St. Louis agreed to teach women Law. In 1869, Arabella Mansfield became the first registered lawyer and began to practise law; since then, most large universities have allowed women to study Law in their schools. The doubt entertained by many as to women's ability to study a difficult subject like Law has almost vanished now. Their capability has been proven by their clear legal arguments, competence equal to that of famous male lawyers, and most of all, their modest conduct in the courts of law. There are hundreds of registered women lawyers in the United States, who work through small firms as men do; there are twenty-one such firms started by couples, of which both husband and wife are lawyers.

There were many who objected that it would be difficult for women to protect their modesty and decorum in law courts where all kinds of cases, good and bad, would be tried. But the objectors should have realized that court cases involve not only men, but also women. Although the female sex does not produce as many culprits as the male sex (which is indeed praiseworthy and creditable to the female sex), some of the culprits do happen to be women. Their true feelings can be better understood by a lawyer of their own sex than by a man. Every thinking person must realize how difficult it is for a woman to be in a place which is full of men, without a single woman around. Moreover, it should not be difficult for a respectable woman to go where respectable men are present—and men in the position of judges and lawyers are bound to be respectable. The probability of getting due justice for women offenders increases with the advent of women lawyers. Be that as it may, experience shows that women lawyers of the United States have not lost their natural modesty and dignity in any way. All the men in the law courts where women lawyers are present treat them with due respect; moreover, the rules that prohibit smoking, [use of] bad language and improper conduct in the court rooms are being more closely observed since women entered them. Nobody can assess women's proficiency in law without seeing for themselves their work in the Supreme Court and other courts of the United States. Men have been practising law for hundreds of years in the United States, and women obtained the right to pass law examinations only twenty years ago. Within this short span of time, these brave women have caught up with highly reputed male lawyers. Women have not yet produced famous lawyers like O'Connel, Curran, Webster and Coats; but they may very well do so in the future. Besides, it is not that all men lawyers are so famous.

Since 1868, a monthly legal journal called *Legal News* has been published in Chicago. It is edited by Myra Bradwell[13], president of the largest publishing house of legal books in the United States. The massive volume known as *Bradwell's Appellate Court Reports*, prepared under this lady's supervision, is very famous and is consulted by most lawyers. Another woman, Caroline White, publishes the fortnightly *Chicago Law Times,* which is also reputed among the legal community for its excellence. In 1886, the women graduates and students of law at Michigan University formed the *Equity Club* with the objective of establishing friendships among women lawyers not only in the United States but in all countries where women have the right to practise law, thus achieving the general advancement of women through mutual help. Although men have been practising law for thousands of years, one has never heard of their having formed a similar association for the common good of the male sex, irrespective of the distinctions of class and nation. This is an excellent example of how women make good use of any power they acquire.

The fourth important profession that women have entered is preaching. During the initial years after the founding of Christianity, Christian women had as much a right to preach as men did. The rule at the time was that only a person—be it a man or a woman—who was chosen by God and endowed with this holy power should preach. The Christian doctrine preached by Christ is simple and its rules apply equally to men and women. The God of Christ imparts His Holy Spirit equally to men and women without distinction of sex. He is not partisan like man and does not entrust the task of preaching only to men. He gives suitable gifts to suitable persons; and distributes such gifts to men and women in many different ways. As regards qualities, like courtesy, artistic skills, intelligence and devotion, it cannot be said that some belong only to men and some to women, as typical of their sex. But when the Christian religion came under the control of the Romans, who regarded women as inferior, they incorporated into it their own beliefs and prejudices. The Roman Catholic bishops and monks regarded women as an enemy, like Satan;

it was they and others like them who deprived women of their right to preach. Until recently, women with a divine urge to preach had to refrain from speaking because of the restriction imposed upon them by partisan men, and listen quietly to what men said. But the light of Reason in this nineteenth century has shown men their mistake. Many non-partisan bishops in most Christian countries have begun to say that women should have the right to preach. In the United States, 165 women of different denominations are registered preachers. The people of this country are beginning to see that on many occasions women are more easily able to evangelize than male preachers. This, and other reasons, have strengthened the public desire for more women preachers.

Stenography, that is shorthand writing, is another occupation taken up by women. They have become so skilful at it that these days great and famous newspaper editors and lawyers in the United States are eager to employ women stenographers in their offices and entrust them with great responsibilities. The women in this occupation earn much more than the average woman school teacher. After learning the system of shorthand writing for a year or so and after completing a short apprenticeship, these women are able to copy down verbatim entire speeches made in law courts and in public meetings. For this work, they earn wages ranging from five to twenty dollars per hour.

When the scholarly Englishwoman Harriet Martineau visited the United States in 1840, the women here were free to engage in seven low-level jobs, namely: (1) Teaching children the alphabet and the mathematical tables (2) Sewing (3) Running boarding houses (4) Domestic service (5) Type-setting in printing presses (6) Folding and stitching pages in book binderies, and (7) Unskilled work in factories. But times have changed. Women have become educated and those who are qualified to do better jobs are no longer content with these. Although they do not receive much help and encouragement from the United States Federal and State Governments, they develop their God-given imagination aided by a sharp intellect, firm resolve and hard work. The census of 1880 shows that the women of the United States were engaged in 300 different occupations. In Massachusetts alone, there were 251,158 women engaged in 284 different occupations, and earning an annual income ranging from 150 to 3,000 dollars.

Some say that women are not imaginative because their brains are smaller, that all the inventions to date are men's. We say that women did not invent things because nobody gave them scope and encouragement to develop their inventiveness, and not because their brains are smaller. It has also happened that women have had new ideas, but, true to their natural generosity, have allowed men to take the credit. For example, the sister of the famous European singer [sic] and musician Beethoven composed many excellent and extraordinarily melodious musical pieces, and allowed them to be made public under her brother's name. They have helped to immortalize Beethoven, but very few know that the compositions were his sister's. Similarly, Caroline Herschell, the sister of the astronomer William Herschell, discovered several planets, and provided able assistance to her brother in his astronomical observations with her extraordinary mathematical abilities. But Caroline Herschell, whose ceaseless efforts and selfless assistance made William Herschell famous, was not credited by the world with a share in her brother's success. One reason why women like Beethoven's sister allowed their own inventions and discoveries to be made public under the names of their male kin or friends was their natural generosity; another reason was the barbaric belief in most countries in the past that it was shameful for women to attract notice either through an invention or any other act. We still hold this belief in our country. In the United States, women's ideas are just beginning to receive a little encouragement. Even in such a short time they have made 1,935 inventions and discoveries which they have patented with the United States Government. They are not minor inventions, but of a kind which clearly display women's deep scientific knowledge. For example, in 1845, a woman invented an underwater telescope, another invented life-jackets and rafts for sea-farers, yet another constructed a steam-making machine. A woman made improvements in the steam engine of the locomotive, another found a solution to reduce the noise of inner city trains, a third thought of a scheme to prevent the loss of standing crops due to flooding, and a fourth made a non-inductive electric cable. Women have made many useful machines for lifting grain on to barges, for winnowing grain, for harvesting fields, etc. Thus there is no room for the charge that women are not inventive.

It must be known to many that in China and in some parts of India, women work as boatmen. It is not customary for women in the United States to work in this capacity, but they are likely to do so in the future. Of the numerous steamers on the large rivers Hudson and Mississippi, some have women navigators as captains who perform their duties efficiently and systematically. It would be difficult to find many occupations in the United states in which women are not engaged. During the last forty years when they have been allowed into different occupations, their means of earning a livelihood have multiplied. Of all the farmers in the United States, seven per cent are women, who manage their own farms. Sixteen per cent of the artisans are women; over 600,000 women support themselves through handicrafts. In addition, there are 60,000 women who are independent traders or their agents. Thousands of women are telegraphists, railway ticket clerks, and post office workers. About 1,370,000 women work as cooks and domestics.

LEGAL RIGHTS

It is both surprising and regrettable that for all the progress in the United States, women have been granted very few legal rights. The social restrictions prevailing in the United States stem mainly from the ancient English law, which in turn is founded on the Commandments of Moses and on Roman law. By recognizing this, one is able to solve the riddle as to why women are treated as greatly inferior by American law. In the new States in the west, there are several changes in laws pertaining to women; [for example] the law stipulates that the house in which a married man lives with his wife should be treated as hers and not his. But in most of the eastern states a widow is not allowed to stay in her late husband's house without paying rent, for more than forty days after his death! The compassionate and learned men in the State of Maine have taken pity on the grieving widow and allowed her to stay in her deceased husband's house for ninety days! These days, many States have granted married women the right to dispose of their self-earned property as they wish. The law states that they do not have a right to the money earned by doing work at home, such as tailoring, sketching, etc., but only to the money earned by paid employment outside the home. In several States, women have a full right to the moveable and immoveable property gifted by their father or brother, and married women have a right to a third of their deceased husband's moveable assets. But in many States, they have no right to self-earned assets or those inherited from the father, and no share whatsoever in the husband's property.

In New York and many other States, a mother has no right over her minor children. A father may give guardianship of his children to whomsoever he wishes during his lifetime or through his last will and testament. Thus the husband has the right to give away the children his wife has borne, against her will. Only if he is of unsound mind or dies intestate, does the mother obtain custody of her minor children. The children born to legally wedded couples are the father's children by law; the mother can claim no right to them. Only the children of unmarried women or prostitutes are regarded as the mother's. A couple of years ago, there was a respectable woman whose heartless husband tried to give away her tender babes against her wishes. The poor mother could not endure the separation from her own flesh and blood. In order to get guardianship of her children, she set aside her modesty and took a false oath in the court of law that they were not her husband's children. Only then did she get her children back. See how the laws of so-called civilized countries insult women's modesty, maternal love and God-given natural rights! . . . Only in the three States of Kansas, New Jersey and Iowa can mothers obtain custody of their children.

A few years ago, in Massachusetts and some other States, women did not have the right to be buried beside their husbands' graves; now this law has changed. Immediately after getting married, a woman becomes her husband's prisoner. The priest makes her take a vow of obedience to her husband. The moveable and immoveable property gifted by her father or brother, her jewellery, and such other possessions go into her husband's hands.†† A few years ago a woman could not claim a right to the clothes she stood in, but now the law has forbidden

††American society still shows vestiges of its ancient barbaric condition, and it may be said that foremost among them is the excessive dependence of married women [on their husbands]. American men are shameless, just like the men of our country. They say, 'We support our households and feed our wives by our daily toil and the sweat of our brow'. Men work for eight, ten, or at the most twelve hours a day; but women have to slog for sixteen to seventeen hours daily, to serve the menfolk, mind

husbands to sell or pawn their wives' dresses in order to fill their own pockets.

The laws governing marriage and divorce differ widely throughout the United States, which causes a great deal of confusion in the social order. The good people of this country, especially The Woman's Temperance Society and its supporters, have been striving for a long time to insist that laws regarding marriage should be just and uniform throughout the country.

There is a law that entitles citizens of the United States to obtain justice in a court of law through a jury of twelve men who are their peers. But women do not have the right to trial by a jury of their own sex, who are their real peers. Men—even though they be a hundred times more foolish than women, or full of vices—do not allow the legislature to lift a finger without consulting them while enacting Federal or State laws. But women—no matter how learned, intelligent, thoughtful and moral—have no right to vote for the Federal or State legislatures. This makes men far superior to women [and not their equals] in the eyes of the law; therefore, if they, as jurors, try a case involving a woman, it does not mean that the woman defendant is tried by a jury of her peers. Except for the Territory of Wyoming, every other part of the United States has denied women this important right of an ordinary citizen, solely on the ground that they are women. Even so, these diligent women are trying to win poltical rights, and there are hopeful signs that their efforts will be crowned with success in the course of time.

---

the children and do household chores. The wives of labourers, farmers and of men in other occupations look after their homes and children first; in addition, they share their husbands' work equally and help them. In spite of all this, a wife has no right to the family income; whenever she needs a little money for her expenses, she has to cajole her husband, supply satisfactory answers to a thousand questions he asks, and beg him for it. If he refuses to give her any money, she cannot claim a right to her hard-earned possessions, either by law or with the support of public opinion. Nor is this all. On the contrary, her husband tells everyone how much she is obliged to him; and society—male society—says, 'Men work hard indeed to earn the money to feed and clothe their wives! Oh, how highly they oblige their wives!' In the absence of a wife in the house, at least two or three servants would need to be employed to do the work that she does singlehandedly; and they would need to be paid wages. Servants are not fed for doing nothing, nor can they be said to be obliged to their master. But a wife, even if she does the work of ten servants, is under an obligation to her husband because he feeds her!

COLLECTIVE EFFORT AND
NATIONAL ORGANIZATIONS

When the democratic republic of the United States was founded, Benjamin Franklin suggested that the national seal be inscribed with the motto 'E pluribus unum' or 'One out of many'. Now, one can see this motto on the national seal everywhere in the United States. Furthermore, we can see, hear and experience it at every step in the actions of these people. The power of the United States lies not in its artillery, cavalry or vast army, but in the people's wisdom and in the truth of the motto 'One out of many'. When women were uneducated and generally inexperienced in worldly matters, they were ignorant of this truth, and therefore did not accomplish great things. With the increase in their education and knowledge, this eternal truth has awakened in their hearts and shines with greater brilliance with every passing day.

Though famous throughout the world for its progressiveness, the United States did not have a single important women's association fifty years ago. Women would just sit at home or gather at a neighbour's house to gossip, or do some sewing in aid of churches, priests or the poor. Nobody even imagined that women were capable of doing anything more important than this. Women themselves, let alone men, had no idea of their real worth, capability and mental powers. Fifty years ago, women supporters of education in England founded an association called The Bluestockings Club, with the aim of promoting general education. It became the laughing stock of the world at the time, and 'bluestockings' became a derogatory word. The self-styled modest women would quake and tremble at the thought of a women's association and of women attending its meetings to discuss educational advancement. Everybody thought it sinful for women to attend public meetings and to address them. But the light of this progressive century has dispelled the darkness of such a belief.

The learned American woman Frances Willard has said that this glorious nineteenth century has seen many wonderful scientific discoveries; but the most wonderful of them all is Woman's discovery of herself. This is borne out by considering the history of women's collective effort during the last forty years to promote their own welfare and that of their society and country, by forming a number of associations. In 1848, a few courageous, progressive and learned women like Lucretia Mott, Elizabeth Cady Stanton, and others established an important women's society to work for women's equal right to education and employment, as well as for their political rights.[14] Women's collective effort can be said to have started from this date. From that time until 1869, perhaps a couple of small women's societies were established, but there is no record of their having done anything special to achieve national stature. No 'National Convention of Women' had come into existence before 1858, not merely in the United States but anywhere in the world. Until that time nobody imagined that women could establish a national association and manage all its work smoothly.

About 1860, signs of a terrible civil war were visible in the United States. A controversy arose between the northern and southern States over the slavery of Negroes, which flared into hostility. In 1860–61, the southern States declared war against the northern ones, and the terrible war which was fought between the two until 1865 devastated American families everywhere. Initially, the Civil War caused untold misery, poverty and suffering; however, they were immediately followed by great good, just as the deadly poison was followed by nectar and the precious gem [when the legendary ocean was churned by gods and demons, according to the Hindu mythology].

President Lincoln became the leader of the northern States, abolished slavery, and called upon strong, able-bodied American men to volunteer for the army to quell the southern rebellion and protect the country's honour. When the brave northern men went to war, honouring President Lincoln's call, they did not have any uniforms (trousers, jackets, socks, etc.) Nor were there any organizations to supply these and other materials for war. When the war started and news came that the soldiers needed uniforms, the women of almost all the towns in the northern States gathered in churches and started sewing uniforms. Initially they supplied uniforms to last the soldiers for three months. This event showed the women the result of collective effort and its tremendous benefit to society and the nation.

A little later, the American Civil War assumed terrible proportions and the fighting spread everywhere. The northern States established a committee called the Christian Commission, with the aim of providing spiritual solace to the soldiers by sending clergymen to the battlefield to preach to them and to administer the last rites. The task of collecting money for the expenses of the Commission fell to the women's lot, while men occupied the positions of president, vice-president, and so on. Women worked very hard to collect large sums of money which they delivered to the Commission, and with which the Commission sent hundreds of clergymen to preach to the soldiers. The Commission's intention was undoubtedly very praiseworthy; but the soldiers, wounded on the battlefield, dying of hunger and thirst and suffering agonies, did not have much interest in listening to sermons. On the other hand, the clergymen who had gone there to ensure the soldiers' spiritual welfare did not know how to promote their physical welfare by alleviating the suffering of their 'temporal' bodies. The poor wounded soldier could not be blamed for not tolerating the chatter of the clergymen who started preaching instead of providing physical aid when he [the soldier] was severely wounded in the arm or the leg. This made many people realize that it was necessary to create a separate organization to give physical aid to wounded soldiers, and that it was desirable for this organization to appoint women to nurse and look after them. This led to the establishment of the Sanitary Commission.

The very existence of this Commission and its great achievements were impressive; but what astonished the world even more was the feat of the American women who supported it, supplied it from beginning to end with all the equipment which was required and managed it. The Commission sent not hundreds but thousands of male and female nurses to the battlefield. They made proper arrangements for the regular meals of the wounded soldiers of the allied army (and also of some destitute enemy soldiers), set up hospitals on the battlefield, buried dead soldiers, and gave succour to the poor and the helpless. It was difficult for the Commission to find the large sums of money and supplies needed for these numerous tasks. The Government treasury had no money, and there was not a single person who possessed the wealth to finance the Commission's formidable expenditure, or at least the generosity to donate it. That was when the prominent women in the working sub-committee of the Commission thought of a clever plan. Mary A. Livermore and a couple of other women proposed to put the plan into practice, and sent an appeal to many people in Illinois and other States informing them of both their aims and plan of action. Shortly, all the newspapers in the northern States published the news that some industrious women of Chicago were proposing to hold a charity bazaar where articles gifted by generous people would be sold at a high price and the proceeds donated to the Sanitary Commission; and that those interested in supporting this admirable enterprise should send whatever they could to the address of a certain lady in Chicago.

The women organizers of the charity bazaar had estimated that, if properly managed, it would yield a profit of at least $ 25,000. This made learned men and respected newspaper editors laugh. They thought that not only did the women lack sense enough to earn $ 25,000, but that they were sure to end up ruining the whole charity bazaar. Some sneered contemptuously. . . . After the bazaar was over, people found out that the sale proceeds, after deducting all expenses, yielded a net profit five times higher than the organizers' estimate. The hardworking women of the Sanitary Commission made a profit of about $ 125,000 (i.e. about Rs 375,000) and dispatched it for the Commission's use. Many such bazaars were held after that in aid of the Sanitary Commission. . . . It was women who thought of the idea of the bazaar, it was they who managed it from beginning to end, and who made all the big and small articles that were sold. This capability, organizational ability, political insight, foresight and perseverance astonished the men who had arrogantly thought that they alone possessed these qualities and who had babbled that women had no capacity for practical work; while the noble people who had recognized women's true worth applauded them.

The Sanitary Commission was a kind of national benevolent association, and it gave women the first opportunity to work alongside men, in positions high and low. The fêtes and bazaars organized in aid of the Commission yielded innumerable benefits and allowed massive tasks to be undertaken and carried through to completion. All this made the women realize the truth that great aims can be achieved if many work together collectively, smoothly and in an organized manner. It also showed the world what mighty deeds women are capable of, when they are given the education, freedom and opportunity to work. The famous English philanthropist Florence Nightingale set aside the English-style seclusion of women, went to [the front in] the Crimean War, nursed wounded soldiers, made proper arrangements for patients on the battlefield, and set an excellent example to all the compassionate women of the world. How well Miss Nightingale's example was followed by the American women is shown by American history of the years between 1860 and 1866. While the Civil War lasted, women of the northern States managed not only their homes but also the jobs and tasks of men; they collected large sums of money and innumerable things required by charitable associations like the Christian and the Sanitary Commissions; and moreover, thousands of them went to the battlefield and worked day and night, to nurse and serve the tired and weary, wounded and half-dead soldiers. At high noon or in the middle of the night, they went personally to help wherever help was needed, even in the thick of battle, ignoring hunger, thirst and physical discomfort. Hundreds of millionairesses left their wealthy homes and went into self-imposed exile to alleviate the suffering of their countrymen on the battlefield, and risked their lives doing a variety of good deeds; at times they lost their physical strength, moveable and immoveable property, and even their invaluable lives! Blessed indeed are these saintly, philanthropic matrons!

Since 1865 to date, a number of women's organizations have been established in the United States, with many more to come. Not only in the United States but also in England, France, Germany, Finland, Norway, Italy, and other countries, local and national organizations have been set up, with a variety of aims. The reason for the existence of these women's national organizations was that women's innate capability was seen by the world through associations like the Civil War Sanitary Commission; and that women recognized their own worth and strength, and realized that enormous tasks could be accomplished if many undertook an enterprise with a single aim and collective effort. . . . The words ['women's organization'] that women were ashamed to utter fifty years ago have become universally acceptable today. Now it would be difficult to find a town of about a thousand inhabitants that does not have at least one women's organization. In every town and city, one finds a variety of women's organizations—for the Promotion of Education, Mutual Improvement, Aid to the Poor, Temperance, . . . Protection of Orphans, Protection of Children, Rehabilitation of Fallen Women, Promotion of Music, Charity, Demand for Legal Rights, Social Progress, Advancement of Women, . . . and so on. . . .

In every country we see that women are the guardians of religion and morality. In all countries and all communities, women are the ones who protect their religion by their pure and pious conduct, charity, devotion to God and total sacrifice in the defence of religion. During the last forty years, these invaluable qualities of women have been discovered in Christian countries, and women have been given the opportunity to conduct religious services independently in the light of their own conscience, which is of great benefit to the world. About twenty-five years ago, the first women's missionary society was founded in this country. Now, most Christian denominations have established their own women's missionary societies. Together these societies have a total of about 1,500,000 women as members; they pay over $2,000,000 (i.e. Rs 6,000,000) annually as membership fees, and utilize this money, through their representatives and presidents, towards evangelical activities and as aid to the destitute. . . . . All the work of these societies and meetings is managed by the women themselves. All the office-bearers, such as the president, vice-president, secretaries, superintendents, speakers, preachers, treasurers, editors of newspapers and magazines, are women; and they alone manage all the work. They are not content with doing charitable work themselves, but also take along their sons and daughters, from a very young age, to attend evangelical meetings; often they arrange meetings only for children, in order to inculcate in them a taste for charitable work. . . . .

Ever since this large body of missionary women came into existence, women have realized their own worth and strength. In the past, only men preachers went to evangelize in other countries as representatives of missionary societies. Only if they were married could their wives join them, without, however, the permission or leisure to preach. The general belief at the time was that women were not capable of preaching, let alone travelling by themselves to far-off lands to evangelize. The orthodox Christian societies still do not ordain women as clergy; however, hundreds of unmarried or widowed women belonging to these societies, who are educated and devout, are ever ready to travel long distances, even alone, within their own country or abroad. Their aim is to emancipate the women there, both rich and poor, from the clutches of falsehood and ignorance. The domestic societies of missionary women bear the expenses of these evangelical women, finance and manage the boys' and girls' schools started by them, and send them all the necessary supplies and aid.

WOMEN'S CLUBS

After women's missionary societies began to be established in this fashion, many learned and far-sighted women developed a strong desire to start women's clubs. Although societies and clubs are generally similar, there is an important difference between them. A society is an association established with a single chief aim, and only those who subscribe to that aim can join it as members. A club is not established with a sole object; it assembles people of diverse beliefs, so that a single club can undertake different types of activities. Because of this diversity of opinions and of ways of thinking among the members, each member gains wide general knowledge from the numerous views expressed on any topic being discussed. Realizing that women need such wide knowledge, some diligent American women founded the first American women's club twenty years ago, under the name Sorosis.[15] . . . When the Sorosis Club came into being, many expressed reservations about its usefulness, considering that women's missionary societies were already in existence. There was no prior model for this club. Although the founders of the Sorosis Club did not acknowledge a specific aim, they had a grand design in mind. At the time, women did not have practical wisdom like men, nor did women of different views communicate with each other; therefore they remained narrow-minded (like frogs in a pond), and were prejudiced and ready to detect and criticize the faults of others. The founders of Sorosis knew that a familiarity with diverse opinions in large gatherings would dispel the prejudices born of ignorance, and that women would be able to act with a single aim and achieve great things.

The establishment of Sorosis showed everybody the numerous advantages of a club; and it soon assumed a variegated and universal character by promoting knowledge and friendship, undertaking charitable work, helping the destitute, and so on. The Club surveyed the condition of orphaned and abandoned infants as well as of infant asylums in New York city, and published the information. The Club also reformed existing infant asylums and earned credit for founding two new ones. It also surveyed the condition of women factory workers in New York city, their treatment by the factory owners, and the reforms necessary to better their condition; it presented these findings before the public, thus greatly benefiting the women workers. The Club was the first to petition the management of the University of New York and of Columbia University, to admit women students along with men. Due to lack of space, it is not possible to give a description of the hundreds of important and beneficial undertakings of this Club. Sorosis prohibits a discussion of three topics: religion, politics, and women's political rights. This has been ensured so as to prevent discord among the members while discussing religion and similar topics, because the Club has been established mainly in order to provide knowledge to ladies and to engage in philanthropy. But this does not mean that its members have no interest in these topics. Numerous other clubs, such as New England Woman's Club, New Century Club, etc. which are the 'daughters' of Sorosis, not only discuss these topics but have vowed to propagate progressive ideas by inviting women of diverse opinions to address them and explain their views, without causing any disagreement.

Some useless fellows say that these women's societies and clubs are but an imitation of men's activities; but the women's societies and clubs which I saw in large numbers in the United States had no connection with those of men. Women's missionary and temperance societies and clubs were founded and developed solely by women. Men's clubs are usually established only with the intention of discussing politics, chatting, or amusing themselves by playing ball-games. They are not much inclined towards charity, promoting education, helping the destitute, comforting sufferers, and so on. Because these men's clubs do not allow ladies, they are infested with harmful and bad practices like drinking, using vulgar language, etc. as I have heard many people say. If this be true, I am happy and proud to say that women's clubs show not the least sign of imitating men's clubs.

Soon after the creation of the Sorosis Club, another very important club known as the Woman's Congress was established. It makes strong efforts to promote women's education, and is therefore also known as The Society for the Advancement of Women. Its members include women from many parts of the United States, who are very learned, far-sighted, experienced and interested in education. There are many local branches of this club, and once every year the members meet at an appointed place. On this occasion, scholarly women read their well-reasoned and thoughtful essays on serious subjects such as politics, social reform, social conditions, education, arts, sciences, poetry and history, and also deliver lectures. This club enjoys great prominence because of the prestige, learning and fame of its members.

There is another famous club known as New England Woman's Club in Boston, which also aims to promote education, as is the case with the Woman's Congress. . . . The New Century Club of Philadelphia is famous for its valuable qualities of progressiveness and philanthropy. Its efforts have led to the formation of The Working Woman's Guild which has over seven hundred working women as its members. Only self-supporting women who work in factories, shops, etc., can become its members. For a couple of hours every evening, classes on different subjects are held in its meeting hall. . . . These days the example of The New Century Club has been followed by respectable, educated women in many other places, who have established organizations like The Working Woman's Guild for the advancement of working women and for the welfare and moral protection of misguided, destitute young women. Nobody will be able to assess the extent of the benefit of such clubs to working women and to society at large. Boston has the Woman's Educational and Industrial Union which is managed by educated, experienced women of good families, who take turns to visit the Union hall and supervise its working. . . .

There are many other societies modelled on this one all over the United States, known as Women's Exchanges. They are all run by women, with the objective of helping poor, destitute women who work for a living, by selling their home-made goods at a fair price. In some places a boarding house is attached to the Exchange, to accomodate women visitors who come from other towns for work. These houses are under the supervision of the respectable, influential women of the town. Its entire management is entrusted to women's societies which are of great help to the working women of the United States.

The Young Women's Christian Association is an excellent philanthropic organization in this country. It has branches in almost all cities, and has hundreds and thousands of young women as members. It has been formed to achieve several praiseworthy and important aims (in which it has been very successful), such as explaining and propagating Christianity among young women, preaching to ignorant women and leading them on the right path, arranging for good and reasonably priced accomodation for self-supporting women, making education available to anyone who is interested in learning languages or getting scientific or vocational information.

In 1848, several active women held a Women's Rights Convention at Seneca Falls in the State of New York, as mentioned above. This was the very first association established for protecting women's rights; all other women's societies have come into being after following its example and with its assistance. The whole world ridiculed the Convention when it was held. So-called gentlemen slung mud at the women who spoke on its behalf, and cursed them; the yellow newspapers drew cartoons of them; public leaders and opinion builders denounced and ostracized them; preachers honoured them with epithets, such as 'irreligious', 'immoral', 'heretical', 'evil', 'witches' and 'Satan's messengers'—epithets that served to expose their own breeding. But the women did not abandon their determination even in the face of such adverse circumstances and public opinion. They sacrificed their happiness, devoted their energies and wealth, and even shared the oppression of the women they helped, in order to continue their work for the abolition of women's slavery. The Convention has now become the National Woman Suffrage Association[16] with branches in hundreds of places in the United States, with its headquarters in Boston. It publishes weekly, fortnightly and monthly newspapers as well as books at several places. The American Woman Suffrage Association publishes a famous weekly paper, the *Woman's Journal*, in Boston. Its example is followed by women in England, Canada, Australia, France, Denmark, Finland, and other countries, with the establishment of similar societies.

The efforts of the National Convention for Women's Rights in the United States have led to several changes and improvements in the laws pertaining to the women of this country. In the State of Kansas, women have obtained all important rights of representation in the municipality. In the Territory of Wyoming, women have received all the political rights that men have, with a clearly beneficial effect. (Also, in Canada, England and the English territory in Australia, unmarried and widowed women have obtained rights in the municipality.) The efforts of these societies have succeeded in large measure, and there are favourable signs that they will be fully successful in the near future. Forty years ago this important Women's Convention founded at Seneca Falls made a small breach in the ramparts of the impenetrable fortress of custom which society had erected around the female community in order to imprison them and block their progress; and it made a small path for women to escape from this terrible fortress. Thousands of women are leaving the fortress in groups in order to reach freedom, and more will continue to do so. This Convention has now become international. At the end of March 1888, women from about ten civilized countries had come to the city of Washington [District of Columbia] at the invitation of the American Woman's Suffrage Association. At that time, the Association called a convention of the International Council of Women and resolved to establish branches in each member country. In some cases this has already been carried out. This International Council of Women has been established not merely in order to obtain political rights for women. It has come into being in order to achieve very important and laudable aims, namely to establish friendly relations among all kinds of women's societies anywhere in the world, to provide mutual help when necessary, to provide mutual encouragement, and to create friendship among women of all nations. . . . There are many other important women's societies in this country, which are not mentioned here because information about all of them will take up considerable space. However, this essay will remain incomplete without at least a little information about the Woman's [Christian] Temperance Union in this country, which I give below.

In November of last year (1887), the National Woman's Temperance Union of the United States held its fourteenth annual convention at the town of Nashville, in the State of Tennessee. The society's president [Frances Willard] had invited me to attend it.[17] I travelled two thousand miles to Nashville to see the great convention and the gathering of eminent women from all the States. For a whole week the city was crowded with women. About three hundred leading women had come there as representatives of the Woman's Temperance Unions of all States in this country. Besides, many men and women had gathered there to see the convention.

The State of Tennessee is situated in the south of the country; and independence, education and diligence are not seen among the women in these parts to the extent seen in the north. Some years ago, nobody there approved of a woman addressing a meeting, and nobody had even dreamt of the words 'women's societies'. There, the female sex has not advanced as much as it should, nor are the means of higher education available to it. On the way to Nashville, I had occasion to stop in the city of Louisville in the State of Kentucky, and to address a meeting at the insistence of the people there. On that occasion, the minister of the church where I was to speak insisted on my sitting on the dais. It was my desire that if I was to sit on the dais, some of the eminent women of the town should also sit with me on the dais. But the women said, 'We have never done such a thing in our lives, how can we bring ourselves to do so now?' I said, 'Ladies, you have never sat on the dais before, but what is the harm in making a beginning now? Just sit there with me once; if it bothers you in any way, don't do it again.' After much hesitation, five or six women agreed to sit on the dais, and stayed there until I finished my speech. Needless to say, they came to no harm. Although women in the south are not secluded, very few of them seem to possess the necessary independence and confidence in company.

On hearing the news that the annual convention of the Woman's Temperance Union of the United States was to take place at Nashville, many people there made many kinds of speculations about it. Nobody really knew much about what the society was and how it worked. Many thought that it would be some kind of play-acting or spectacle produced by the unimaginative ideas of half-sane and half-insane women. Many clergymen refused them permission to hold meetings in their churches on the grounds that it was an irreligious act and that the women were engaging in unwomanly conduct in contravention of biblical injunctions. At last, it was decided to hold the meetings in the hall of a public library. The local [chapter of the] Woman's Temperance Union of Nashville exerted itself extremely hard to coax the local women to help with the convention. These generous women invited to their homes the women who had come from afar and entertained them very hospitably.

On the morning of 16th November, the marvellous convention began. Seven hundred chairs had been arranged in a semi-circle in the meeting hall; there was no room for more. All the walls of the hall were decorated with the flags of different States and the colourful banners of the Woman's Temperance Unions of each State, embroidered and inscribed with their mottos. The spot where the president and other prominent women were to sit was decorated with the star-spang led banner of the United States, flower bouquets and green wreaths.

By nine in the morning, the meeting hall was full. The audience also included a number of men. Then the president, Frances E. Willard, called everybody's attention and started the meeting. Some eminent women said excellent, absorbing prayers, sang sweet songs, gave touching advice, and Miss Frances made an absorbing, deeply meaningful and beautiful speech. A great poet should have been present there to do justice to all this.

Before the first day's meeting was concluded, many clergymen in the town changed their minds and sent invitations to this unparalleled Woman's Union, insisting that they should hold meetings in their churches, make speeches, and oblige them. The men in the audience stopped ridiculing the Union and began to show it respect. Then, throughout that week, the prominent women in the Union went to about six different places every morning, noon and night, to make speeches and give advice; even so, the people were not content. During that week, people saw resolutions being passed in the meeting, reports of the previous year's activities being read out, and an efficient manner of conducting the proceedings; the overall beauty and excellent management of all this would have made even the British parliament and the United States Congress envious of this Temperance Union. On that occasion, Miss Frances Willard's talent for public speaking, leadership, managerial skill, organizational capacity, and extraordinary knowledge of the old rules of parliament [were fully displayed]. . . .

On the evening of 24th November, the convention was concluded. On that occasion, while bidding farewell to the women gathered there, prominent men and clergy of Nashville recounted how they had changed their minds about women and how the procedure and excellent organization of the Union, its good advice and benevolent moral philosophy surprised and gladdened them; and, with high praise and great honour, they bade the National Woman's Temperance Union of the United States farewell and invited it to come there again the following year.

The whole convention passed off happily. I had not seen such a marvellous, charming and vast scene ever before in my life, and it made me feel that my life was now fulfilled. This great convention and Union cannot be compared to any association or convention other than the convention of the International Council of Women held at Washington, at the end of last March.

WOMAN'S CRUSADE

Demoness Liquor and her brother Tobacco had forced their way into people's houses and begun to devastate them. Almost every single man began to give imaginary justifications, such as, 'I am a man, I can do anything with impunity; liquor helps to ease tiredness; chewing and smoking tobacco relaxes the brain; it is scientifically proven that a small drink for medicinal purposes or to help digestion is perfectly harmless;' and began drinking and using intoxicants to his heart's content and squandering money on them. Saloons, which were the gateways to hell and the causes of total ruin, grew everywhere. Their stained glass windows and decorated doorways beckoned men temptingly. Saloon-keepers, who filled their pockets by exploiting others, invented thousands of ways to increase their business by luring the young and the old, the ignorant and the wise, in many different ways. Day by day, more and more men were caught in their noose, lost all they had, and forfeited their happiness, respectability, and sometimes life itself. Because of them, their poor wives and their tender, newborn babes were reduced to a wretched state. Thousands of devoted wives suffered inwardly, as they watched their husbands being totally ruined by the vice. Millions of mothers suffered in their hearts, as they saw their sons, dearer than their own lives, abandoning religion, morality and their happiness in this world and the next, while heading for eternal hell because of their addiction to liquor. Even so, all those poor women endured their agonies in silence. Scriptures and custom—the two arbiters of society—have issued women an injunction to stay at home and put up with everything quietly; in obedience to it, women have endured endless, intolerable agonies and mental suffering without so much as a moan, until today.

But there is a limit to everything in this world. When oppressed too heavily, even a worm turns once in a while and prepares to fight the enemy in self-defence. It is not very surprising, then, that a time comes when human beings—even women, who are accustomed to enduring oppression patiently—are driven to put up a resistance against oppression when the oppression reaches a limit. Such an occasion arose in the case of women in the State of Ohio, when they dispensed with their seclusion and silence, and resolved to fight the saloon-keepers who had heartlessly caught their husbands and sons in their coils and dragged them away, in order to protect their babes and their dear ones. Hundreds of well-born, forbearing and virtuous women girded themselves and assisted the crusade against saloon-keepers; and vowed not to return from the battlefield until they had defeated the enemy and protected their sons and their homes. In this war, nobody slit another's throat or snatched a morsel of food from another's mouth through deceit; nobody's blood was spilt and nobody's heart was pierced by harsh words; nobody terrified another with deadly weapons like guns, swords or cannons. Even so, its name made the liquor-sellers and their partisans—those irreligious tormentors and plunderers of others' property—tremble; the crusaders' banner of peace made Satan quake; and their sweet, logical exhortations shook the foundations of Satan's citadels until they crumbled and fell. The Crusades†† of the eleventh and twelfth centuries pale before the marvellous and unparalleled, peaceful crusade of women in the nineteenth century. There can be no comparison between the two. Men's crusades, during the barbaric times of the past, were aimed at cutting people's throats, sprinkling the whole earth with human blood, and tarnishing the name of religion. The women's crusade of the nineteenth century was aimed at saving people's lives, rescuing them from hell, and establishing happiness, peace and joy in their homes. Men's crusades of the eleventh and twelfth centuries destroyed millions of lives; the women's crusade of the nineteenth century employed the means to pull billions of people out of the jaws of death. Those barbaric crusades sullied the religion of Christ, the Angel of Peace; this modern crusade made that holy religion shine like burnished gold.

††A crusade is a war fought in the name of the Cross. At the close of the eleventh century, Mahommedans conquered Jerusalem and prepared to occupy Christian countries like Spain. The followers of Christianity then fought wars against the Mahommedans in defence of their religion, which are known as the Crusades. These wars continued until the thirteenth century AD.

This marvellous crusade started on 24th December, 1873. A man named Dio Lewis had come to the town of Hillsboro in the State of Ohio to make a speech. On the evening of the 24th, he delivered a lecture on the subject 'Our Girls' for the Lecture Association there, at the Washington Court-House. On that occasion, he described the extent to which the human race was harmed by the use of liquor, other intoxicating drinks, tobacco, etc. and narrated his own experience. His mother, a devout and righteous woman, was deeply grieved at the harm caused in the world by this vice. Dio's father was addicted to liquor and had lost everything. Mrs Lewis, seeing her happiness and family life ruined, decided to save her husband; and she thought of a new solution to cure the townspeople of this vice. Taking some women friends along, she herself visited saloons which sold liquor and other intoxicants, prayed and preached there, and entreated their owners to give up their low and ruinous trade. Her efforts were eventually successful and all the saloon-keepers in the town closed down their saloons. After narrating this story, Dio Lewis said to the women in the audience that if they followed suit, their good efforts would also be successful, and that all the saloons there would be closed down within a week; and that, if the women wanted to undertake the deed, their leaders should indicate their consent. On hearing Lewis' words, about fifty women stood up to show their consent for the undertaking. Then Lewis turned to the men, who opposed drinking, sitting nearby, and asked how many of them would help the women if they undertook the deed, upon which about seventy men stood up. When it was thus decided to undertake this deed, it was resolved to call a meeting on the morning of Christmas Day, that is, 25th December, for this great deed.

On Christmas Day, at ten in the morning, a large gathering met at the Presbyterian Church there, in accordance with the previous night's resolution. After a psalm was sung and the service held, Dio Lewis made an hour-long speech in which he narrated his mother's story, described how much strength women possess to undertake important tasks, and how their tolerance, diligence and affectionate nature are the useful means to accomplish such tasks. All the people gathered there approved highly of Dio Lewis' suggestion and the Woman's [Temperance] Crusade was launched that very morning.

Like other societies, this Crusade also made rules, elected a president, vice-president, secretary and treasurer; needless to say, all of them were women. One committee from this women's society was sent to war. This was a committee of fifty-two women who took a vow to fight to the finish. A resolution was passed to form a Committee of Visitation to present appeals at hotels and saloons to give up the evil trade and start another respectable business, and also hold prayers and sermons.[18] A group of 'backers' was set up to help the Committee of Visitation, in which thirty-seven men accepted the responsibility of providing financial aid to the women crusaders. After making all these preparations, it was resolved that a sub-committee should be formed to write an appeal to be sent to all saloon-keepers.

The Committee of Visitation made Mrs E. J. Thompson its leader and decided to attack the enemy. Mrs Thompson describes the first battle as follows:[19]

On the morning of 25th December 1873, we turned our faces towards the first-class saloon (as it was called) kept by Robert Ward, on High Street, a resort made famous by deeds, the memory of which unnerved the heart and paled the cheek of some among us, as the seventy entered the open door of the . . . [saloon]. Doubtless he had learned of our approach, as he not only propped the heavy door open, but with the most perfect suavity of manner held it until the ladies all passed in; then, closing it, walked to his accustomed stand behind the bar.

Seizing the strange opportunity, the leader [i.e. Mrs Thompson herself] addressed him as follows: 'Well, Mr Ward, this must seem to you a strange audience! I suppose, however, that you understand the object of our visit?' 'Robert' by this time began to perspire freely, and remarked that he would like to have a talk with Dio Lewis. Mrs Thompson said: 'Dr Lewis has nothing whatever to do with the subject of our mission. As you look upon some of the faces before you, and observe the marks of sorrow, caused by the unholy business that you ply, you will find that it is no wonder we are here. We have come, however, not to threaten, not even to upbraid, but in the name of our Divine Friend and Saviour, and in his spirit, to forgive, and to commend you to his pardon, if you will but agree to abandon a business that is so damaging to our hearts and to the peace of our homes!'

The hesitation and embarrassment of the famous saloon-keeper seemed to afford (as the leader thought) an opportunity for prayer; so, casting her eye around upon that never-to-be-forgotten group of earnest faces, she said, *very softly*: 'Let us pray.' Instantly all, even the poor liquor-seller himself, were upon their knees. . . .

The scene that followed, in a most remarkable manner portrayed the spirit of our holy religion. Poor wives and mothers, who the day before would have crossed the street to avoid passing by a place so identified with their heartaches, their woes, and their deepest humiliation, in tearful pathos were now pleading with this deluded brother to accept the world's Redeemer as his own. Surely, 'God is Love'!

The greatness of that other-worldly love and forgiveness cannot be described enough. The prophecy of Dio Lewis came true. Thanks to the unceasing efforts of this marvellous Committee of Visitation, all the saloons in Hillsboro closed down within a week!

On hearing the report of the Hillsboro Crusade, women of many other places in the United States followed their example. But these crusades were not long-lasting; therefore, some far-sighted women decided to make a collective effort. In 1874, some of the successful women crusaders met at a summer camp at Chautauqua and established the Woman's Christian Temperance Union with the purpose of making continuous efforts to eradicate the vice of drinking. Soon it became a national association thanks to the efforts of some good, diligent and upright women; and assumed the name, The National Woman's [Christian] Temperance Union of the United States. . . .

I have no hesitation in saying that this is the best and greatest of all the associations prevalent among all civilized countries. It would be rare to find a good deed that it has not undertaken, difficult to cite any example of its motherly love being denied to anyone, and impossible to imagine that the virtues of bravery, seriousness, courage and forgiveness can have reached perfection anywhere else, except in God. It is not that the women's missionary societies in this and other countries are insignificant; they have spent millions of rupees and have been selflessly engaged in the task of leading foreign people on to the path of the holy religion, for which they cannot be praised enough. But there are denominational differences among these societies, which is why they lack unity, and are unable to perform as many good deeds as the Temperance Union does. Women's Christian societies include only so-called 'evangelical' sects, and do not assist others. All other societies for the promotion of education and philanthropic works may be excellent and beneficial in their own ways, but cannot be compared to the Union, because their numbers are small and aims limited. But the aims of the Woman's Temperance

Union are many and very important. It has no internal differences of opinion; here women of all opinions, classes and kinds work together unitedly. Its successive local, state, national and international levels; its simple but strict rules, which are excellent, acceptable to all and easy for all to observe; its extraordinary management, superior to the administration of any country and holding everything and everybody together—considering all these, one feels that this Union is the crown of all the marvellous miracles on God's earth in the present age. . . .

For many years now, the State Governments of Maine and Iowa have passed temperance laws to prohibit the brewing and sale of liquor; but the Governments are helpless before the wickedness of the liquor-sellers. A clandestine traffic in liquor still goes on there. About two years ago, the women of Kansas won important political rights with regard to the municipality. The first important task for which they exercised their rights was to put a complete stop to the liquor traffic in the State. About half these women were members of the Woman's Temperance Union; they made efforts to prevent the clandestine traffic in liquor. What the men in the State of Maine, lacking the support of women, were unable to achieve in twenty-five years, was accomplished by the people of the State of Kansas almost within two years, on the strength of the united power of men and women. . . .

When the women of Kansas obtained political rights, some mischievous men of a town in the State elected a well-born young housewife as their Mayor, in order to demonstrate that women did not deserve political rights and were not capable of important political work. The very next day the people who had elected her Mayor realized that their assumption, that women were unable to carry on administration and implement laws, was wrong. Immediately upon assuming the office of Mayor, the woman made a search for all the saloons, gambling dens and other places of illegal activities, and closed them down. The good men and women of the town assisted her greatly in locating clandestine places. The townspeople are very happy with her administration, and she manages her duties in a proper and excellent manner. The members of the National Woman's Christian Temperance Union of the United States used to think that women did not need political rights. But, during the past fifteen years, their intensive efforts have not yielded the expected results; and they have realized that the lack of political rights is the sole reason. The liquor traders are almost all men, and they have invested millions of dollars in this trade. There are also many men who support them. All of them have political rights, and they vote against the women's efforts to introduce temperance laws. The law supports the majority vote. In the matter of making laws, women have no power, and men, especially liquor-sellers and drinkers, enjoy political rights as well as financial advantage. Many men and women have begun to think that unless women obtain some of the political rights, they will not be able to defeat the demon of liquor. Therefore they are making unceasing efforts to obtain political rights for women.

The International Woman's Temperance Union has been established thanks to the vision and organizational ability of Miss Frances E. Willard, the respected president of the National Woman's [Christian] Temperance Union of the United States, and with the help of her friends. Miss Willard had this idea in 1883. . . . And then, in 1884, this International Woman's Temperance Union was established. Mrs Mary Clement Leavitt, an adventurous, brave and resolute woman, became its representative and started on a journey around the world with the intention of establishing temperance unions everywhere. She went first to the island of Hawaii, then to countries like Australia, Japan, China, Ceylon, India, Madagascar, Africa [sic], etc., and established hundreds of temperance unions. Now she intends to visit all the countries of Europe. When this single, unsupported, helpless woman started on this great enterprise, she had neither money nor a companion; but she is accompanied by her God and her strong resolve to do good. Wherever she goes, she receives the assistance she needs. Now Woman's Temperance Unions are being established in most of the civilized countries. The women of England were also inspired by American women's enthusiasm and sense of duty. They have established the national union, called the British Woman's Temperance Association, and it does a lot of good work. Canada also has the National Woman's Temperance Union; it is engaged in intense efforts to prohibit traffic in liquor in that country. Similar unions exist in Australia, the Hawaiian islands, Madagascar and Africa. My Indian sisters, why do you lag behind? Such a national union is essential in our country. The International Woman's Temperance Union proposes to send a strong appeal to all heads of nations, in which women of all nations plan to request them to stop traffic in liquor and intoxicants. All our Indian women must sign this appeal; everybody must try to circulate the appeal and obtain signatures. May there be no Indian who refuses to assist this great enterprise directly or indirectly. This is our prayer to the Almighty.

Now Miss Frances E. Willard is president of the International Woman's Temperance Union. Under her leadership, at least one million women are engaged in activities related to temperance, throughout the world. This [International Woman's Christian] Temperance Union is the 'United Democratic State of Women'. These women unite the whole world by connecting them with a bond of friendship, with the sacred bond of their white ribbon, a symbol of peace and love.†† They propagate the three precious virtues, which are the source of all happiness—peace, love and friendship—among women of all nations. The great deed which could not be done by men, who have been kings and emperors, and who, for thousands of years, have been armed with weapons, have possessed bodily strength, and have been rulers of society, has been been done by these women, [who have been] derided as ignorant and weak. O God, You are great indeed! You make such people, who are shunned by the world, into the instruments which humble the conceit of the arrogant. In Your hands even a blade of grass becomes immeasurably powerful like a thunderbolt!

NOTES

1. Haihayarjuna was supposed to have a thousand arms. As is well-known, Sita did not kill Ravana or any other demon; one is therefore tempted to see this as an attempt at a feminist rewriting of mythology.
2. The comparison between Martineau's book and Ramabai's own is implicit. Incidentally, Martineau's book was actually published in 1837.
3. Significantly, Ramabai uses the term 'native' (or *etaddeshiya* in Sanskritized Marathi) in its original sense as a local inhabitant, rather than in the imperial sense as a colonial subject, as was usually done by her Maharashtrian contemporaries.
4. This ostensible quote does not appear in Martineau's book and was obviously intended as a gist of her argument. According to Yates (1985:

††Women members of the Temperance Union—both the national union of the United States and the international union—wear its sign, the white ribbon, on their chest. It indicates that these women do the holy work of the Union with sincerity and love in their hearts, and that they love all humanity.

18), Martineau was 'the first Englishwoman to make the analogy between the American woman's lot and the slave's'.

5. The World Anti-Slavery Convention held in London in 1840 ruled, in spite of strong objections, that only male delegates should be seated. The American women delegates, including Lucretia Mott and Elizabeth Cady Stanton, were compelled to sit in the galleries and were unable to participate in the proceedings (Flexner 1975: 71).

6. Oberlin College was founded in 1833 as a seminary and developed into a rudimentary college. It 'offered women a curriculum even remotely comparable to that available to men on the college level', and was 'the first such institution to open its doors to all comers, regardless of race, colour or sex' (Flexner 1975: 29).

7. Emma Willards' efforts resulted in the establishment of the Troy Female Seminary in New York State in 1821. It was 'the first endowed institution for the education of girls' (Flexner 1975: 26).

8. Vassar College was opened in 1865, Smith and Wellesley in 1875, Harvard Annex in 1879 and Bryn Mawr in 1885 (Flexner 1975: 36). Antioch College became co-educational in 1852, the State University of Iowa accepted women in 1858, Wisconsin admitted women to its normal school training course in 1863. Cornell was founded in 1868, and a special branch for women, Sage College, was added in 1874; the first woman student entered the University of Michigan in 1870 (Flexner 1975: 124–25).

9. Alice Freeman (later Mrs Palmer) graduated from the University of Michigan and became President of Wellesley in 1882; when the University of Chicago opened in 1892, she was appointed Dean of Women (Solomon 1987: 57, 69).

10. Mrs Quincy Shaw as well as Miss Frances Willard were office-bearers of the Ramabai Association of Boston.

11. Dr Mary Putnam Jacobi's essay won Harvard's Boylston Prize in 1876 (Solomon 1987: 57).

12. Elizabeth Blackwell's New York Infirmary for Women and Children, staffed entirely by women, was opened in 1857 and also provided medical training for women; it served as a model for similar institutions (Flexner 1975: 119; Solomon 1987: 35).

13. Mrs Myra Bradwell of Illinois was one of the first women lawyers in the USA. Her application in 1870 to the Supreme Court of Illinois for a licence to practise law was refused; she finally won the right in 1873 after a protracted battle involving the United States Supreme Court (Flexner 1975: 122–3).

14. The Woman's Rights Convention at Seneca Falls, New York, was called in July 1840 by five women: Lucretia Mott, Elizabeth Cady Stanton, Martha Wright (Mrs Mott's sister), Jane Hunt and Mary Ann McClintock, most of whom were Quakers (Flexner 1975: 71–77).

15. Sorosis was founded in 1868 by Mrs Jennie C. Croly, a recognized journalist who was refused a ticket to the dinner hosted by the New York Press Club in honour of Charles Dickens' visit, because she (like other women journalists) did not belong to the Press Club (Flexner 1975: 182–83).

16. The American Equal Rights Association which was formed out of the Woman's Rights Convention split in 1869 into the National Woman Suffrage Association and the American Woman Suffrage Association; their merger began to be negotiated in 1887 and finally took place in 1890 (Flexner 1975: 155, 226).

17. The Woman's Christian Temperance Union (WCTU) was formed in 1874. Frances Willard became its president in 1879; she organized WCTU chapters in every State and increased its membership to over 2,00,000 (Deckard 1983: 264).

18. Thompson's account, on which Ramabai has relied heavily in this section, has been liberally used in translating it; see Thompson, *et al.* (1906).

19. Thompson (1906: 75–76).

PART IV

KEDGAON

Famine Experiences
(1897)

To the Friends of Mukti School and Mission
(1900)

A Short History of Kripa Sadan, or Home of Mercy
(1903)

A Testimony of Our Inexhaustible Treasure
(1907)

The Word-Seed
(1908)

8

FAMINE EXPERIENCES*

I have long been wishing to thank the kind friends who have so generously sent help at this time of our need and now I am glad to be able to write a few lines to express my gratitude. . . .

Several friends have asked me to give an account of my visit to the famine districts, which I do very gladly, and hope that you will find it convenient to give a little space in your columns and publish it. I must, however, preface this account with a few of my recollections of the last famine. Many people who lived and worked in it will remember how millions of poor people were starved to death, and how the great part of Madras Presidency and the Southern Marathi [sic] country were laid waste by the famine of 1876. When I heard of the present famine and its havoc in the Central Provinces, my heart sank within me, and I cried to God for help on behalf of those dear countrypeople of mine.

I feel deeply for these poor dying people, because I have myself known what it is to suffer from hunger and thirst, and have seen my dearest relatives die of starvation. My recollections carry me back to the hard times some twenty-two years ago. The last great famine of

---

*Portions of the Letter which deal in detail with the demoralization of the people consequent upon the famine have been omitted, according to the note in the printed pamphlet from which this piece is reproduced.

the Madras Presidency reached its climax in the years 1876-77, but it began at least three years before that time. I was in my teens then and so thoroughly ignorant of the outside world, that I cannot remember observing other people's condition, yet saw enough of distress in our own and a few other families to realize the hard-heartedness of unchanged human nature.

High-caste and respectable poor families who are not accustomed to hard labour and pauperism, suffered then, as they do now, more than the poorer classes. My own people among many others fell victims to the terrible famine. We had known better days. My father was a landholder and an honoured Pandit, and had acquired wealth by his learning. But by and by, when he became old and infirm and blind in the last days of his earthly life, he lost all [his] property in one way or another. My brother, sister, and myself had no secular education to enable us to earn our livelihood by better work than manual labour. We had all the sacred learning necessary to lead an honest, religious life, but the pride of caste and superior learning and vanity of life prevented our stooping down to acquire some industry whereby we might have saved the precious lives of our parents.

In short, we had no common sense, and foolishly spent all the money we had in hand in giving alms to Brahmans to please the gods, who, we thought, would send a shower of gold mohurs upon us and make us rich and happy. We went to several sacred places and temples, to worship different gods and to bathe in sacred rivers and tanks to free ourselves from sin and curse, which brought poverty on us. We prostrated ourselves before the stone and metal images of the gods, and prayed to them day and night; the burden of our prayer being that the gods would be pleased to give us wealth, learning, and renown. My dear brother, a stalwart young fellow of twenty-one, spoilt his health and wasted his fine well-built body by fasting months and months. But nothing came of all this futile effort to please the gods—the stone images remained as hard as ever, and never answered our prayers. . . .

We knew the Vedanta and knew also that we worshipped not the images but some gods whom they represented—still, all our learning and superior knowledge was of no avail. We bowed to the idols as thousands of learned Brahmans do. We expected them to speak to us in wonderful oracles. We went to the astrologers with money and other presents to know from them the minds of [the] gods concerning us. In this way we spent our precious time, strength and wealth in vain. When no money was left in hand we began to sell the valuable things belonging to us—jewelries [sic], costly garments, silverware, and even the cooking vessels of brass and copper were sold to the last, and the money spent in giving alms to Brahmans till nothing but a few silver and copper coins were left in our possession. We bought coarse rice with them and ate very sparingly, but it did not last long. At last the day came when we had finished eating the last grain of rice—and nothing but death by starvation remained for our portion. Oh the sorrow, the helplessness, and the disgrace of the situation!

We assembled together to consider what we should do next, and after a long discussion, came to the conclusion that it was better to go into the forest and die there rather than bear the disgrace of poverty among our own people. And that very night we left the house in which we were staying at Tirpathy [Tirupati]– a sacred town situated on the top of Venkatghiri [sic]—and entered into the great forest, determined to die there. Eleven days and nights—in which we subsisted on water and leaves and a handful of wild dates— were spent in great bodily and mental pain. At last our dear old father could hold out no longer; the tortures of hunger were too much for his poor, old, weak body. He determined to drown himself in a sacred tank nearby, thus to end all his earthly suffering. It was suggested that the rest of us should either drown [our]selves or break the family and go our several ways. But drowning ourselves seemed most practicable. To drown one's self in some sacred river or tank is *not* considered suicide by the Hindus, so we felt free to put an end to our lives in that way. Father wanted to drown himself first, so he took leave of all the members of the family one by one. I was his youngest child, and my turn came last. I shall never forget his last injunctions to me. His blind eyes could not see my face, but he held me tight in his arms, and stroking my head and cheeks, he told me in a few words broken with emotion, to remember how he loved me, and how he taught me to do right and never depart from the way of righteousness. His last loving command to me was to lead an honourable life if I lived at all, and serve God all my life. He did not know the only true God but served the—to him—unknown God with all his heart and strength; and he was very desirous that his children should serve Him to the last. 'Remember, my child,' he said, 'you are my youngest, my most beloved child. I have given you into the hands of our God, you are His and to Him alone you must belong and serve all your life.' He could speak no more. My father's prayers for me were, no doubt, heard by the Almighty, the all-merciful Heavenly Father whom the old Hindu did not know. The God of all flesh did not find it impossible to bring me, a great sinner and an unworthy child of His, out of heathen darkness into the saving light of His love and salvation. I can now say to the departed spirit of the loving parent, 'Yes, dear father, I will serve the only true God to the last.' But I could not say so when my father spoke to me for the last time. I listened to him, but was too ignorant, too bewildered to understand him or make an intelligent answer. We were after this dismissed from my father's presence; he wanted an hour for meditation and preparation before death.

While we were placed in such a bewildering situation, the merciful God, who so often prevents His sinful children from rushing headlong into the deep pit of sin, came to our rescue. He kept us from the dreadful act of being witnesses to the suicide of our own loved father. God put a noble thought into the heart of my brother who said he could not bear to see the sad sight. He would give up all caste pride and go to work to support our old parents, and as father was unable to walk, he said he would carry him down the mountain into the nearest village, and then go to work. He made his intentions known to father and begged him not to drown himself in the sacred tank. So the question was settled for that time. Our hearts were gladdened and we prepared to start from the forest. And yet we wished very much that a tiger, a great snake, or some other wild animal would put an end to our lives. We were too weak to move and too proud to beg or work for earning a livelihood. But the resolution was made, and we dragged ourselves through the jungle as best we could.

It took us nearly two days to come out of the forest into a village at the foot of the mountain. Father suffered intensely throughout this time. Weakness caused by starvation and the hardships of the life in the wilderness, hastened his death. We reached the village with great difficulty, and took shelter in a temple, but the Brahman priests of the temple would not let us stay there. They had no pity for the weak and helpless. So we were obliged again to move from that temple and go out of the village into the ruins of an old temple where no one but the wild animals dwelt in the night. There we stayed for four days. A young Brahman, seeing the helplessness of our situation, gave us some food.

The same day on which we reached that village, my father was attacked by fever from which he did not recover. On the first day, at the beginning of his last illness, he asked for a little sugar and water. We gave him water, but could not give sugar. He could not eat the coarse food, and shortly after he became unconscious and died in the morning of the third day.

The same kind young Brahman who had given us some food, came to our help at that time. He could not do much. He was not sure whether we were Brahmans or not,[1] and as none of his co-villagers would come to carry the dead, he could not, for fear of being put out of caste, come to help my brother to carry the remains of my father. But he had the kindness to let some men dig a grave at his own expense, and follow the funeral party as far as the river. Father had entered the order of a Sannyasin before his death. So his body was to be buried in the ground according to the commands of the Shastras. As there was no one else who could help carry the dead, my brother tied the body in his dhoti like a bundle, and carried it alone over two miles to its last resting place. We sadly followed [him] to the river bank, and helped him a little. So we buried our father outside the village, away from all human habitation, and returned with heavy hearts to the ruins of the old temple where we had taken our abode. That same evening our mother was attacked by fever, and said she would not live much longer. But we had to leave the place; there was no work to be found and no food to be had. We walked with our sick mother for a while, and then some kind-hearted people gave us a little food and money to pay our fare as far as Raichur. There we stayed for some weeks, being quite unable to move from the town owing to the illness of our mother. Our life at Raichur was a continuous story of hopelessness and starvation. Brother was too weak to work, and we could not make up our minds to go to beg. Now and then, kind people gave us some food. Mother suffered intensely from fever and hunger. We too suffered from hunger and weakness, but the sufferings of our mother were more than we could bear to see. Yet we had to keep still through sheer helplessness. Now and then, when delirious, mother would ask for different kinds of food. She could eat but little, yet we were unable to give her the little that she wanted.

Once she suffered so much from hunger that she could bear it no longer, and sent me into a neighbour's house to beg a little piece of coarse *bajree* cake. I went there very reluctantly. The lady spoke kindly to me, but I could on no account open my mouth to beg for that piece of *bajree* bread. With superhuman effort and a firm resolution to keep my feelings from that lady I kept the tears back, but the expression of my face told its own story. The kind Brahman lady, guessing what was on my mind, asked me if I would like to have some food, so I said, 'Yes, I want only a little piece of *bajree* bread.' She gave me what I wanted and I felt very grateful, but could not say a word to express my gratitude. I ran to my mother in great haste and gave it to her. But she could not eat, she was too weak. The fever was on her, she became unconscious and died in a few days after that. Her funeral was as sad as that of my father, with the exception that two Brahmans came to help my brother and me, to carry her body to the burning ground, about three miles from the town.[2]

I need not lengthen this account with our subsequent experiences. My elder sister also died of starvation, after suffering from illness and hunger. During those few months before our sister died, we three travelled on foot from place to place in search of food and work, but we could not get much of either. My brother and myself continued our sad pilgrimage to the northern boundary of India, and back to the east as far as Calcutta. Brother got work here and there, but most of the time we lived an aimless wanderer's life. Very often we had to go without food for days. Even when my brother had got some work to do, he got so little wages, only four rupees a month, and sometimes much less than that, that we were obliged to live on a handful of grain soaked in water, and a little salt. We had no blankets or thick garments to cover ourselves, and when travelling we had to walk barefoot, without umbrellas, and to rest in the night, either under the trees on the roadside, or the arches of bridges, or lie down on the ground in the open air. Once, on the banks of the Jhelum, a river in the Punjab, we were obliged to rest at night in the open air, and tried to keep off the intense cold by digging two grave-like pits and putting ourselves into them, and covering our bodies—except the heads—with dry sand of the river bank. Sometimes the demands of hunger were so great, that we would satisfy our empty stomachs by eating a handful of wild berries, and swallowing the hard stones together with their coarse skins.

Four long years we suffered from scarcity. We did not mind it much as we were young and strong, we could stand it much better than our poor old parents and weak sister. The Heavenly Father very mercifully removed them from this earth, and that none of their children, whom they loved so much, died or were separated from them in their lifetime, gave us some satisfaction, but the memory of the last days of their life, full of sorrow, almost breaks my heart. I would never have written this account had not the necessity of my present situation obliged me to do so. None of my friends can ever understand what my feelings are for the famine people unless they know that I have had once to go through the same experience as that of the starving thousands of Central India. Yet I must say that suffering alone is not able to produce sympathy for other sufferers. My own experience of the unconverted state of mind [3] and the present knowledge of my fellow countrywomen and girls, whom I have ample opportunity to study, shows that suffering in itself has rather a hardening effect on the human heart. It takes away almost all delicate feelings from the soul, making it as hard as a stone. I can quite understand now what God meant when He said to Israel, 'I will take away the stony heart out of your flesh, and I will give you a heart of flesh.' Unless God changes our hearts through the wonderful regenerating action of His Holy Spirit, we never have true love and sympathy for our fellow men. Later on, I shall give an example of this. But now I must pass on to the chief subject of this article.

A little over four months ago [September 1896], I heard of the distress of the people in Central India, and at once my heart went out to them in sympathy. The human common sense said, 'You had better stop here,' and 'Whatsoever thy hand findeth to do; do it, here. You have no means and no strength to do what you wish. Your powers are limited and you will not be held responsible for not doing anything to help those famished people. Indeed, what can a weak woman do to help the dying thousands? Besides the Government of India and other benevolent people are doing what they can do to relieve the poor and the needy. There is nothing for you to do.' I tried to quiet my conscience in this manner, but louder and louder spoke the voice of God from within my heart. 'Remember the days of old.' 'Thou shalt remember that thou wast a bondsman in the land of Egypt, and the Lord thy God redeemed thee,' and 'Who knoweth whether thou art come to the kingdom for such a time as this?'

A missionary lady, Mrs Drynan, of Rajputana, accompanied me part of the way, to gather some children for mission orphanages of Poona. We went to Sohagpur first, and began the work at once. We found out from the good people there that we could not get the orphan children without the permission of the Government. So our first business was to go and see the physician in charge at the Hospital, and the Tahsildar in charge of the Poor House. We went to the Hospital too early, at about 8.30 in the morning. The doctor was not there, but right before that hospital were walking three little famished skeleton-like forms, and this first sight of their distress I shall never forget. The three children, we found out, were of the Chamar caste. Their father had died some time ago, and the mother had died only the day before. The eldest was a girl of about seven, the second a boy of five, and the youngest a baby boy three years of age. The girl was protecting herself from the intense cold with a covering of rags, and the two boys had nothing on their bodies. Their wrinkled faces and the ghastly death-like expression told the story of the terrible suffering they were in.

The agony and dismay I felt at seeing that sight cannot be told in words. I was perfectly powerless, and could do nothing but cry to the Father to help me. As we could do nothing, we had to harden our hearts and turn our step toward the Poor House, where we expected to find the Tahsildar. The memory of the three little ones, especially the youngest child, who I am sure could not have lived many days after that, haunts me to this day. Whenever I think of them my heart is filled with indescribable sorrow. I could neither sleep nor rest for the thought of them for many days. We did not get the children, though we tried our best. It took us such a long time to go and see the officer in charge of the Poor House, and by the time we returned, they had gone somewhere, and no one could tell us where they were. I went again to that place, made a thorough search all over the town, and round about it, but did not find them. Perhaps they fainted on their way to the town in quest of food, and fell down in some ditch on the roadside, and died there of hunger. The Lord have mercy upon us all and give us repentance for not going to help such innocent little sufferers. It will take me too long to describe all that I saw and heard at the Poor Houses and relief camps I visited. So I will say in general what most affected my mind.

The first Poor House we saw was no house at all. It was a grove in the outskirts of the town. Groups of famished people were seen sitting or lying in ashes on dirty ground. Some had rags to cover their bodies, and some had none. There were old and young men, and women and children, most of them ill, too weak to move about, and many suffering from leprosy and other horrible diseases. Bad men, and women, pure young girls, innocent children and old people, good, bad, and indifferent, were freely mixing and conversing with each other. They slept in the open air or under the trees at night, and ate the scanty and coarse food provided by the Government. The food was nothing but dry flour and some salt. There were several starving orphan children who could not cook for themselves, and had no one to work for them. So they had either to eat the dry flour or depend upon the tender mercies of their fellow sufferers, the older persons, who took as much of their food as they could, with the right of their might.

The poor people seem to have lost all human feeling. They are most unkind toward each other and the little children around them. They do not care even for their own children. Some parents eat all the food they get for themselves and for their little ones, and become quite fat, while their children are starved and look like skeletons, and some are even in a dying state and yet their fathers and mothers feel no affection for them.

Parents can be seen taking their girl children around the country and selling them for a rupee or a few annas, or even for a few seers of grain. The food given to the children is snatched from their hands, and eaten by their stronger neighbours. In some places, the Government officials give two pice or more to each child, or old or sick person [who is] unable to work, but what can a baby of two or three years of age do with two copper pieces in hand? The pice are soon stolen and the little ones left to die of starvation. In other places, food, i.e. wheat or jowari flour, and some kind of pulse, are cooked into *dal* and *roti* and then distributed to the poor.

The Government officials are kind, and are doing what they can to help the poor people at the relief camps and in the Poor Houses. But the means at their disposal make it impossible to meet the demands of the needy ones. What are a few thousand rupees among so many thousands, to be supported for months? Perhaps about eight or ten annas, or at the most, a rupee per month is allowed for each person; and how much and what kind of grain will that sum bring?

Alas! alas! for the poor who are obliged to eat all the food given to them at the Poor Houses. Few of the subordinate officers, such as the Mukadams [overseers] and cooks who have it in their power to give or withhold from the poor the food sent for them, have any heart or conscience. The grain, the very cheapest kind, is bought and ground into flour, without being cleaned of the sand and earth it contains. Then the heartless cooks steal the flour and put a quantity of earth into it, while they cook the *dal* and *roti*—and nobody notices that the food is thus adulterated. The poor people are too afraid of the Mukadams to complain to the higher officials. The flour and pulse so adulterated, then made into *roti* and *dal*, do not look any better than cakes of cowdung.

The people in the Poor Houses are in such a degraded condition, that even the pigs who wander round about our villages do not begin to be compared with them in filthiness. The absolute nakedness of almost all [the] little children, and hundreds of older people covered with dirt, and sometimes with filthy rags, their skeleton-like bodies full of frightful sores, and their sad wrinkled faces wearing a ghastly, death-like expression, and their forlorn condition, are all an indescribably sad sight.

The European and Native officers employed to look after the interests of the dying thousands are hard at work, and try to do as much as they can. But it is impossible for them to find out what goes on behind their backs. The sepoys and Mukadams are the real masters and rulers of these places. Take for instance a Poor House containing over two thousand poor people, and a relief camp where over 15,000 people are working. What can one or two, or half-a-dozen superior officers, do for these thousands? They are obliged to leave the work in the hands of the Mukadams, who can do whatever they like. They use their sticks and tongues freely. They pull and push the working coolies, even women.

This is no good sign at all. Wicked men and women are everywhere on the lookout for young women and girls. They entice them by offering sweetmeats and other kinds of food, clothing, and fair promises to take them to nice places and make them happy. So hundreds of girls, young widows and deserted wives, are waylaid as they go to the relief camps and Poor Houses, in search of food and work, and taken away before they place themselves in the custody of the Government. The wicked are not afraid of the judgment of God, they are sinning away their lives in the midst of the fearful scenes of famine and pestilence. May the merciful Father help these children! One of my workers was walking on the road one day, when she saw a little girl of about twelve years sitting on the roadside. She looked sad and hungry. My worker spoke kindly to her and found out that she was an orphan. When the worker asked her if she would like to come to me, the girl said she had an older sister, and would go anywhere with her. In the meanwhile, the sister, who had gone to wash, came back to the place where the child was sitting. From her my worker heard their pathetic story. Their father had died about three weeks ago. They had no one to take care of them, and did not know where to go to get food. They were on their way to the relief camp. Someone had told them that there was a lady near the place, who had come to gather some children to give them a home, so they had come to the Sarai to look for her. From this statement we knew they were looking for me, but I left the Sarai before they came, and so missed seeing them. My worker then asked the older girl, who is about fourteen, if she and her sister would like to come and stay under my care. The girl said she would. She begged of my worker with tears in her eyes, that she should be placed under the care of good people. For she had met with so many bad people after her father's death, and they had tried to tempt her into evil. But she had resolutely refused to go with them. While the conversation was taking place, half-a-dozen or more wicked men had gathered around my worker, and were about to take the girls away, by frightening them out of their wits, but God saved the children from the dreadful fate and they were safely brought to me.

God help the young girls and young women who are obliged to go to the relief camps and Poor Houses. The sight of the pitiable condition of these poor orphan girls brought to my memory the state which I was in some twenty-two years ago. I bless and thank God for not having allowed us to go to the relief camps in the days of our need. My sister, a fine young woman of twenty-five, and myself, a girl of sixteen, would have easily fallen into the cruel hands of the wicked people of such places. The very remembrance of relief camps and Poor Houses and the condition of our sisters there makes me shiver, and I tremble with fear for several thousands of young women and girls, who are being sacrificed to the devil in these hard times.

There are not many girls who will resist the devil in the face of starvation and death. God be thanked for protecting the virtue of these innocents. But it has been my sad lot to see many little girls ruined for life. Even the little children seemed to have lost all their innocence and were acting like little devils. What lies, what thefts, what indecent language! 'Oh God,' I exclaimed, when I saw them. 'Save us, save our nation from utter destruction.' It seemed as if nothing short of a great flood would be able to wash away all this sin from the face of our country. I wonder at the mercifulness and long suffering of our Father, who is still bearing with us.

It is impossible for the Government officers alone to look after the little children and to protect the virtue of young women and girls. There is a large field of work for you and for me if only we undertake to do it. Old people and middle-aged persons, and delicate women, who are unable to break twelve baskets of stone, and carry it to the appointed place, and who cannot get their wages at the relief camps unless they do so much work every day, need our help. The sad sight of aged men and delicate women stretching forth their sore hands and begging you to help them, pouring out their sorrow into your ears, and lamenting over their hard fate while their tearful eyes look straight into yours to find out if there is a particle of sympathy for them, is altogether too much to bear, for a person having a heart of flesh.

Why do not good Christian people in England and America send money to the missionaries in this country, who are so anxious to help the poor people, and are trying hard to do as much as they can for them, but cannot do more for want of means? The great motherly heart of missionary ladies is yearning for the dying children and other poor of the Central Provinces. Let benevolent people send generous donations to them for feeding and caring for the Lord's little ones. Men can do much, but all godly women must come forward at this time and care for little children and protect young women whom the Government officials are not able to help and care for. It is woman's work and cannot be left to the officers and their subordinates.

My sympathies are excited by the needs of young girl widows especially at this time. To let them go to the relief camps and Poor Houses, or allow them to wander in the streets and on the highways, means their eternal destruction. Ever since I have seen these girls in the famine districts—some fallen into the hands of wicked people; some ruined for life and turned out to die a miserable death in a hopeless, helpless manner; some in the hospitals only to be taken into the pits of sin there to await a cruel death; some bearing the burdens of sin utterly lost to the sense of shame and humanity—hell has become a horrible reality to me, and my heart is bleeding for those daughters of fond parents who have died leaving them orphans. Who with a mother's heart and a sister's love can rest without doing everything in her power to save at least a few of the girls who can yet be saved from the hands of the evil ones! So, regardless of the trying financial state of my school, I went to work in the Central Provinces to get a few of the helpless young widows.

The Father, who is a very present help in trouble, has enabled me to get some sixty widows, forty-seven of whom will go to school to study, and others will work. Over eight hundred and fifty rupees were spent in fetching them here. Of this amount, about five hundred and twenty five rupees were given me by friends, and I thank them for it. To go to work to get these widows, to fetch them here from Central India and to feed them and clothe them is an awfully expensive business. Harder still is the work of civilising them and teaching them habits of cleanliness. They are no better than brute animals. The filthy habits they have acquired during these years of famine have become second nature with them. It will take a long time to civilise and teach them. We can do all things in the Power of the Lord. The Lord has put it into my mind to save three hundred girls out of the famine district and I shall go to work in His name. The funds sent to me by my friends in America are barely enough to feed and educate fifty girls, and several people are asking me how I am going to support all these girls who may come from Central India. Besides their food and clothing, new dormitories and dining rooms must be built. Our present school-house is not large enough to hold more than one hundred girls, at the most. And how are these emergencies to be met?

I do not know, but the Lord knows what I need. I can say with the Psalmist—'I am poor and needy, but the Lord thinketh upon me' and He has promised that 'Ye shall eat in plenty and be satisfied and praise the name of the Lord your God that hath dealt wonderfully with you; and My people will not be ashamed.' My girls and I are quite ready to forego all the comforts, give up luxuries and live as plainly as we can. We shall be quite contented to have only one meal of common coarse food daily if necessary, and so long as we have a little room or a seer of grain left in this house, we shall try and help our sisters who are starving. It seems a sin to live in this good house and eat plenty of good food and be warmly clothed, while thousands of our fellow creatures are dying of hunger and are without shelter. If all of us do our part faithfully, God is faithful to fulfil His promises and will send us the help we need at this time.

I humbly request you to pray for me and mine that we may be made strong in the Lord, and walk by faith and not by sight.

Believe me yours
In the Lord's service
Ramabai

PS: The good missionaries at Hoshangabad, Itarsi, Narsingpur, Jabalpur and Bina, have been very kind to me and helped me a great deal in my work. Our dear friend Miss Richardson, of Bombay, went to work with me and has aided me by giving passage money for the girls whom I brought here. I thank all these good friends for extending their help and for their goodness to me.

Ramabai

Poona, January 20th, 1897

NOTES

1. It is surprising that the Dongre family's Brahman origins were doubted; ordinarily, recitations from the sacred texts would have immediately proved their bona fides in an age when Sanskrit learning was strictly limited to Brahmans.

2. Ramabai does not mention here another harrowing fact about this event. She had to help carry the bier of her mother (which high-caste women did not do; they did not even accompany the funeral party to the cremation ground and still do not do so). Being the youngest and the shortest, she had to place the end of the wooden pole on her head instead of her shoulder (as is usually done), which was physically much more painful (Vaidya 1988: 51).

3. Ramabai obviously links voluntary famine relief efforts with a Christian ethos.

9

TO THE FRIENDS OF MUKTI SCHOOL AND MISSION[*]

Dear Friends,

A year has passed since I wrote the last year's account of Mukti. Several friends have again and again asked me to write more about this School. It is a little over three years since the Lord called me to take up famine relief work. From a small beginning of temporal character, the Mukti School has grown into a permanent and large institution. Three hundred girls rescued from starvation in 1897 have received regular secular and Christian instruction. They are the children of many prayers; much love and labour has been bestowed on them, and now I am able to say, with great joy, that the workers have not laboured in vain. The money which so many friends have sent for them has not been spent in vain. The Lord is very good to let us see the fruit of our labour, and He is giving us abundant joy as we see the girls growing in grace and proving themselves worthy of the love and labour spent on them.

Five hundred and eighty [girls] in the Mukti Sadan and sixty girls in the Kripa Sadan are being trained to lead a useful Christian life. The number of the inmates of these Homes is doubled and will increase as days pass by. God is greatly blessing the work here, and

[*]Reproduced from a pamphlet in the Archives of the Pandita Ramabai Mukti Mission.

the prayers of our friends in all parts of the world are answered daily. Including the hundred girls of the Sharada Sadan I have altogether nearly seven hundred and fifty girls under training. It will be easily imagined that they need a large number of teachers and helpers to train them. I have only sixteen paid teachers from outside, in these Homes. There are eighty-five other persons to help me in the three institutions. Thirty-three teachers, ten matrons and forty-two workers in different branches of Industry are daily labouring for the good of their sisters and their own improvement. Although they are dependent on these Schools for their daily bread, they may be said to earn their own living as most of them receive no pay or have but nominal pay. The Sharada Sadan has trained seventy teachers and workers in the past eleven years, and the Mukti School has trained nearly eighty girls to earn their own living in the past three years. Eighty-five of the old and new girls have found work in their own mother institutions, and sixty-five of the old girls are either married or earning their living as teachers and workers in different places.

A question has often been asked, namely, what is going to become of all these girls? It is not difficult to answer it. India is a large country, and a vast amount of ignorance prevails everywhere. Men and women of education and character are needed to enlighten this and the coming generations. I have had a hundred requests from missionaries and superintendents of schools to give them trained teachers, Bible-women and matrons. I had quite as many and more requests from young men to give them educated wives. It will not be difficult to find good places and comfortable homes for all these young girls when the proper time comes. Our first duty is not to think of what may happen tomorrow, but what can we do for and how shall we train these young lives today. Each day brings fresh need and new hopes and new work with it. So the lives of the workers here are full of today's work and care. We have but little time left to think of the morrow. My heart is burdened with the thought that there are more than 145 millions of women in this country who need to have the light of the knowledge of God's love given them. All the work that is being done by missionaries and their assistants in this vast country is but a drop in the ocean. It will be very small help to add our particle to that drop. But every particle added will increase the drop, so it will be multiplied and permeate the ocean until it becomes a stream of the living water that flows from under the throne of God, to give life and joy to this nation. My aim is to train all these girls to do some work or other. Over two hundred of the present number have much intelligence, and promise to be good school teachers after they receive a few years' training. Thirty of the large [i.e. older] girls have joined a training class for nurses. Some girls have mastered the trade of oil making. Others have learnt to do laundry work and some have learnt dairy work. More than sixty girls have learnt to cook very nicely. Fifty or more have had some training in field [i.e. farm] work, but want of rain has stopped that branch of our industry which will, I hope, be started again after the rain falls. Forty girls have learnt to weave nicely and more than fifty girls have learnt to sew well and make their own garments. The rest [of the] small and large girls are learning to do some work with the three Rs.

One of the smaller girls rescued from starvation in the last famine is taking charge of a few of our blind girls. Miss Abrams very kindly taught her to read the blind characters. The girl herself is studying hard while engaged in teaching the blind girls to read the Scripture. Besides reading the Scripture she teaches them tables, mental arithmetic and geography in her spare hours. She sees to their bathing, taking meals at [the] proper time, and can be seen going about her work with her family of the blind and feeble-minded girls. Her heart goes out to the feeble and friendless and, as soon as she sees someone who is not loved by other girls, she befriends her and takes charge of her at once. She is a truly converted Christian girl trying to follow in the steps of her Divine Saviour. This and other instances of converted girls trying to do what they can to alleviate the sufferings of their sisters, while yet in school and busy with their work, is a great encouragement to us workers who thank God for being so good as to let us see that our labours are not lost.

Some girls who are not intellectually bright are learning other work. Some of them have a mother's heart which is full of love for children. They are appointed as matrons and have small groups of children under their charge, and love and care for them like their own mothers. These very girls who are so gentle and loving now were very wild, greedy and selfish before their conversion to Christ. One would have hardly believed that they could ever be so changed and be what they are now. But the Scripture says, 'Nothing is impossible with God.' His love has won their hearts and He has made them new creatures in Christ. It must not, however, be understood that our School and Mission and the workers connected with them are models of perfection. We are all very defective, make many mistakes, and our flesh many a time gets the better of us. You will find many faults in us if you look out for them. The Lord knows that we are nothing but dust. But He in His supreme love does not give us up for lost but chastises us back into the right way and lets us know why He chastised us. We thank Him with all our hearts for His unspeakable love and mercy. Most of my helpers have joined the Bible Training Class taught by Miss Abrams. The daily study of the Word of God has made them willing workers. 'The Law of the Lord is perfect, converting the soul.' We have found that nothing helps so much to make matters straight as the study of God's Word. Out of this Bible Training Class I hope there will rise a trained band of Bible-women who will take the Gospel to their sisters in their own homes. Some girls have already begun to go about in the villages around here. They are working as Zenana Bible-women and Sunday School teachers in their spare time.

No one who has not lived here for some time can have any idea as to how many different kinds of work the Mukti girls have to do. Kedgaum [i.e. Kedgaon] is by no means a romantic place. The girls have to walk a long distance in the burning sun, bare-footed and without umbrellas on their heads, to go to bathe by the wells. They have to rise as early as four and work in the morning in order to get their day's work done. The following are the hours assigned to different [kinds of] work:

A.M.	4	to	4.30	Washing.
"	4.30	to	5	Singing.
"	5	to	7	Preparation of lessons.
"	7	to	8	Breakfast.
"	8	to	10	School.
"	10	to	10.30	Prayers.
"	10.30	to	11	Recess.
"	11	to	2 P.M	School.
P.M.	2	to	2.30	Recess and midday meal.
"	2.30	to	3.30	Bible study or other work.
"	3.30	to	5.30	Bathing and washing clothes.
"	5.30	to	6	Evening prayers.
"	6	to	7	Dinner.
"	7	to	8	Rest and play.
"	8	to	4 A.M.	Retire for the night.

The hour of bathing and school are changed in different seasons. The girls cannot bathe in cold water early in the morning in cold and rainy seasons, so they have school in the morning. In very hot months, from March to the end of June, they have their bath in the morning and have school for four hours only. They have their holidays in the month of May, and a fortnight's vacation at Christmas time, and school is always closed on Saturdays, Sundays and other festival days. In long holiday, as in May and December, they have to do some little work in order to keep their minds busy. The girls who cook in the morning have to rise as early as two o'clock in the morning. Two classes having twenty-five or thirty girls in each have to cook and serve by turns. Those who cook in the morning have their rest in the afternoon and can retire early. Their time of work is changed after a few weeks. When one class has mastered the work assigned to it, another takes up the work and the former one begins to learn something else. In this way all the girls are trained to do almost every kind of work done here. All get sleep from seven to eight hours. They are neither over-fed nor get too delicate food, but none of them are under-fed. They get three good meals a day as a rule. The weak and sick ones, as well as the very little children, have milk and other nourishing food. We have a regularly trained hospital nurse—a good Christian woman—to look after the sanitary conditions of the place. She has a large band of girls working under her. Some of the girls who need and desire for hospital treatment in their sickness are sent to Poona to the Zenana Mission Hospital or to the Sassoon General Hospital. But most of the girls know the Lord as the Saviour of their souls as well as their bodies and ask for prayers in their sickness and are healed according to their faith.

Yet, I have [had] to record thirteen deaths during the past year; eleven died from the effects of famine, one died of fever and one of small-pox. Chicken-pox, small-pox and measles were brought by the new girls arrived from the famine districts this year. I have tried my best to separate them from the older girls. Arrangements have been made to quarantine the newcomers—and all the small-pox and measles cases are placed in a separate compound by themselves. New sheds have been built and the houses enlarged as fast as help came. No time, labour or money have been spared to save life and make the girls comfortable. But weakness, produced by prolonged starvation and the extreme heat caused by want of rain, has been too difficult to cope with. Yet I cannot but thank God out of the fullness of my heart in so wonderfully protecting so many hundreds of lives from plague and famine. Although life at Kedgaum is hard, the girls look fat and healthy and are full of spirits. I find that hard work makes better women of the girls. The easy and comfortable city life is, of course, preferable to the flesh, but life in places like Kedgaum with fewer comforts and harder work is more conducive to bodily and spiritual health.

You have heard and are still hearing about the great famine which is devastating this country. The land has not yet recovered its former state; it is still suffering from the effects of the last great famine; and yet a greater famine has come upon it so soon. The people are too weak to bear it and are dying like so many animals in times of epidemics. The condition of Gujerat and Rajputana is worse than that of any other famine-stricken part of India. The land for hundreds of miles is quite dry with no crops and no grass growing. Small streams and rivers which form a network all over the country have dried up long ago, and the large rivers have dwindled down into threads of small streams of water. Large wells too have scarcely any water. Trees in the jungles have been shorn of their foliage and deprived of their branches, [and] a few stumps are left standing here and there; they look very much like the starving people around the country. Only a few green bushes which are perhaps poisonous and will not be touched by man or beast are left here and there, and their leaves are almost the only green things seen on the dry land. The fertile country of Gujerat was never so dry and destitute as it looks now. Large herds of hungry and thirsty cattle move about like armies of ghosts. I have never seen such a ghastly sight in my life. They have nothing but skin and bones left and fall down dead at any moment. I have passed trains upon trains loaded with cowhides. Piles of bones of dead animals and of men and women can be seen near railway stations. The traffic in cowhides and bones has been flourishing in Gujerat and Rajputana for months. Some people are profiting by it, but the death of so many cattle means a great loss to the agriculture of this country for years to come.

But, turning from the cattle, we see a more pitiful and heart-rending sight in the human skeletons moving about in search of food. Nearly six millions of people are at work in Government relief camps, and the number is fast increasing. But there are many more poor people who are too weak to work and too helpless. Many high-caste people who are too proud to work in relief camps are dying of famine in their own homes.

Life in relief camps is very hard. The people are asked to break twelve basketsful of stone in small pieces and have from three to five pice or 3/4 to 1 and 1/4 penny a day. Digging of the ground, breaking stone, carrying earth to a long distance, is the work they have to do in relief camps. The money they get for a hard day's labour is not enough even to give them one coarse meal a day. Out of this money they have to bribe the Mukadams, in order to get work, and the Marwari who measures out so much grain for the money deceives them and gives them a very small quantity of old and bad grain. The camps have no shady trees or sheds to protect [them] from cold or heat. They have to work in the burning sun all day and sleep in open air all night. They cannot get water to bathe and wash and have very little of it to drink. Small children under eight years of age get a little food from the Government kitchen. They have very insufficient shelter and almost no clothing on their bodies. No one can blame the Government for such a state of things, for the famine is very great and the means at their disposal are small. They have to depend largely on the subordinate workers and employees, most of whom have little or no conscience. The Mukadams and Clerks are mostly busy in filling up their own purses and the higher officials, who know what the grievances of the poor people are, feel very helpless for want of good conscientious workers. Everyone is not able to stand this hard camp life; so many of the weak, poor men and women go about begging or seek admittance in Poor Houses.

Many of the starving people wandering in jungles have eaten up all the fruit of the cactus and sycamore and wild berries found in the land and are now eating leaves, barks and small twigs of the trees. Vast numbers of children and famished old people can be seen picking a few grains from the dusty roads over which carts of grain have passed. They are found gathering and winnowing manure and dust in the bazaars and on highways in hope of finding a few particles of grain for satisfying their hunger. They are filling their empty stomachs with sand and small stones in order to escape the pangs of hunger. They are drinking filthy and muddy water wherever they can find it. They cry out continuously for food and water, and strike their stomachs and their heads in great agony. Many who have no strength left in them to say even a word to express their suffering lie down on the roadsides and in the Poor Houses and suffer silently. Some of them simply stare at you when you see them—their poor, lightless eyes so deeply sunk in their sockets through which their death agonies are expressed haunt you day and night. They are so silent and still that their very silence speaks loudly of how very great sufferings they have gone through. Numberless such skeletons are lying down everywhere, and dying away without even a groan or sigh, for they have no strength even for that! Who will understand what these poor people must have suffered and are suffering? Filthiness caused by want of water to wash bodies and clothes is added to starvation. The sores on the bodies and heads of children and grown up people are fearful. Their rags and hair and skin are full of insects and sores. Dirt and filth seem to have become a part of their lives, and their dreadful smells are unbearable. Some people have a few rags, but they are no protection to their bodies. As there is nothing to protect their bodies from cold or heat, hundreds die from cold in the cold months. This famine began to be felt since the beginning of last July, but it was not officially admitted and few dared to say that there was any famine. When the poor people and cattle actually began to die of starvation, and their dead bodies [began] to fall down everywhere, the existence of famine could not be denied any longer and the Government and others commenced to take active measures to help famine sufferers.

We have heard true stories of many cruel people and their devilish acts in the days when Sati burning was allowed. If after inducing the poor unwilling widow to mount the funeral pyre of her husband, her relatives saw that her heart failed her and she began to flee from those destroying flames, they used to force her back into the fire and hold her down with long bamboo sticks until she was suffocated and her body fell into the fire and was burnt to ashes. How you and I have shuddered at these acts of cruelty and said that nothing but heathenism and uncivilized, unrefined minds would have done it. But what civilization and how much of humanity and refinement do you find in the acts of certain authorities who shut their eyes and ears and force the fleeing people back into their own villages and States to suffer the unspeakable agonies of starvation? They are held down there not with bamboo sticks but by bayonet points until they are burnt down by the flames of hunger and their lifeless bodies can no longer move away. When the famine set in by the beginning of last July, thousands of poor people from the native States of Rajputana, Gujerat and Kathiawar began to pour into British territory, in hopes of saving their lives from starvation. But an alarm was taken at it. Collectors, magistrates and their subordinates were ordered to drive the people back into their own States and the Princes were ordered to feed their own poor—to which they officially consented with their lips, and many of them did the best they could. But it must be remembered that the extravagant expenses incurred by the Rajas and Chiefs on grand occasions like marriages and deaths, as well as at times of visits from Governors and other Government officials, have had a good deal to do with the impoverishment of the States and their people. The inhabitants had to pay large taxes and the treasuries were emptied and the States burdened with debt. Most of the Chiefs and their ministers have little strength and less desire to feed and care for the perishing poor. There are of course Poor Houses and relief works opened quite lately but for months the starving poor were allowed to die like rats and dogs. There is a Marathi proverb which says, 'The mother will not give food and the father will not allow to beg'; what is the child to do then but to die without uttering a single word? This is exactly what happened to the poor people of many native states of Rajputana, Gujerat and Kathiawar. The British Government would not allow them to come to beg in their territory and their Mother States did not give them food to eat. So they died of starvation, quite unintentionally but cruelly forced upon them.

Now that the Poor Houses and relief camps are opened everywhere it may be supposed that the lives of the remaining are saved. This is quite a mistake in many, many cases. First, because though the hungry ones are flocking to the Poor Houses, most of these have been suffering from starvation for months, so much [so] that even if they get food they will not live. They have very poor, coarse food given them which their stomachs are not able to digest. No attention is paid to keep their bodies clean and covered to protect them from cold or from sores or other fearful diseases. In many cases it so happens that the poor are gathered and fed only when some British officer is present, and as soon as he turns to go away—quite satisfied that everything is being done to save their lives—they are turned out of the Poor Houses and camps, driven into jungles to die horrible deaths. The able-bodied men and women who can work in relief camps, and are able to hold their own, will live through this famine, but the poor defenceless widows, deserted wives, orphans and old people are, alas! dead and dying by the thousands.

Now that the Rajas and Chiefs know that these poor people of their States will have no room in British territories, they have found it easy to manage their affairs. They will not allow kind Christian people to rescue the starving widows and orphans—because their ministers and other grand people have brought their influence to bear on them for the defence of the Hindu religion. They are saying that the orphans taken by Christian Missionaries will be Christianized and so they will not be allowed to be taken out of the States. But many of us know that these poor children are not cared for. Many are actually dying by neglect. Young widows are being enticed away by wicked people and sold to sin, and the infirm people cannot do anything to save their own lives. It were a noble thing for the Hindu religion to have so many thousands of Martyrs, if only they were willing Martyrs, but these poor defenceless thousands are sacrificed on the unholy altar of caste prejudice by sheer force brought to bear upon them by both the British and native States. The Government's policy of non-interference with religious customs is an admirable and a noble one, but in such cases as these forced deaths of thousands, it is to say the least, inhuman. What difference is there between allowing people to burn their widows alive, or to sacrifice their children to Kali, and to force women and children and weak people back into the States where they will surely die or be sold to sin to die a dog's death later on? My language may seem strong, perhaps unwise, but, dear friends, you must remember I am speaking for those thousands who are too feeble and powerless to lift up their voices—and am speaking the truth. I do not blame individual officials, for they can only do what they are told; but the policy of non-interference mis-applied in this case is blameworthy. I am deeply grateful to the individual officials who are not only helping the poor officially, but feeding and saving them with their own money when they find the Government money is not available. It is these righteous officials who are helping missionaries and others to save the lives of the perishing ones and I know God will bless them. Let us pray very earnestly that all of them—including the law-makers and administrators—be filled with this Christ-like spirit and shew mercy to the poor. They will bring a rich blessing upon themselves and upon the Government.

But woe to those who have never felt the pang of hunger, neither suffered from cold and from heat and coolly allow so many poor to die and the girl children and young women to be sold to the agents of the devil for hellish purposes. May God give them a repenting heart, or it will go very bad against them in the last day. I have visited Poor Houses and seen men, women and children dying of hunger on highways and byeways. Their ghastly appearance, their dumb appeal—Oh, those pitiful eyes which speak volumes—haunt me day and night, and the appealing voices, the agonized cries and the hopeless expressions are all so burnt down into my heart that I cannot but speak a few words for them. The Word of God says (Prov. 31: 8), 'Open thy mouth for the dumb in the cause of such as are appointed for destruction.' And woe to me if I do not obey the command, even at the cost of losing the favour of the high and mighty of this world. Many a careless official has allowed children to be taken away by people who will turn the boys and girls into slaves and concubines. The children who have been sheltered in Poor Houses are supposed to have lost their caste—and caste Hindus will never re-admit them into their community and to all their caste privileges! Men of education and means among the Hindus have found it next to impossible to get into their caste when they have once lost it by crossing the sea or by openly associating with Christians or by marrying widows. The poor children who have been sheltered in Poor Houses and eaten food from the hands of people of other castes will not be taken back into their caste, but will be in lifelong slavery if they are 'adopted' by Hindus or Mahommedans. The Contagious Diseases Act, which has again come into force under the name of Cantonments Act, is a great force on the side of the devil and enables wicked people to carry on their wicked traffic in girls for the 'benefit' of the British soldiers.[1] Missionaries and others have found it much more difficult to get girls than boys from famine districts; men and women who are engaged in this traffic in flesh and blood were very busy for months gathering girls before any of the relief works and Poor Houses were started. Whenever they saw any of the Christian people coming to the rescue of the girls, they started such alarms and told such dreadful stories about Christians that in many cases the girls have refused to place themselves in charge of Christians' schools and have gone to their destruction.

It is hard work to gather and save girls and young women. Their minds have been filled with such a dread towards Christian people that they cannot appreciate the kindness shewn them. For instance, many of the unconverted girls in my homes have a great fear in their mind. They think that some day after they are well-fattened, they will be hung downward—and a great fire will be built underneath and oil will be extracted from them to be sold at a fabulously great price for medical purposes. Others think they will be put into oil mills and their bones ground. It is only lately that our girls gathered from the last famine have begun to lose these dreadful thoughts, but the minds of the new ones are filled with more dreadful ideas than these. They cannot understand that anyone would be kind to them without some selfish purpose.

Bad men have succeeded in gathering large numbers of girls by enticing them away, and [have] sold them to a bad life. It is too shocking to the refined feelings of refined people, but facts are facts, and Christian mothers ought to know them [so] that they may be prompted to pray and to work hard for the Salvation of young girls— perhaps of the same age as their own sweet daughters. Let the thought and love of our daughters move our mother-hearts to come forward and save as many of the perishing young girls as we can. I have found out to my great horror and sorrow that over twelve per cent of the girls rescued by my workers have been ruined for life and had to be separated from the other girls and placed in the Rescue Home. The bodies of some of these poor girls are so frightfully diseased that there is no hope for their recovery. Half a dozen of them have died already and some more will die soon. If you could only see them yourself you will understand what I say.

It seems very necessary under these circumstances to save as many precious lives as we can get hold of. Orphanages and schools are filled to the overflowing with great numbers of children taken in. My own homes among others have had their share of girls. I have already received over three hundred and fifty young widows, deserted wives and girls from the present famine, and shall not refuse to take a larger number if necessary. The number of girls in my three homes together has increased from 375 last year to 750 this year. The support and education of all these and many more girls to come will, I know, cost a great deal, and the responsibility of so many souls on hand is greater still. But I know also that the silver and gold of this world is the Lord's and He cares for them all. Not one of them falls without the Father knowing it, and He will somehow or other supply all their needs, temporal and spiritual. My present duty seems to be to rescue and save as many young girls as I can and prevent them from falling into the hands of wicked people.

The enemy is very busy in starting bad reports about this work among people around us, and they believe them with all their hearts. Hindus, Parsees and Mahommedans have heard that I deceive the girls, take them by force without permission of their parents and compel them to become Christians. They have also said I have deceived the Hindus, the English and the Americans and am filling up my purse with money. They sneer at my workers and myself, point the finger of scorn at us when we go about doing the Lord's work and say, 'here are these dreadful people'. They laugh and talk about us, turn their faces, as if from some loathsome objects, and say, 'Why does Ramabai take all these animals to her home; what is she going to do with them?' Then they answer their own question and say, 'Yes, we see she is taking them to make Christians and out castes of them, and make money and fill her purse!' The poor women and girls rescued from the famine districts are so terribly dirty and have such bad smells about them that the passengers in trains and other clean people cannot bear the very sight of them. Houses cannot be hired to shelter them at the chief stations where my workers are working, because owners of bungalows and small houses object to have these dirty people staying in their houses. There are some very highly educated and over-clean people who despise us and do not let us stand near them because we associate with such dirty, ghastly looking women and girls. But though thus despised and rejected by society we know that He who came to save the fallen and call sinners to repentance—the Man acquainted with sorrows and the Friend of the poor sinners—is with us. He has promised to be with us even unto the end of the world. We consider it a great privilege to be counted worthy to be despised by the world like our Master, and thank God for His goodness.

I must say a few words about my fellow workers, sharers of all the hardships in the famine relief work. . . . They are doing work from which many a mighty man would shrink. It is but a small thing to fight a great battle and win a victory with many titles, compared with the heroism of such women. They are true heroes and heroines who suffer with the poor and cast their lot with the despised ones. It takes great courage to stand by the rejected dirty and loathsome people. God bless these and other such workers whose works are not recorded in the reports here but for whom the Master has a crown of victory ready and will place it on their heads when they have finished the battle of this life. . . . It rejoices my heart to see some of the girls saved from the last famine going out into the famine districts with my workers to save the lives of their perishing sisters in the present famine.

Before taking up famine relief work this year, the writer waited on God to know His mind about it. The treasury was quite empty, and when the quarterly balance-sheet was prepared in the middle of October last there was no balance left at all. Reports of the widespread famine and the wicked traffic in girls reached me from many sides. Still there was nothing to be done except to wait and pray. The Lord did not try my faith very long. The very next day a cheque for Rs 272-2-0 [272 rupees, 2 annas, 0 pice] was sent for Mukti and another daily need was supplied in a wonderful manner. It was then made clear to me that I must step out in faith and receive as many girls as the Lord would have me reach. So the work was begun at once. Workers were stationed at different places to search for young girls. There was no money for buying material to build new sheds, so some old material was gathered and a shed was prepared to shelter the newcomers. Our girls had to give up a good many comforts. Little children and older people had to go without milk and butter; only a few small babies who could not eat solid food and the very sick girls got milk, the rest had a little buttermilk with a great deal of water mixed in it. The store-room was almost empty and the saries [sic] of our girls and most of their blankets had turned into old rags—there was no money to buy new saries and blankets. But saries had been ordered from the cloth merchants with the understanding that they were to take all the saries back if by a certain date their bills were not paid; not one of them however was touched. Grains and other necessities of life were not ordered for the month. Many people could not understand why I had to make certain changes in food, etc. But the Lord knew all about it. He let the trials come at certain times and let the house and treasury be quite empty only to fill them again. He made me realize from time to time that His 'hand is not shortened that it cannot save; neither His ear heavy that it cannot hear' Is.59. . . .

The work of rescuing girls went on and is still going on in spite of all difficulties and trials, for God makes it very plain to me from time to time by removing obstacles when they come that it is His will that this work should not be stopped until He Himself stops it. Augur's prayer, Prov.30: 8,9, is being answered in our case. We are not allowed too much or too little of food and clothing and other comforts. Moreover the Lord is teaching our Christian girls to deny themselves a little for the sake of others that they may meet the expenses of their Christian instruction and other church expenses. He sent us a message one day to give up one of our meals on Sundays to save money to feed the hungry and poor and to help His work in other missions. Most of the girls very cheerfully came forward with the request to cut off their one meal on Sundays, which was of course granted and the money thus saved has been used to feed the Lord's poor and to help His work in other places.

The question of self-support of the Native Christian Churches in India is becoming a very serious one. The Indian Christians are very poor, it is true, and will not be able to pay very high salaries and bear heavy expenses of fashionable churches. But it must be remembered that these Christians are mostly converts from Hinduism or children of converts. As Hindus they or their parents did not look to some other nation or to the high priests for the support of their temples, and their priesthood and the wandering religious beggars. As Christians there is no reason why they should not train themselves and their children to deny themselves and to systematic giving. The Lord showed me this was my opportunity to practise and teach what I believed, and I am very thankful to say that the experiment has proved to be a success and the Lord's promise, Mal.3: 10, has been literally fulfilled. . . . If we give one-twentieth or fiftieth part and call it a 'tithe', or give very little with great reluctance we are robbing God of His dues and robbing ourselves of great blessings which He is eager to give us if we only accept them by fulfilling the conditions. This, to me, seems to be the only true cause of the material poverty of the Native Christian Church in India. We must not expect that God will give us many spiritual and temporal blessings unless we cheerfully fulfil the conditions on which He has promised them to us.

Our honoured friends, the Rev. Albert and Mrs Norton, felt called to God to start a Christian Home for famine boys, so they left Mukti for Dhond and are being blessed by God in their loving work for the poor famine-stricken boys. Miss Edmonds who stayed and helped us over a year felt that she must have a separate home, and has gone to Belgaum and is carrying on her blessed work of rescuing and training poor destitute girls and winning them over to Christ. I am very grateful to these friends for the help they gave me while they were here.

You may remember what I said about Mrs Baker in my last year's account. God prompted her to go and work for the Rescue Home started in connection with this Mission, and as the result of her labour of love, 390 pounds were received toward the Rescue Home building. The Rescue Home building which is called Kripa Sadan is progressing slowly; part of it will (D.V.) [Deo Volente; god willing] be finished and occupied before the rainy season sets in. I am very grateful to Mrs Baker for the help she has given me in building the Kripa Sadan.

The Rev. W.E. Robbins of the M.E. Church, Rev. D.G. Malhar of the Presbyterian Church, and Rev. D.K. Shinde of the Church of England have incessantly laboured for the spiritual welfare of my Christian girls. I owe a great debt of gratitude to these and other Christian friends who have visited us from time to time and fed us with the heavenly Manna from the Word of God. Miss Abrams, who has charge of the Christian instruction in this Mission and School, is greatly blessed of God in her labour of love for my girls. We all love her and are very grateful to her for all that she is doing for us. The friends who have helped the Lord's work in Mukti with their means and prayers are daily remembered with great thankfulness, before the throne of grace. My special thanks are due to The American Ramabai Association, to the Proprietor of the *New York Christian Herald*, and of the *London Christian,* to the Editors of the *Bombay Guardian, The Record of Christian Work, The Vanguard, The Missionary Review of the World,* and to other Editors of papers and hundreds of other good friends who have helped us with their words, prayers and sent money to support the girls here. My special thanks are due to Rev. D.O. Fox and Mrs Fox who audit my accounts, for the help they render to this work. The teachers and other helpers, especially the noble Christian women who have laboured to rescue the girls from famine and death, have my gratitude and prayers. God gave me a special message from His Word a few days ago to give all the friends who are helping the Lord's work at Mukti and other missions, which I pass on to you. It is this: 'He that giveth unto the poor shall not lack.' You have denied yourselves in many ways for the sake of giving money for the poor women and children sheltered in our Homes, but you have this rich promise from the Lord as your reward. God bless you all. As for me, I have His sure word to depend upon. 'He that spared not His own Son, but delivered Him up for us all, how shall He not with Him also freely give us all things?' VII.32. Now, 'Unto Him that loved us, and washed us from our sins in His own blood, and hath made us kings and priests unto God, and His Father; to Him be glory and dominion forever and ever, Amen.'

Believe me, dear friends,
Yours gratefully
in the Lord's Service,
Ramabai

Mukti, April 1900

NOTES

1. The Contagious Diseases Act was designed to protect enlisted men from venereal disease, and penalized the prostitute who was found to be the source of the disease. The Act also allowed a woman to be identified as a prostitute on the word of a plainclothes policeman (the onus of proving her innocence was on the woman), and to be compelled to submit to examination by army or navy doctors. The first Act, passed in England and Ireland in 1864, caused a feminist protest led by Josephine Butler and others (Spender 1983: 472–80). Similar Acts were subsequently passed in all parts of the British Empire.

10

A SHORT HISTORY OF KRIPA SADAN, OR HOME OF MERCY*

As a Hindu, I was totally a stranger to the condition and needs of the so-called 'fallen' women in this country. The Hindu women of higher castes and upper ranks are kept in ignorance of the condition of their less favoured sisters. The caste system and the Hindu Shastras, society and social customs, all unite in despising and condemning these women who have fallen because they were deceived by fallen men. Yet the men are allowed to go without any punishment for their sins. Society and religious rules condemn a man for honourably marrying a widow, but men are allowed to have illegal connexion with women of different castes, and force their lawful wives to serve them. A man can marry several women of his own caste at a time, but divorce and re-marriage of widows are not allowed. So no woman is free to marry another man in the life-time of her husband, nor after his death. Child-marriage, polygamy and enforced widowhood are the great sources of social evil and force thousands of young girls and women either to commit suicide or live a life of shame.

When I first landed in England early in 1883, I was met by the kind Sisters of Wantage, who took me to their Home. Later they sent me for a change to one of the suburbs of London where they

*Reproduced from the Archives of the Pandita Ramabai Mukti Mission.

have several Homes. They took me to see the rescue work carried on by them. I met several of the women who were in their Rescue Home once, but who had so completely changed and were so filled with the love of Christ and compassion for suffering humanity, that they had given their life for the service of the sick and the infirm. Here for the first time in my life, I came to know that something should be done to reclaim the so-called fallen women, and that Christians, whom Hindus considered outcastes and cruel, were kind to these unfortunate women, degraded in the eyes of society. I had never heard, or seen, anything of the kind done for this class of women by the Hindus in my own country. I had not heard anyone speaking kindly of them, nor making any effort to turn them from the evil path they had chosen in their folly. The Hindu Shastras do not deal kindly with these women. The law of the Hindus commands that the king should cause the fallen women to be eaten by dogs in the outskirts of the town. They are considered as the greatest sinners, and not worthy of compassion.

After my visit to the Homes at Fulham, where I saw the work of mercy carried on by the Sisters of the Cross, I began to think that there was a real difference between Hinduism and Christianity. I asked one of the Sisters of Wantage what made them care for and reclaim the 'fallen' women. She read the story of Christ meeting the Samaritan woman and His wonderful discourse on the nature of true Worship and explained it to me. She spoke of the Infinite Love of Christ for sinners, who did not despise them but came to save them. I had never read or heard anything like this in the religious books of the Hindus. I realized after reading the 4th Chapter of St. John's Gospel, that Christ was truly the Divine Saviour He claimed to be, and no one but He could transform and uplift the downtrodden womanhood of India and of every land.

About the beginning of October 1894, I paid a visit to Brindaban. This place is sacred to Krishna and visited yearly by millions of pilgrims of the Vaishnava sect. I had known something about the condition of widows in this and other places, but I had no real idea of the terrible facts which I came to know after my visit there. I went about the place and made a thorough investigation of the matter and found out that thousands of the Hindu widow[ed] pilgrims visiting that place, are allured and captured by the priests who carry on a trade in flesh and blood and make much money out of it. The Hindu religion, as taught by these avaricious priests, teaches that women fulfilling the lustful desires of Brahmans in the sacred places, do not commit sin. A class of women consecrated to the service of the temples, who are married to the gods, live in sin with priests and with the pilgrims and are said to be leading worthy lives. Customs of Hindu society permit the existence of another class of prostitutes whose religion is to lead an evil life. These women are considered perfectly good and honourable, as they are said to be following their own peculiar religion. The women belonging to the caste of dancers and singers, and temple girls are honoured by Hindu religion and by society, who invite them to dance and sing on festive occasions such as marriage, or the birth of a son or the celebration of the birthdays of gods and goddesses and other religious festivals. These and many such social customs have encouraged immorality in the country and bad women wander about in the land increasing the social evil.

Ever since I opened a home and school for widows in Poona, I had come to know of the miserable condition of many destitute young widows who had fallen prey to the evil desires of man. As I could not admit them in my home, I used to find shelter for them in the late Miss Richardson's Industrial Home for Women. She was always kind and ready to help me out of my difficulties and I sent several widows to her Home. But when I took up the famine relief work at the end of 1896, there was quite a large number of women rescued from Central India who could not be safely placed among the Mukti girls. The dear servant of God, Major Yuddhabai, of the Salvation Army, took care of over twenty-five of them in her home for women. I can never be thankful enough for this invaluable help rendered me by her in the time of my need. When she was about to leave for England, it became necessary to bring some of the girls back to be placed in a separate home at Kedgaon. Several of the girls were left in the Salvation Army's Home for women to be trained as Christian workers. I am thankful to know that they have given their hearts to God and are willing to do His work. My grateful thanks are due to Major Yuddhabai and her helpers for their kindness to me.

I quote the following account of the beginning of the Home of Mercy from my report of Mukti Mission written in March 1899: 'An unexpected help came to us in a new worker, Miss Edmonds of America. It was like Him who gives beyond all that we can ask or think, to send her here, just when we needed such a helper. The Lord had laid it on the writer's heart for some time to do something for the destitute women of this country, who are led astray by the devil and his messengers. Yet she did not know how or what to do for them. The chief want was a worker who had specially prepared herself for this branch of Christian work, that of seeking and saving the lost girls. Miss Edmonds came in answer to a call from God to work in this mission. A new home has been opened, since her arrival, for destitute women and girls. Miss Edmonds and two Christian helpers are in charge of it. At present, it has thirteen inmates who attend school regularly and receive Christian instruction. They are taught some industrial work according to their abilities. God is doing wonderful work among them in healing their sin-stricken souls and bodies. All the needs of the new Home have been provided for up to this time in answer to prayer. A beautiful incident of divine leading must be mentioned in connection with this new home. An earnest Christian missionary—Mrs Baker, of Rochester, USA—was led by God to come to India when Mr and Mrs Norton started from America to come to Kedgaon about six months ago. She did not know for some months why God had told her to go to India. But she left her large training home for Christian workers, and came away in obedience to God's order. When she arrived at Kedgaon we were all glad to see her though she was a complete stranger to us. She had thought of staying here just one day, but God did not allow her to go away anywhere else. For some days after, she kept enquiring of God what she had to do here. He told her to help this Mukti Mission. Then it dawned upon her that she might be a help in starting the new home for destitute women. Miss Edmonds was trained in her home for Christian workers. Although they were both totally unacquainted with the earnest desire of my heart, God led them both to help me greatly in planning for this new home. We are all confident that God is going to bless this new branch of Christian work started here. The new home cannot be a part of the Mukti Home, but the Lord gave us a piece of land for it some months ago. A new house will be built in that ground. At present the inmates of the new home are living in sheds with a thorn fencing around for security. The writer was waiting for the money to come before planning the house and laying the foundation stone. But the Lord spoke to her and rebuked her unbelief and told her to go forward in faith and lay the foundation stone. We had a very impressive Christian service on the evening of March 20th, 1899 on the new ground, with many missionaries and nearly one hundred workmen present. Mrs Baker read Scripture portions and was followed by a Christian helper reading the same portions from the Marathi Bible. Hymns were sung in praise to God and earnest prayers offered for a blessing on the future house. Mr Norton, assisted by another Christian man, laid the foundation stone, and praises were sung to God. A worker in the Mukti Mission told the workmen the story of the home, making it plain to them that although there was not a single pice in hand to build this new house, yet the foundation stone was laid in obedience to God's order—that His word is sure and He promises to build this new house. It was meant for the good of our fellow creatures and to the glory of our God. We shall look to God alone to provide for it. As for the Mukti School and Mission, Mrs Baker seems to have finished her work in this country. She has received her order from God to go home without seeing another place in all India, excepting this unattractive Kedgaon and a little of Poona. She expects to sail very soon. God's ways and thoughts are very different from ours. He may yet use Mrs Baker in doing grand, good work for India. We shall miss her very much, but hope that she will come back to be present at the opening of the new house when it is completed.'

The Home of Mercy, which was christened Kripa Sadan, made good progress from that time. Miss Edmonds took great pains with the girls and cared alike for their bodies and souls. Many of them received great benefit while under her care and the number of inmates of the Kripa Sadan rose from 13 to about 25. About the end of 1899 we had a visit from two godly women who have consecrated their lives to serve the cause of the downtrodden womanhood of India. We workers at Mukti were profited by their visit, and encouraged to go on with the work which God has placed in our hands. It became evident at that time that they were, for some reason, not satisfied that Miss Edmonds should work here; after much prayer and consultation they decided that she should start a separate Rescue Home. I owe a debt of gratitude to Miss Edmonds for all that she did for me while she was working with me. She left Mukti at the end of 1899 and established a Rescue Home at Belgaum. About the time when Miss Edmonds was to leave the place, I was much perplexed how to find a worker to take her place; I prayed to God to send me a good Christian woman who was fitted by education and training to look after the Rescue Home girls. The Lord heard and answered my prayer and sent a nice, motherly Christian woman to help me in this special work. Mrs Marybai Aiman is a very godly woman and has rendered most excellent services both in the Rescue Home and in the Mukti hospital for the past three years.

Mrs Baker paid us another visit just before Miss Edmonds left and helped strengthen my heart and hands, and encouraged me to go on with the Rescue work. She was very enthusiastic over it and interested many friends both in England and America, who gave money to build the Kripa Sadan. Another great famine came on us in the year 1900, and among nearly 2,000 girls gathered from famine districts in that and in the following year, there were more than 350 girls and women who had to be placed in the Kripa Sadan. Many of these died after their arrival here for they were greatly reduced by starvation and afflicted with incurable disease.

There are at present about two hundred girls in the Home of Mercy. The younger ones must be separated from the older and more hardened cases. One half of the square of the Home of Mercy building has been finished. As there are seventy-five girls under 16 years of age, it is advisable to have two departments. The foundation for another Rescue Home has been laid. In the meanwhile many of the rescued girls who are too sick to do anything are kept in the Rescue hospital for treatment. This hospital has no building. A few temporary sheds have been put up in a separate compound. At this time there are 86 large and small girls in the Rescue Hospital, suffering from terrible diseases. Most of the two hundred girls have been more sinned against than sinning. Only a few of them seem to be very hardened; the majority have improved greatly and show a desire to try to be good girls. I give a few extracts from the entries in my books which will show how these poor girls have suffered owing to the terrible customs of child-marriage, polygamy and enforced widowhood. Their tales are told in a few words. But oh! what volumes of tragic stories could be written if one had time to listen to what the girls have to say about their sad experiences. What sufferings, what shame, what diabolical treatment they have received at the hands of heartless men and women.

> S: I was given in marriage when ten years of age and sent to my husband's house where I lived for seven years. My husband had more wives. They and my sister-in-law persecuted me very much. My husband also treated me very cruelly. He used to beat me with a large stick and whip me with

ropes. I have the marks on my body to this day. No one loved me in my husband's home. I had to work hard and keep a herd of buffaloes and do all the household work from early morning till midnight, and I had not enough food given me. They gave me a little piece of bread. I could not stand this suffering and starvation, so I wanted to go home to my parents. My husband gave me permission to go away. But when I went home, my parents refused to take me in. They said they were too poor to support me. There was nothing for me to do but to take to the streets. I wandered from place to place and begged people to give me food. I had no home, respectable people refused to admit me in their houses, because I had nothing but rags on me. For months, I wandered about in this way. I would beg for my food in the day and lie down in the night wherever I found a little space either on the roadside or in any other open place, where wicked men troubled me continually. I had no one to protect me or care for me. My cries were not heeded and I had no rest or refuge. That is why I have become so ill and weak. Sometime ago I heard about the Kripa Sadan and found my way here. Now I am so glad I do not have to beg for my food and I am loved and cared for; I am willing to do any work when I get well.

J: I was given in marriage when only four years old and became a widow just three months after. I lived with my parents, but they were very poor. When I grew a little older, I had to work hard in order to get my living. My parents did not get me married again as our custom forbids that but they gave me into the hands of a wicked man, who used to drink whisky and eat opium. He kept many other women in the house. As I was the youngest, the others made me work hard and beat me mercilessly. They subjected me to many kinds of abuse, and when I became very ill and had boils and sores all over my body, they just turned me out of the house and I was obliged to wander about and beg for my food. I found my way to this home and now I thank God that He brought me here.

G: I was married when ten years old. My husband was a drunkard and kept another woman. Both he and she used to beat me very cruelly. I bear marks of wounds received at their hands. Some years after my marriage, I left my husband and went home to my father's; I had a step-mother. She did not like my coming home. Whatever I did or said was bad in her eyes and she used to find fault with me in everything. She persecuted and treated me cruelly in many ways. She used to make special bread for me with flour and ashes mixed together. I could not bear this hard life. My father was not kind to me; one day he told me to leave his house and live in the house of another man. This man's mother was worse than my own step-mother. She and her son treated me very badly. They made me do all sorts of hard work and did not give me enough to eat. So I became very weak and ill and was driven away by them. So again I went home to my father, but he died soon after my return home. I was thrown out in the world, all alone. I cannot describe all that I have suffered. One day while wandering about in search of food I went to a missionary lady who sent me here. And now I am very happy and free from troubles.

R. Age 15: My parents were very poor. I was married when 6 years old, and three years after my marriage I became a widow. As there were none to support me, I went out into the town, begging. I did not get much to eat for a time. I carried water for some people, when I fell ill and was not able to work. Still I supported myself by eating sparrows and other small birds, and [also] sold them. But wicked men were after me all the while and troubled me very much. A child was born to me and suffered much. The baby died after a month. I became a skeleton and dreadfully diseased. A good missionary woman found me and brought me to this house of refuge. I have barely escaped death and owing to my sinful life have become disfigured for life. It is a miracle of God's grace that I am still alive, feeling strong and able to help myself. I thank God for all His mercies. He rescued me out of many many troubles and sorrows. He is my father and I am His child.

T. Age 17: I was married when very young, about 5 years old. Soon after this, my mother sent me to my husband's house. I lived there for a year. As I was a small child my husband married another woman, who treated me very badly. She made me work all day long and gave me a piece of bread to eat at night. But it was not good bread, it was made of husks, specially prepared for me. One day I refused to eat this kind of bread. When my husband came home from his work he listened to that woman and beat me cruelly. [T]here are many marks on my body that bear witness to his cruelty. After this, I sought an opportunity to escape from the house and ran away. I was then wandering about and was enticed away by many wicked men and forced to commit sin. When I was dreadfully diseased, it was hard for me to get bread. One day while I was begging, a missionary saw me and sent me to this place. Now I am glad to say that I am improving in my health. I get good bread and nice clothing. I never expected to have such a good place to live in. I had only a small piece of a rag when I came here, it was very dirty and had several holes in it; I thank God for sending me to this happy home. . . . [1]

D.S. Age 11:†† I was married when 5 years of age. After my mother died, I had to suffer much and had to attend to all household work. One

††D.S. was terribly mutilated and diseased, and the child's life was saved with great care. The Lord heard prayers on her behalf. She is better now, and learning to read and to work as much as her strength will permit.

day I went into the field to gather firewood, where I was met by an old woman. She spoke very kindly to me. She caressed me and said she felt very sorry for me as my mother had died and there was no one to love me. But [she] said she would love me like a mother, give me sweets, nice clothes, jewels and take me to some good place. She coaxed me to go with her and I believed in what she said and ran away with her. She took me to the railway station and brought [me] to Bombay. All went on well for a few days, and then one night she locked me in a room with a big man. I was frightened and screamed for help, but he stuffed my mouth with a cloth and hushed my voice. I was quite helpless. I cannot tell you all that I had to suffer that night and for another fortnight. I was kept locked up in the room a helpless prisoner and could not get away. The old woman would not let me go. I fell ill and the old woman thought I would not recover. So she sold me to a Brahman for 20 rupees and left me with him. While in his house I got acquainted with a kind good woman in the neighbourhood. I told her my sad story and begged her to save me from the cruel people, and take me away. The good woman helped me out of that hell and sent me to a missionary, who sent me here. I have learnt to love Jesus. I heard of Him and of His love for sinners since I came here and I am happy. I know Jesus loves me and has saved me from death, and given me life. I have learnt to sing and read, and I feel very happy when I tell all my troubles to Jesus.

The parents of a little girl about nine years of age married her off to a young boy and left her with him. As the famine grew bad, he deserted her and went away. The child was then taken by a Mahommedan to his house and was used very badly. She was shut up in his house for a number of days but finally escaped from her prison and was brought to my Rescue Home by my workers. The child had suffered a great deal and it took months of careful nursing to restore her to health.

Another little girl about the same age was brought to me some months ago; her poor little body bore marks of cruel treatment. She was beaten, bruised, and branded, and could not walk steadily. Her mother-in-law had turned her out of her home after punishing her severely. She is a child widow, her boy-husband died a year ago. His relatives, especially the mother, cursed her and made her work hard and would not give her food. She had beaten and branded the little widow and sent her away. The child soon fell into the hands of some cruel policemen who, after accomplishing their diabolical purpose, left her to die on the roadside. She was found by a Bible-woman and brought to my home. It was a wonder that the child recovered from her illness after some months of good treatment and careful nursing.

Another little girl of about twelve years of age was brought to me from the famine districts. Her parents and husband had died. She lived in her uncle's house. She had to do all the household work, there being no other woman to do that. Besides this, she was cruelly used by her cousins during the day and by the uncle at night. She had suffered untold miseries and, at last, when she became useless to them, the cruel men turned her out of their house and left her to die in the jungle. Her poor tender body was so dreadfully mutilated and so rotten that the sight of it was unbearable. She lived a few months after her arrival, but her life was full of agony. Nothing could be done to save her, so she died an innocent victim sacrificed to man's lust. I could relate several stories of this kind; but let me turn away from this sad narrative.

One would suppose, by reading these sketches, that all the girls rescued from such a terrible fate must be very grateful, that they appreciate the kindness shown to them, that they must feel like being in heaven and must be giving themselves to their studies and improving their time and opportunities. But I must say that this is far from being the case. Many of the girls, when they get angry and when something in the rules of the school crosses their will, get so wild that they actually threaten to rise against us in a body, to kill us workers, to set the house on fire and go away. Scarcely a day passes without one of them getting angry with the workers and with me— when she [that girl] gives vent to her feelings, she curses us almost all day, and sometimes for weeks her anger does not leave her. She might be seen making ugly faces, spitting at us, and speaking as bad words as she can think of. She uses all dirty epithets in speaking our names. She blames the workers who went into famine districts and brought her here. She says that they deceived her—that she was very happy in her home in a large bungalow, had a loving husband and relatives and fields, but she was enticed away by these wicked women who told her that she would have many jewelries[sic]; so forth and so on! One [of them] says that she had gone to the bazaar to buy some brown sugar *for her cattle*, when one of my workers met her and brought her away by force. She is more than 25 years of age, a very stout and strong woman and the worker who brought her looks very small compared with her size. Another says she was comfortably sitting in a large two-storied house when one of my workers went and forced her to come away. One young woman says she was sitting by the side of her husband chatting happily with him when my Bible-woman brought her away by force. A young girl, who is a mere skeleton, is so discontented and displeased with the restrictions put on her wandering life, that she keeps cursing and speaking ugly words to the worker who brought her from the famine district. There are not a few even among our old girls, rescued from the famine of 1897, who have forgotten all about their terrible sufferings in the famine from starvation, all the ill treatment which they were subjected to as widows and deserted wives. The poor women do not know what they do or talk about. So we smile at them and thank them for coming here and for favouring us with their company and go about our work.

Our Brahman brethren have organized a movement to break down this work. They are giving false reports to the Government, that the girls are very badly treated and want to be set free. The persons in authority who are quite new in the country [i.e. region] and do not know much about the feelings of our Brahman countrymen, have implicitly believed in their stories and have sided with them. The intention of the Brahmans seems to be to overthrow this work. We workers here are having much trouble from without and from within. Some of the worst girls in the Kripa Sadan are delighted to find that the authorities do not look upon this work with favour, and in their excitement they tried to set the house and sheds on fire three times since last year. But the Lord smiled on us and sent help in time to save the house. No evidence could be found at the time to charge anyone of this guilt, but when the excitement had subsided, the guilty ones confessed their crime and asked to be forgiven. Some of these girls are discontented, and the worst of them organize a rebellion in the Home, get a few of their friends in the class to rally together and run away in a body. Several such girls have left the Home; especially since certain people living around us began to give us trouble in many ways. Our fellow-countrymen do not do anything to help these poor creatures. The orthodox Hindu does not even [utter the] name [of] such fallen girls. The very thought of helping such girls is repulsive to them. If a child-widow or deserted wife falls into temptation and her sins come to light, she is either secretly murdered, or cast away. The usual mode of casting away a fallen woman is to burn an effigy of her and perform funeral ceremonies; thenceforth, she is considered as dead to the family and the relatives or people belonging to her caste never help her. Everybody, even her own parents, curse her and wish her dead. They rejoice in any affliction that may befall her; and when dead, they leave her body to be eaten by dogs, but the humane English Government employs low-caste men to bury the dead at their expense for the sake of preserving public health. Such is the hatred of the high-caste men and orthodox Hindus toward a fallen woman. . . .

But what about the modern reformers, you may ask, for you [would] have heard of the great National Social Conference which yearly passes dozens of resolutions in favour of social reform. Our most advanced reformers have never been heard talking about the necessity of establishing rescue homes and reclaiming the fallen women. I have seen many of them in Poona, Bombay and other great cities living within a stone's throw of streets full of the houses of ill fame. But I have never heard any of them taking steps towards rescuing and reforming the poor prisoners of the devil in those houses.

It is a pity that our Brahman countrymen should consider it their duty to overthrow such a work as this. I am sorry for them. Our countrymen do not choose to understand my motives in carrying on this work, nor are they willing to be fair and you know that none are so blind as those who will not see. The non-Christian people of this country are shocked to hear of the conversion of many of the girls to Christ. It is natural for them not to wish their people to go into another faith, but I do not see the reasonableness of their wish when they are doing nothing to enlighten and save those people. Women and low-caste people are utterly neglected by the high-caste Hindus. These neglected people have no knowledge of their religion and practically there is no religion for them. The low-caste people have to serve the high-caste people, that is said to be their religion. To serve their husbands is the women's religion.

The Hindus do not, as a rule, allow their women to worship their gods independently of their husbands. The husband is *the god* of a Hindu woman. She worships him in person while he lives, and when dead she worships his spirit. The high-caste man alone is considered good enough to approach the gods with his offering and prayers, etc. His wife can accompany him to the temples and sit or stand by his left side while he worships the gods. The Tulsi plant is almost the only god that can be worshipped by orthodox Hindu women. But there are certain heretics among the Hindu women who have usurped the right of worshipping the gods independently of their husbands. Such women carry their little idols with them either tied up in a cloth or packed up in a box of copper or brass. They unpack them at the time of worship, bathe them with water, offer flowers, sandalwood paste and food, then pack them up again and put them away. The Brahmans wink at the heretics, for they get money and other presents from these religious members of the Hindu community. But the idols worshipped by women, Shudras and low-caste men are never worshipped by Brahman men. The household gods are considered as defiled and dead if accidentally touched by women members of the family, and have to be purified with an ablution of the five products of the cow and the divine life [has] to be brought into the idols by the chanting of the mantras before they are again fit to be worshipped by Brahmans. Women are not allowed to enter the inner part of the temples where the idols are enshrined, nor to touch them. . . .

Again, widows who do not shave their heads are considered as unholy and are excluded from any and every religious rite. Orthodox Brahmans will not take food and water from them. The deserted wives, having committed the sin of displeasing their husbands, are considered as very irreligious, and the gods do not accept their worship. Widows who have their heads shaven regularly twice a month, keep fasts, etc. do sometimes worship the Tulsi and some other idols which they can carry about. . . . There are so many different ways of worshipping the gods, but all women who have been separated from their husbands, and the widows [who have] not [been] shaving their heads cannot worship them as their worship is [deemed] not acceptable to the gods. Women therefore have very little religious consolation. Fasting on certain days and giving presents to the Brahmans, keeping caste rules, bowing before the idols in the shrines from a distance, worshipping their husbands and pleasing them [in] every way is the religion of women among the Hindus. Women are not taught to read and understand religious books. The Shudras and women are not allowed to read the books considered most sacred by the Hindus. Among them are the Vedas, the Upanishads, the Brahmanas, the Brahma Sutras and the mystic monogram 'Om'. With the exception of a part of the Vedas, none of these books are translated in the vernacular languages. They are written in the most ancient Sanskrit, not understood, even by those learned in modern Sanskrit, without the help of commentaries. The great epics Mahabharata and Ramayana, and all but two or three of the Puranas and Upapuranas, the Tantras and all the sacred laws of the Hindus, and other such religious works are sealed books to the women and Shudras. . . . Like their numerous gods, the religious books of the Hindus are many, and are inaccessible to the women. Women are not supposed to be good enough even to read books written in modern Sanskrit. They must hear them read by the priests. Many Hindu women go to the temples where the Puranas are read and explained by priests called Puranikas, who with a few exceptions, are by no means the models of good moral character. Among those who attend the temples where Puranas are read are men and women of all classes, except the low-castes. Temple girls, dancing girls and professional singers of bad reputation come to the temples, apparently to hear the Purana reading, but in reality, to catch foolish men in their snares. The young widows and girls who go to the temples to hear the Purana reading, get acquainted with dancing girls and public women, who are nicely dressed and decked with costly jewellery. The poor child widows get their heads turned at the dazzling sight of the dancing girls, [and] are tempted to leave their homes, throw away the hard rules of widowhood, which subject them to untold sufferings and lifelong slavery, adopt a new mode of life imitating the dancing girls, which they think better than the degrading life of Hindu widows, and earn their livelihood by giving themselves to a life of shame in streets of large and small cities. This is how the number of prostitutes is increased year by year. Few of the child widows who attend the reading of Puranas in temples are capable of resisting the temptation to go into a bad life.

Some people have impressed it upon the minds of certain men and women of the West that the position of a Hindu woman is superior to that of an English or American Christian woman. I pity the people who believe such a story as this, for it is not true. Those people who have never been in the place of the Hindu woman, that of a widow or a wife not loved by her husband, can never know the hardship of their lot, and to idealize the position and life of a widow, for talk about the honour given her is nothing but an idle story. . . .

A superficial knowledge of the philosophies and religious books of India has been misleading many Western people to think that the Hindus are the sole possessors of superior spirituality. I am not surprised that the good men and women of the West, who only see the outside of the grand structures of the Oriental philosophies, are charmed with them. These philosophies are not meant for women and Shudras and low-caste people. . . .

Some eight years ago, I visited Agra in company with a very dear friend of mine. One day we went into the Fort, to see the grand palaces of the Moghul emperors. There we saw the great Khas Mahal, or the emperor's private palace, where he used to keep hundreds of beautiful women shut up for life. The guide showed us the Rani's private rooms, the gardens and grand marble buildings once occupied by the kings and queens. He also showed us the beautiful pleasure-tower called Samman Burj. Visitors are shown all that is beautiful there, and they go away carrying very pleasant impressions of Agra with them. I was not satisfied with seeing the outside beauty of those 'poems in marble,' but wished to see the dungeons, and the place where the unfortunate women used to be confined and hanged at the pleasure of the king. The guide at first denied the existence of such places in the palace; but, finally—on obtaining a promise to get a little more money for his trouble—he consented to show [us] the dungeons. He opened a trap-door on one side of the basement of the palace, let us in, and guided us about, showing us the many small and large under-ground rooms where the queens, who had incurred the king's displeasure, used to be shut up, tortured, and starved, until it pleased his majesty to set them free. The guide then lighted a big torch, and took us to the furthest end of the prison, into a room underneath the Samman Burj, or Jasmine Tower. The room was very dark and octagonal, with a deep, dark pit in the centre, and a big beam placed on the walls across the room right over that pit. This beam was beautifully carved and served for hanging the unfortunate women who once occupied the throne of the king as his queens, but had by some unknown cause fallen under his displeasure, and had to suffer such a cruel and ignoble death. Their lifeless bodies were thrown into that dark pit, whence the waters flowing in the moat surrounding the castle, carried them to the waters of the Jumna, to be eaten by crocodiles. Thus the poor, miserable wives of the Moghul emperors suffered torture and death in that dark hell-pit under the pleasure-gallery, while their cruel masters and rivals sang songs, enjoyed life, and made merry over their grave in the beautifully decorated, grand Samman Burj. I think but little of those lovely palaces, but always remember seeing that dark room, and compare it with similar places of torture which exist in many sacred towers of India. If the walls of that horrible room had the power of speech, oh, what stories of human cruelty and misery would they tell today!

I beg of my Western sisters not to be satisfied with looking on the outside beauty of the grand philosophies, and not to be charmed with hearing the long and interesting discourses of our educated men. . . . The teachers of false philosophies and lifeless spiritualities will do no good to our people. Nothing has been done by them to protect the fatherless and judge the widow. If anything has been done by anybody at all, it has been done by those people who have come under direct influence of Christianity. Education and philosophies are powerless to break down caste rules, ancient customs, and priestcraft. That is why our educated men and our learned Sadhus are so indifferent toward their own brothers and sisters. The educated men and learned priests do not like to move about. They don't want to take the trouble to go about to see how dreadfully the widows have to suffer and how many thousands of lives are destroyed by their priestly brethren. They mourn over a few women who have the boldness to declare themselves as free women, and to follow their conscience by confessing Christ as their Saviour. But they say nothing of the thousands who die every year or lead shameful lives. My Brahman brethren are mourning for the girls who have become Christians, for they think that they are lost to society, and that the nation has been made weak by this loss of strength. These good people never think of the thousands of young widows who are yearly led astray, and whose lives are wantonly destroyed by men like themselves.

The *Hitabadi*, a Hindu paper of good standing, describes the famous Kalighat of Calcutta and other such places in the following terms:

> If we consider what takes place in this holy place, we can only call it a place of sin. When we see in a Hindu country a place of Hindu pilgrimage in such a deplorable condition there is no limit to our shame. For this reason we mention this subject again and again, and shall continue to do so as long as it is not remedied. In the shops where fruits and sweets are sold, all manner of sin is committed. Pilfering, stealing, pick-pocketing, are common occurrences, but in addition to this, the modesty of women is outraged in this hell. In the adjoining rest-houses these sins are committed. Shopkeepers, by force or by trickery, rob the pilgrims of all

their money. The Brahmins, with their marked foreheads, their bead necklaces, their silk cloths and garments, stamped with the names of their gods—wolves in sheep's clothing—joining hands with shopkeepers, make it their chief business to rob the pilgrims, sharing the gains with them. Being considered a holy people they are allowed to enter any part of the temple; taking advantage of this privilege they make it an opportunity to sin. These Brahmins are of the lowest character. Their daily custom is to drink, and to smoke ganja. Such are the priests of our places of pilgrimage. We bow our heads with shame as we say it.

. . . I earnestly beg of the women of England and America to come to India and live in our sacred cities—not living in European and American fashion, but living like the poor beggar-women, going in and out of their dirty huts, hearing the stories of their miserable lives, and seeing the fruits of the 'sublime' philosophies. Let not my Western sisters be charmed by the books and poems they read. There are many hard and bitter facts which we have to accept and feel. All is not poetry with us. The prose we have to read in our own lives is very hard. It cannot be understood by our learned brethren and comfortable sisters of the West.

An American lady, who very kindly came to visit this place, asked me the other day whether it was true that Hindu religion is better than the religion of Jesus Christ and if the position of Hindu women is a very happy and glorious one? She had heard some disciples of the yellow-robed Swamis say so! Oh, said I, it is all very well to say so, but it is not quite so lovely to experience it. To praise Hindu religion quite blindly without regard to the truth, to declare themselves either Hindus or Buddhists, is becoming quite a fashion among certain Western people. . . .

'He that hath an ear, let him hear what the Spirit saith unto the Churches.' Rev. II.7.

Believe me yours,
In the Lord's Service
Ramabai

Mukti, Kedgaon, India
March 1903

NOTES

1. Ten more similar case studies follow.

11

A TESTIMONY OF OUR INEXHAUSTIBLE TREASURE[*]

'Jesus . . . saith . . . Go home to thy friends, and tell them how great things the Lord hath done for thee, and hath had compassion on thee.' Mark 5: 19. 'Come, and hear, all ye that fear God, and I will declare what he hath done for my soul.' Psalm 66: 16.

AN HONOURABLE HERITAGE

My father, though a very orthodox Hindu and strictly adhering to caste and other religious rules, was yet a reformer in his own way. He could not see why women and people of the Shudra caste should not learn to read and write the Sanskrit language and learn sacred literature other than the Vedas.

He thought it better to try the experiment at home instead of preaching to others. He found an apt pupil in my mother, who fell in line with his plan and became an excellent Sanskrit scholar. She

[*]Reproduced from the booklet published by the Pandita Ramabai Mukti Mission, 11th edition, 1992.

performed all her home duties, cooked, washed, and did all the household work, took care of her children, attended to guests, and did all that was required of a good religious wife and mother. She devoted many hours of her time in the night to the regular study of the sacred Puranic literature, and was able to store up a great deal of knowledge in her mind.

The Brahman Pandits living in the Mangalore District, round about my father's native village, tried to dissuade him from the heretical course he was following in teaching his wife the sacred language of the gods. He had fully prepared himself to meet their objections. His extensive studies in the Hindu sacred literature enabled him to quote chapter and verse of each sacred book, which gives authority to teach women and Shudras. His misdeeds were reported to the head priest of the sect to which he belonged, and the learned Brahmans induced the guru to call this heretic to appear before him and before the august assemblage of the Pandits, to give his reasons for taking this course, or be excommunicated. He was summoned to Krishnapura and Udipi, the chief seat of the Madhva Vaishnava sect.

My father appeared before the guru, the head priest, and the assembly of Pandits and gave his reasons for teaching his wife. He quoted ancient authorities, and succeeded in convincing the guru and chief Pandits that it was not wrong for women and Shudras to learn Sanskrit Puranic literature. So they did not put him out of caste, nor was he molested by anyone after this. He became known as an orthodox reformer.

My father was a native of Mangalore District, but he chose a place in a dense forest on the top of a peak of the Western Ghats, on the borders of Mysore State, where he built a home for himself. This was done in order that he might be away from the hubbub of the world, carry on his educational work and engage in devotion to the gods in a quiet place, where he would not be constantly worried by curious visitors.

He used to get his support from the rice-fields and coconut plantations which he owned. The place he had selected for his home happened to be a sacred place of pilgrimage, where pilgrims came all the year round. He thought it was his duty to entertain them at his expense, as hospitality was a part of his religion. For thirteen years he stayed there and did his work quietly, but lost his property because of the great expense he incurred in performing what he thought was his duty.

So he was obliged to leave his home, and lead a pilgrim's life. My mother told me that I was only about six months old when they left their home. She placed me in a big box made of cane, and a man carried it on his head from the mountain top to the valley. Thus my pilgrim life began when I was a little baby. I was the youngest member of the family.

Some people honoured him for what he was doing, and some despised him. He cared little for what people said, and did what he thought was right. He taught and educated my mother, brother, sister, and others.

A UNIQUE EDUCATION

When I was about eight years old, my mother began to teach me and continued to do so until I was about fifteen years of age. During these years she succeeded in training my mind so that I might be able to carry on my own education with very little aid from others. I did not know of any schools for girls and women existing then, where higher education was to be obtained.

Moreover, my parents did not like us children to come in contact with the outside world. They wanted us to be strictly religious and adhere to their old faith. Learning any other language except Sanskrit was out of the question. Secular education of any kind was looked upon as leading people to worldliness which would prevent them from getting into the way of Moksha, or liberation from the everlasting trouble of reincarnation, in millions and millions of animal species, and undergoing the pains of suffering countless millions of diseases and deaths. To learn the English language and to come in contact with the Mlenchchas, as the non-Hindus are called, was forbidden on pain of losing caste, and all hope of future happiness. So all that we could, or did learn was the Sanskrit grammar and dictionaries, with the Puranic and modern poetical literature in that language. Most of this, including the grammar and dictionaries, which are written in verse form, had to be committed to memory.

Ever since I remember anything, my father and mother were always travelling from one sacred place to another, staying in each place for some months, bathing in the sacred river or tank, visiting temples, worshipping household gods and the images of gods in the temples, and reading Puranas in temples or in some convenient places.

The reading of the Puranas served a double purpose. The first and foremost was that of getting rid of sin, and of earning merit in order to obtain Moksha. The other purpose was to earn an honest living, without begging.

The readers of Puranas—Puranikas as they are called—are the popular and public preachers of religion among the Hindus. They sit in some prominent place, in temple halls or under the trees, or on the banks of rivers and tanks, with their manuscript books in their hands, and read the Puranas in a loud voice with intonation, so that the passers-by, or visitors of the temple might hear. The text, being in the Sanskrit language, is not understood by the hearers. The Puranikas are not obliged to explain it to them. They may or may not explain it as they choose. And sometimes when it is translated and explained, the Puranika takes great pains to make his speech as popular as he can, by telling greatly exaggerated or untrue stories. This is not considered a sin, since it is done to attract common people's attention, that they may hear the sacred sound, the names of the gods, and some of their deeds, and be purified by this means. When the Puranika reads the Puranas, the hearers, who are sure to come and sit around him for a few moments at least, generally give him presents. The Puranika continues to read, paying no attention to what the hearers do or say. They come and go at their choice.

When they come, the religious ones among them prostrate themselves before him and worship him and the book, offering flowers, fruits, sweetmeats, garments, money, and other things. It is supposed that this act brings a great deal of merit to the giver, and the person who receives does not incur any sin. If a hearer does not give presents to the Puranika, he loses all the merit which he may have earned by good acts. The presents need not be very expensive ones, a handful of rice or other grains, a pice, or even a few cowries, which are used as an exchange of pice (64 cowrie shells are equal to one pice) are quite acceptable. A flower, or even a petal of a flower or a leaf of any good sacred tree, is acceptable to the gods. But the offerer knows well that his store of merit will be according to what he gives, and he tries to be as generous as he can. So the Puranika gets all that he needs by reading the Puranas in public places.

My parents followed this vocation. We all read Puranas in public places, but did not translate or explain them in the vernacular. The reading and hearing of the sacred literature is in itself believed to be productive of great merit—'Punya,' as it is called by the Hindus. We never had to beg, or work to earn our livelihood. We used to get all the money and food we needed, and more; what remained over after meeting all necessary expenses was spent in performing pilgrimages and giving alms to the Brahmans.

FAMINE, DEATH AND DOUBTS

This sort of life went on until my father became too feeble to stand the exertion, when he was no longer able to direct the reading of the Puranas by us. We were not fit to do any other work to earn our livelihood, as we had grown up in perfect ignorance of anything outside the sacred literature of the Hindus.

We could not do menial work, nor could we beg to get the necessities of life. Our parents had some money in hand. If it had been used to advance our secular education, we might have been able to earn our living in some way. But this was out of the question. Our parents had unbounded faith in what the sacred books said. They encouraged us to look to the gods to get our support. The sacred books declared that if people worshipped the gods in particular ways, gave alms to the Brahmans, repeated the names of certain gods, and also some hymns in their honour, with fasting and performance of penance, the gods and goddesses would appear and talk to the worshippers, and give them whatever they desired. We decided to take this course of meeting our temporal wants. For three years, we did nothing but perform these religious acts. At last, all the money which we had was spent but the gods did not help us.

We suffered from [the effects of the] famine, which we had brought upon ourselves. The country too, that is, the Madras Presidency, where we lived at that particular time, had begun to feel the effects of famine. There was scarcity of food and water. People were starving all around, and we, like the rest of the poor people, wandered from place to place. We were too proud to beg or to do menial work, and ignorant of any practical way of earning an honest living. Nothing but starvation was before us. My father, mother, and sister, all died of starvation within a few months of each other.

I cannot describe all the sufferings of that terrible time. My brother and I survived, and wandered about, still visiting sacred places, bathing in rivers and worshipping the gods and goddesses, in order to get our desire. We had fulfilled all the conditions laid down in the sacred books, and kept all the rules as far as our knowledge went, but the gods were not pleased with us, and did not appear to us. After years of fruitless service, we began to lose our faith in them and in the books which prescribed this course, and held out the hope of a great reward to the worshippers of the gods. We still continued to keep caste rules, worshipped gods and studied sacred literature, as usual.

But as our faith in our religion had grown cold, we were not quite so strict with regard to obtaining secular education and finding some means of earning an honest livelihood. We wandered from place to place, visiting many temples, bathing in many rivers, fasting and performing penances, worshipping gods, trees, animals, Brahmans and all that we knew for more than three years after the death of our parents and elder sister. We had walked more than four thousand miles on foot without any sort of comfort; sometimes eating what kind people gave us, and sometimes going without food, with poor, coarse clothing, and finding but little shelter except in Dharma Shalas, that is, free lodging places for the poor which are [open and] common to all pilgrims and travellers of all sorts except the low-caste people. We wandered from the south to the north as far as Kashmir, and then to the east and west to Calcutta in 1878.

INTRODUCTION TO CHRISTIANITY

We stayed in Calcutta for about a year and became acquainted with the learned Brahmans. Here my brother and I were once invited to attend a Christian gathering. We did not know what it was, for we had never come in social contact with either the Hindu Reformers, nor with Christians before that time. We were advised by our Brahman acquaintances to accept this invitation. So we went to the Christian people's gathering for the first time in our life. We saw many people gathered there, who received us very kindly. There were chairs and sofas, tables, lamps—all very new to us. Indian people curiously dressed like English men and women, some men like the Rev. K.M. Banerji and Kali Charan Banerji, whose names sounded like those of Brahmans but whose way of dressing showed that they had become 'Sahibs', were great curiosities. They ate bread and biscuits and drank tea with the English people and shocked us by asking us to partake of the refreshment. We thought the last age, Kali Yuga, that is, the age of quarrels, darkness, and irreligion, had fully established its reign in Calcutta since some of the Brahmans were so irreligious as to eat food with the English.

We looked upon the proceedings of the assembly with curiosity, but did not understand what they were about. After a little while one of them opened a book and read something out of it and then they knelt down before their chairs and some said something with closed eyes. We were told that was the way they prayed to God. We did not see any image to which they paid their homage but it seemed as though they were paying homage to the chairs before which they knelt. Such was the crude idea of Christian worship that impressed itself on my mind.

The kind Christians gave me a copy of the Holy Bible in Sanskrit, and some other nice things with it. Two of those people were the translators of the Bible. They were grand old men. I do not remember their names, but they must have prayed for my conversion through the reading of the Bible. I liked the outward appearance of the Book and tried to read it, but did not understand [it]. The language was so different from the Sanskrit literature of the Hindus, the teaching so different that I thought it quite a waste of time to read that Book, but I have never parted with it since then.

CALCUTTA—DEEPER HINDU STUDIES AND SCEPTICISM

While staying in Calcutta we became acquainted with many learned Pandits. Some of them requested me to lecture to the Pardah women on the duties of women according to the Shastras. I had to study the subject well before I could lecture on it; so I bought the books of the Hindu law published in Calcutta. Besides reading them, I read other books which would help me in my work. While reading the Dharma Shastras, I came to know many things which I never knew before. There were contradictory statements about almost everything. What one book said was most righteous, the other book declared as being unrighteous. While reading the Mahabharata I found the following, 'The Vedas differ from each other; Smritis, that is, books of sacred laws, do not agree with one another; the secret of religion is in some hidden place: the only way is that which is followed by great men.'

This I found true of about everything, but there were two things on which all those books, the Dharma Shastras, the sacred epics, the Puranas and modern poets, the popular preachers of the present day and orthodox high-caste men, were agreed, that women of high- and low-caste, as a class were bad, very bad, worse than demons, unholy as untruth; and that they could not get Moksha as as men [did]. The only hope of their getting this much-desired liberation from Karma and its results, that is, countless millions of births and deaths and untold suffering, was the worship of their husbands. The husband is said to be the woman's god; there is no other god for her. This god may be the worst sinner and a great criminal; still HE IS HER GOD, and she must worship him. She can have no hope of getting admission into Svarga, the abode of the gods without his pleasure, and if she pleases him in all things, she will have the privilege of going to Svarga as his slave, there to serve him and be one of his wives among the thousands of the Svarga harlots who are presented to him by the gods in exchange for his wife's merit.

The woman is allowed to go into higher existence thus far but to attain Moksha, or liberation, she must perform such great religious acts as will obtain for her the merit by which she will be reincarnated as a high-caste man, in order to study the Vedas and the Vedanta, and thereby get the knowledge of the true Brahma and be amalgamated in it. The extraordinary religious acts which help a woman to get into the way of getting Moksha are utter abandonment of her will to that of her husband. She is to worship him with whole-hearted devotion as the only god; to know and see no other pleasure in life except in the most degraded slavery to him. The woman has no right to study the Vedas and Vedanta, and without knowing them, no one can know the

Brahma; without knowing Brahma no one can get liberation, therefore no woman as a woman can get liberation, that is, Moksha. QED. The same rules are applicable to the Shudras. The Shudras must not study the Vedas, and must not perform the same religious act which a Brahman has a right to perform. The Shudra hearing the Vedas repeated must be punished by having his ears filled with liquified lead. The Shudra who dares to learn a verse or verses of the Vedas must be punished by having intensely hot liquor poured down his throat. This would no doubt be done to the Shudra violating the sacred law, if he were left to the tender mercies of the Brahman. His only hope of getting liberation is in serving the three high castes as their lifelong slave. Then he will earn merit enough to be reincarnated in some higher caste, and in the course of millions of years, he will be born as a Brahman, learn the Vedas and Vedantas, and get knowledge of the Brahma and be amalgamated in it. Such is the hope of final liberation held out by the Shastras to women and to the Shudras.

As for the low-caste people, the poor things have no hope of any sort. They are looked upon as being very like the lower species of animals, such as pigs; their very shadow and the sound of their voices are defiling; they have no place in the abode of the gods, and no hope of getting liberation, except that they might perchance be born among the higher castes after having gone through millions of reincarnations.

The things which are necessary to make it possible for them to be born in higher castes are that they should be contented to live in a very degraded condition serving the high-caste people as their bond servants, eating the leavings of their food in dirty broken earthen vessels, wearing filthy rags and clothes thrown away from the dead bodies of the high-caste people. They may sometimes get the benefit of coming in contact with the shadow of a Brahman, and have a few drops of water from his hand or wet clothes thrown at them, and feel the air which has passed over the sacred persons of Brahmans. These things are beneficial to the low-caste people, but the Brahmans lose much of their own hard-earned merit by letting the low-caste people get these benefits!

The low-caste people are never allowed to enter the temples where high-caste men worship gods. So the poor degraded people find shapeless stones, broken pots, and smear them with red paint, set them up under trees and on roadsides, or in small temples which they build themselves, where Brahmans do not go for fear of losing their caste, and worship, in order to satisfy the cravings of their spiritual nature. Poor, poor people! How very sad their condition is no one who has not seen [it] can realize. Their quarters are found outside every village, or town where the sacred feet of the pious Brahmans do not walk!

These are the two things upon which all Shastras and others are agreed. I had a vague idea of these doctrines of the Hindu religion from my childhood, but while studying the Dharma Shastras, they presented themselves to my mind with great force. My eyes were being gradually opened; I was waking up to my own hopeless condition as a woman, and it was becoming clearer and clearer to me that I had no place anywhere as far as religious consolation was concerned. I became quite dissatisfied with myself. I wanted something more than the Shastras could give me, but I did not know what it was that I wanted.

One day my brother and I were invited by Keshab Chandra Sen to his house. He received us very kindly, took me into the inner part of the house, and introduced me to his wife and daughters. One of them was just married to the Maharaja of Cuch Behar, and the Brahmos and others were criticising him for breaking the rule which was laid down for all Brahmos, that is, not to marry or give girls in marriage under fourteen years of age. He and his family showed great kindness to me, and when parting, he gave me a copy of one of the Vedas. He asked if I had studied the Vedas. I answered in the negative and said that women were not fit to read the Vedas and they were not allowed to do so. It would be breaking the rules of religion, if I were to study the Vedas. He could not but smile at my declaration of this Hindu doctrine. He said nothing in answer, but advised me to study the Vedas and Upanishads.

New thoughts were awakening in my heart. I questioned myself, why I should not study the Vedas and Vedanta. Soon I persuaded myself into the belief that it was not wrong for a woman to read the Vedas. So I began first to read the Upanishads, then the Vedanta, and the Vedas. I became more dissatisfied with myself.

In the meanwhile my brother died. As my father wanted me to be well-versed in our religion he did not give me in marriage when [I was] a little child. He had married my older sister to a boy of her own age, but he [the boy] did not want to study, or to lead a good religious life with my sister. Her life was made miserable by being unequally yoked, and my father did not want the same thing to happen to me. This was of course against the caste rules, so he had to suffer, being practically put out of Brahman society. But he stood the persecution with his characteristic manliness, and did what he thought was right, to give me a chance to study and be happy by leading a religious life. So I had remained unmarried till I was 22 years old.

Having lost all faith in the religion of my ancestors, I married a Bengali gentleman of the Shudra caste [Bipin Behari Das Medhavi]. My husband died of cholera within two years of our marriage, and I was left alone to face the world with one baby in my arms.

MARRIAGE AND LIFE IN BENGAL

I stayed in Bengal and Assam for four years in all and studied the Bengali language. While living with my husband at Silchar, Assam, I found a little pamphlet in my library. I do not know how it came there but I picked it up and began to read it with great interest. It was St. Luke's Gospel in the Bengali language.

There was a Baptist missionary, Mr Allen, living at Silchar. He occasionally paid visits to me and preached the gospel. He explained the first chapter of the Book of Genesis to me. The story of the creation of the world was so very unlike all the stories which I read in the Puranas and Shastras that I became greatly interested in it. It struck me as being a true story, but I could not give any reason for thinking so or believing in it.

Having lost all faith in my former religion, and with my heart hungering after something better, I eagerly learnt everything which I could about the Christian religion, and declared my intention to become a Christian, if I were perfectly satisfied with this new religion. My husband, who had studied in a Mission school, was pretty well acquainted with the Bible, but he did not like to be called a Christian. Much less did he like the idea of his wife being publicly baptized and joining the despised Christian community. He was very angry and said he would tell Mr Allen not to come to our house any more. I do not know just what would have happened had he lived much longer.

I was desperately in need of some religion. The Hindu religion held out no hope for me; the Brahmo religion was not a very definite one. For it is nothing but what a man makes for himself. He chooses and gathers whatever seems good to him from all religions known to him, and prepares a sort of religion for his own use. The Brahmo religion has no other foundation than man's own natural light and the sense of right and wrong which he possesses in common with all mankind. It could not and did not satisfy me; still I liked and believed a good deal of it that was better than what the orthodox Hindu religion taught.

WIDOWHOOD—AND POONA

After my husband's death, I left Silchar and came to Poona. Here I stayed for a year. The leaders of the reform party, and the members of the Prarthana Samaj treated me with great kindness and gave me some help. Messrs Ranade, Modak, Kelkar and Dr Bhandarkar were among the people who showed great kindness to me. Miss Hurford, then a missionary working in connection with the High Church, used to come and teach me the New Testament in Marathi. I had at this time begun to study the English language, but did not know how to write or speak it. She used to teach me some lessons from the primary reading books, yet sometimes I was more interested in the study of the New Testament than in the reading books. The Rev. Father Goreh was another missionary who used to come and explain the difference between the Hindu and Christian religions. I profited much by their teaching.

ENGLAND—BEING DRAWN TO
RELIGION OF CHRIST

I went to England early in 1883 in order to study and fit myself for my life-work. When I first landed in England, I was met by the kind

Sisters of Wantage, to one of whom I had been introduced by Miss Hurford at St. Mary's Home in Poona. The Sisters took me to their Home, and one of them [Sister Geraldine], who became my spiritual mother, began to teach me both secular and religious subjects. I owe an everlasting debt of gratitude to her, and to Miss Beale, the late Lady Principal of Cheltenham Ladies' College. Both of these ladies took great pains with me and taught me the subjects which would help me in my life-work. The instruction which I received from them was mostly spiritual. Their motherly kindness and deeply spiritual influence have greatly helped in building up my character. I praise and thank God for permitting me to be under the loving Christian care of these ladies.

The Mother Superior once sent me for a change to one of the branches of the Sisters' Home in London. The Sisters there took me to see the rescue work carried on by them. I met several of the women who had once been in their Rescue Home, but who had so completely changed, and were so filled with the love of Christ and compassion for suffering humanity, that they had given their life for the service of the sick and infirm. Here for the first time in my life, I came to know that something should be done to reclaim the so-called fallen women, and that Christians, whom Hindus considered outcastes and cruel, were kind to these unfortunate women, degraded in the eyes of society.

I had never heard or seen anything of the kind done for this class of women by the Hindus in my own country. I had not heard anyone speaking kindly of them, nor seen anyone making any effort to turn them from the evil path they had chosen in their folly. The Hindus Shastras do not deal kindly with these women. The law of the Hindus commands that the king shall cause the fallen women to be eaten by dogs in the outskirts of the town. They are considered the greatest sinners, and not worthy of compassion.

After my visit to the Homes at Fulham, where I saw the work of mercy carried on by the Sisters of the Cross, I began to think that there was a real difference between Hinduism and Christianity. I asked the Sisters who instructed me to tell me what it was that made the Christians care for, and reclaim the 'fallen' women. She read the story of Christ meeting the Samaritan woman, and His wonderful discourse on the nature of true worship, and explained it to me. She spoke of the Infinite Love of Christ for sinners. He did not despise them but came to save them. I had never read or heard anything like this in the religious books of the Hindus; I realized, after reading the 4th Chapter of St. John's Gospel, that Christ was truly the Divine Saviour He claimed to be, and no one but He could transform and uplift the downtrodden womanhood of India and of every land.

Thus my heart was drawn to the religion of Christ. I was intellectually convinced of its truth on reading a book written by Father Goreh, and was baptized in the Church of England in the latter part of 1883, while living with the Sisters at Wantage. I was comparatively happy, and felt a great joy in finding a new religion, which was better than any other religion I had known before. I knew full well that it would displease my friends and my countrymen very much; but I have never regretted having taken the step. I was hungry for something better than what the Hindu Shastras gave. I found it in the Christians' Bible and was satisfied.

After my baptism and confirmation, I studied the Christian religion more thoroughly with the help of various books written on its doctrines. I was much confused by finding so many different teachings of different sects; each one giving the authority of the Bible for holding a special doctrine, and for differing from other sects.

For five years after my baptism, I studied these different doctrines, and made close observations during my stay in England and in America. Besides meeting people of the most prominent sects, the High Church, Low Church, Baptist, Methodist, Presbyterian, Friends, Unitarian, Universalist, Roman Catholic, Jews, and others, I met with Spiritualists, Theosophists, Mormons, Christian Scientists, and followers of what they call the occult religion.

No one can have any idea of what my feelings were at finding such a Babel of religions in Christian countries, and at finding how very different the teaching of each sect was from that of the others. I recognized the Nastikas of India in the Theosophists, the Polygamous Hindus in the Mormons, the worshippers of ghosts and demons in the Spiritualists, and the Old-Vedantists in the Christian Scientists. Their teachings were not new to me. I had known them in their old eastern nature as they are in India; and when I met them in America I thought they had only changed their Indian dress and put on Western garbs, which were more suitable to the climate and conditions of the country.

As for the differences of the orthodox and non-orthodox Christian sects, I could not account for them, except that I thought it must be in the human nature to have them. The differences did not seem of any more importance than those existing among the different sects of Brahmanical Hindu religion. They only showed that people were quarrelling with each other, and that there was no oneness of mind in them. Although I was quite contented with my newly-found religion, so far as I understood it, still I was labouring under great intellectual difficulties, and my heart longed for something better which I had not found. I came to know after eight years from the time of my baptism that I had found the Christian *religion*, which was good enough for me; *but I had not found Christ, Who is the Life of the religion*, and 'the Light of every man that cometh into the world'.

FINDING CHRIST

It was nobody's fault that I had not found Christ. He must have been preached to me from the beginning. My mind at that time had been too dull to grasp the teaching of the Holy Scriptures. The open Bible had been before me, but I had given much of my time to the study of other books about the Bible, and had not studied the Bible itself as I should have done. Hence my ignorance of many important doctrines taught in it. I gave up the study of other books about the Bible after my return home from America, and took to reading the Bible regularly.

Following this course for about two years, I became very unhappy in my mind. I was dissatisfied with my spiritual condition. One day, I went to the Bombay Guardian Mission Press on some business. There I picked up a book called 'From Death unto Life', written by Mr Haslam, the Evangelist. I read his experiences in this book with great interest. He, being a clergyman of the Church of England, had charge of a good parish and was interested in all Christian activities connected with the Church. While he was holding conversation with a lady, a member of his Church, she told him that he was trying to build from the top. The lady meant to say, he was not converted, and had not experienced regeneration and salvation in Christ.

I read his account of his conversion, and work for Christ. Then I began to consider where I stood, and what my actual need was. I took the Bible and read portions of it, meditating on the messages which God gave me. There were so many things I did not understand intellectually. One thing I knew by this time, that I needed Christ, and not merely His religion.

There were some of the old ideas stamped on my brain; for instance, I thought that repentance of sin and the determination to give it up was what was necessary for forgiveness of sin: that the rite of baptism was the means of regeneration; that my sins were truly washed away when I was baptized in the name of Christ. These and such other ideas, which are akin to the Hindu mode of religious thoughts, stuck to me. For some years after my baptism, I was comparatively happy to think that I had found a religion which gave its privileges equally to men and women; there was no distinction of caste, colour, or sex made in it.

All this was very beautiful, no doubt. But I had failed to understand that we are of 'God in Christ Jesus, who of God is made unto us wisdom, and righteousness, and sanctification and redemption.' 1 Cor. 1: 30. I had failed to see the need of placing my implicit faith in Christ and His atonement in order to become a child of God by being born again of the Holy Spirit, and justified by faith in the Son of God. My thoughts were not very clear on this and other points. I was desperate. I realised that I was not prepared to meet God, that sin had dominion over me, and I was not altogether led by the Spirit of God, and had not therefore received the Spirit of adoption and had no witness of the Spirit that I was a child of God. 'For as many as are led by the Spirit of God, they are the sons of God. For ye have not received the spirit of bondage, again to fear; but ye have received the Spirit of adoption whereby we cry, "Abba, Father." The Spirit itself beareth witness with our spirit, that we are the children of God.' Romans 8: 14–16.

What was to be done? My thoughts could not, and did not help me. I had at last come to an end of myself, and unconditionally surrendered myself to the Saviour; and asked Him to be merciful to me, and to become my Righteousness and Redemption, and to take away all my sin.

Only those, who have been convicted of sin and have seen themselves as God sees them under similar circumstances, can understand what one feels when a great and unbearable burden is rolled away from one's heart. I shall not attempt to describe how and what I felt at the time when I made an unconditional surrender, and knew I was accepted to be a branch of the True Vine, a child of God by adoption in Christ Jesus my Saviour. Although it is impossible for me to tell all that God has done for me, I must yet praise Him and thank Him for His loving-kindness to me, the greatest of sinners. The Lord, first of all, showed me the sinfulness of sin and the awful danger I was in, of everlasting hell-fire and the great love of God with which He 'So loved the world, that He gave His only begotten Son'. And He gave this Son to be the propitiation for my sin: for does not the inspired Apostle say, 'We have an Advocate with the Father, Jesus Christ the Righteous: and He is the Propitiation for our sins: and not for ours only but also for the sins of the whole world.' 1 John 2: 1–2.

The Bible says that God does not wait for me to merit His love, but heaps it upon me without my deserving it. It says also that there is neither male nor female in Christ.

'The righteousness of God which is by faith of Jesus Christ, unto all and upon all of them that believe: for there is no difference: for all have sinned, and come short of the glory of God; being justified freely by His grace through the redemption that is in Christ Jesus: Whom God hath set forth to be a propitiation through faith in His blood to declare His righteousness for the remission of sins that are past, through the forbearance of God; to declare I say at this time His righteousness: that He might be just, and the justifier of him which believeth in Jesus.' Romans 3: 22–6.

I do not know if anyone of my readers has ever had the experience of being shut up in a room where there was nothing but thick darkness and then groping in it to find something of which he or she was in dire need. I can think of no one but the blind man, whose story is given in St. John, chapter nine. He was born blind and remained so for forty years of his life; and then suddenly he found the Mighty One, Who could give him eyesight. Who could have described his joy at seeing the daylight, when there had not been a particle of hope of his ever seeing it? Even the inspired evangelist has not attempted to do it. I can give only a faint idea of what I felt when my mental eyes were opened, and when I, who was 'sitting in darkness saw Great Light,' and when I felt sure that to me, who but a few moments ago 'sat in the region and shadow of death, Light *had* sprung up'. I was very like the man who was told, 'In the name of Jesus Christ of Nazareth rise up and walk . . . And he, leaping up, stood, and walked, and entered with them into the temple, walking and leaping and praising God.'

I looked to the blessed Son of God who was lifted up on the cross and there suffered death, even the death of the cross, in my stead, that I might be made free from the bondage of sin, and from the fear of death, and I received life. O the love, the unspeakable love of the Father for me, a lost sinner, which gave His only Son to die for me! I had not merited this love, but that was the very reason why He showed it to me.

How very different the truth of God was from the false ideal that I had entertained from my earliest childhood. That was that I must have merit to earn present or future happiness, the pleasure of Svarga, or face the utterly inconceivable loss of Moksha or liberation. This I could never hope for, since a woman, as a woman, has no hope of Moksha according to Hindu religion. The Brahman priests have tried to deceive women and the Shudras and other low-caste people into the belief that they have some hope. But when we study for ourselves the books of the religious law and enquire from the higher authorities we find that here is nothing, no, nothing whatever for us.

They say that women and Shudras and other low-caste people can gain Svarga by serving the husband and the Brahman. But the happiness of Svarga does not last long. The final blessed state to which the Brahman is entitled is not for women and low-caste people. But here this blessed Book, the Christians' Bible says:

'When we were yet without strength, in due time Christ died for the ungodly. For scarcely for a righteous man will one die: yet peradventure for a good man some would even dare to die. But God commendeth His love toward us, in that, while we were yet sinners Christ died for us. . . . For . . . when we were enemies, we were reconciled to God by the death of His Son.' Romans 5: 6–10.

'In this was manifested the love of God toward us, because that God sent His only begotten Son into the world, that we might live through Him. Herein is love, not that we loved God, but that He loved us, and sent His Son to be the propitiation for our sins.' I John 4: 9, 10.

How good, how indescribably good! What good news for me, a woman, a woman born in India among Brahmans, who hold out no hope for me and the likes of me! The Bible declares that

Christ did not reserve this great salvation for a particular caste or sex.

'But as many as received Him, to them gave He power to become the sons of God, even to them that believe on His name: which were born, not of blood, nor of the will of the flesh, nor of the will of man, but of God.' John 1: 12,13.

'For the grace of God that bringeth salvation hath appeared to all men.' Titus 2: 11.

'The kindness and love of God our Saviour toward man appeared, not by works of righteouness which we have done, but according to His mercy He saved us.' Titus 3: 4.

No caste, no sex, no work, and no man was to be depended upon to get salvation, this everlasting life, but God gave it freely to anyone and everyone who believed on His Son Whom He sent for the 'propitiation for our sins'. And there was not a particle of doubt left as to whether this salvation was a present one or not. I had not to wait till after undergoing births and deaths for countless millions of times, when I should become a Brahman man, in order to get to know the Brahma. And then, was there any joy and happiness to be hoped for? No, there is nothing but to be amalgamated into Nothingness Shunya, Brahma.

The Son of God says,

'Verily, verily, I say unto you He that heareth my word, and believeth on Him that sent me hath everlasting life, and shall not come into condemnation but is passed from death unto life.' John 5: 24.

'If we receive the witness of men, the witness of God is greater; for this is the witness of God which he hath testified of His Son. He that believeth on the Son of God hath the witness in himself: he that believeth not God, hath made Him a liar: because he believeth not the record that God gave of His Son. And this is the record, that GOD HATH GIVEN TO US ETERNAL LIFE, and This Life is in his Son. He that hath the Son hath life; and he that hath not the Son of God hath not life. These things have I written unto you that believe on the name of the Son of God; that ye may know that *ye have eternal life* and that ye may believe on the name of the Son of God.' 1 John 5: 9–13.

The Holy Spirit made it clear to me from the Word of God, that the salvation which God gives through Christ is present, and not something future. I believed it, I received it, and I was filled with joy.

TELLING OTHERS

Sixteen years ago, a new leaf was turned in my life. Since then I have come to know the Lord Jesus Christ as my personal Saviour, and have the joy of sweet communion with Him. My life is full of joy, 'For the Lord Jehovah is my strength and my song; He also is become my salvation.' Now I know that what the Prophet means by saying, 'Therefore with joy shall ye drew water out of the wells of salvation.' I can scarcely contain the joy and keep it to myself. I feel like the Samaritan woman who 'left her waterpot, and went her way into the city, and saith to the men, Come, see a Man, which told me all things that ever I did: is not this the Christ?'

I feel I must tell my fellow-creatures what great things the Lord Jesus has done for me, and I feel sure, as it was possible for Him to save such a great sinner as I am, He is quite able to save others. The only thing that must be done by me is to tell people of Him and of His love for sinners and His great power to save them.

My readers will not therefore find fault with me for making this subject so very personal. The heart-experiences of an individual are too sacred to be exposed to the public gaze. Why then should I give them to the public in this way? Because a 'necessity is laid upon me; yea, woe is unto me, if I preach not the gospel!' 1 Corinthians 9: 16. I am bound to tell as many men and women as possible, that Christ Jesus came to save sinners like me. He has saved me, praise the Lord! I know 'He is able to save them to the uttermost that come unto God by Him, seeing He ever liveth to make intercession for them.' Hebrews 7: 25.

God has given me a practical turn of mind. I want to find out the truth about everything including religion by experiment. I experimented on the religion in which I was born. I did not leave a stone unturned, as it were, as far as I knew; not only in the way of studying books, but of doing myself what the books prescribed. I have seen many others also doing the same thing. I saw them doing everything that was commanded them. The sad end was, that I found that they were not saved by it, nor was I. It was a dire spiritual necessity that drove me to seek help from other sources. I had to give up all pride of our ancestral religion being old and superior, which is preventing many of my countrypeople from finding Christ although they know well that they have not got the joy of salvation. They can never have it except in Christ.

There are I know many hungry souls, and maybe, some of them might be helped by reading this account. I would urge upon such brothers and sisters to make haste and come forward, and accept the great love of God expressed in Christ Jesus and not to neglect 'so great salvation', which God gives freely. Hebrews 2: 1–3

'Neither is there salvation in any other: for there is none other name under heaven given among men, whereby we must be saved.' Acts 4: 12.

Do not therefore lose time through pride or because of any other difficulty. The caste may put you out, your near and dear ones will perhaps reject you and persecute you, you may very likely lose your temporal greatness, and riches: but never mind, the great salvation which you will get in Christ by believing on Him, and confessing Him before men, is worth all the great sacrifices you can possibly make. Yes, and more than that, for all the riches and all the gain, and all the joys of the world, do not begin to compare with the JOY OF SALVATION.

On the other hand, of what use are all the riches and greatness of the world, if you are condemned to the second death, and are to live in the lake of fire for ever and ever suffering indescribable agonies from which there is no relief?

'For what shall it profit a man, if he shall gain the whole world and lose his own soul? Or what shall a man give in exchange for his soul?' Mark 8: 36–37.

I would urge on you, dear brother and sister, to make haste and get reconciled with God through Christ. For the great day of judgment is fast coming on us, so make haste and flee from the wrath of God, which you and I have justly merited. God is Love, and He is waiting patiently for you to accept His great salvation, so despise not 'the riches of His goodness and forbearance and longsuffering', and know 'that the goodness of God leadeth thee to repentance'. Romans 2: 4.

It would make the story too long if I were to tell all that happened to me after I found Christ. I was greatly helped in my spiritual life by attending several Mission services conducted by Dr Pentecost, Mr Haslam, Mr Wilder, Mr Reeve, and other missionaries. I received another spiritual uplift by attending religious services conducted by Rev. Gelson in 1895 at Lonavala Camp meeting.

I found it a great blessing to realize the personal presence of the Holy Spirit in me, and to be guided and taught by Him. I have experienced the sweet pleasure promised by the Lord in Psalm 32: 8, 'I will instruct thee and teach thee in the way which thou shalt go: I will guide thee with mine eye.'

The Holy Spirit taught me how to appropriate every promise of God in the right way, and obey His voice. I am sorry to say that I have failed to obey Him many a time, but He tenderly rebukes and shows me my faults. Many a time He finds it most necessary to punish me in various ways. His promise is: 'I will correct thee in measure, and will not leave thee altogether unpunished.' Jeremiah. 30: 11.

I have many failures and am corrected as the Lord sees fit. It is always helpful to be shown that His hand is in everything that happens. Then no room is left for murmuring. Whenever I heed and obey the Lord's voice with all my heart, I am very happy and everything goes right. Even the tests of faith, and difficulties, and afflictions become great blessings.

Since the year 1891, I have tried to witness for Christ in my weakness, and I have always found that it is the greatest joy of the Christian life to tell people of Christ and of His great love for sinners.

About twelve years ago, I read the inspiring books, 'The Story of the China Inland Mission', 'The Lord's Dealings with George Muller', and the 'Life of John G. Paton', founder of the New Hebrides Mission. I was greatly impressed with the experiences of these three great men, Mr Hudson Taylor, Mr Muller and Mr Paton, all of whom have gone to be with the Lord within a few years of each other. I wondered after reading their lives, if it were not possible to trust the Lord in India as in other countries. I wished very much that there were some missions founded in this country which would be a testimony to the Lord's faithfulness to His people, and the truthfulness of what the Bible says, in a practical way.

I questioned in my mind over and over again, why some missionaries did not come forward to found faith-missions in this country. Then the Lord said to me, 'Why don't you begin to do this yourself, instead of wishing for others to do it? How easy it is for anyone to wish that someone else would do a difficult thing, instead of doing it himself.' I was greatly rebuked by the 'Still Small Voice' which spoke to me.

I did not know then that there were some faith-missions in India. Since then I have come to know that there are a few faith-missions working in this country, and I thank God for setting them up here and there, as great beacon lights.

At the end of 1896, when the great famine came on this country, I was led by the Lord to step forward and start new work, trusting Him for both temporal and spiritual blessings. I can testify with all my heart that I have always found the Lord faithful. 'Faithful is He that calleth you.' 1 Thessalonians 5: 24. This golden text has been written with the life-blood of Christ on my heart. The Lord has done countless great things for me. I do not deserve His loving-kindness. I can testify to the truth of Psalm 103: 10, 'He hath not dealt with us after our sins; nor rewarded us according to our iniquities.'

Here are some of the things which the Lord has been teaching me during the past sixteen years, especially in the last decade since He brought this Mukti Mission into existence.

1. 'Men have not heard, nor perceived by the ear, neither hath the eye seen, O God, beside Thee, what He hath prepared for him that waiteth for Him.' Isaiah 64: 4.
2. 'All the promises of God in Him are yea, and in Him Amen, unto the glory of God by us.' 2 Corinthians 1: 20.
3. 'The gifts and calling of God are without repentance.' Romans 11: 29.
4. My unbelief shall not 'make the faith of God without effect.' Romans 3: 3.
5. 'The secret of the Lord is with them that fear Him; and He will shew them His covenant.' Psalm 25: 14.
6. 'The blood of Jesus Christ His Son cleanseth us from all sin.' 1 John 1: 7.
7. 'This is a faithful saying, and worthy of all acceptation, that Christ Jesus came into the world to save sinners; of whom I am chief.' 1 Timothy 1: 15.

In short, the Lord has been teaching me His Word by His Spirit, and unfolding the wonders of His works, day by day. I have come to believe the Word of God implicitly, and I have found out by experience, that IT IS TRUE. I praise God and thank Him for His mercies to me and mine. Hallelujah!

I feel very happy since the Lord called me to step out in faith, and I obeyed. To depend upon Him for everything; for spiritual life, for bodily health, for advice, for food, water, clothing, and all other necessities of life—in short, to realise by experiment, that the promises of God in Philippians 4: 6, 19 and in other parts of the Holy Scriptures are true, is most blessed.

'Be careful for nothing; but in everything by prayer and supplication with thanksgiving, let your requests be made known unto God.' Philippians 4: 6.

'I am the Lord thy God, which brought thee out of the land of Egypt: open thy mouth wide, and I will fill it.' Psalm 81: 10.

'It is better to trust in the Lord, than to put confidence in man. It is better to trust in the Lord, than to put confidence in princes.' Psalm 118: 8–9.

I am spared all trouble and care, casting my burden upon the Lord. There are over 1,500 people living here. We are not rich, nor great, but we are happy, getting our daily bread directly from the loving hands of our Heavenly Father, having not a pice over and above our daily necessities, having no banking account anywhere, no endowment or income from any earthly source, but depending altogether on our Father God; we have nothing to fear from anybody, nothing to lose, and nothing to regret. The Lord is our *Inexhaustible Treasure.*

'The Eternal God is thy refuge, and underneath are the everlasting arms.' Deuteronomy 33: 27. We are confidently resting in His arms, and He is loving and faithful in all His dealings with us. How can I express in words the gratitude I feel toward such a Father, and the joy that fills my heart because of His goodness?

'Bless the Lord, O my soul, and all that is within me bless His holy name. Bless the Lord, O my soul, and forget not all His benefits: Who forgiveth all thine iniquities; Who healeth all thy diseases; Who redeemeth thy life from destruction; Who crowneth thee with loving-kindness and tender mercies; Who satisfieth thy mouth with good things; so that thy youth is renewed like the eagle's.' Psalm 103: 1–5.

BOMBAY—FOUNDING OF MUKTI MISSION— HOME OF SALVATION

Nineteen years ago in this month of July, I started from the city of Philadelphia, and went to San Francisco, in response to the kind invitation sent by some good friends, who took a deep interest in the well-being of the women of India. I lived in the latter city for more than four months; and sailed from the Golden Gate for Bombay, via Japan and China.

God in His great goodness gave me faithful and true friends in America, who promised to help me in my work. My work in the beginning, was a purely educational one, and religious liberty was to be given to the inmates of my school, and all plans were made to start the Home for Widows as soon as I should land in Bombay.

The day for sailing from San Francisco arrived. I felt as if I were going to a strange country and to a strange people. Everything seemed quite dark before me. I fell on my knees, committed myself to the care of our loving Heavenly Father, and sailed.

My religious belief was so vague at the time that I was not certain whether I would go to heaven or hell after my death. I was not prepared to meet my God then. How can I describe my feelings when I heard of the disaster at San Francisco by the terrible earthquake, and of the great destruction of human life in the harbour of Hong Kong not long ago. How I thanked God for letting me live all these years, and not sending the terrible earthquake and the dreadful storms when I was not prepared to meet Him. I deeply sympathise with the people living in both these places in their afflictions, and pray to God that He may save each and all of the surviving inhabitants of San Francisco and Hong Kong.

When starting from San Francisco, and on landing in Bombay, I had resolved in my mind, that although no direct religious instruction was to be given to the inmates of my home, yet I would daily read the Bible aloud and pray to the only True God in the name of Christ; that my countrywomen, seeing and hearing what was going on, might be led to enquire about the true religion, and the way of salvation.

There were only two day-pupils in my school, when it was started a little more than eighteen years ago. No one was urged to become a Christian, not was anyone compelled to study the Bible. But the Book was placed in the library along with other religious books. The daily testimony to the goodness of the True God awakened new thoughts in many a heart.

After the first ten years of our existence as a school, our constitution was changed slightly. Since then, every pupil admitted in the school has been receiving religious instruction, retaining perfect liberty of conscience.

Many hundreds of the girls and young women who have come to my Home ever since its doors were opened for them have found Christ as I have. They are capable of thinking for themselves. They have had their eyes opened by reading the Word of God, and many of them have been truly converted and saved, to the praise and glory of God. I thank God for letting me see several hundred of my sisters, the children of my love and prayer, gloriously saved. All this was done by God in answer to the prayers of faith of thousands of His faithful servants in all lands, who are constantly praying for us all.

I was led by the Lord to start a special prayer-circle at the beginning of 1905. There were about 70 of us who met together each morning, and prayed for the true conversion of all the Indian Christians including ourselves, and for a special outpouring of the Holy Spirit on all Christians of every land. In six months from the time we began to pray in this manner, the Lord graciously sent a glorious Holy Ghost revival among us, and also in many schools and Churches in this country. The results of this have been most satisfactory. Many hundreds of our girls and some of our boys have been gloriously saved, and many of them are serving God, and witnessing for Christ at home, and in other places.

I have responded to the Lord's challenge, 'Prove Me now,' Malachi 3: 10, and have found Him faithful and true. I know He is a prayer-hearing and prayer-answering God. His promise, 'My people shall never be ashamed', Joel 2: 27, and all the thousands of His promises are true. I entreat you, my readers, to prove the Lord as I have proved Him.

'O taste and see that the Lord is good; blessed is the man that trusteth in Him. O fear the Lord, ye His saints; for there is no want to them that fear Him. The young lions do lack, and suffer hunger:

but they that seek the Lord shall not want any good thing.' Psalm 34: 8–10.

'O give thanks unto the Lord for He is good: for His mercy endureth for ever. Let the redeemed of the Lord say so, whom He hath redeemed from the hand of the enemy: And gathered them out of the lands, from the east and from the west, from the north and from the south. They wandered in the wilderness in a solitary way; they found no city to dwell in. Hungry and thirsty, their soul fainteth in them. Then they cried unto the Lord in their trouble, and He delivered them out of their distress. And He led them forth by the right way, that they might go to a city of habitation. Oh that men would praise the Lord for His goodness, and His wonderful works to the children of men! For He satisfieth the longing soul, and filleth the hungry soul with goodness.' Psalm 107: 1–9.

GLORIOUS NEW HOPE

This has been literally fulfilled in me and mine. I praise the Lord Who has done great things for us. Hallelujah, Amen.

The most precious truth which I have learnt since my conversion is the second coming of the Lord Jesus Christ. I firmly believe, as taught in the Bible, that the Lord Jesus Christ is coming soon. He will most certainly come, and will not tarry. The signs of the times in the last decade have taught me to be waiting for Him. I was totally ignorant of this particular subject. It is not generally taught in this country. The missionaries connected with some denominations do not believe in it at all. They believe that Christ will come to judge the quick and the dead at the time of the last judgement but they do not think He will come for His servants before the time of the resurrection of the dead, and before the final judgement.

I do not remember just how I came to know about it at first. But shortly after my conversion, I began to read many books on the subject. The works of Mr Middleton, Mr Newberry, Dr Grattan Guinness, and others, have greatly helped in fixing this subject in my mind. I have studied and continue to study the Book of Revelation with greatest interest and spiritual profit. There is nothing like the Word of God, which teaches everything clearly. Other good books written by godly men and women are quite helpful in that they help to make this subject of special interest, and increase the desire for its study. But there is nothing so very helpful as to study the Bible itself, aided by a good concordance, and the 'Treasury of Scripture Knowledge'.

The hope of the appearing of our Saviour to take His redeemed ones to be with Him has been a great help to me in my Christian life. I praise the Lord for the great promise of His coming, and His counsel to watch and pray.

'Watch therefore: for ye know not what hour your Lord doth come.' Matthew 24: 24.

'Take ye heed, watch and pray; for ye know not when the time is.' Mark 13: 33.

UNEXPECTED VISIT FROM THE GOVERNOR

One day, during this month, as I was getting ready for my afternoon work, one of my fellow-workers came to the door of the office, followed by the Collector of Poona. Both told me that His Excellency the Governor of Bombay had come to visit Mukti. I was taken by surprise, for I never thought that the Governor would ever come to such an out-of-the-way place, and visit an unpretentious institution, which had not earned popularity by great achievements, and by courting the favour of the great men of the country. In a few moments my surprise vanished, giving way to perfect pleasure, at finding the Governor so simple and natural in his manner, though he was very dignified and grand.

It was delightful to see the greatest man of this Presidency taking kindly notice of everyone who happened to come in his way, enquiring with interest of every little detail concerning the work. He seemed to be well acquainted with what was going on here. After inspecting all parts of the Mission, he bade us goodbye, and went away. It was a very pleasant surprise, and we shall never forget his visit and kindness to us all.

As we did not know about his visit, we had not made any preparations to receive him; so he saw us as we were; some walking about, some idly sitting where they were, some doing their work properly, some sweeping the ground and doing other housework, some dressed well and tidily, others in rags with unkempt hair, some giving themselves to their lessons and industry with diligence, and some just looking into the air and doing nothing and thinking about nothing in particular.

It does one good to be taken by surprise in this way. The one great thought that filled my heart while the Governor was here, and after he went away, leaving a very pleasant impression on our mind, was that our Lord Jesus Christ is coming some day just in this manner, and those of us who are prepared to meet Him will have the joy of being caught up in the air to be with Him. How blessed it will be, not to have anything to be afraid of, or anything that belongs to the enemy. How nice to be able to say with our Blessed Saviour, 'The prince of this world cometh, and hath nothing in me.'

'The grace of God that bringeth salvation hath appeared to all men, teaching us that, denying ungodliness and wordly lusts, we should live soberly, righteously, and godly, in this present world; looking for that blessed hope, and the glorious appearing of the great God and our Saviour Jesus Christ; Who gave Himself for us, that He might redeem us from all iniquity, and purify unto Himself a peculiar people, zealous of good works.' Titus 2: 11–14.

A LOVING INVITATION

'And take heed to yourselves, lest at any time your hearts be overcharged with surfeiting, and drunkenness, and cares of this life, and so that day come upon you unawares. For as a snare shall it come on all of them that dwell on the face of the whole earth. Watch ye therefore, and pray always, that ye may be accounted worthy to escape all these things that shall come to pass, and to stand before the Son of Man.' Luke 21: 34–36.

If I were to write all that the Lord has done for me, even as much as it lies in my power to do so, the book would be too large for a person to read; so I have made the account of my spiritual experience as short as possible. I am very glad and very thankful to the Lord for making it possible for me to give this testimony of the Lord's goodness to me. My readers will scarcely realise the great spiritual needs of all my countrywomen and of my countrymen too. The people of this land are steeped in sin, and are sitting in a terrible darkness. May the Father of Light send them light and life by His chosen ones. We need witnesses for Christ and His great salvation freely offered to all men.

Dear brother and sister, whoever may happen to read this testimony, may you realise your responsibility to give the gospel of Jesus Christ to my people in this land, and pray for them, that they may each and all be cleansed from their filthiness, and from all their idols, that they may find the true way of salvation.

My prayer for those readers who have not yet been saved is that they may seek and find Christ Jesus, our Blessed Redeemer, for the salvation of their souls.

'Our citizenship is in heaven, from whence also we wait for the Saviour, the Lord Jesus Christ.' Philippians 3: 20.

'Unto Him that loved us, and washed us from our sins in His own blood, And hath made us kings and priests unto God and His Father; to Him be glory and dominion for ever and ever. Amen.' Revelation 1: 5–6.

Ramabai

March 1907

12

THE WORD-SEED*

'In the morning sow thy seed, and in the evening withhold not thine hand: for thou knowest not whether shall prosper, either this or that, or whether they both shall be alike good.'

Eccl. II: 6.

I praise and thank God with all my heart for sending Christian missionaries to preach the blessed Gospel of our Lord Jesus Christ to my people, and I pray God, to bless them abundantly and let them see the fruit of their labours for the people of India.

I want to write a few words to give my humble testimony to the wonderful saving power of our Blessed Lord Jesus. I cannot do better than express my feelings by quoting the words of Mary: 'My soul doth magnify the Lord and my spirit hath rejoiced in God my Saviour.'

I want to bear my testimony to the wonderful power of the blessed name of Jesus Christ to save sinners. About forty years ago, when I was a little girl, my parents visited Benares as pilgrims, to get merit, for they thought they would save themselves, and us their children, by bathing in the Ganges, and by worshipping the idols in that place. As orthodox Brahmans, they most religiously avoided coming in contact with Christians and the Mlechchhas, i.e. the foreigners. But one day in

---

*Reproduced from a pamphlet in the Archives of the Pandita Ramabai Mukti Mission.

the providence of God, a Christian man came to see my father while we were at Benares. I do not remember whether he was an Indian or an European Christian, nor what he spoke to my father. But I remember two words which I heard him say while he was conversing with my father. The words were: 'Yeshu Khrista', i.e. Jesus Christ. He shook hands with my father when taking his leave, and said something which I do not remember. But I found myself repeating the two words 'Yeshu Khrista,' which I heard from him, after he went away. I must have repeated them many times, because my sister was much alarmed and drew my mother's attention to what I was whispering to myself. Mother asked me what it was that I had been repeating; but I was afraid to answer her question and kept silence. She warned me against repeating the name of the God of the Mlechchhas, and told me not to bring His name to my lips again. But I never forgot that Name.

About thirteen years after this, a Baptist Missionary living at Silchar, Assam, sent a little printed card to me by my husband. The card had these words on it 'INCLINE YOUR HEART UNTO THE LORD.' I read them and pondered over them in my heart. I had lived without God and without hope for many years. I felt as if there was a great big emptiness within me which needed to be filled, and no one but the God Who was full of love and compassion for sinners would be able to fill it. I felt I needed His help, and for the first time in my life I prayed to the Unknown God to incline our hearts unto Him.

I did not know how to pray, but without my knowing it the Holy Spirit converted the Words of the Scripture into a prayer in my heart, and God did answer that prayer in His appointed time, when it pleased Him to bring me into the light of the blessed Gospel.

A few weeks after the above incident I found a little booklet, the Gospel of St. Luke in my room. I do not know who had brought it or left it there, but I began to read it, and greatly liked the story told in it. About this time my husband introduced me to the Missionary, who, some weeks before, had sent the card for me. The Missionary read the first chapter of Genesis and explained it to me. There was a wonderful attraction in the words which he read. My soul responded to the message of God's Holy Spirit. I resolved then without knowing the reason why, that I would become a Christian. Sixteen years after the time when I first heard the Name of Jesus Christ, I realized that 'There is none other name under heaven given among men whereby we must be saved.'

Some unknown friend, whose name is written in the Book of Life, made me acquainted with that Name at Benares, and another unknown friend left a small Gospel in my room for me to read, that I might come to know the Son of God 'who loved me and gave Himself for me'. These dear people who are well known to God and whom I expect to meet soon in the presence of the King, sowed the seed, others watered, and God gave the increase, and I was born in His Kingdom. How I thank God with a full heart to-day for sending His messengers in order to make Himself known to me. I realize more and more the wonderful power that is in the Name of Jesus, and in the Word of God which converted me. It will be an encouragement to the dear children of God, who have toiled long in this country without seeing any visible fruit of their labours, to know that the Word-seed, faithfully and prayerfully sown, does surely bear fruit.

'For as the rain cometh down, and the snow from heaven, and returneth not thither, but watereth the earth, and maketh it bring forth and bud, that it may give seed to the sower, and bread to the eater: So shall My Word be that goeth forth out of My mouth; it shall not return unto me void, but it shall accomplish that which I please, and it shall prosper in the thing whereto I sent it.' Isaiah 55: 10–11.

'Therefore, my beloved brethren, be ye steadfast, unmoveable, always abounding in the work of the Lord, for as much as ye know that your labour is not in vain in the Lord.' I Cor.15: 58.

I am convinced more and more that the Gospel given to our people freely will be the means of their salvation. It will be eternally profitable to spend time and money in giving the Gospel to many thousands of pilgrims, and to many others. Please pray that all those who read in the Gospel the Word of God, and all who have heard the Name of our Lord Jesus Christ, may be saved and gathered into His fold quickly, before He comes again to meet His elect Bride.

Ramabai

REFERENCES

Adhav, S.M. (1979), *Pandita Ramabai*, Madras: The Christian Literature Society (Confessing the Faith in India Series, No.13).

Agarkar, Gopal Ganesh (1984–86), *Agarkar-Vangmaya*, edited by M.G. Natu and D.Y. Deshpande, 3 vols., Bombay: Maharashtra State Board of Literature and Culture.

Bodley, Rachel (1887), 'Introduction', *The High-Caste Hindu Woman*, Bombay: Maharashtra State Board of Literature and Culture (reprint 1977).

Burton, Antoinette (1995), 'Colonial Encounters in Late Victorian England: Pandita Ramabai at Cheltenham and Wantage, 1883–86', *Feminist Review* (Spring), pp. 29–49.

——(1998), *At the Heart of the Empire: Indians and the Colonial Encounter in Late-Victorian Britain*, Berkeley: University of California Press.

Dall, Caroline Healey (1888), *The Life of Dr Anandabai Joshee: A Kinswoman of Pundita Ramabai*, Boston: Roberts Brothers.

Deckard, Barbara Sinclair (1983), *The Women's Movement: Political, Socioeconomic and Psychological Issues*, 3rd edn., New York: Harper & Row.

Doerksen, Lilian (1967), 'Foreword', *Stri Dharma Niti*, 3rd edn., Kedgaon: Ramabai Mukti Mission.

Dnyanodaya (an Anglo-Marathi weekly), several issues, Bombay: American Marathi Mission.

Dongre, R.K. and J.F. Patterson (1963), *Pandita Ramabai: A Life of Faith and Prayer*, Madras: The Christian Literature Society.

Flexner, Eleanor (1975), *Century of Struggle: The Woman's Rights Movement in the United States*, revised edn., Cambridge, Mass., and London: Harvard University Press.

Fuller, (Mrs) Marcus B. (1900), *The Wrongs of Indian Womanhood*, New Delhi: Inter-India Publications (reprint 1984).

The Gazetteer of Bombay City and Island (1909), 3 vols., Pune: Government Photozinco Press (facsimile reproduction 1978).

Gidumal, Dayaram (1889), *The Status of Woman in India*, Bombay: Fort Publishing Press.

Glover, Susanne L. (1995), 'Of Water and of the Spirit', unpublished PhD thesis, University of Sydney.

Hartshorne, Henry (1888), 'Professional Tribute', *In Memoriam Rachel L. Bodley*, pp. 20–22, Pennsylvania: Archives of the Medical College of Pennsylvania.

The *Indu-Prakash* (an Anglo-Marathi weekly), several issues, Bombay.

The *Kesari* (a Marathi weekly), several issues, Pune.

Kosambi, Meera (1988), 'Women, Emancipation and Equality: Pandita Ramabai's Contribution to Women's Cause', *Economic and Political Weekly*, 29 October, pp. WS 38–49.

——(1991), 'Girl Brides and Socio-Legal Change: The Age of Consent Bill (1891) Controversy', *Economic and Political Weekly*, 3–10 August, pp. 1857–68.

——(1992a), 'An Indian Response to Christianity, Church and Colonialism: The Case of Pandita Ramabai', *Economic and Political Weekly*, 24–31 October, pp. WS 61–71.

——(1994), 'The Meeting of the Twain: The Cultural Confrontation of Three Women in Nineteenth Century Maharashtra', *Indian Journal of Gender Studies*, vol.1, no.1, pp.1–22.

——(1995), *Pandita Ramabai's Feminist and Christian Conversions: Focus on Stree Dharma Neeti*, Bombay: Research Centre for Women's Studies, SNDT Women's University.

——(1996a), 'Gender Reform and Competing State Controls Over Women: The Rakhmabai Case (1884–1888)', *Contributions to Indian Sociology* (n.s.), vol. 29, nos. 1–2, pp. 265–90.

——(1996b), 'Anandibai Joshee: Retrieving a Fragmented Feminist Image', *Economic and Political Weekly*, 7 Dec., pp. 3189–97.

——(1998a), 'Child Brides and Child Mothers: The Age of Consent Controversy in Maharashtra as a Conflict of Perspectives on Women' in Anne Feldhaus (ed.), *Images of Women in Maharashtrian Society*, Albany, NY: State University of New York Press.

———(1998b), 'The Home as a Social Universe' in Irina Glushkova and Anne Feldhaus (eds), *The House and Home in Maharashtra,* New Delhi: Oxford University Press.

———(1998c), 'Multiple Contestations: Pandita Ramabai's Educational and Missionary Activities in Late Nineteenth Century India and Abroad', *Women's History Review,* June.

———(forthcoming), 'Life After Widowhood: Two Radical Reformist Options in Maharashtra', in Meera Kosambi (ed.), *Intersections: Socio-cultural Trends in Maharashtra,* Delhi: Orient Longman.

Lerner, Gerda, ed. (1992), *The Female Experience: An American Documentary,* New York and Oxford: Oxford University Press.

The Letters and Correspondence of Pandita Ramabai, edited by A.B. Shah, Bombay: Maharashtra State Board of Literature and Culture.

Macnicol, Nicol (1926), *Pandita Ramabai,* Calcutta: Association Press (Builders of Modern India Series).

The Mahratta (an English weekly), several issues, Bombay.

Mueller, F. Max (1899), *Auld Lang Syne* (second series), *My Indian Friends,* London: Longmans, Green & Co.

Phadke, Y.D. (1975), *Social Reformers of Maharashtra,* New Delhi: Maharashtra Information Centre, Government of Maharashtra.

———(1989), *Women in Maharashtra,* New Delhi: Maharashtra Information Centre, Government of Maharashtra.

The Philadelphia Evening Bulletin (a daily), several issues, Philadelphia, Pennsylvania.

Ramabai, Pandita, (1883), *Pandita Ramabai Yancha Englandcha Pravas* edited by D.G. Vaidya, 2nd edn., Bombay: Maharashtra State Board of Literature and Culture (1988).

———(1900), 'Introduction', in M.B. Fuller, *The Wrongs of Indian Womanhood,* New Delhi: Inter-India Publications (reprint 1984).

Ranade, Ramabai (1910), *Amchya Ayushyatil Kahi Athavani,* 7th edn., Pune: K.G. Sharangapani (1953).

Sathe, Tarabai (1975), *Aparajita Rama,* Pune: D.P. Nagarkar.

Second Annual Report (1890), Boston: Ramabai Association.

Sengupta, Padmini (1970), *Pandita Ramabai Saraswati: Her Life and Work,* Bombay: Asia Publishing House.

Shah, A.B. (1977), 'Introduction' in A.B. Shah (ed.), *The Letters and Correspondence of Pandita Ramabai,* Bombay: Maharashtra State Board of Literature and Culture.

Shepherd, Verene, Bridget Brereton and Barbara Bailey, eds (1995), *Engendering History: Caribbean Women in Historical Perspective,* Kingston: Ian Randle Publishers, London: James Currey Publishers.

Shinde, Tarabai (1882), *Stri-Purusha Tulana,* edited by S.G. Malshe, Bombay: Bombay Marathi Grantha Sangrahalaya (1975).

Solomon, Barbara Miller (1987), *In the Company of Educated Women: A History of Women and Higher Education in America*, New Delhi: Asian Books (first Indian reprint).

Spender, Dale (1983), *Women of Ideas (And What Men Have Done to Them): From Aphra Behn to Adrienne Rich*, London: Ark Paperbacks.

Sunthankar, B.R. (1993), *Maharashtra, 1858–1920*, Bombay: Popular Book Depot.

Telang, Kashinath Trimbak (1886),'Must Social Reform Precede Political Reform in India?', Bombay: The Bombay Jam-E-Jamshed Printing Press.

Thackeray, K.S. (Prabodhankar). (1905), *Pandita Ramabai*, Bombay: V.R. Baum.

Thompson, Eliza, Frances E.Willard *et al.* (1906), *Hillsboro Crusade Sketches and Family Records*, Cincinnati: Jennings and Graham.

Tilak, D.N. (1960), *Maharashtrachi Tejaswini Pandita Ramabai*, Nasik: Nagarik Prakashan.

Vaidya, D.G. (1988), 'Biographical Appendix' in (parts II and III) *Pandita Ramabai Yancha Englandcha Pravas*.

Vaidya, Sarojini (1991), *Shrimati Kashibai Kanitkar: Atmacharitra ani Charitra*, 2nd edn., Bombay: Popular Prakashan.

Yates, Gayle Graham, ed. (1985), *Harriet Martineau on Women*, New Brunswick, NJ: Rutgers University Press.

INDEX

DATE DUE